Designing
Secure
Web-Based
Applications
for Microsoft®
Windows® 2000

Michael Howard
with Marc Levy and
Richard Waymire

PUBLISHED BY
Microsoft Press
A Division of Microsoft Corporation
One Microsoft Way
Redmond, Washington 98052-6399

Library of Congress Cataloging-in-Publication Data
Howard, Michael, 1965-
    Designing Secure Web-Based Applications for Microsoft Windows 2000 / Michael Howard.
        p.   cm.
    Includes bibliographical references and index.
    ISBN 0-7356-0995-0
    1. World Wide Web--Security measures. 2. Web sites--Security measures. 3. Microsoft Windows (Computer file) I. Title.
    TK5105.888. H66 2000
    005.8--dc21   00-038661

Printed and bound in the United States of America.

1 2 3 4 5 6 7 8 9   MLML   5 4 3 2 1 0

Distributed in Canada by Penguin Books Canada Limited.

A CIP catalogue record for this book is available from the British Library.

Microsoft Press books are available through booksellers and distributors worldwide. For further information about international editions, contact your local Microsoft Corporation office or contact Microsoft Press International directly at fax (425) 936-7329. Visit our Web site at mspress.microsoft.com. Send comments to mspinput@microsoft.com.

Intel is a registered trademark of Intel Corporation. Active Directory, ActiveX, Authenticode, BackOffice, BizTalk, JScript, Microsoft, Microsoft Press, MSDN, MSN, NetMeeting, Outlook, Visual Basic, Win32, Windows, and Windows NT are either registered trademarks or trademarks of Microsoft Corporation in the United States and/or other countries. Other product and company names mentioned herein may be the trademarks of their respective owners.

Unless otherwise noted, the example companies, organizations, products, people, and events depicted herein are fictitious. No association with any real company, organization, product, person, or event is intended or should be inferred.

Acquisitions Editor: Eric Stroo
Project Editor: Devon Musgrave
Technical Editor: Jim Fuchs
Editorial Assistant: Melissa von Tschudi-Sutton

To Cheryl, who selflessly sacrificed our time together so that
I could write this book. The person who taught me about living,
and the kindest, most beautiful woman I know. I love you.

—Michael

This one (and the next) is for Julia, Simone, and my little apricot.

—Marc

I'd like to thank my colleagues at Microsoft for helping me understand
the complicated world we work in. I'd also like to thank my wife and
children for their love and understanding while I took time away from
them to work on the book. And last but not least, I'd like to thank
Michael and Marc, as well as all the helpful folks at Microsoft Press.

—Richard

Contents

Table of Contents

Foreword

Over a period of about three years, Internet applications have evolved quickly, starting as simple information distribution Web sites serving up mostly static HTML content (with a small amount of server-side scripting used to address differences between Web browsers), providing simple site personalization, or being used by search engines as query processors. Today, multitiered, distributed applications use the scripting capabilities of Microsoft Internet Explorer or Netscape Navigator to form Web server–based "middle tier" servers. These applications are often implemented as CGI, ASP, or ISAPI programs accessing database or messaging servers. Replacing legacy client/server applications within corporate internal networks and opening up new strategic business-to-business applications, these applications are beginning to change supply chain systems and provide much more productive ways to collaborate with business partners.

As director of Windows NT security at Microsoft, I've witnessed a corresponding increase in the number and severity of security-related attacks on these Web-based applications. Pubic interest in security centered on privacy as it relates to financial transactions and identity protection—and the rapid spread of computer viruses capable of compromising data integrity—has increased pressure to make Internet applications and operating systems more secure. I believe three key things need to be done to improve the overall security of these applications. First, system administrators and data center operations staff need increased awareness of security threats and the associated best practices for securing computing systems against these threats. Second, application developers need to build security into their code up front rather than after the fact. Finally, the foundation components, comprising base operating systems (client and server), Internet browsers, Web servers, communication middleware, and database and collaboration servers, need to provide the necessary security functions, eliminating the need for applications to implement them. The high volume of questions on the security-related discussion aliases indicates a growing interest by end users, developers, and IT professionals in understanding and improving the overall security of their systems. The challenge they've faced is that too much information is spread across too many books, white papers, and Web sites for most people to be able to find the information needed in an understandable form. Security education within most college or university computer science curricula focuses on security theory, which addresses only a portion of system security, and industry consulting groups lack the capacity to meet demand.

With Microsoft Windows 2000 and the corresponding releases or availability of Internet Explorer, Internet Information Services (IIS), Exchange, and SQL Server, I believe Microsoft has made significant progress toward offloading security functionality from application developers and helping with security administration. This book goes a long way toward providing the necessary information to administrators and application developers. The combination of "just enough" security theory, security-focused functional descriptions of Internet Explorer, IIS, COM+, and SQL Server, and the pragmatic step-by-step lists for deploying the recommended configurations provide the complete picture required for configuring and monitoring the system for attacks. I highly recommend *Designing Secure Web-Based Applications for Microsoft Windows 2000* to every application developer and system administrator. After reading this book, you'll have a much better security awareness and an understanding of how to build secure applications by taking advantage of the security capabilities available in Microsoft products.

Doug Bayer
Director, Windows NT Security

Preface

WHY WE WROTE THIS BOOK

Although numerous books on security are available, many of them cover only theory or perhaps a security silo—that is, an island of security based on a particular tool, application, or technology. It should be obvious that no complete security solution is a silo; all secure business applications touch many tools and many technologies. Also, designing, building, and deploying any secure solution as a series of silos is difficult and unwise because getting the silos to talk to one another can be time-consuming and expensive.

The focal point of this book is a holistic view of how to build secure Microsoft Windows 2000–based solutions that use various Web technologies. We cover soup to nuts: from the browser to servers to middleware servers to database servers and back. As it turns out, this is a reasonably complex task to address; there are many moving parts and our goal is to make sure you understand how it all fits together. Accordingly, this book is part reference, part tutorial, and part cookbook for building secure Web applications by using Microsoft technologies. We also cover some of the trade-offs you need to make when building such end-to-end solutions. For example, choosing the appropriate authentication and identity mechanisms can have a performance impact on your solution. For this reason, it's important that you choose the correct technologies to meet your business requirements.

WHO SHOULD READ THIS BOOK?

This book's target audience is primarily Web developers and administrators developing, deploying, supporting, and using Windows 2000–based Web applications. Web developers will learn how to build security into their applications up front rather than after the fact; adding security features at the end of the development process is an often-made mistake that almost always jeopardizes security. They'll also learn how to approach and make the trade-offs between functionality, speed, and security. Web administrators will learn how to deploy Web applications securely, how to determine whether a computer is coming under attack, and how to respond to attacks.

Any reader of this book will gain a greater understanding of the security capabilities in Windows 2000, COM+, Internet Information Services (IIS), and Microsoft SQL Server and will learn a great deal about bedrock security principles. This knowledge is invaluable beyond building and deploying Web applications; all computer-based solutions require security of some sort.

ORGANIZATION OF THIS BOOK

We loosely based the format of this book on a successful security paper we delivered at Tech·Ed, a Microsoft-sponsored event for corporate developers, in Dallas, Texas, in May 1999. It was the first public demonstration of a multitier Web-enabled application performing Kerberos delegation. This book is organized into four parts.

Introduction and Design

Chapter 1, "Security 101," outlines core security principles and a taxonomy of security categories and threats. Chapter 2, "A Process for Building Secure Web Applications," describes a process for designing secure applications and follows up with an example scenario used as the basis for much of the rest of the book. The security solution design process is applied to the example application so that you can see how the process works. Security experts can possibly skip Chapter 1; however, everyone should read Chapter 2 because it serves as the cornerstone for the rest of the book.

Technologies and Trade-Offs

Chapters 3 through 7 cover the security features and capabilities of Windows 2000, Microsoft Internet Explorer 5, Internet Information Services 5, SQL Server 7, SQL Server 2000, and COM+ 1.0. This is highly recommended reading. Even if you've been using these products for some time, we know you'll find some new material in these chapters. Each chapter covers the security capabilities of the product in detail, offering many insights into how the product works.

Chapters 8 and 9—"Practical Authentication and Authorization" and "Practical Privacy, Integrity, Auditing, and Nonrepudiation"—investigate the practical side of security technology. Rather than focusing on pure technology, these chapters look at trade-offs you can make when choosing different types of technology to satisfy the core security requirements described in Chapter 1. The trade-offs are considered in terms of functionality, scalability, and "deployability," as well as the security implications of the requirements you choose to satisfy and how you go about satisfying them.

In Practice

Chapter 10, "Building a Secure Solution," looks at how to build an application for the scenario defined in Chapter 2 by using the technologies and strategies discussed in Chapters 3 through 9. This is a critical chapter in the book because it covers one of the most common questions people have asked us over the years: how do you securely flow identity throughout a secure application? Chapter 11, "Troubleshooting Secure Solutions," explains one of the most important aspects of building any application—how to troubleshoot the architecture. We explain how to read event log entries, describe tools that can help you look for problems, and discuss some common errors, including what they mean and how to remedy them.

Chapter 12, "Securing Against Attack," focuses on what to expect when you put an application on the Web. It is based on experiences gained—some painful!—while building and deploying secure Web applications and placing them on the Internet. If you're going to the trouble of putting an application on the Web, do yourself a service by reading this chapter!

Reference

Chapter 13, "Security Administration with ADSI, WMI, and COM+," covers how to use the tools and scriptable interfaces in Windows 2000 to build custom, remotable administration scripts by using Microsoft JScript, Microsoft VBScript, and Perl. Finally, Chapters 14 and 15—"An Introduction to Kerberos Authentication in Windows 2000" and "An Introduction to Cryptography and Certificates in Windows 2000"—introduce the reader to Kerberos authentication and cryptography and certificates in Windows 2000. Both chapters are pragmatic and easy to follow.

ABOUT THE COMPANION CD

The companion CD includes sample code and numerous tools to help build secure Web-based applications by using the tools we outline in the book. It also includes an electronic version of the book, which includes six appendixes that do not appear in the printed book. First, let's look at the appendixes.

Appendix A, "Windows 2000 Well-Known SIDs," lists the accounts installed on all Windows 2000–based computers and the tasks they perform, if applicable. Appendix B, "Strong Passwords," shows how to create strong, but memorable (to you!), passwords. Appendix C, "Windows 2000 Default Ports," is a list of TCP and UDP ports used by Windows 2000–based computers. This is important information for firewall administrators. Appendix D, "Internet Information Services Authentication Summary," lists the characteristics of all the authentication protocols supported by IIS 4 and IIS 5. Appendix E, "Security-Related IIS Server Variables," explains all the server variables that can be used to help you develop secure Web applications. Appendix F, "Secure Web Server Checklist," is the IIS 5 version of the famous IIS 4 security checklist. It's designed to work with the Hisecweb.inf configuration file found on the companion CD.

The tools and files included on the companion CD are described in the following table.

Tool	*Comments*
Hisecweb.inf	A Security Configuration Editor template for a secure Web server. You can deploy the template as outlined in Chapter 3.
KList	Kerberos ticket listing tool.
KerbParser	A Kerberos parser for Microsoft Network Monitor.
RUAdmin	A tool that warns you if you have administrator-like privileges when you log on.
TPFX2	A tool to add a Secure Sockets Layer/Transport Layer Security (SSL/TLS) certificate to IIS 5 from the command line.
CryptUtil	A COM+ component to generate cryptographically sound random numbers in Active Server Pages (ASP). Includes source code.
RandomGoo	A Microsoft Windows CE 3.0 application for MIPS and SH3 Pocket PCs to produce random data. Useful for deriving strong passwords.
WhatIf	A DHTML tool to determine which security settings support delegation.
WFetch	A highly configurable client tool that behaves like a browser. You can configure many settings, including authentication protocol requirements, SSL/TLS ciphers and protocols, client authentication certificate types, and proxy server information.
TranslateName	A tool that performs Active Directory lookups to translate between various name types such as SAM-compatible and UPN names. Includes C++ source code.
PerlScripts	Various Perl scripts for maintaining a secure server. The scripts include: ■ **Attacks.pl** Analyzes IIS W3C log files for common attack signatures.

Tool	*Comments*
PerlScripts *(continued)*	■ **Buffy.pl** Analyzes C and C++ source code for common buffer-overrun problem APIs.
	■ **IP.pl** Pings a subnet. For use with Network Monitor.
	■ **Parselog.pl** Parses IIS W3C log files, and displays all unique fields.
	■ **Pingsubnet.pl** Pings a subnet and looks for open ports.
	■ **Syn.pl** Parses netstat output looking for SYN floods.
	■ **Scan** A port scanning tool.
	■ **Uptime** A tool that generates HTML pages showing Web server uptime.
End2End	Code for building the sample end-to-end solution defined in Chapter 10 and sample administration scripts.
	There are four directories, each relating to a specific computer used in the solution defined in Chapter 10.
	00-WebServer:
	■ **ExAirConfig.vbs** Creates the Exploration Air sample virtual directories on IIS 5.
	■ **WebContent** Contains the two files used to make up the IIS Web site.
	01-Middleware:
	■ **DBQuery.dll** The COM+ DLL that implements data access with SQL Server. The DLL exposes two methods, the more important of which is *WhoAmI*, which returns the name of the user determined by SQL Server.
	■ **Source** Contains the Visual Basic 6 source code for DBQuery.
	02-DBServer:
	■ **ExAirHR.sql** Contains the SQL Server script to set up the ExAir database
	03-DomainController:
	■ **AddUsers.js and Accounts.xml** Set the default users, Alice, Bob, Cheryl, and AppAccount in Active Directory.
	■ **SetDelg.js** Sets or resets the Trusted For Delegation capability of a computer.

SYSTEM REQUIREMENTS

To use this book, you need either Microsoft Windows 2000 Server, Microsoft Windows 2000 Advanced Server, or Microsoft Windows 2000 DataCenter Server. A second computer running Windows 2000 Professional or any Web browser capable of Basic authentication is highly recommended. Although an intranet with at least four computers is necessary to run the sample application, you can understand its operation even if you don't have such a setup.

No programming knowledge is required to run the utilities included on the companion CD. (Some knowledge of a scripting language such as VBScript, Jscript, or Perl is very helpful to understand the code fragments in the book.)

ACKNOWLEDGMENTS

Writing a book is a slow, painstaking process involving long nights and lots of coffee. It's also an incredibly rewarding process. Three authors have their names on the front of this book, but without the help of many other people this book would be, at best, often inaccurate and usually lacking important detail. The authors would sometimes like to think they know everything about security and the English language, but they don't!

First, we thank the Microsoft Press crew. Without Eric Stroo and Ben Ryan, the acquisitions editors, this book would not exist. Eric was instrumental in getting the initial proposal running. Devon Musgrave and Jim Fuchs turned our geek-babble into technically accurate English with such finesse that the reader won't realize their impact. You are consummate professionals; we'll work with you any time you please. Of course, you might not feel the same way about us!

We would like to single out Jaroslav Dunajsky for recognition. Jaro is, without a doubt, the best security tester there is. He continues to prove that if you really want to know how something works, you should ask a tester.

Huge thanks go to David LeBlanc for answering so many questions about intrusion detection, hacking, and system security. Do not give this guy your IP address. You have been warned! We also greatly appreciate the help Paul Leach, John "PacMan" Brezak, and Richard Ward provided by answering questions about Windows 2000 security. Of course, having Paul in the next office is useful too! You guys rock. Thanks! Thanks also to Angus Freeman for his insights into Internet Explorer caching and for providing some of the core material for the topic. His real-world experience with this topic was invaluable. Nicola Martelli and Mark R. Harrison reviewed more material than anyone else. We thank them both for their enthusiasm and wisdom.

Part I

Introduction and Design

Many others contributed to the book by answering numerous questions, providing unique insights, telling us when we were plain wrong, or reviewing drafts of the manuscript. These people included: Andrew "If it moves, script it" Clinick, Balasubramanian Sriram, Ben "SQL Server can do that, but faster" Thomas, Brad Shantz, David Anselmi, David Mowers, Don Schmidt, Henrik "HTTP" Frystyk Nielsen, J.D. Meier, Jason Fossen, Jeff "Bovine" Lawson, Jeff Spelman, Jim Allchin, John Banes, Justin Grant, Kirk Soluk, Kris Frost, Leon Braginski, Mark Ingalls, Mike Webb, Praerit Garg, Richard Harrington, Rudolph Balaz, Saji Abraham, Scott Field, Sekar Chandersekaran, Steven Hu, Thomas "Got my old job" Deml, Todd Stecher, Tony Andrews, Trevor "X.509" Freeman, Van "Jean-Claude Van DAV" Van, Vic Heller, Wade "ISAPI" Hilmo, and William Dixon.

Michael Howard
Marc Levy
Richard Waymire

Redmond, Washington
May 2000

Chapter 1

Security 101

WHY BUILD SECURE APPLICATIONS?

Everybody's heard that the world would be a wonderful place if we could all get along and just trust one another. Unfortunately, this is not possible. If you're a businessperson, imagine relying on trust to "protect" information you want to keep private, such as commercially sensitive product designs or a five-year business plan. If you work in the medical field, imagine relying on trust to keep patient records from being tampered with. And now imagine the disaster caused by a hacker altering a hospital's data to indicate that a patient has an illness that requires a high dose of a restricted drug.

Like it or not, trust can be a dangerous proposition. Furthermore, leaving aside extreme examples for the moment, any successful attack on your organization's information or Web presence will lead to a loss of confidence in your organization. Hence, you have little choice but to secure your applications from malicious use or damage.

The Internet is a different place than it was ten years ago—it's a much more perilous realm for the incautious. Just try putting a new Web site with an interesting Domain Name System (DNS) name on the Net and waiting a few hours. You'll see what we mean as your server is probed and then possibly attacked by unidentified assailants. Long gone are the days of security through obscurity, or "if we don't tell them it's there, they'll never find it!" It simply doesn't work. In fact, the need for Internet security knowledge has never been greater.

SECURITY DEFINED

Security involves the protection of assets, where assets are defined as *anything with value*. This is an important issue that we'll come back to in more detail in Chapter 2, "A Process for Building Secure Web Applications"—if something has no value, it's probably not worth the cost and effort of securing it.

Some assets are tangible and have a monetary value, and others are intangible but still valuable. For example, it's easy to see why you should defend a tangible asset, such as inventory, that everybody agrees is "worth something." But it's also important to realize that certain intangibles, such as the reputation associated with your company's name, are also important. Below are some examples of assets:

- Business plans
- Chattels (possessions)
- Confidential source code
- Private cryptographic keys
- Ideas
- Identity
- Money (physical and digital)
- Privacy
- Reputation and name

Intangible assets—such as identity, privacy, and reputation and name—can be very difficult to place a value on. It's easy to place a value on your car or your house, but what is your privacy worth to you? The nature of this kind of question begins to reveal the complexity of our topic. As you'll see, security is a multifaceted discipline that involves determining the value of assets, which assets to protect, how to go about protecting them (that is, what methods to use), and what technologies to use. Obviously, all of this must be tempered with business rationale because deploying security for the sake of using cool technology is a bad idea. The rest of this book addresses many of these concerns.

WHY IS SECURITY DIFFICULT?

It's likely that all applications would be secure if security were easy! However, security is not easy for a myriad of reasons, some of which are listed here:

- An attacker need only find one weak point to enter the system; a defender needs to make sure that all possible entry points are defended.

- The usability of a system is inversely proportional to its security.

- Security is often tacked on to an application as an afterthought.

Examining each of these security challenges is a worthwhile exercise.

Attackers and Defenders

A scenario: You are the keeper of a castle, with vast treasures to defend from marauding bandits. The castle is defended by various means, including a deep moat, extremely thick walls, a drawbridge made of solid oak, and hundreds of archers placed on the battlements. As far as you're concerned, the castle's wealth is secure.

Here comes the attacker. Through a little reconnaissance, the attacker realizes that a brute-force attack would be futile owing to the number of archers you have. Attempting to swim the moat would also prove prickly. And the walls and drawbridge are so thick that a battering ram would also fail. After a few more days of snooping, the attacker realizes that your water supply is fed from an underground stream. While the castle's populace is sleeping, the attacker and his cronies enter the stream and wade through the water until they reach the bottom of the well inside the castle. They then throw a grappling hook that attaches to the rim of the well. You can imagine what happens next.

Now back to computing! Our systems are often like castles in that they utilize multiple defenses such as firewalls, proxies, secure channels, authentication schemes, and so on. However, all it takes is for an attacker to find one—just one—weak spot, and he or she has access to your system. This makes securing systems a complex proposition because Web site developers and information technology personnel must stay one step ahead of assailants. In doing so, they must choose from a dizzying array of constantly evolving products, tools, and technologies.

Security is a journey, not a destination. You must keep abreast of the environment, risks, business drivers, and the state-of-the-art security attacks affecting you. Failure to do so will render your Web applications vulnerable to attack.

Usability vs. Security

We want our systems to be usable—indeed, it's very good business practice to have practical computer systems! Another challenge for security, however, is that as a system becomes more secure, it becomes harder to use, as shown in Figure 1-1.

An old security adage states that the most secure computer system is turned off and buried in a concrete bunker. This is undeniably true, but clearly such a security solution is ridiculous. The point is that every security configuration represents a usability compromise.

Perhaps the most common example of ease-of-use vs. security is the use of passwords. Passwords are notoriously difficult to manage. If you force users to use

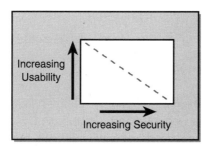

Figure 1-1. *A trade-off exists between security and usability. Secure systems are usually less usable.*

complex passwords, such as *T^1Qam-Za9*, they'll tend to write them down because the password is so hard to remember (that is, hard to use). A password like the word *Hello* is not only easy to remember and use but also easy to guess and utterly insecure. In the first case, the more secure, less easy-to-use solution actually backfires when the users write down their passwords. Such a possibility is another element to consider in the compromise you must make between usability and security.

Balancing usability and security is difficult, but a happy medium must be found to satisfy your business requirements. For example, your business's operating realities might require that all sales personnel have access to confidential sales and forecast data. A security solution by which the data is so well secured that only the executive staff has access is of little use to the business. (Chapter 2 will discuss business requirements in greater detail.)

Security as an Afterthought

Over the years, we've seen many cases in which an application has been nearly completed and during a status meeting someone asks the question, "So, when is the security going to be enabled?" Why is security often added so late in the product life cycle? Usually the reason is that security is difficult to implement and, as a result, the company developing the application leaves off making the hard security decisions to focus first on easier-to-implement aspects of the application. That way it looks like a lot of progress is being made!

Of course, this is bad practice—you should never leave difficult items until late in product development. You should work on the harder, riskier, and less well-known aspects of the application as soon as possible, and that includes security. Failure to address an application's security early in the application's development should be at the top of any project manager's list of things to worry about.

Security is also often an afterthought because developers usually see it as "plumbing"—that is, technology that adds no business value but that enables business processes. For example, open database connectivity (ODBC) is plumbing. It in itself adds no value to the business, but applications using ODBC do provide business

value. In the most pathological case, security is seen as unnecessary work offering no financial return. This attitude (or, as already mentioned, the tendency of development teams to avoid difficult tasks) more often than not creates the need for security to be retrofitted in an application. Of course, having to retrofit security makes security solutions even more difficult to create. By now, most developers know that adding a component to an existing technology is far more difficult than designing it into the system during the early stages of design and development.

We've addressed only a few of the reasons security is difficult, but we feel that these reasons perhaps contribute the most to security difficulties. In the rest of this chapter, we'll define a critical security taxonomy that we'll use in the rest of this book. It's imperative you understand what the elements of the taxonomy mean and how they interrelate—this understanding will help you identify the aspects of your own security solutions requiring the most attention.

THE GOLDEN RULES (AND SOME OTHERS)

Before we continue, it's important to define some core security vocabulary. Although we've generally defined security, the concept can still be somewhat nebulous. No doubt you've heard that "a system is secure" or that "system A is more secure than system B," but what do such phrases mean? Specifically, security is often thought of as comprising the following categories:

- Authentication
- Authorization
- Auditing
- Privacy
- Integrity
- Availability
- Nonrepudiation

The first three categories are sometimes referred to the "Golden Rules" because they start with the letters *Au*, the chemical symbol for gold in the periodic table of elements. In the following sections, we'll describe these categories in detail.

Authentication

Authentication is the process by which an entity, also called a *principal*, verifies that another entity is indeed who or what it claims to be. A principal can be a user, some executable code, or a computer. Authentication requires *evidence* in the form of *credentials,* and evidence can be in one or more of the following forms:

- Something known (such as a password or a secret)
- Something possessed (such as a smart card)
- Something unique about the entity (in the case of humans, a signature, for example)

Proving that a principal is not an imposter depends upon the trustworthiness of the credentials. Credentials are trustworthy to the extent that they are correct or not—that is, absolutely. If a principal possesses the correct credentials, identity is verified regardless of who the principal is. In other words, authentication is a black-and-white process, resulting in a positive or negative response to a claim of identity.

However, the *strength* of the credentials is also important. For example, access to highly secure data might require credentials such as biometrics—for example, your thumbprint, a voice analysis, or a retinal scan, all of which are incredibly difficult to forge. Because biometrics are hard to counterfeit, they are often referred to as *strong credentials*. Passwords, on the other hand, are a weak credential because they are relatively easy to falsify.

Examples of some current authentication technologies include the following:

- **Kerberos** Kerberos is the default network authentication scheme for Microsoft Windows 2000.

- **Windows NTLM** This is the default protocol for Microsoft Windows NT 4 and is included in Windows 2000 for backward compatibility. It's also referred to as Windows NT Challenge/Response authentication.

- **Basic** Basic authentication is part of the HTTP 1.0 specification supported by most Web servers and Web browsers. It's insecure, because passwords are not encrypted. All versions of Microsoft Internet Information Services (IIS) support Basic authentication.

- **Digest** Digest authentication is part of the HTTP 1.1 specification and resolves many of the insecurities in Basic authentication. Internet Information Services 5 supports Digest authentication.

Chapter 3, "Windows 2000 Security Overview," Chapter 4, "Internet Explorer Security Overview," Chapter 5, "Internet Information Services Security Overview," Chapter 6, "SQL Server Security Overview," Chapter 7, "COM+ Security Overview," and Chapter 8, "Practical Authentication and Authorization," will further cover authentication issues.

Authorization

Once a principal's identity is authenticated, the principal will want to access resources, such as printers, files, Registry keys, Active Directory attributes, and tables in a database. Access is determined by performing an access check to see if the authenticated entity has access to the resource being requested.

Access is determined by comparing information about the principal with access control information associated with the resource—this information, for example, might be held in an access control list (discussed in Chapter 3). If Alice is given full access to the file Info.txt, she can read, write, and delete that file. Suppose Bob has read-only access to this same file. If he attempts to write to or delete the file, he will be denied access.

As you can see, degrees of authorization exist—Alice might have complete access to A, B, and C, while Bob might have only read access to B, and so on.

Examples of authorization mechanisms include

- **Windows 2000 access control lists (ACLs)**   An ACL describes the capabilities (such as read, write, execute) of a principal on a resource.

- **Windows 2000 privileges**   Such as the ability to debug or log on across the network.

- **Permissions**   Permissions (that is, create, read, update, and delete) such as in a Microsoft SQL Server database.

- **Role checking in a COM+ component**   The ability to programmatically determine whether a principal can perform an action (such as withdraw funds); based on the principal's membership in an administrative-defined role.

Chapter 3 and Chapter 8 will describe authorization in detail.

Auditing

The aim of auditing, also called *logging,* is to collect information about successful and failed access to objects, use of privileges, and other important security actions and to log them in some form of file for later analysis. Logging also aids in debugging applications because without logging you can only guess why someone was denied access to a resource.

Examples of audit logs include

- **The Windows 2000 Security Event Log**   Contains data about who logged on, what files they accessed, which COM+ objects were accessed, and so on.

- **The Internet Information Services 5 log**   Contains data about Web page hits, how long the access took, and from what IP address the request came. IIS also writes to the Windows 2000 security event log files.

- **SQL Server log**   Contains information about who logged on and off SQL Server. SQL Server uses the Windows 2000 log files as well as its own custom text files for auditing purposes.

Chapter 3 and Chapter 9, "Practical Privacy, Integrity, Auditing, and Non-repudiation," cover auditing in detail.

Privacy

Privacy, sometimes referred to as *confidentiality,* is a means of hiding information from prying eyes and is usually performed using encryption. By using privacy technologies, Alice can send a secret message to Bob, and anyone using a network protocol analyzer, such as Microsoft Network Monitor, cannot see what Alice has sent. Examples of privacy technology include

- **Secure Sockets Layer (SSL) or Transport Layer Security (TLS)**   Both use encryption algorithms to scramble data as it travels across insecure networks such as the Internet.

- **Internet Protocol Security (IPSec)**   An IETF (Internet Engineering Task Force) standard and a new security feature in Windows 2000 that provides data encryption of low-level IP packets.

Chapter 3 and Chapter 9 go into privacy in detail.

Integrity

Integrity refers to the ability to protect data from being deleted or changed either maliciously or by accident. If Alice orders 100 widgets from Bob, she doesn't want an attacker to modify the order en route to Bob to 1000 widgets. In the worst case, integrity checks determine whether the data has been changed.

> **NOTE**   Maliciously adjusted data is usually more serious than deleted data. If data is missing because it has been deleted, you know you need to use the last backup made to reinstate the missing data. However, if data is maliciously changed, you might not notice the change for a long time and the erroneous data might be used to make critical business decisions.

Examples of integrity technology include

- **SSL/TLS** Both use Message Authentication Code (MAC) algorithms to verify that data is not tampered with.
- **IPSec** Provides integrity checking of low-level IP packets.

Chapter 9 covers integrity in detail.

Availability

Another important aspect of security is availability, or the ensuring that a legitimate user is not denied access to a requested resource. For example, Alice, a valid user, won't be able to place an order by using your Web-based application if Bob, a malicious user, has launched an attack against your Web site that consumes all your network bandwidth. As far as Alice is concerned, your Web site is unavailable, so she might go elsewhere, perhaps to a competitor, to place her order.

Examples of availability technology include

- **Load-balancing hardware and software** Spreads heavy workloads over multiple devices to help ensure access
- **Failover hardware and software** Allows work requests to be switched from a failed device to a backup device

Please note that load-balancing and failover technologies are beyond the scope of this book.

Nonrepudiation

Nonrepudiation is a technique for providing proof that an action occurred so as to prevent a principal from fraudulently reneging on a transaction. For example, if Alice purchases an item, she might have to sign for the item upon receipt. The vendor can then use the signed receipt as evidence that Alice did indeed receive the package.

A complete nonrepudiation plan requires providing authentication, authorization, auditing, and data integrity. Nonrepudiation also requires that you inform the principal that the action he or she is about to take is legally binding. As you can imagine, nonrepudiation is extremely important for e-commerce.

We'll cover nonrepudiation in Chapter 9.

THREATS, SAFEGUARDS, VULNERABILITIES, AND ATTACKS

Security doesn't involve only the components we've just discussed, which make up part of the operation of the application you're creating. You must also place your system in the context of the environment in which the system will operate, such as on a corporate intranet or on the Web. Once you've determined what that context is, you need to determine how your system might be attacked, what threats exist to your business, and how you might attempt to counter them with technology, policy, and procedure. The security terms used when performing such an analysis are *threat, safeguard, vulnerability,* and *attack,* each of which we'll quickly describe here. We'll explain how to perform such an analysis in detail in the next chapter.

A *threat* is a possibility that poses danger to business assets (such as privacy or data integrity). An example of a threat is the possibility that an unauthorized person might get access to confidential company data or maliciously adjust account details. All threats are determined in relation to *business risk.* The greater the risk—that is, the greater the impact on the business should the threat be realized—the greater the threat. High-risk outcomes include public embarrassment, loss of credibility or good will, death or injury, loss of money, and so on.

A *safeguard* is a means to counter the threat, through technology, policy, or procedure. For example, requiring personnel to carry identification badges is a safeguard used to counter the threat that unauthorized people might enter a secure building.

A *vulnerability* is a weakness in a safeguard that can lead to a threat being realized as an attack. For example, if an administrator doesn't log off a secure terminal when she leaves, a nonadministrator might be able to perform administrative tasks such as changing passwords. In this case, the administrator logging off is the safeguard against the threat of unauthorized changes, and the fact that she might fail to do so is a vulnerability in the safeguard.

An *attack* is a threat that is brought to fruition through the exploitation of a vulnerability (or vulnerabilities) in the system. For an attack to take place, the following must occur:

- The attacker must have a motive. For example, an attacker might attack your Web site because he dislikes your stance on trade policy.

- The attacker must be able to justify the attack. For example, an attacker might believe that by attacking your site with antitrade policy graffiti she will heighten awareness of your policies.

■ An opportunity must arise. The attacker must find a weakness in the system by which he can attack your site. When a server is on the Web, the opportunity for attack is 24 hours a day, so the risk is vulnerability-based rather than time-based—meaning, how secure is your system?

Each of these requirements is covered in detail in Chapter 12, "Securing Against Attack."

Three main categories of attacks exist: denial of service, disclosure, and integrity. We'll discuss these categories in the following sections.

Denial of Service

Denial of service (DoS) attacks are common on the Internet today because such attacks can be launched remotely and with a good degree of anonymity. Two of the most common forms of DoS attacks are

■ Consuming all resources on the system so that no resources are available for other authorized users. An example of this is flooding a print queue with thousands of massive print jobs so that the printer runs out of paper and can no longer function.

■ Crashing the system. An example of this is attempting to find a flaw in the system that creates an access violation (AV) and causes a crash.

Disclosure

Disclosure attacks involve unauthorized access to data. For example, a nonemployee might gain access to a company's personnel databases. Imagine the damage an attacker could cause by accessing your personal data, such as your address, telephone number, salary, birthday, social security number or tax identification number, bank account details used for salary direct deposit, and so on. All this information could be used to impersonate you.

Integrity

The final type of attack is an integrity attack, in which data is changed maliciously. Often, the only way to survive a successful attack of this kind is to have a good backup policy. Fortunately, most Internet-based attackers do not want to destroy data; hence, this kind of attack is rare.

SUMMARY

In this chapter, we looked at the importance of security: you have assets to protect. Some assets are tangible and easy to value. Others are intangible, which does not mean they have no worth. Possibly the most important intangible asset you must protect is your name and reputation. If your name is tainted, you're likely to lose clients and be forced to endure serious financial ramifications.

Security can be grouped into seven main technology fields: authentication, authorization, auditing, privacy, integrity, availability, and nonrepudiation. When considering any security solution, you must consider all these disciplines and the eventual environment for your solution. All systems are subject to attack. Threats in vulnerable systems with inappropriate countermeasures are simply waiting to be acted on.

It's generally appreciated that three types of attack exist. A disclosure attack yields data to an attacker who should not have access to the data. An integrity attack involves malicious changing of data. And a denial of service attack prevents valid users from accessing a resource by maliciously consuming all the resources.

A Process for Building Secure Web Applications

Although building secure Web applications can seem daunting, following a few simple steps will make the task a little easier. In this chapter, we'll thoroughly describe the security design process that we'll advocate and use throughout this book. Following that discussion, we'll take a look at general application design—at first divorced from security concerns—and then map the process for building secure Web applications to the application design model we've described. To tie everything together, we'll end the chapter with a fairly detailed example, tracing the development of a security solution from a particular set of business requirements through the creation of a product list for the solution. This is the example that Chapter 10, "Building a Secure Solution," will pick up again following the chapters in Part II, "Technologies and Trade-Offs," which describe the pros and cons of the Microsoft technologies and strategies you might consider using.

A SECURITY DESIGN PROCESS

You'll note in Figure 2-1, which diagrams the security design process, that the process is cyclical. The rationale for this is quite simple: threats, both business and technical, change rapidly, and it's important that you stay on top of old and new threats to your applications and understand their security implications.

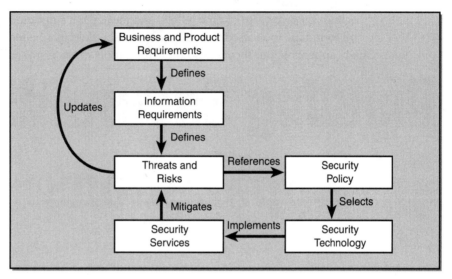

Figure 2-1. *An iterative process for determining security requirements and technologies.*

As you can see, the process begins (and begins again) with business and product requirements: the details of what you want your business and its tools to be able to do. The process has no room for the notion of technology for technology's sake. You must choose technology because it's the right tool for the job, not because it happens to be the technology de jour.

Note also how much of the process involves information gathering and decision making prior to any actual development work. Only at the last step—indicated by the Security Services box—does the nuts-and-bolts development begin. This is not a fluke; the process comprises a lot of research and planning to help ensure that the solution you ultimately build is the best response to your security needs. I hope you'll see that each step is necessary and commonsensical, and I strongly encourage you not to take any shortcuts in this process.

Each part of the process is described in further detail in the following sections.

Business and Product Requirements

Determining your business and product requirements is by far the most important stage in developing a security solution for your applications. No solution is useful unless it solves a business requirement, meets users' needs, and creates a practical business solution. Of course, this is heresy to some technical people, who feel that technology is a playground of intellectual stimulation. So let's get something straight: the best technology is a waste of time, effort, and money if it's not the right tool for the job. The incredible tools used to build the space shuttle might be technically and intellectually appealing, but they're also the wrong tools to fix a broken fan belt on an automobile!

Examples of high-level business requirements include the following:

- The ability to provide insurance information to field personnel quickly and effectively—most notably, the capacity to create insurance quotes for clients within five minutes of gathering all requisite client data

- The capability to determine the most cost-effective combination of goods and shipping methods based on quantity, shipping schedules, special offers, and previous sales history

- The need to optimally define medical operation timetables based on surgeon timetables, patient needs, and, where applicable, donor organs

- A requirement to take orders from clients, based on inventory and credit, in a timely fashion with a goal of taking market share from competitors

Now let's turn our attention to the next step in developing security solutions and another important aspect of business processes: determining the data and information required to back up the business requirements.

Information Requirements

Once you've defined your business requirements, you need to determine the information required to support those business processes. Each business process requires raw data, which it turns into useful information. Without that data, the business process is meaningless. Hence, the data and intellectual capital that a company owns needs protecting. Also, the information used by a business helps it gain competitive advantage, which is another reason protecting information is so important. Obviously, without competitive advantage a business might eventually cease to exist.

Examples of information requirements include a sales-oriented application requiring access to sales history, product, client, commission, discount, and delivery schedule information and a medical application requiring access to surgeon timetables, private patient medical histories, drug interaction data, insurance company policies, and so on.

Threats and Risks

Now that you know the capabilities your application must provide—dictated by your business requirements—and the information required by the application, you can turn your attention to the first of the security-related topics: threats and risks to the company. A discussed in Chapter 1, "Security 101," a threat is a possibility that poses danger to business assets, and all threats are determined in relation to business risk. The greater the risk—that is, the greater the impact on the business should the threat be realized—the greater the threat.

Different companies have differing threats. Banks don't want money stolen, hospitals don't want patient records maliciously adjusted, and software development companies don't want source code destroyed, yet these sorts of companies face these threats every day. (The risks faced by these companies vary with the particularities and business contexts for the companies.) Furthermore, having some form of Web presence exposes companies to even more threats and risk.

The first order of business at this step of the security design process is to establish your company's risk tolerance—that is, the degree to which the company is willing to take risks to achieve its objectives. A high-profile bank's risk tolerance might be low as it has a reputation to uphold. However, a small start-up company might be willing to take more risks to gain exposure or market share. Once you have a general feel for what your company's risk tolerance is, you can better analyze the threats and risks for the business.

Analyze the threats

Analyzing threats can be difficult, but it's important that a good deal of effort be spent in this phase. Indeed, you simply cannot build a secure application without understanding the threats to your application. Without such understanding, you can't determine the appropriate technology to use to counter the threats, as covered in the remaining steps of the process.

A basic taxonomy of attacks—that is, threats that have been carried out—was discussed in the previous chapter, and it included

- Denial of service

- Disclosure

- Integrity

This taxonomy serves as a good starting point, but I'll use a much more granular taxonomy used at Microsoft called STRIDE. The STRIDE model includes

■ Spoofing user identity

■ Tampering with data (integrity)

■ Repudiability

■ Information disclosure (disclosure)

■ Denial of service

■ Elevation of privilege

As the bulleted list indicates, the STRIDE model includes the three types of threats I've discussed before and adds some others that need to be considered when you're designing an application. As you'll see, this model is more usable and applicable in the current era of Internet application development.

Let's look at each threat in a bit more detail.

Spoofing user identity

An example of user identity spoofing is the breaching of a user's authentication information. In this case, the hacker has obtained the user's personal information or something that enables him or her to replay the authentication procedure. Spoofing threats are usually associated with a wily hacker being able to impersonate a valid system user or resource to get access to the system and thereby compromise system security.

Tampering with data

Tampering with data involves the malicious modification of system or user data with or without detection. An unauthorized change made to stored or in-transit information, the formatting of a hard disk, the introduction by a malicious intruder of an undetectable network packet in a communication, and an undetectable change made to a sensitive file are all examples of tampering threats.

Repudiability

Repudiability threats are associated with users—malicious or otherwise—who can deny performing an action without administrators having any way to prove otherwise. An example of a repudiability threat is a user performing an illegal operation in a system that lacks the ability to trace such operations.

Information disclosure

Information disclosure threats involve the compromising of private or business-critical information through the exposure of that information to individuals who are not supposed to see it. A user's ability to read a file that she or he was not granted access to and an intruder's ability to read data in transit between two computers are both disclosure threats. Note that this threat differs from a spoofing threat in that in this case the perpetrator gets access to the information directly rather than by having to appear as a legitimate user.

Denial of service

Denial of service (DoS) threats when carried out deny service to valid users—for example, by making the system temporarily unavailable or unusable or by forcing a reboot or restart of the user's machine. You must protect against certain types of DoS threats simply to improve system availability and reliability. Other types of DoS threats, however, are very hard to protect against; at a minimum, you should identify and rationalize such threats.

Elevation of privilege

In this type of threat, an unprivileged user gains privileged access and thereby has sufficient access to compromise or destroy the entire system. The more dangerous aspect of such threats is the compromising of the system in undetectable ways whereby the user can take advantage of privileges without the knowledge of system administrators. Elevation of privilege threats include those situations in which an attacker has effectively penetrated all system defenses and become part of the trusted system itself—at that point, the attacker can cause extreme system damage.

Because it requires thorough understanding of numerous technologies, threat and risk determination is somewhat of a specialized field, and you might need to spend time with a security consultant or risk specialist to determine the threats to your application.

Prioritize the threats

Once you've determined which risks and threats prevail, you might be amazed at the number of them. Chances are you won't be able to address every threat. Therefore, after compiling your list of threats, you need to prioritize them.

Prioritization is a simple process of determining how much it will cost to counter the threat and comparing that cost to the cost of the asset the countermeasure will protect. Is it worth spending $100,000 to protect an asset worth only $1,000? Probably not! Of course, you might decide that the cost is outweighed by the possible loss of credibility with the public if the asset is successfully attacked.

It's also important to note that it's likely at this stage that you won't know the real cost of protecting the asset because the technology you'll use for the protection hasn't been chosen. In other words, your countermeasure costs are only estimates at this point.

Because certain aspects of the prioritization process—such as intangibles like public image and the fact that you might decide to pay the price of protecting an asset if the chance of attack on it is high—make the process a little complicated, you should apply a simple formula to each threat:

Risk = Criticality / Effort

Criticality is the overall importance of the resource being protected, and *effort* is the degree of difficulty required to mount an attack on the resource. *Risk,* then, gauges the overall danger a particular threat poses. You'll use this risk rating in conjunction with your analysis of security cost vs. asset value to make your prioritization decisions.

For example, a threat is found regarding access to client medical data—an information disclosure threat. Obviously, if the data is compromised in any way, there could be serious implications for both the patient and the hospital or doctor's office in question. Therefore, this threat's criticality is given a rating of 10, on a scale of 1 (least critical) through 10 (most critical). You determine that the effort to mount an attack based on this threat is minimal, so you rate the threat's effort at 1, on a scale of 1 (attack easiest to mount) through 10 (attack most difficult to mount).

The risk posed by this threat is 10 / 1, or 10. This is a very high-risk threat indeed; in fact, it's the highest rated threat possible. When you're prioritizing your threats, such a rating would balance any discrepancy between countermeasure cost and asset value and would encourage you to rank the threat as one crucial to address. For a more detailed discussion of this formula, see Edward Amoroso's *Fundamentals of Computer Security Technology* (Prentice Hall, 1994).

Once you have a list of raw prioritized threats, you've completed the third stage of the security design process. The next phase, application of the company's security policy, will help you fine-tune the list of prioritized threats and begin determining what to do in response to each threat.

Security Policy

The next step is to refer to corporate security policy to see which threats are tolerable and which are not. Despite a threat's low-risk rating, for example, security policy might dictate that the threat must be addressed no matter what. A medical institution will probably determine that the threat of an attacker maliciously changing patient medical data (a data-tampering threat and possibly a disclosure threat) must be remedied at any cost despite its risk rating or cost.

You have three choices with regard to a threat, each of which will be driven by taking into account your threat prioritization list and security policy:

■ You can *accept* the threat if, say, the cost of protecting the asset is too high or the risk is too low. If you decide to accept a threat, you might want to inform your users that the threat exists and that the feasibility of it being exploited is low.

■ You can *assign* the threat to another party, such as an insurance company. In other words, the threat is someone else's problem should it be carried out. Once again, since you've decided not to counter the threat, consider informing your users that the threat exists.

■ You can *defend* against the threat by implementing countermeasures, such as education, informing users of the threat in documentation, and the use of technology.

Security policy documents should be drafted by every company and regularly updated because

■ Business landscapes change rapidly

■ The Internet changes rapidly (rabidly?)

■ Internet security is constantly evolving

An old security policy is useless; the policy document should be a living document, evaluated at least every six months. I've seen a number of instances in which a company had either

■ No corporate security policy and hence no idea how to build secure systems mapped to its business processes, or

■ A security policy that was hopelessly out-of-date. In one such case, the company made incorrect security decisions because no one referred to the security policy document for direction (because it was irrelevant). Obviously, referring to the document wouldn't have helped either.

Make sure you have a security policy document, and make sure it's up-to-date! Now that you have guidance from your security policy on how to deal with each threat—that is, whether to accept, assign, or defend against it—you can begin to look at the technologies you'll use to counter those threats you've chosen to defend against.

Security Technology

There are many security technologies to choose from when building solutions, so many in fact that it can be difficult to determine which ones to choose. To make this process easier, break it into two steps. First, before considering the actual products you'll use, determine the generic types of technology that can be used to solve specific threats—that is, map general countermeasures (not yet linked with specific products) to the threats you're defending against. For example, Table 2-1 maps various possible countermeasures to each of the threats in the STRIDE model.

Threat	*Countermeasures*
Spoofing user identity	Strong authentication.
	Don't store secrets (such as passwords) in configuration files. If you must store secrets, use secure mechanisms.
Tampering with data	Strong access control mechanisms.
	Hashes/digital signatures on resources.
	End-to-end tamper-resistant data transfer protocols.
Repudiability	Secure logging.
	Digital signatures and time stamping.
Information disclosure	Strong access control mechanisms.
	Perform correct file canonicalization.
	Limit specific file operations.
	End-to-end encrypted data transfer protocols.
	Don't store secrets (such as passwords) in configuration files. If you must store secrets, use secure mechanisms.
Denial of service	Bandwidth throttling.
	Resource throttling.
	Quality of service.
	Packet filtering.
Elevation of privilege	Run process in low privileged account.
	Safe buffer management.

Table 2-1. *Countermeasures mapped to each threat in the STRIDE model.*

Microsoft Windows 2000 includes many technologies, most of which are discussed in subsequent chapters in this book, to help create the countermeasures listed in Table 2-1. Table 2-2 maps technologies and capabilities offered by Windows 2000, as well as some best practices, to many of those countermeasures.

Countermeasure	*Technologies and Best Practices*
Strong authentication	■ Don't design your own authentication scheme; most of the time such schemes are very weak and flawed. ■ Use digest, certificates, or Kerberos authentication, if possible.
Storing secrets	■ Use the data protection APIs: *CryptProtectData* and *CryptUnprotectData*.
Access control	■ Access control lists (ACLs) on resources such as files and registry settings.
Hashes and digital signatures	■ CryptoAPI 2.0 provides functions such as *CryptHashData* and *CryptSignHash* for creating hashes from data.
Secure end-to-end protocols	■ Secure Sockets Layer/Transport Layer Security (SSL/TLS), which is built into most Web servers and browsers such as Microsoft Internet Explorer and Microsoft Internet Information Services (IIS). ■ Internet Protocol Security (IPSec), which is the industry-standard IP security protocol built into Windows 2000.
File canonicalization	■ Use the Windows 2000 functions to open files rather than writing your own. If you perform your own work you may make incorrect assumptions about file names.
Limiting specific file operations	■ You should consider whether '..' (parent directory) is allowed in a filename. Allowing this might allow an attacker to access files otherwise not accessible.
Bandwidth throttling	■ Windows 2000 thread pools. ■ IIS 5 bandwidth throttling. ■ HTTP compression, built in to IIS 5, conserves bandwidth and provides faster data transmission between the Web server and compression-enabled clients.
Resource throttling	■ IIS 5 CPU throttling. IIS 5 uses Windows 2000 *job objects* to perform this task. A job object is described in MSDN like so: "A job object allows groups of processes to be managed as a unit. Job objects are namable, securable, sharable objects that control attributes of the processes associated with them. Operations performed on the job object affect all processes associated with the job object." You can set CPU, time, user interface restrictions, and memory limits on a job object.

Table 2-2. *Some Windows 2000 security technologies mapped to the countermeasures in Table 2-1.*

Countermeasure	*Technologies and Best Practices*
Quality of service (QoS)	■ Windows QoS controls how network bandwidth is allotted to applications; time-critical applications can be given more bandwidth, less important applications less bandwidth.
Packet filtering	■ Packet filtering is used to specify what type of traffic is allowed into and out of the computer. For example, you can limit a computer to accept only Web traffic (which uses TCP port 80) and *ping* traffic (which uses the Internet Control Message Protocol [ICMP]).
Buffer management	■ Windows 2000 structured exception handling and good programming practices, such as ❑ Making sure buffers are large enough to copy data into ❑ Analyzing safe usage of C/C++ functions that copy data such as *strcpy*, *strcat*, *memcpy*, and *sprintf*
Low privilege context	■ Run the application under a non-administrator and non-local-system account. ■ Use restricted tokens, such as *CreateRestrictedToken*, to remove privileges and security identifiers (SIDs) from the user's token. ■ Use Windows 2000 secondary logon.

Security Services

The final step of the security design process is designing security services that use security technologies. The purpose of security services is to mitigate all risks to a tolerable level. Any security service that does not mitigate one or more risks should not be built; if the service doesn't counter a threat, there's no reason to build it.

In a well-designed solution, security services are constructed by using security technologies as discrete components or building blocks rather than tightly interweaved tools. This is a classic software engineering principle called *loose coupling:* components are written to have minimal dependence on each other. Loosely coupled solutions do not rely on a large number of public methods, variables, and properties.

You can find more information on loose coupling and other good software development practices in the Microsoft Solutions Framework (MSF), a software development framework produced by Microsoft Consulting Services (MCS) based on Microsoft's internal development methodology and find-tuned from the best practices of many MCS corporate clients. For more information about MSF, visit *http://www.microsoft.com/msf.*

APPLICATION DESIGN

This section deals with pure application design rather than the design of security solutions. The information here is intended to round out the process of designing and developing Web applications and to help you build better, more robust, and cheaper Web applications.

First, all applications—Web or otherwise—should be designed initially with no technology in mind. Too often, designers have a tool or technology they like and they limit themselves to looking for problems that can be solved with that tool. This is an easy trap to fall into, especially if you're a technical person. When you know how to use a tool well, you use it. But many applications have been designed with the wrong tool for the job, because that was the only tool known to the company. Typically, this greatly increases cost because the application developed must be either abandoned later or adjusted to accommodate the correct technology for the task.

A good application design pattern comprises three phases, as illustrated in Figure 2-2. In the first phase, called the business model, you determine your business requirements (including security requirements and risk/threat analysis) and information requirements. At this stage, you're concentrating on business needs, not theorizing an application to meet those needs. In the next phase, the logical model, you begin to look at how an application called for by the details in the business model might be designed. At this point, you're working out the capabilities of the application without considering the technologies you'll use to build the application. Finally, in the physical model phase, you choose the technologies you'll use to build the application and you build it. This framework is in accord with many large-scale design methods, including the Microsoft Solutions Framework.

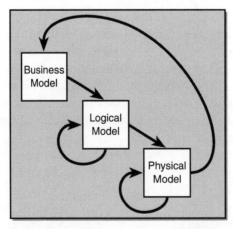

Figure 2-2. *The process involved in building any application.*

Note from Figure 2-2 that the logical and physical models are iterative. This is because you learn a great deal at each stage, invalidate previous assumptions, and address issues with fresh ideas. By repeating your analysis at these stages, you can save a good bit of money and time and prevent a number of headaches. It's much cheaper to fix problems and handle "unknowns" during the logical design model phase or even during the physical model's design phase than it is to patch mistakes while developing code, which is very expensive.

Also, note that the physical model should ultimately lead you back to consideration of your business model; this is because any technology introduced into a business changes that business's environment. Consider a bank that historically has performed standard "brick and mortar" banking functions that decides to create a Web site to handle online account balances, allow for bills to be paid on line, and so on. Once the Web site is completed, the bank's business environment changes radically— for example, the competition might adopt strategies to counter the new Web site, and bank clerks might have time to perform other tasks.

THREATS AND BUSINESS REQUIREMENTS

Security threats are a special form of business requirement, but, unlike business requirements, they tend to be overlooked. Remember this: failure to incorporate solutions for security threats within the application is a failure just like shipping a pilot program three months late.

Take a look at Figure 2-3 to see how the application design model and the security design process I discussed earlier in this chapter interrelate.

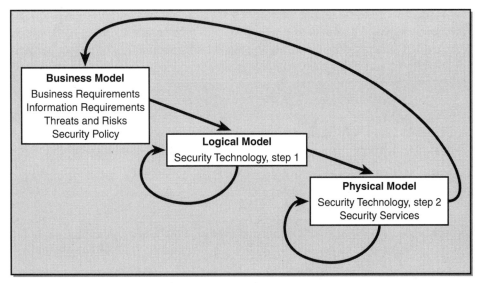

Figure 2-3. *The security design process mapped to the application design process.*

As you can see, determination of business and product requirements, determination of information requirements, threat and risk analysis, and application of security policy all fall within the business model phase. All of these steps take place prior to consideration of how to design an application, which takes place during the logical model phase. Step 1 of the security technology phase—that is, the mapping of possible countermeasures to the threats you'll address—makes up the logical model. Step 2 of the security technology phase—the mapping of specific technologies to countermeasures—and the security services phase make up the physical model of the application design process.

Enough theory! Let's look at an example to illustrate how to develop a secure application.

AN EXAMPLE

The following example relates to issues faced by the sales arm of a fictitious company named Exploration Air. First we'll turn our attention to the most important aspect of the solution: the information gathered during the business model phase.

The Business Model

During this stage, Exploration Air gathers information, analyzes and rates threats and risks, and applies its security policy.

Business, product, and information requirements

First, appropriate company personnel—the sponsor and clients of the project—consult and develop the following problem statement: Sales personnel do not have access to up-to-the-minute airline reservation information and therefore cannot determine what discounts to give clients and what products need to be aggressively marketed. This situation leads to lost sales opportunities, less than optimal client relations, and an inability to confirm orders.

The company comes up with the following list of requirements:

- Sales personnel must be able to access flight schedule and planning and booking information from anywhere in the world, such as at the office, at home, or at a hotel room, at any time of the day or night.

- Sales personnel must be able to access data from many devices in many ways, such as with a Pocket PC, a laptop, or a desktop by using a modem or a LAN connection.

- Sales personnel will be restricted to accessing only their own sales data relating to their clients; however, they'll also be able see aggregate data (such as total bookings for Exploration Air as a whole).

- Because risk tolerance is low, security must be very strong.

- The sales data already exists in a Microsoft SQL Server 7 database. (Technically, this isn't a requirement; it's a situation within which company personnel work because the company is not likely to switch databases any time soon!)

- The Information Technology (IT) department wants to be able to define authentication and authorization at various points in the application as needs change over time. For example, if in the future an offline version of the application is created, authentication and authorization will need to be performed locally (on the user's computer). (At present, the offline scenario is not a requirement, but it might become one in the future.)

- The IT department does not want to create multiple user account databases. These can lead to support issues if a new user is added, changed, or deleted, because information must be updated in multiple places, a step that is both time-consuming and prone to errors.

Now that they have a list of business, product, and information requirements, Exploration Air personnel can look at the security threats that might be faced by an application that matches those requirements.

Threats and risks

Putting corporate sales data on the Web is a dangerous proposition. The Internet is a proving ground for hackers, and, because of weaknesses in the TCP/IP protocol, attacks can be launched virtually anonymously. (See Chapter 12, "Securing Against Attack," for more information on countering such attacks.) Let's take a look at a subset of some of the threats to the application called for by the company's business, product, and information requirements and at some of the countermeasures that can be employed to counter those threats. The threats are listed in order of risk; the most dangerous risks are listed first.

Information disclosure threat (risk level 5)

This information disclosure threat involves sales data being made available to unauthorized users such as hackers. The value of the attacked assets is presently unknown, but the value is probably high owing to the possible loss of faith by Exploration Air clients and, worse, the damage that can be done if the data is accessed and used maliciously. Based on these factors, the threat's criticality is extremely high: 10. The effort required to perform such an attack is considered low: 2. So, the risk rating of this threat is 5 (10 / 2 = 5). This is the highest risk rating calculated during the company's threat analysis sessions, and it should be addressed immediately.

Methods to use to counter this threat include the following:

- Strong authenticating protocols to validate the user

- Appropriate ACLs on all resources

- Privacy of the communication channel between a valid user and the Web site, thus preventing unauthorized data snooping with technologies such as SSL/TLS or the secure version of IP, IPSec

Denial of service threat (risk level 2)

This DoS threat involves the server hosting the Web server being rendered unusable through malicious TPC/IP-level attacks, such as SYN-flooding, distributed denial of service attacks, fragment attacks, and so on. (See Chapter 12 for more information on this type of attack.) Currently, the company rates the value of the Web site at approximately $100,000. This is the cost of business lost during a one-hour Web server blackout. But the figure is inaccurate because the company has considered only how much business will be attributed to the Web site, which is currently somewhat of an unknown. The company intends to re-evaluate this value in the next 6, 12, and 24 months and update the risk document accordingly.

Company personnel determine that the Web site is somewhat critical to the business now but will certainly be mission-critical to the business in the future (within 18 to 24 months, they think), so they give the threat a criticality rating of 6. Because the ability to mount such an attack is pretty simple—there are many automated DoS tools available on the Web that require little skill to use—effort is rated at 3. The threat's overall risk rating, then, is 2.

Technologies to counter this threat are easy to choose from and well understood; one of these is a packet-filtering firewall placed before the Web server that can be configured to discard suspected TCP/IP packets.

Spoofing user identity threat (risk level 2)

This spoofing user identity threat is very common and probably applicable to most Web applications: an attacker uses an employee's password to gain access to a system. The threat's criticality is rated at 10 because the value of the assets being protected is immeasurable and there are multiple secondary threats associated with this threat:

- The attacker gains access to confidential data (information disclosure).

■ If the attacker gains access to the administrator's password (elevation of privilege), he or she can mount many other attacks, including

  ❑ Changing log files to cover their tracks (repudiability)

  ❑ Shutting down the Web site (denial of service)

  ❑ Changing the Web site's pages (integrity)

The good news is that the effort that's required to access passwords on a well-maintained Windows 2000–based Web server is nontrivial. (By "well-maintained," I mean a server whose administrator is staying abreast of security updates to the operating system and Web server.) So, the threat's effort rating is 5, which results in a risk rating of 2.

This threat can be countered by using strong authentication protocols requiring strong credentials. If you determine that passwords are too weak, either a stronger password policy can be enforced or a non-password-based scheme can be used, such as client authentication certificates perhaps using smartcards.

Integrity threat (risk level 1.66)

This integrity threat involves data being improperly modified by attackers. For example, say an attacker accesses the home page of the company's Web site (an information disclosure threat) and modifies it to contain political or defamatory messages. The implications of such an attack are probably worse than the DoS attack (hence the threat is given a criticality of 10), but the attack is harder to perform (effort is 6), so the threat's overall risk rating is 1.66.

Tools and technologies to counter this threat include

■ Data-entry validation in the server application to verify data ranges and data format validity before committing to permanent storage.

■ Performing regular backups in case of data integrity compromise. Backup policy dictates that regular backups be held off-site at a secure location.

■ Strong authentication protocols to validate the user before resources are accessed.

■ Access control mechanisms such as ACLs to limit users access to resources.

■ Audit trails to help locate what resources were accessed, when they were accessed, and by whom.

■ System integrity tools (such as Pedestal Software's Intact) to quickly verify that Web content has changed.

Information disclosure threat (risk level 1)

This information disclosure threat relates to a Web site that takes input from users; the input data is accessed as it travels from the user to the server. The value of the disclosed data is difficult to ascertain, but it's probably high owing to loss of customer faith if the confidential customer data is accessed, so criticality is rated 6. Because the effort required to mount such an attack is quite high, also a 6, the threat's overall risk rating is 1.

The technologies to counter this threat are easy to implement and commonly available; they involve encrypting the data channel between the client and the Web server. The technologies include SSL/TLS and IPSec or similar technologies.

Repudiability threat (risk level 1)

This repudiability threat involves a sales person fraudulently acquiring airline tickets for private use, which causes both loss of business and loss of income. Criticality is more minor, rated a 4, and the effort required to carry out the threat is reasonably easy, also a 4, so the overall risk rating is 1.

To help counter this threat, security policy says that all audit logs are to be analyzed regularly for suspicious activity and archived for five years. In addition, clocks on all computers are synchronized to help analyze audit logs across multiple computers. Out-of-step clocks make such analysis much harder. At present, the company does not want to use time stamping and digital signatures, but this is to be investigated later.

Elevation of privilege threat (risk level 1)

This elevation of privilege threat relates to an attacker becoming an administrator through odious means on Exploration Air's Web server. Damage could be significant because so many other attacks are possible if this attack is successful, so criticality is extreme: 10. Luckily, this attack is normally not easy to perform and requires extensive skills, so effort is also rated 10 and the threat's overall risk rating is 1.

In the case of defects in third-party components, the threat can be alleviated by keeping abreast of appropriate security updates to affected components of the Web solution. Other aspects of this threat can be offset by good administrative practices, such as strong passwords and strong access control mechanisms on resources used to store secrets such as passwords.

The Logical Model

Let's turn our attention from security for a moment to the core application that needs to be built to meet the business requirements defined earlier in this example. Obviously, company personnel need to access a database (such as SQL Server), and they need to use the Web. In this case, SQL Server is the database of choice for the company, so that's the database that will be used for the application. In addition, SQL

Server is a popular database on servers running Windows 2000. The application will use the Web because it provides many access points and satisfies the following business requirements (from the list of requirements that appeared earlier in "Business, Product, and Information Requirements"):

■ Sales personnel must be able to access flight schedule and planning and booking information from anywhere in the world, such as at the office, at home, or at a hotel room, at any time of the day or night.

■ Sales personnel must be able to access data from many devices in many ways, such as with a Pocket PC, a laptop, or a desktop by using a modem or a LAN connection.

It's fair to say that virtually every Web application today follows the high-level design shown in Figure 2-4.

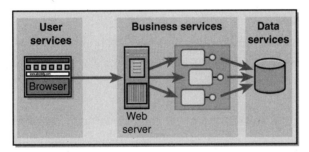

Figure 2-4. *A common high-level design for Web applications.*

In this scenario, sales personnel use a Web browser to communicate with a Web server. The Web server calls on some business logic residing in reusable components that in turn manipulate data and return results to the user. This is a very well understood model because it has been around since client/server days.

Figure 2-5 shows the logical model diagram that emerges when threats and related countermeasures are applied to the application in Figure 2-4.

As you can see, security comes into play at many points in the application's operation. These points can be categorized using the security categories introduced in Chapter 1—see "The Golden Rules (and Some Others)," beginning on page 7. The categories applicable in this case are authentication, authorization, privacy, integrity, and audit. In the physical model phase, company personnel will choose appropriate technology to address each of these security areas. One of main objectives of this book is to show which technologies are appropriate in particular areas of security and how to use those technologies to build business solutions based on Microsoft products.

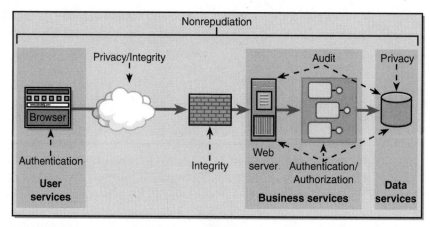

Figure 2-5. *Security requirements of a Web application.*

The Physical Model

Now that Exploration Air has a feel for the security and business requirements of the Web application to be developed, it's time to choose some technologies. Table 2-3 outlines the relevant core security categories and some technologies that map to those categories.

Category	Example Technologies
Authentication	■ Kerberos
	■ Windows NT Challenge/Response
	■ Basic (HTTP 1.0 Protocol)
	■ Digest (HTTP 1.1 Protocol)
	■ X.509 certificates
Authorization	■ Access control lists
	■ Permissions (SQL Server)
	■ Web access permissions (IIS)
	■ Role checking (COM+)
Privacy	■ SSL/TLS
	■ IPSec
	■ Encrypting File System (EFS)
Integrity	■ SSL/TLS
	■ IPSec
	■ Packet-filtering firewall

Table 2-3. *Applicable technologies mapped to the security categories (the "golden rules") relevant to the application in Figure 2-5.*

Category	Example Technologies
Audit	■ Windows 2000 Security Event Logs
	■ IIS Web logs
	■ SQL Server logs and Profiler traces
Nonrepudiation	■ Audit logs
	■ Law and policy

Various Microsoft products, as described in Table 2-4, can provide all the technologies listed in Table 2-3.

Product or Technology	Comments
Windows 2000 Server	Windows 2000 Server includes improved network, application, and Web services, as well as increased reliability and scalability. One of the most important additions is improved security technology, such as public key infrastructure, Kerberos authentication, IP Security, and the Active Directory.
	Windows 2000 also includes IPSec, which lets you set up port rules to determine which IP packets can enter which ports. It's not a replacement for a firewall, but it's a great line of defense. IPSec is covered in Chapter 3, "Windows 2000 Security Overview."
Internet Explorer 5.0	Internet Explorer 5.0 is the Web browsing technology provided in Windows 2000. Internet Explorer includes support for many security technologies, including digest and Kerberos authentication, SSL/TLS support, and Fortezza. (Fortezza is a set of cryptographic functions mandated by the U.S. federal government for sensitive but nonclassified communication.)
Internet Information Services 5	IIS 5 is the latest version of Microsoft's award-winning Web server. It includes many new security tools and technologies, including digest authentication, Kerberos authentication integration, SSL/TLS support, Fortezza support, and two new security tools: the Permissions wizard and the Server Certificate wizard.

Table 2-4. *Some Microsoft products and their security features.*   *(continued)*

Table 2-4. *continued*

Product or Technology	Comments
COM+	Building on the success of COM, COM+ makes it easy for developers to create location-independent software components in virtually any programming language.
	COM+ provides the component technology for the Microsoft Windows Distributed interNet Applications (Windows DNA) architecture, enabling developers to integrate Web-based and client/server applications in a single, unified architecture.
SQL Server 7 or SQL Server 2000	SQL Server provides integrated security with the Windows 2000 operating system. It supports using all available security protocols and provides authentication for each user. Permissions are discretionary and are extremely granular.
Certificate Services 2.0	Certificate Services provides customizable services for issuing and managing certificates ▸ used in security systems employing public key technologies.
	The role of Certificate Services is to create a certificate authority (CA) that receives certificate requests from clients and servers, verifies the information in the request, and issues a corresponding X.509 certificate. This will all be explained in detail in Chapter 15, "An Introduction to Cryptography and Certificates in Windows 2000."
X.509 certificates	X.509 certificates contain public information about a user or computer and associate a public key to the user or computer. Certificates are issued by certification authorities such as Thawte (*www.thawte.com*), VeriSign (*www.verisign.com*), or your own corporate CA using Microsoft Certificate Services; certificates are used to authenticate users and computers. SSL/TLS uses certificates for authentication purposes. See Chapter 15 for more information on certificates.
SSL/TLS	SSL is a security technology developed by Concensus and Netscape, and TLS is the IETF-ratified version of SSL. SSL/TLS allows you to encrypt the channel between two points, making it tremendously difficult for a malicious user to spy on the communication.

When the details in Table 2-4 are applied to the application illustrated in Figure 2-5, the physical model solution looks like that shown in Figure 2-6.

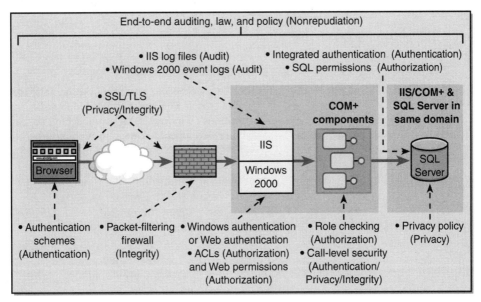

Figure 2-6. *The application's physical model solution.*

Table 2-5 describes the core components of the solution.

Product/Technology	*Where It Fits in the Solution*
Internet Explorer 5.0	Allows the user to enter username and password (or some other credentials) and send them to the Web server. The session will be conducted over an SSL/TLS connection.
	Other browsers such as Pocket Internet Explorer could be used on Microsoft Windows CE devices to satisfy the businesses requirement that the application run on many devices.
	Note that browsers less capable than Internet Explorer could be used, but the resulting fidelity might be somewhat reduced. Company personnel need to handle this eventuality in the solution as determined by business requirement number two.
SSL/TLS	SSL/TLS will be used between the browser and the Web server when sensitive data is sent across the Internet.

Table 2-5. *How some Microsoft products map to the physical model solution.*   *(continued)*

Table 2-5. *continued*

Product/Technology	Where It Fits in the Solution
Internet Information Services 5	IIS hosts a number of Active Server Pages (ASP) that call COM+ components. Most of the user interface layout is provided by ASP as it generates HTML (or dynamic HTML).
Windows 2000 Server	IIS 5 runs as a service on Windows 2000 Server and leverages many of the security technologies in Windows 2000 (such as ACLs) and Windows 2000 authentication (such as Windows NT Challenge/ Response authentication [NTLM] and Kerberos).
COM+ components	The COM+ components will perform most, if not all, of the business work as well as query SQL Server by using ADO.

COM+ is language-neutral, but Exploration Air will create the components using Microsoft Visual Basic 6. |
ADO	ADO, or Active Data Objects, provides a high-level, flexible interface to various databases such as SQL Server.
Visual Basic 6	Microsoft Visual Basic 6 is a high-level rapid application development (RAD) tool for creating applications and COM+ components. It was chosen for its speed of development and execution as well as its excellent debugging capability. Visual Basic was also chosen because it is supported by third-party companies and because it is one of the most popular development tools in the world.
SQL Server 7 or SQL Server 2000	SQL Server will store all of the corporate sales data, and, like IIS, it runs as a service on top of Windows 2000.

INTERNET VS. INTRANET VS. EXTRANET

Notice that I've made little or no distinction between Internet, intranet, and extranet scenarios. Although they are differing deployment settings, the scenarios call for use of the same technologies. You can draw a security line between the situations only in that some of the threats are different; intranet scenarios have different audiences from, say, extranet scenarios and hence their threats will differ somewhat.

At this stage, the company is in a good position to build the solution. It's followed a path from a business requirements information-gathering phase through a logical model design phase to a physical model design phase informed by actual products. This process has allowed risks to be rated, prioritized, and planned for early, and it's helped the company find a better, more informed solution to the problem, thus saving time and money. However, before committing to the final product list, it's important that the personnel building the application understand in significant detail what each tool and technology being considered for deployment can do, the tradeoffs between the technologies (their pros and cons), and the implications of strategies regarding security's golden rules. Those matters are the subject of Part II of this book; Chapters 3 through 7 will describe the security capabilities and implications of using the major Microsoft products mentioned in this chapter—more specifically, Windows 2000, Internet Explorer, IIS, SQL Server, and COM+—and Chapters 8 and 9 will address authentication, authorization, privacy, integrity, auditing, and nonrepudiation.

Part II

Technologies and Trade-Offs

Chapter 3

Windows 2000 Security Overview

Microsoft Windows 2000 was designed as an extremely secure operating system and includes numerous security tools and technologies to aid in the development and deployment of secure solutions. It's important to understand these core security features so that you'll know how and why security solutions work and why they sometimes don't work. Each product that runs on the operating system can take advantage of these features.

In the following sections, as listed below, we'll give an overview of the security technologies implemented in Windows 2000 and explain the terminology related to each technology:

- Authenticated logon
- Authentication
- Privileges
- User accounts and groups
- Domains and workgroups
- DOMAIN/Account names and user principal names
- Managing accounts
- Security identifiers (SIDs)

- Tokens
- Access control lists (ACLs)
- Impersonation
- Delegation
- Miscellaneous Windows 2000 security features

However, before we get started, it's important to discuss the security implications of a significant technology included with Windows 2000: the Active Directory service. (For non-security-related information about the Active Directory, see this book's bibliography.)

WHAT IS A SERVICE?

Services are processes that start up when Windows 2000 starts up or on demand and that do not require any user interaction. Examples include Microsoft SQL Server, Internet Information Services (IIS), and the print spooler. You can look at the currently available services on your system by opening the Services tool.

One of the important new capabilities in Windows 2000 is the ability to perform a task in the event that a service fails:

1. Right-click the service in question (for example, the IIS Admin Service).

2. Choose Properties from the context menu.

3. Click the Recovery tab.

4. Look at the First Failure, Second Failure, and Subsequent Failures options.

THE IMPACT OF ACTIVE DIRECTORY

Active Directory is both a database about resources on a network—such as computers, users, and printers—and a directory service that makes the information in the database available to users and applications. Active Directory provides enterprise-level directory service features such as an extensible information source, naming conventions for directory objects, a common set of policies, and tools for administering the service from a single point of access. Secure, distributed, partitioned, and replicated, it is designed to work well in any size installation, from a single server with a few hundred objects to thousands of servers and millions of objects. Active Directory has many features that make it easy to manage large amounts of information, reducing management overhead for administrators and making the service easier to use for end users.

By default, a machine running Windows 2000 Server does not have Active Directory installed. To install it, you must run the Active Directory Installation wizard, either by using the Dcpromo.exe tool at the command line or like so:

1. Click Start.

2. Select Programs, Administrative Tools, and then Configure Your Server.

3. Select Active Directory, and click Start to start the wizard.

Once Active Directory is installed, a world of security possibilities opens up, as described in Table 3-1.

Feature	*Benefits*
Kerberos V5 authentication	Single sign-on to multiple Windows 2000–based servers and other operating systems running the MIT Kerberos V5 authentication protocol. (Kerberos V5 is a fast, secure authentication protocol.)
Account delegation	Kerberos authentication allows Windows 2000 to delegate user's account information from one machine to another. This capability was not available in previous versions of Windows, including Microsoft Windows NT.
Extensive public key support	Windows 2000 supports certificates and other public key technologies, but it is much more scalable and flexible when Active Directory is used because certificates can be associated automatically with the user accounts and machine accounts in the directory.
Smartcard logon	Windows 2000 can use smartcards as an authentication mechanism when used in conjunction with Active Directory.
Easier administration	Group Policy can be used to define default settings that will be automatically applied to users and computers. These settings can determine security options and control what software can be installed on particular computers and what software is available to particular groups of users.
	In addition, an entire domain can be managed from a small number of tools.
Scalability	Active Directory is designed to hold millions of objects, such as users, computers, and printers, stored across thousands of machines.

Table 3-1. *Some of the advantages of Active Directory.*

AUTHENTICATED LOGON

Authentication is the process of verifying the identity of something or someone, otherwise known as a *principal*. Windows 2000 requires that all principals be authenticated before they can use services in the operating system. A principal can be authenticated in two ways: interactively and across the network.

An interactive logon is generated when a user is physically present at the computer and enters credentials, such as a username and password or a smartcard and personal identification number (PIN). The account logging on must have the Logon Locally logon right; if it does not, the account will fail to log on.

A network logon is generated when the user is connecting to a network computer. The account logging on must have the Access This Computer From The Network logon right or the logon will fail. For example, when a user accesses a resource, such as a printer, on a network computer running Windows 2000, the remote Windows 2000 operating system will automatically attempt a network logon.

Two other types of logon exist—batch logon and service logon—but they are less used by users. Batch logon is usually reserved for applications that run as batch jobs, such as bank account reconciliation programs or very large print jobs. It is seldom used by Windows. Service logon is required by accounts used to start a Windows service such as Microsoft SQL Server or the print spooler service. The appropriate logon right is required to log on as a batch job (Logon As A Batch Job) or as a service (Logon As A Service).

AUTHENTICATION

Windows 2000 supports many authentication protocols, including those used for dial-up authentication, Internet authentication, and network authentication. In the case of network authentication, Windows 2000 supports two protocols: Windows NT Challenge/Response (also called NTLM) and Kerberos V5.

NTLM is supported by Windows 95, Windows 98, Windows NT, and Windows 2000. In Windows 2000, it is the authentication mechanism used for computer communication between machines running Windows NT and Windows 2000. Kerberos V5 authentication is supported on Windows 2000 when Active Directory is installed, and it is the default authentication protocol.

For more information about NTLM, see "User Authentication with Windows NT" at *http://support.microsoft.com/support/kb/articles/q102/7/16.asp*. For an explanation of how Kerberos V5 works in Windows 2000, see Chapter 14, "An Introduction to Kerberos Authentication in Windows 2000."

PRIVILEGES

Privileges, which, along with the logon rights mentioned in "Authenticated Logon," make up a general category called rights, relate to the authorization to perform an operation that affects an entire computer rather than specific objects only. (Access to specific objects is controlled by permissions.) Privileges are defined in a computer's security policy.

To view user privileges, log on using an account that has administrative authority and then open the Local Security Policy tool, which lets you view and edit security policies. Figure 3-1 shows this tool and the user rights assignment, or the granting of privileges, for the local computer.

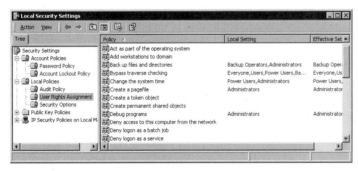

Figure 3-1. *User rights assignment in the Local Security Policy tool.*

NOTE   You can grant and revoke user rights from the command line by using the NTRights.exe tool in the *Microsoft Windows 2000 Server Resource Kit.*

There are a number of user rights in Windows 2000 that are not available in Windows NT 4, including

- Deny access to this computer from the network

- Deny logon as a batch job

- Deny logon as a service

- Deny logon locally

These are the opposite of the normal logon rights discussed in "Authenticated Logon" and override those logon rights. If a user has both the Logon Locally right and the Deny Logon Locally right, he or she will not be able to log on locally. The main purpose of these privileges is to support the "allow everyone but *x*" type of scenario. If you wanted to support this scenario in Windows NT, you'd have to create a new group, add valid users and groups to the new group, and then apply the privileges to the group. This kind of situation is easier to implement with the new scheme of deny privileges in Windows 2000.

USER ACCOUNTS AND GROUPS

In Windows NT and Windows 2000, users can be members of groups. A group is a collection of user accounts. By making a user account a member of a group, you give that user all the rights and permissions granted to the group. Also, note that groups can be members of other groups.

Information about user accounts and groups is held in a user account database. The database is called the Security Accounts Manager (SAM) database in Windows NT 4, Windows 2000 Professional, and Windows 2000 Server running without Active Directory. The SAM is a file stored in the Registry, which is implemented as files in the %windir%\system32\config directory.

When Active Directory is installed, the user and group account information is stored in the Active Directory itself as User and Group objects. These objects can be accessed by using the Active Directory administration tools as well as the Active Directory Services Interface (ADSI). Information regarding ADSI and how to remotely administer security can be found in Chapter 13, "Security Administration with ADSI, WMI, and COM+."

A NOTE ON PASSWORDS

Users can log on to Windows 2000 by using their user account name and a password. Passwords are limited to 14 characters in Windows NT; this limit is increased to 127 characters in Windows 2000 when Active Directory is installed. It's therefore recommended that sensitive accounts, such as administrative accounts, take advantage of this security enhancement. See Appendix B, "Strong Passwords," which you can find in the companion CD's electronic version of this book, for more information on how to enforce strong passwords and how to remember them.

DOMAINS AND WORKGROUPS

Since the advent of Windows NT 3.1, people have been somewhat perplexed about the difference between a domain and a workgroup. The simplest way to discern the difference is to ask, "Where are the user accounts authenticated?" If each account is authenticated on each computer, you have a workgroup. If the accounts are authenticated at a central location, you have a domain. Servers performing centralized authentication are often referred to as *domain controllers*.

Here's another way of looking at it: A domain is a grouping of accounts and network resources under a single domain name and security boundary. A workgroup is a simpler grouping, intended only to help users find objects such as printers and shared folders within that smaller group. Domains are the recommended choice for all networks except small ones with few users.

In a workgroup, users might have to remember multiple passwords, one for each network resource. In a domain, passwords and permissions are simpler to maintain, since a domain has a single, centralized database of user accounts and permissions. The information in this database is replicated automatically among domain controllers. You determine which servers are domain controllers and which are simply members of the domain.

As mentioned, a domain can have one or more domain controllers. A small organization using a single local area network (LAN) might require only one domain with two domain controllers for high availability and fault tolerance (that is, the ability of the system to recover from errors without losing data). A large company with many geographical locations will require one or more domain controllers in each location to provide high availability and fault tolerance.

DOMAIN/ACCOUNT NAMES AND USER PRINCIPAL NAMES

Prior to Windows 2000, all account names were of the form *DOMAIN/Account*—for example, *EXAIR/Michael*. This is also called the *SAM account name*. Although this form worked well, it did have two shortcomings:

- The user's logon name and e-mail name are different.

- Two organizations might have the same domain name, and hence there's a possibility of user names clashing if the two domains needed to talk to each other.

Windows 2000 introduces the notion of user principal names (UPNs), which follow the now-classic, well-understood e-mail address format of *user@domain*—for example, *michael@exair.com*.

By default, the UPN name of a user is *username@DNSDomainName*, where *DNSDomainName* (also called the UPN suffix) is the Domain Name System (DNS) name of the organization. However, the name is somewhat arbitrary and is configurable using the Active Directory Domains And Trusts tool, as shown in Figure 3-2.

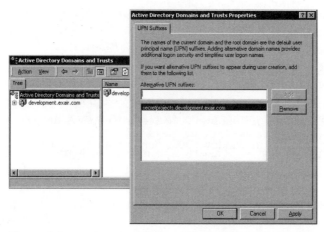

Figure 3-2. *Configuring different UPN suffixes in Active Directory.*

Once you've set the UPN suffixes, you can set the UPNs for users. For example, Cheryl's account might be in the *development.exair.com* domain, but her UPN can be *cheryl@web.development.exair.com*. When Cheryl logs on to Windows 2000, she can log on as either *DEVELOPMENT/Cheryl* or *cheryl@web.development.exair.com*. The UPN name is configurable in Active Directory by editing the *userPrincipalName* attribute of the user's object or by using the User Logon Name option, as shown in Figure 3-3.

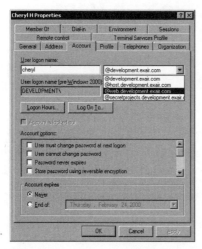

Figure 3-3. *Setting a user's UPN in Active Directory.*

Some applications, including SQL Server 2000, might not recognize UPN names—that's why Windows 2000 supports both DOMAIN/Account naming and UPN naming. We expect that this situation will be resolved as more developers port their applications to Windows 2000 and more users deploy solutions requiring UPNs.

MANAGING ACCOUNTS

Windows 2000 offers new tools for user and group account management. These tools cover three scenarios, and each tool is optimized for its environment:

- Managing accounts in Windows 2000 Professional
- Managing accounts in Windows 2000 Server without Active Directory
- Managing accounts in Windows 2000 Server with Active Directory

Let's take a moment to look at each in turn.

Managing Accounts in Windows 2000 Professional

User accounts are managed using User Manager in Windows NT 4 Workstation. In Windows 2000 Professional, user accounts are configured using the Users And Passwords tool accessed via Control Panel. The purpose of this tool is to make local administration simple and foolproof. Defining users with this tool only sets up local user accounts; stored in the machine's SAM database, the user accounts are not users in Active Directory.

The beauty of this tool is that both types of credentials used by Windows 2000—passwords and private keys (and the associated certificates)—are administered seamlessly from the one tool, as shown in Figure 3-4.

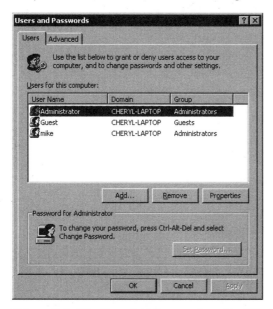

Figure 3-4. *The Users And Passwords tool in Windows 2000 Professional.*

Managing Accounts in Windows 2000 Server Without Active Directory

User accounts are managed using User Manager For Domains in Windows NT 4 Server. In Windows 2000 Server, you use the Local Users And Groups tool. Like the tool available in Windows 2000 Professional, the accounts are local to the computer and are granted rights and permissions on the computer.

This tool is also available as an advanced option when using Windows 2000 Professional. To open it, click the Advanced tab of the Users And Passwords dialog box; then click Advanced in the Advanced User Management area.

Managing Accounts in Windows 2000 Server with Active Directory

In Windows 2000, domain accounts are managed using the Active Directory Users And Computers tool; in Windows NT 4 Server, they are administered using User Manager For Domains. The Active Directory Users And Computers tool looks similar to the Local Users And Groups tool, but the similarity is skin-deep—the tools' implementations are very different.

EXTENDING THE ACTIVE DIRECTORY SCHEMA

Extending the Active Directory schema is not to be taken lightly; in fact, this functionality is disabled by default. Perform the following steps to extend the schema:

1. From the command line, go to the %winnt%/system32 directory.

2. Type *regsvr32 schmmgmt.dll*. (You don't need to type this command every time you want to extend the Active Directory schema; you need to type it only once.)

3. From the command line or the Start menu, run *mmc /a*.

4. Choose Add/Remove Snap-in from the Console menu.

5. Click Add.

6. Select Active Directory schema.

7. Click Add.

8. Click Close.

9. Click OK.

The format of the SAM is inflexible (you cannot change the data format or add your own field definitions), but Active Directory is richer and can be extended to include user-defined extensions. This is called extending the Active Directory schema. For example, you might have a user attribute relating to a user's access to a human resources database; this information could be added to the Active Directory user object.

SECURITY IDENTIFIERS (SIDS)

Administrators, of course, refer to user names and group names by their easy-to-remember verbal names. Internally, the operating system refers to each account by a number that uniquely identifies that account. Every account on the network is issued a unique SID when the account is first created. If you create an account, delete it, and then create another account with the same name, the new account will not have the rights or permissions previously granted to the old account because the accounts' SIDs will be different.

A SID has the following format:

S-R-A-S-S-S-S

Table 3-2 explains this format.

Section	Name	Comments
S	SID	This means we are referring to a SID.
R	Revision	Think of this as the SID format version number. Windows 2000 creates version 1 SIDs.
A	Authority	This is a 48-bit identifier authority value that identifies the authority, such as a Windows NT/Windows 2000 domain, that issued the SID. Example authorities include Everyone/World (1) and Windows NT/2000 (5).
S	Subauthority	This is a series of numbers that uniquely identify the principal.

Table 3-2. *SID structure.*

Two types of SIDs exist in Windows 2000: created SIDs and well-known SIDs. Created SIDs are created by Windows 2000 itself or by Windows 2000 administrators. The format of these SIDs is the same as that defined in Table 3-2, but the subauthority numbers have a special meaning. Take, for example, the following SID, which Table 3-3 translates:

S-1-5-21-397661181-626881882-18441761-1009

Section	Comments
S	This is a SID.
1	Version level 1.
5	Identifier authority value of 5 (NT authority).
21	First subauthority—this is a domain or workgroup.
397661181-626881882-18441761	Second, third, and fourth subauthorities—these uniquely identify the domain or workgroup.
1009	The last subauthority, a counter starting from 1000, which identifies the account in the domain. This number is incremented whenever a new account is created.

Table 3-3. *The makeup of a created SID.*

Well-known SIDs identify generic groups and generic users. For example, well-known SIDs exist to identify the following groups and users:

- The Everyone group, which is a group that includes all users. You do not need to add users to this group—everyone is a member of the group by default.

- The Administrators group for the built-in domain on the local computer.

- The Interactive group, which includes all users that have logged on to the system interactively. Like the Everyone group, there's no need to add users to this group; all authenticated users are automatically a member of this group.

Refer to Appendix A, "Windows 2000 Well-Known SIDs," in the companion CD's e-book for a list of well-known SIDs.

TOKENS

When a user logs on to a computer running Windows 2000 and the account is authenticated, a *token* is created for that user, and this token is applied to every process and thread within each process that the user starts up. The token contains the information in Table 3-4.

Field	*Comments*
User SID	The user's security identifier, or SID.
Group SIDs	The list of SIDs of all the groups of which the user is a member. In Windows 2000, group membership in a token is flattened. In other words, if the account is a member of group A, which in turn is a member of group B, the token will contain SIDs for A and B, not just A.
Privileges	The list of privileges the user has on this computer.
Owner SID	The SID of the user or group who, by default, is the owner of any object that the user either creates or takes ownership of. This is usually the same as the user SID, except in the case of an administrator, in which case it is the administrator's group SID.
Primary group	This is not used by any part of Windows 2000 but the POSIX subsystem.
Default access control list	A list of permissions that Windows 2000 applies to objects created by the user if no other access control information is available. By default, it grants full control to creator/owner, and system.
Source	An 8-byte string that identifies the process that created the token.
Type	One of two types: either a primary token or an impersonation token. A primary token is the token associated with the process and is the default token for each thread in the process. The token associated with a thread becomes an impersonation thread when a thread calls an impersonation function, such as *ImpersonateLoggedOnUser* or *RpcImpersonateClient*.
Impersonation level	Governs the degree to which a server process can act on behalf of a client. The levels are as follows: **Anonymous** The server process cannot obtain identification information about the client, and it cannot impersonate the client.

Table 3-4. *The contents of a Windows 2000 token.* (continued)

Table 3-4. *continued*

Field	Comments
	Identification The server process can obtain information about the client, such as security identifiers and privileges, but it cannot impersonate the client.
	Impersonation The server process can impersonate the client's security context on its local system. The server cannot impersonate the client on remote systems.
	Delegation The server process can impersonate the client's security context on local and remote systems.
Statistics	Information about the token, usually used only by the operating system.
Restricted SIDs	The token is often referred to as a restricted token if this optional field is not empty.
	When a thread tries to access a secured object, the system performs two access checks: one using the token's enabled SIDs and another using the list of restricting SIDs. Access is granted only if both access checks allow the requested access rights.
	Restricted SIDs are new to Windows 2000 and can be created using the *CreateRestrictedToken* API. This function will also allow you to remove privileges from the token.
Session ID	Only applicable for a session created by Terminal Server, this is a unique nonzero numeric value for each connected client.

You can look at some of the critical data in your own token by using the WhoAmI.exe tool included with the Windows 2000 Resource Guide. Below is some sample output:

```
C:\WINNT>whoami /all
[User]     = "DEV\Cheryl"   S-1-5-21-392915311-626881126-188441333-1191
[Group  1] = "DEV\Domain Users"  S-1-5-21-392915311-626881126-188441333-513
[Group  2] = "Everyone"  S-1-1-0
[Group  3] = "BUILTIN\Power Users"  S-1-5-32-547
[Group  4] = "BUILTIN\Users"  S-1-5-32-545
[Group  5] = "LOCAL"  S-1-2-0
[Group  6] = "NT AUTHORITY\INTERACTIVE"  S-1-5-4
[Group  7] = "NT AUTHORITY\Authenticated Users"  S-1-5-11
[Login ID] = S-1-5-5-0-6553
```

```
(X) SeChangeNotifyPrivilege         = Bypass traverse checking
(0) SeSystemtimePrivilege           = Change the system time
(0) SeShutdownPrivilege             = Shut down the system
(0) SeProfileSingleProcessPrivilege = Profile single process
(X) SeUndockPrivilege               = Remove computer from docking station
```

This output tells you that

- Cheryl logged on interactively. (She is a member of the Interactive group.)

- She is a member of the Everyone, Authenticated Users, Domain Users, Users, and Power Users groups.

- Her account was the 1191st account created in this domain. (Look at the last subauthority in the user SID.)

- Her logon identifier is 6553.

- She has a number of privileges, but only Bypass Traverse Checking and Remove Computer From Docking Station are currently enabled.

To fully understand the content of the token, cross-reference the SIDs defined above with the SIDs detailed in Appendix A.

ACCESS CONTROL LISTS

Windows 2000 protects securable resources from unauthorized access by employing discretionary access control, which is implemented through discretionary access control lists (DACLs). DACLs, usually abbreviated to ACLs, are a series of access control entries (ACEs). Each ACE lists a principal and contains information about the principal and the operations that the principal can perform on the resource. Some people might be granted read access, and others might have full control. The type of ACE depends on the type of securable object.

A securable object is any object that has a security descriptor containing security information, such as the owner's SID and ACL data, about the object. Examples of securable objects include the following:

- NTFS files and directories
- Named and anonymous pipes
- Processes and threads
- Registry keys
- Services
- Printers

- Network shares

- Job objects

An ACL is a simple data structure. It contains a series of owner information and zero or more ACEs. Each ACE contains a SID and access information pertaining to that SID, such as read, write, open, create, and so on. ACLs are applied to resources requiring protection and are referred to as discretionary because deciding who has what degree of access to the object is at the discretion of the object owner. For example, you might decide that only three other people should have access to a file you control: Bob (Read Only), Alice (Read Only), and Cheryl (Full Control).

In this case, the ACL contains three ACEs: two that give Bob and Alice read-only access to the resource, and one that gives Cheryl full control, as shown in Figure 3-5. Note that in this case an administrator will be denied access if he or she attempts to access the resource because no explicit ACE exists that would allow anyone but Bob, Alice, and Cheryl access; this is what is meant by discretionary access.

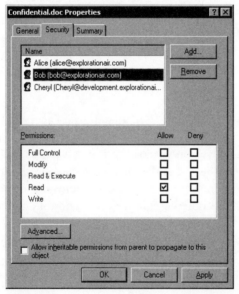

Figure 3-5. *The ACL for a file named Confidential.doc.*

Windows 2000 also includes support for explicitly denying access to an object by using deny permissions. For example, if you want all users (Everyone) except for

Richard to have access to a file, you'd set the following: Everyone (Read) and Richard (Deny Full Control).

Because denies are always checked before allows, Richard will always be denied access to this object. For this reason, never deny Everyone access to an object. You will be warned of the ramifications if you do this from the Windows shell.

In addition, different objects have different permission types:

- Files can have their permissions set and can be written to, read from, and created.

- Printers can be printed to or managed.

- Active Directory objects can have specific settings on object properties such as the ability to read a user's certificates or set their e-mail address.

- Registry keys can be queried, written to, and have subkeys created and deleted.

WHAT HAPPENS TO SECURED RESOURCES IF THE OWNER LEAVES?

Imagine that an employee creates some secured resources that do not allow the administrator to access the resources, and then the employee leaves. What happens to the files? The owner of an object can always create any ACL on any resource he or she owns, but an administrator can always take ownership of that resource. Note, however, that the administrator cannot give ownership back. Instead, the administrator can take ownership of the resource and then set new ACLs. Because the administrator cannot take ownership of a resource, change ACLs, and then reassign ownership of the resource back to the original owner, the possibility of abusing the ability to take ownership is slim.

To look at the owner of a file, perform the following steps:

1. Right-click the resource.

2. Choose Properties from the context menu.

3. Click the Security tab.

4. Click the Advanced button.

5. Click the Owner tab.

If you either have permission to take ownership—there is a Take Ownership permission that an owner can apply to a resource—or are an administrator, you can take ownership by selecting yourself in the Change Owner To: list box, as shown in Figure 3-6.

Figure 3-6. *Viewing a file's owner.*

How Access Is Determined

When a principal attempts to access a resource, Windows 2000 performs a simple DACL check. It does this by checking the SIDs in the user's token for the type of access requested (for example, a call to *CreateFile* or *OpenRegKey* for read, write, and so on) against the SIDs in each ACE of the resource's ACL. Windows 2000 denies access to the object if none of the ACEs allow the user access or if an ACE denies the user access; otherwise access is allowed.

There is one other step in Windows 2000. When a restricted process or thread tries to access a securable object, the system performs two access checks: one using the token's enabled SIDs and another using the list of restricting SIDs. Access is granted only if both access checks allow for the requested access. (We'll discuss restricted tokens shortly.)

It's important to note that an application acting on behalf of a user (that is, impersonating the user) should ask only for the access rights it requires to perform its tasks and no more. If the application asks for read, write, and delete access but the resource allows read access only, the application will be denied access—it won't be granted read access.

ACLs at the Command Line

You can view and update ACLs on an NTFS partition from the command line by using the CACLs.exe tool. The CACLs.exe tool lets you display, edit, or replace ACLs on files and directories. The following is an example of how to grant the Everyone group read access and the Administrators group full control for a file named info.txt:

```
cacls info.txt /G Everyone:R Administrators:F
```

You can display the ACLs on a file if you type *cacls info.txt*:

```
C:\WINNT>cacls info.txt
C:\WINNT\info.txt Everyone:R
                  BUILTIN\Administrators:F
```

ACL TOOLS IN THE RESOURCE KIT

The *Microsoft Windows 2000 Server Resource Kit* includes a number of ACL-related tools, including PermCopy.exe, ShowACLs.exe, SubInACL.exe, SvcACLs.exe, and XCACLs.exe, to make command-line administration easier. (As with CACLs.exe, these tools work only on NTFS partitions.)

PermCopy.exe copies share-level (Full Control, Read, Change) and file-level (Full Control, Modify, Read & Execute, Read, Write, Traverse Directory) ACLs from one share to another.

ShowACLs.exe details access rights for files and folders. The most useful feature of ShowACLs.exe is the ability to show permissions for a particular user.

SubInACL.exe administrators can obtain security information on files, registry keys, and services, and transfer this information from user to user, from local or global group to group, and from domain to domain.

SvcACLs.exe sets ACLs on service objects, enabling administrators to delegate control of services when using the Services administration tool. For example, an administrator could grant a nonadministrator such as EXAIR/Marc the rights to control the Web server with the following command line:

```
svcacls w3svc g:exair\marc rx
```

XCACLs.exe is a finer grained version of CACLs.exe; it offers more control over how you set and manipulate ACLs than CACLs.exe.

The Principle of Least Privilege

As a user, you should always execute code with just enough privilege to get the job done and no more. This helps prevent accidental or malicious damage. Because all user code executes in the context of the user, if the user is a privileged account, damage can be massive.

The simplest solution is to never log on as an administrator unless you absolutely must. Any code you run, whether good or malicious, will run with all the privileges assigned to the administrator account, which might cause serious damage if you execute code infected with a virus.

Windows 2000 extends support for the concept of least privilege by providing restricted tokens and secondary logon, which the following sections will describe.

Restricted tokens in practice

If you require only privileges X and Z to perform a task but your token is capable of performing tasks requiring X, Y, and Z, you should remove privilege Y from your token. Restricted tokens support the concept of reducing the default capability of a token.

A good example of this is Web browsing: While you're browsing the Web, your application should run at the lowest possible privilege just in case you accidentally execute malicious code. If you execute such code, the damage will be contained because the code runs with fewer privileges than you normally have. The APIs supporting restricted tokens are available in Windows 2000 only and are described in Table 3-5.

API	*Comments*
CreateRestrictedToken	The *CreateRestrictedToken* function creates a new access token that is a restricted version of an existing access token. It can be called to remove privileges, set deny attributes to SIDs, and specify restricted SIDs.
IsTokenRestricted	The *IsTokenRestricted* function indicates whether a token contains a list of restricting SIDs.
CheckTokenMembership	The *CheckTokenMembership* function determines whether a specified SID is enabled in a token.

Table 3-5. *Restricted token APIs in Windows 2000.*

Secondary Logon

As already mentioned, you should always log on to a computer running Windows 2000 using a nonadministrator user account. You should not add yourself to the Administrators local group, and you should avoid running your computer while logged on as an administrator. One of the authors wrote a small program he places in the Startup group for all users on his computers—it reminds him if he is logged on as an administrator. This simple tool, RUAdmin.exe, is included on the companion disc.

For most computer activity, log on as a member of the Users or Power Users group. If you need to perform administrative tasks, you can log off and log on again as an administrator, in which case you would lose your current work, or you can use the Secondary Logon service, which is also called the RunAs service in Windows 2000.

RunAs allows a user to run specific tools and programs with different permissions than the user's current logon provides. For example, the following command will start another command shell but run it as the local administrator rather than the currently logged on user:

```
runas /user:EXAIR\administrator cmd
```

After entering the command, the user is prompted to enter the administrator's password for the EXAIR domain. Figure 3-7 shows a command shell created by RunAs running as administrator.

Figure 3-7. *A command shell created by RunAs running as administrator.*

If you create a shortcut to an application on your desktop, you can invoke the RunAs service by holding down the shift key and right-clicking the shortcut on the desktop and choosing Run As from the context menu. You are then prompted to enter the account information; by default, the user name will be the local administrator, as shown in Figure 3-8.

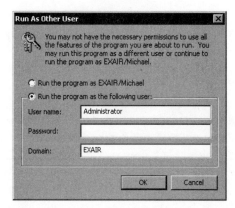

Figure 3-8. *Selecting a user account to run a command under.*

You can make the Run As Other User dialog box appear each time you acti-vate a shortcut by selecting the Run As Different User option—see Figure 3-9—in the Properties option of a shortcut, like so:

1. Right-click the shortcut in question.

2. Choose Properties from the context menu.

3. Select the Run As Different User check box.

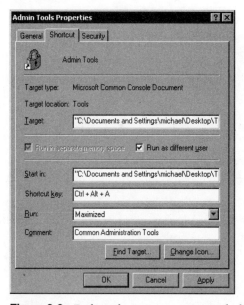

Figure 3-9. *Desktop shortcut properties, including the ability to run as a different user.*

NOTE You will not be given the opportunity to use RunAs if you hold down the shift key and right-click the Microsoft Internet Explorer icon on your desktop. You can work around this by creating a shortcut to IExplore.exe; all shortcuts have the RunAs capability.

As already mentioned, the general philosophy is to perform day-to-day tasks as a user or power user, perform dangerous tasks with low privilege, and perform administrative tasks by using RunAs. Figure 3-10 shows an example of how you can accomplish this and use your Windows 2000 computer securely.

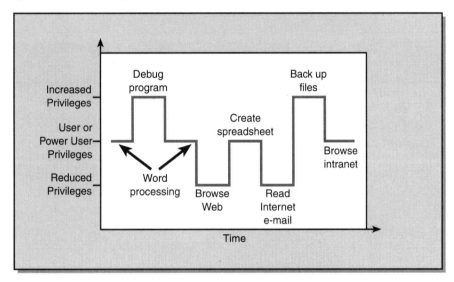

Figure 3-10. *Changing privileges while performing day-to-day tasks.*

In this example, the user is running as a user or power user for most tasks, such as word processing, spreadsheet work, and browsing the corporate intranet. However, for tasks that involve communicating with unknown and distrusted users, the user drops down to a lower privilege by using either restricted tokens or a lower privilege account through the RunAs service. For higher privilege requirements, such as backing up files (which requires the Back Up Files And Directories right) and debugging programs (which requires the Debug Programs right), the user can use RunAs to run as an account with greater privilege for the duration of the task. To use the RunAs functionality, the RunAs service must be running.

WOULDN'T IT BE EASIER JUST TO RUN AS AN ADMINISTRATOR?

Yes, it would be easier; there'd be no need to use RunAs or similar functionality. However, you'd also be more vulnerable to attack. One of the reasons viruses spread and Trojan horse programs do so much damage is because the user account under which the malicious code is executing is a privileged account. Restricting the account's capabilities helps limit the damage caused by such malware.

In short, do not run as the administrator or as a user in the local administrator's group unless you absolutely must do so.

Checking process access tokens

You can check the default token, and hence the user account, associated with a process by using the Pulist.exe tool in the *Microsoft Windows 2000 Server Resource Kit*. The following Pulist.exe sample output is interesting because it shows that three copies of Internet Explorer are running, each as a different account:

```
C:\WINNT>pulist
Process          PID   User
Idle             0
System           8
smss.exe         160   NT AUTHORITY\SYSTEM
csrss.exe        184   NT AUTHORITY\SYSTEM
winlogon.exe     204   NT AUTHORITY\SYSTEM
services.exe     232   NT AUTHORITY\SYSTEM
lsass.exe        244   NT AUTHORITY\SYSTEM
scardsvr.exe     364   NT AUTHORITY\SYSTEM
inojobsv.exe     608   NT AUTHORITY\SYSTEM
llssrv.exe       644   NT AUTHORITY\SYSTEM
regsvc.exe       792   NT AUTHORITY\SYSTEM
mstask.exe       812   NT AUTHORITY\SYSTEM
explorer.exe     1388  EXAIR\cheryl
wcescomm.exe     1180  EXAIR\cheryl
dnetc.exe        1496  EXAIR\cheryl
OUTLOOK.EXE      1168  EXAIR\cheryl
MAPISP32.EXE     988   EXAIR\cheryl
IEXPLORE.EXE     1628  CHERYL-LAPTOP\Administrator
cmd.exe          1616  EXAIR\cheryl
IEXPLORE.EXE     868   CHERYL-LAPTOP\LowPriv
IEXPLORE.EXE     1868  EXAIR\cheryl
WINWORD.EXE      1696  EXAIR\cheryl
pulist.exe       832   EXAIR\Cheryl
```

Audit ACEs

Windows 2000 includes another kind of ACL called a System ACL (SACL). SACLs are often referred to as audit ACEs. Rather than checking access to a resource, a SACL generates audit messages for attempts to access the resources. The results are then stored in the security event log.

To audit access to specific files (or parts of the Registry or Active Directory), you must apply SACLs to the files in question and configure Windows 2000 to log such auditing events. The following sections describe the required steps.

Step 1: Applying SACLs to files and/or directories

You need to perform the following steps on every object or group of objects you want to audit:

1. Open Windows Explorer.

2. Navigate to the directory or files in question.

3. Right-click the directory or files in question.

4. Choose Properties from the context menu.

5. Click the Security tab.

6. Click Advanced.

7. Click the Auditing tab. You do not have appropriate privileges if the tab is not available (or the directory or files are not on an NTFS partition).

8. Click Add.

9. Select a user, computer, or group; commonly, you'll select the Everyone group.

10. Click OK.

11. Select the access type you want to audit. Don't forget that you can audit both successful and failed events.

12. Click OK three times.

Step 2: Configuring Windows 2000 to audit file/object access events

You need only perform this step once. However, you should turn off this option if you're not auditing for file and object access, because the security logs can fill up quickly.

1. Open the Local Computer Policy tool.

2. Navigate to Computer Configuration, Windows Settings, Security Settings, Local Policies, Audit Policy.

3.   Double-click Audit Object Access.

4.   Select Success And/Or Failure Attempts.

5.   Click OK.

6.   Close the Local Computer Policy tool.

Note that local policy is overridden if you have defined a domain-level policy through Group Policy.

IMPERSONATION

Impersonation is the ability of a thread to execute in a security context different from that of the process owning the thread. Typically, a thread in a server application impersonates a client before performing work on behalf of the client, thus allowing the server thread to act on behalf of that client to access objects or validate access to its own objects.

You might choose to have a server impersonate a client when connecting to a database so that the database can authenticate and authorize the client. Or your application can impersonate the client before accessing files that are protected with an ACL so as to ensure that the client can obtain only authorized access to information in these files. This process is shown in Figure 3-11.

First, a process starts up under a security context. This is either the context of the user, or, if the process is a service (similar to a UNIX daemon), the context of a service account is defined and controlled by the service control manager.

The application's security context is the security token associated with the process. Any threads that start inside the process automatically inherit the parent process's token. This is shown in the left column of the diagram where a pool of threads is waiting for client connections.

In the middle column of the diagram, a client connects and attempts to use a secured resource. To perform this action, a thread is removed from the pool, calls a Win32 API to impersonate the client, and then performs the required tasks. Impersonating is literally the act of swapping tokens on the thread. If the calling user is not allowed access to a resource, an access denied error occurs.

Finally, the client drops the connection because the work is completed, and the thread reverts to the token of the parent process.

> **NOTE**   If a remote application or service impersonates a client, it can access only resources local to the service on behalf of the client. Attempts to access resources on remote computers while impersonating the client will usually fail. See the next section, "Delegation," for further details.

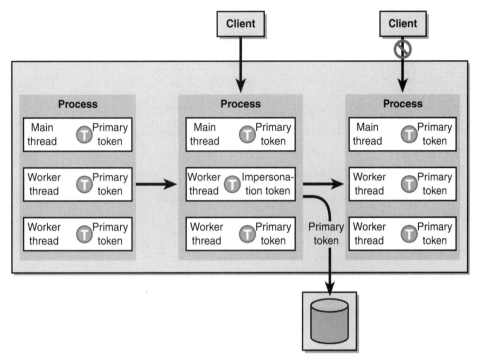

Figure 3-11. *The impersonation process.*

DELEGATION

Delegation is the next step up from impersonation. Rather than just being able to access local resources on behalf of the client, delegation supports the accessing of remote resources on behalf of the client. Indeed, there's no limit to how many computers you can delegate your account to, so long as they are configured correctly.

Delegation is supported in Windows 2000 only, and only when the Kerberos authentication protocol is used, which requires Active Directory. The key to delegation is the concept of delegatable or forwardable tickets. Refer to Chapter 14 for more information about Kerberos and tickets.

Supporting Delegation

The following three sections describe the steps and settings required to support delegation.

Step 1: Verify that the user's account can be delegated

The Account Is Sensitive And Cannot Be Delegated option on each user account in question must not be checked. This is a property of the user's account object in Active

Directory, as shown in Figure 3-12. You can verify this setting by performing the following steps:

1. Open the Active Directory Users And Groups tool.

2. Right-click the User object in question.

3. Choose Properties from the context menu.

4. Click the Account tab.

5. Scroll down until you see Account Is Sensitive And Cannot Be Delegated in the Account Options box.

6. Make sure the option is not checked.

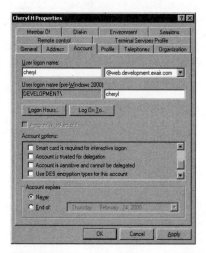

Figure 3-12. *Verifying that the user's account can be delegated.*

Step 2: Verify that the application account can act as a delegate

If you're running a service or application under an account other than *LocalSystem*, you need to verify that the account is permitted to act as a delegate, as shown in Figure 3-13:

1. Open the Active Directory Users And Groups tool.

2. Right-click the User object in question.

3. Choose Properties from the context menu.

4. Click the Account tab.

5. Scroll down until you see Account Is Trusted For Delegation in the Account Options box.

6. Make sure the option is checked.

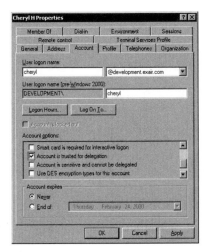

Figure 3-13. *Verifying that an account can be used to delegate other credentials.*

NOTE You do not need to perform this step if the service is running as *LocalSystem* because this account automatically supports the trusted for delegation capability. You can verify the account under which the service is running in the Services tool.

Step 3: Verify that all computers are trusted for delegation

You also need to make sure that all computers used within the distributed application are trusted for delegation. For example, if you want to delegate credentials across four servers running Windows 2000, each of these must be configured as trusted for delegation. To configure a computer as trusted for delegation, do the following:

1. Open the Active Directory Users And Computers tool.

2. Expand the Domain Name node.

3. Expand the Computers node.

4. Right-click the computer you want to configure.

5. Choose Properties from the context menu.

6. Check the Computer Is Trusted For Delegation option.

   CAUTION Delegation is a very powerful feature and is disabled by default. Computers and user accounts that are trusted for delegation should be under controlled access to prevent the misusing of delegation to make network connections on behalf of users or computers.

In summary, delegation works in a distributed application only if the following is true:

- Active Directory and Windows 2000 are being used.

- All computer and user accounts are in the same domain or in a trusted domain.

- The user account being delegated is not marked as sensitive.

- The account under which any services or processes that handle the user's requests are running are configured as trusted to delegate the user's credentials.

- All computers involved in the distributed application must be marked as trusted for delegation, except the first and last computers in the chain.

Delegation will fail if any of these aspects are not set correctly. Figure 3-14 outlines the required settings.

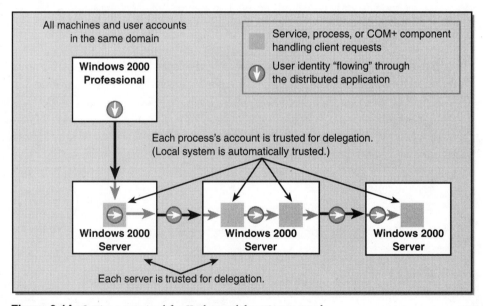

Figure 3-14. *Settings required for Kerberos delegation to work.*

NOTE   Don't confuse the term *delegation* as it relates to delegation of authentication with administrative delegation in Active Directory. The former is what we've been discussing; the latter relates to controlled delegation of control over users, groups, policy, and so forth. Administrative delegation disseminates the administrator's workload without granting dangerous privileges to delegates. There are two wizards available to make delegation easier: the Delegate Administration wizard in the Active Directory Users And Computers tool, and the Delegation Of Control wizard in the Active Directory Sites And Services tool.

MISCELLANEOUS WINDOWS 2000 SECURITY FEATURES

This section gives overviews of other important aspects of Windows 2000 security; the overviews are not to be considered complete tutorials. The topics covered in the following sections include Encrypting File System (EFS), IP Security (IPSec), the Security Configuration Editor (SCE), and Windows File Protection (WFP).

Encrypting File System

The Windows 2000 Encrypting File System, an integral part of the Windows 2000 file system, NTFS, lets users encrypt files and folders on a computer for added protection. EFS automatically decrypts the file for use and encrypts the file when it is saved. No one can read EFS-encrypted files except the user who encrypted the file or a user, such as an administrator, with an EFS Recovery certificate. EFS's main purpose is to protect files on high-risk devices such as laptops where physical attack is a greater possibility than on a desktop or server computer.

Note that files under the %windir% directory and files with the SYSTEM attribute set cannot be encrypted. You can determine the value of %windir% by typing the following at the command line:

```
echo %windir%
```

You can encrypt files by following these steps:

1. Right-click the file or folder you want to encrypt, and then click Properties.

2. Click Advanced, select the Encrypt Contents To Secure Data check box, and then click OK.

You can also use the Cipher.exe tool included with Windows 2000 to display or encrypt files and directories from the command line. For more information about EFS, refer to the online Windows 2000 help and the EFS white paper at

http://www.microsoft.com/windows2000/library/howitworks/security/encrypt.asp

> **CAUTION**   Do not encrypt your C:\Temp directory if you use Offline folders, also called client-side caching. Doing so can make Offline folders behave inconsistently.

IP Security

Once you've read Chapter 12, "Securing Against Attack," you'll know that the TCP/IP protocol suite is insecure. There is no authentication, no authorization, no privacy, and no data integrity for IP packets. Because of this, all protocols in the TCP/IP protocol, including ICMP, IGMP, TCP, UDP, and IP packets, can be forged. Fake packets cause havoc on the Web; many denial of service (DoS) attacks rely on malicious use of such packets. IPSec is designed to address many of these issues by protecting IP packets and providing defense against network-based attacks.

Protecting IP packets

IPSec protects IP packets by using cryptography to provide authentication, privacy, replay defense, and data integrity. Authentication, integrity, and antireplay are provided by the Authentication Header (AH) protocol, and privacy is provided by the Encapsulating Security Payload (ESP) protocol. ESP can be used alone or in conjunction with AH.

IP packet authentication

IPSec supports many authentication mechanisms, including Kerberos V5 authentication protocol (requires Active Directory), a public key certificate, or a preshared secret key. The latter requires that you enter a secret phrase or key into the IPSec administration tool on each computer you want to use; this is a simple method for authenticating computers not running Windows 2000, stand-alone computers, or any clients not running the Kerberos V5 authentication protocol. The key is used for authentication only, not for encrypting IP packets.

IP packet integrity and privacy

IPSec can use the MD5 or SHA-1 digest algorithms for message integrity and DES or Triple-DES (also referred to as 3DES) for encryption. IPSec can also be configured to generate new encryption keys after a predetermined amount of time or after a number of bytes have been transmitted or received using IPSec. New keys are derived using the Diffie-Hellman protocol.

NOTE Windows 2000 includes a graphical tool called IPSecMon.exe to show real-time IPSec security associations. Refer to the online help or Knowledge Base article Q231587 at *http://support.microsoft.com/support/kb/articles/Q231/5/87.asp* for details about using this tool.

Why use IPSec?

The main purpose of using IPSec is verifying that the server you're communicating with is the server it says it is and, optionally, that all data between the two or more hosts is private and has not been tampered with.

Let's take a moment to look at an example of IPSec in action: you have a server running Microsoft SQL Server that can be accessed only from a Web server in the "demilitarized zone" (DMZ) and from administration servers on an intranet. Figure 3-15 illustrates this scenario.

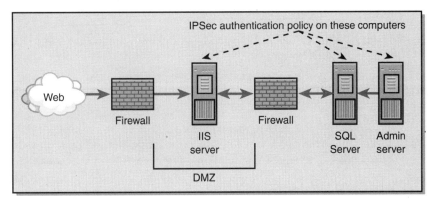

Figure 3-15. *A Web-based scenario using IPSec to authenticate connections between computers.*

THE DEMILITARIZED ZONE EXPLAINED

A DMZ is the area on a network that lies between the internal network and the Internet. Often a DMZ is implemented between two firewalls or as a small, private network that is connected to one network card in the firewall.

In this example, only the IIS and administration servers can communicate directly with the SQL Server box. Direct access to the SQL Server computer will fail because the attacker must be in the Kerberos domain, must have a trusted certificate, or must know the preshared secret, depending on how IPSec is configured to authenticate other IPSec computers.

> **NOTE** IPSec does not secure all IP-based protocols. IPSec exempts Internet Key Exchange (or IKE, formally known as ISAKMP/Oakley), Kerberos authentication, and IP multicast and broadcast packets.

Providing defense against network-based attacks

IPSec also provides support for blocking access to protocols ports; this is more often referred to as *packet filtering*. IPSec implements such filtering by using a series of rules, and each rule determines whether communication can take place between the server and a remote host based on source IP address, destination IP address, port number, and IP protocol.

For example, say you want to disallow all traffic except HTTP traffic to the network card with IP address 172.12.99.61. Setting up this policy is simple:

1. Set a rule that allows all TCP traffic to and from port 80, from any IP address to IP address 172.12.99.61.

2. Disallow all other traffic.

These two rules will enforce the policy defined.

> **NOTE** IPSec is not a replacement for a dedicated firewall because IPSec does not support the ability to perform low-level packet inspection such as the IP or TCP flags or Internet Control Message Protocol (ICMP) subcodes.

IPSec from the command line

The *Microsoft Windows 2000 Server Resource Kit* includes a tool that makes it easy to deploy IPSec policy from scripts. The tool, IPSecPol.exe, configures IPSec policy in Active Directory and in a local or remote server's Registry.

One area where the tool shines is setting up packet filtering policy. For example, the following code will lock all ports except the HTTP port, port 80:

```
IPSecPol \\exair1 -w REG -p "Web" -o
IPSecPol \\exair1 -x -w REG -p "Web" -r "BlockAll"
    -n BLOCK -f 0+*
IPSecPol \\exair1 -x -w REG -p "Web" -r "OkHTTP"
    -n PASS -f 0:80+*::TCP
IPSecPol \\exair1 -x -w REG -p "Web" -r "OkICMP"
    -n PASS   -f 0+*::ICMP
```

This code needs a little explaining, because there are no port-blocking examples in the resource kit documentation.

The first line removes the IPSec policy named Web and deletes any associated filters and filter actions. The next three lines block all IP traffic other than HTTP traffic and ICMP traffic, based on the syntax in Table 3-6.

Argument	Comments
IPSecPol	The tool name.
\\exair1	The name of a remote server to configure. The local machine is assumed if this option is missing.
-x	Activate the policy.
-w REG	Write the data to the registry. The other option is to write the data in Active Directory, but in this example the computers are not in a domain and therefore have no Active Directory access.
-p "Web"	The name of the policy.
-r "BlockAll" and *-r "OkHTTP"* and *-r "OkICMP"*	Policies are made of rules—in this case, the "Web" policy is made of three rules, *"BlockAll"*, *"OkHTTP"*, and *"OkICMP"*.
-n BLOCK -f 0+, *-n PASS -f 0:80+*::TCP, and *-n PASS -f 0+*::ICMP*	These rules set negotiation policy—in this case, the first blocks access to and from all ports and protocols, the second passes (that is, allows) access to port 80, and the last allows all ICMP traffic (for example, ICMP echo, or ping). *-f* means a filter list. *0* means my IP address(es) or all the IP addresses assigned to this computer. *0:80* means my address(es) using port 80 (HTTP port). *+* means create two filters, one for inbound traffic and the other for outbound traffic. * means all ports. *::TCP* means all IP addresses, on any port using TCP. (The port is not included between the two : characters.)

Table 3-6. *IPSecPol command line syntax.*

The format of the *-f* argument is as follows:

SourceAddr:SourcePort+DestinationAddr:DestinationPort:Protocol

It doesn't matter in what order you list the rules because the IPSec engine will order the rules such that the most specific rules are first and the most general are last.

For further information about IPSec, refer to the IP Security white paper at

http://www.microsoft.com/windows2000/library/howitworks/security/ip_security.asp

and the step-by-step guide to IPSec at

http://www.microsoft.com/windows2000/library/planning/security/ipsecsteps.asp

Security Configuration Editor

Because it can be time-consuming and difficult to set up, configure, enforce, and maintain distributed security environments, management errors are one of the prime causes of security problems in any network or internetwork. The SCE toolset is designed to alleviate this situation by providing an easy-to-use and consistent set of tools for security administration. Not only can the SCE deploy security policy, it can also audit that policy to verify that nothing has changed. The only audit tool available in Windows NT is the Event Viewer, but it's not designed to verify the security policy of Windows NT servers.

Security policy is created using the Security Template tool and then applied to a computer using the Security Configuration And Analysis tool. The latter tool can also analyze a system and verify that it complies with the security policy defined in the template.

Security templates allow you to configure the following security categories:

- Account policies: password, account policy, and Kerberos policy

- Local policies: audit policy, User Rights assignment, and security options

- Event logs: event log policy

- Restricted groups: Restricted group membership

- System services: security and startup policy

- Registry: Registry security settings

- File system: file access and audit security

The default installation of Windows 2000 Server includes the templates in Table 3-7.

Name	Comments
basicdc	This template contains basic security settings for Windows 2000 domain controllers. It requires that you set the DSDIT, DSLOG, and SYSVOL environment variables. The target computer must be in a domain in order for this template to work. This template does not modify the User Rights or the Restricted groups.
basicsv	This template applies basic security settings for computers running Windows 2000 Server. It does not modify the User Rights or the Restricted groups.
basicwk	This template applies basic security settings for computers running Windows 2000 Professional. It does not modify the User Rights or the Restricted groups.

Table 3-7. *Default security templates.*

Name	*Comments*
compatws	This template applies default permissions to the Users group so that legacy applications are more likely to run. It assumes you've done a clean install of the operating system and the registry ACLs to an NTFS partition. The template relaxes ACLs for members of the Users group and empties the Power Users group.
DC Security	This template applies default security settings for domain controllers.
hisecdc	This template assumes you've done a clean-install of the operating system and the Registry ACLs to an NTFS partition. The template includes SecureDC settings (see below) with Windows 2000–only enhancements. It empties the Power Users group.
hisecws	This template offers increased security settings over those of the securews template. It restricts Power User and Terminal Server ACLs and empties the Power Users group.
notssid	This template removes the Terminal Server User SID from Windows 2000 Server. It sets no other policy.
ocfiless	This template contains file security settings for optionally installed components on machines running Windows 2000 Server. Because all the files defined in this template are optional, many of the files might not be installed. This template is used if you install an optional Windows 2000 component after initial setup to make sure that the ACLs on the newly installed files are secure.
ocfilesw	This template contains file security settings for optionally installed components on machines running Windows 2000 Professional. Because all the files defined in this template are optional, many of the files might not be installed. This template is used if you install an optional Windows 2000 component after initial setup to make sure that the ACLs on the newly installed files are secure.
securedc	This template assumes you've done a clean-install of the operating system and the registry ACLs to an NTFS partition. The template provides higher security settings than those in the basicdc and the DC Security template.
securews	This template assumes you've done a clean-install of the operating system and the registry ACLs to an NTFS partition. The template provides higher security settings than those in the basicwk template and empties Power Users group.
setup security	This template contains "out of box" default security settings

Security Configuration Editor deployment process

Designing and deploying security policy is straightforward using the SCE toolset. If you want to modify an existing security policy, use the Security Templates tool. (There's no need to use this tool if you want to use an existing template.) You can load the Security Templates tool by following these steps:

1. Start Mmc.exe.

2. Choose Add/Remove Snap-in from the Console menu.

3. Click Add.

4. Select Security Templates.

5. Click Add, click Close, and click OK.

To use the SCE, first load the Security Configuration And Analysis tool by following the steps below:

1. Start Mmc.exe.

2. Choose Add/Remove Snap-in from the Console menu.

3. Click Add.

4. Select Security Configuration And Analysis.

5. Click Add, click Close, and click OK.

Now create an SCE database. SCE databases are used to track changes made to a computer and to allow you to audit against those settings. Create the database by following these steps:

1. Right-click the Security Configuration And Analysis tool.

2. Choose Open Database from the context menu.

3. Enter the name of the database, and click Open.

4. Select the name of the security template you want to use.

Now right-click the Security Configuration And Analysis tool and do the following:

1. Choose Analyze Computer Now from the context menu.

2. Enter the name of a file to write progress information to. The default file location is \Documents and Settings\<user>\Local Settings\Temp\delta.log.

3. Click OK.

Wait a moment while the tool analyzes your system, as shown in Figure 3-16. At this stage, the tool is comparing the system security with that defined in the template.

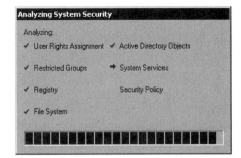

Figure 3-16. *The Security Configuration Editor analyzing a computer.*

You can browse the results when the analysis phase is complete, as shown in Figure 3-17, to see which settings do not comply with the policy you've defined.

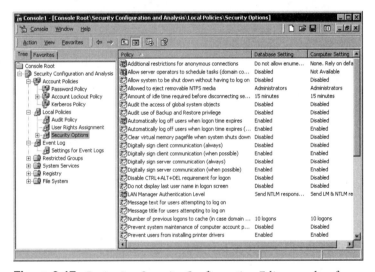

Figure 3-17. *Reviewing Security Configuration Editor results after an analysis.*

If you're happy with the settings, right-click the Security Configuration And Analysis tool again and choose Configure Computer Now from the context menu.

NOTE Security policy can also be deployed as part of Windows 2000 Group Policy by extending the Group Policy Editor. Group Policy is propagated to computers in a domain or organizational unit and applied to the computers. This configuration information is applied to affected computers regularly to ensure that they comply with corporate policy.

You can also analyze and configure a system by using the SecEdit.exe command line tool. Refer to the Windows 2000 online help and to the Security Configuration Editor Toolset white paper at *http://www.microsoft.com/windows2000/library/howitworks/ security/sctoolset.asp* for further details on this command.

Windows File Protection

Windows File Protection is a new feature of Windows 2000 designed to help make the operating system more stable. Technically, it's not a security feature, but it does offer the ability to detect when system files have been modified, possibly by an attacker.

All SYS, DLL, EXE, and OCX files that ship on the Windows 2000 CD are protected, as are the Micros.ttf, Tahoma.ttf, and Tahomabd.ttf TrueType fonts. If WFP detects that a system file has changed, it will silently replace the updated file with a copy of the file from the system32\dllcache directory or from the Windows 2000 installation CD.

Windows 2000 also includes a tool called System File Checker, Sfc.exe, that allows an administrator to scan all protected files to verify that they are valid versions. As this tool operates, it displays a status window and writes any file discrepancy information to the event log.

WFP knows which system files are valid and which are not through a mechanism called *driver signing*. All Windows 2000 files are hashed and then signed by Microsoft. The signed data is held in catalog files (not in the drivers themselves) in the System32\CatRoot directory. Each catalog file contains the signatures of valid system files. For example, the NT5IIS.CAT file stores all the signatures for the files that make up IIS 5. Double-clicking this file will display the signature information.

You can verify system file signatures at any stage by using the SigVerif.exe tool. After the tool runs, it will display a list of files that have either no signature or an invalid signature. Any file listed by the tool should be viewed with caution. Virtually all files shipped with Windows 2000 are signed; a very small number are not.

SUMMARY

- Windows 2000 builds on the core security principles in Windows NT.

- All accounts, often referred to as principals, in Windows 2000 must be authenticated by the operating system. An account is allowed to log on if the account's principals are valid and it has the appropriate privileges to access the computer.

- Windows 95, Windows 98, Windows NT, and Windows 2000 all support the Windows NT Challenge/Response authentication protocol.

- Windows 2000 supports the Kerberos V5 authentication protocol if Active Directory is installed.

- Windows NT 4, Windows 2000 Professional, and Windows 2000 Server or Windows 2000 Advanced Server without Active Directory installed store user and group account information in the Security Accounts Manager database, the SAM. When Active Directory is installed, user and group information is stored as objects in Active Directory.

- When Active Directory is installed, user accounts can be known by their SAM name in the form *DOMAIN/Name* or by their user principal name (UPN) in the form *name@DNSName*.

- All user accounts and groups are represented internally as security identifiers or SIDs. SIDs have the form S-R-A-S-S-S-S—for example, S-1-5-21-397661181-626881882-18441761-1009.

- Some SIDs are well-known SIDs; in other words, they are common to all instances of Windows 2000. An example includes the SID for the Everyone group: S-1-1-0. The Everyone group has the same SID on all computers running Windows NT and Windows 2000.

- When a user logs on, Windows 2000 creates a token to represent that account. A token contains the user's SID, SIDs of the groups to which the user belongs, privileges, and so on.

- Access or authorization in Windows 2000 is governed by access control lists. ACLs are associated with resources such as files. An ACL contains access control entries (ACEs), and each ACE contains information about what principal can do what to the resource.

- Windows 2000 helps support the concept of least privilege by providing restricted tokens and secondary logon. Restricted tokens are normal tokens that have privileges and SIDs removed. Secondary logon allows a user to log on normally as a low privilege account yet perform high privilege actions by performing a secondary logon as a more privileged account before invoking the program. The RunAs command is one way to use secondary logon. You can also hold down the shift key and right-click a shortcut on the desktop, and choose Run As from the context menu.

- Never log on to Windows 2000 as an administrator or as a member of the local administrators group unless you absolutely must do so. Instead, log on as a lower privilege account and use the secondary logon facility when you must run programs requiring higher privileges.

- Windows 2000 supports impersonation, or a program's ability to act on behalf of a user. Impersonation is used to access local resources. Impersonation is usually implemented as a server with a pool of worker threads; when the server receives a client request, it takes a thread from the pool, authenticates the user, impersonates the user, accesses the resources on behalf of the user, and then reverts to the security context of the server. This means that all ACLs are honored appropriately.

■ Windows 2000 can delegate the client identity to remote computers. Rather than just being able to access local resources on behalf of the client, as in the case of impersonation, delegation supports the ability of accessing remote resources on behalf of the client. Delegation is supported on Windows 2000 only, and only when using the Kerberos authentication protocol, which requires Active Directory. The key to delegation is the concept of delegatable or forwardable tickets.

■ For delegation to work, the user account in question must not be marked as sensitive, all servers must be marked as trusted for delegation, and all processes handing the client request must start up with accounts trusted to delegate the client request.

■ Encrypting File System is a new feature in Windows 2000; it allows files and directories to be automatically encrypted and decrypted by the file owner. Recovery administrators have the ability to recover protected files if required.

■ IP Security, IPSec, is a new open standards–based feature of Windows 2000 for ensuring secure communication between computers. It can also be used to protect against attack by blocking IP protocols and ports.

■ The Security Configuration Editor toolset alleviates many administrative errors by providing an easy-to-use, consistent set of tools. It can deploy and audit security policy.

Chapter 4

Internet Explorer Security Overview

In the previous chapter, we looked at the foundation for building secure Web services, Microsoft Windows 2000. In this and the following three chapters, we'll discuss the security capabilities of Microsoft Internet Explorer, Internet Information Services (IIS), Microsoft SQL Server, and COM+.

Internet Explorer 5 is the Web-browsing technology incorporated into Windows 2000. It's used to access Web data and FTP data, as well as Windows networking information. Most people think of Internet Explorer as the process called Iexplore.exe; however, you must consider that the Internet Explorer Web-browsing technology is deeply integrated with many aspects of the Windows 2000 graphical shell. This is because the technology is highly componentized. It's possible, for example, to include links to your favorite Web sites in Microsoft Management Console (MMC). One of the authors has a standard set of tools he uses all the time in an MMC console, one of which is a link to the Microsoft security pages at *www.microsoft.com/security*, as shown in Figure 4-1.

The following sections regarding Internet Explorer security include

- ■ Privacy

- ■ Code safety and malicious content

- ■ Security zones

- ■ SSL/TLS and certificates

- ■ Cookie security

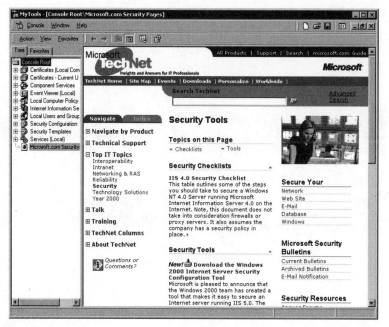

Figure 4-1. *A set of standard tools in MMC, including a link to the Microsoft security pages.*

PRIVACY

A major threat facing all Web browser users is invasion of privacy; your privacy can be violated by malicious users snooping browser-to-Web-server communications. For example, by default the communication channel from the browser to the server is not encrypted, which might enable malevolent users to "sniff" the channel and possibly gain access to credit card information, passwords, confidential data (such as personal medical records), and the like as it travels across the Internet. The simplest way to defend against this threat is to use a secured channel using the Secure Sockets Layer/Transport Layer Security (SSL/TLS) protocol. This must be configured at the Web server, not at the client, because it is the server's responsibility to determine whether the information being transferred to the client is to be encrypted.

NOTE   Even though a Web site might require SSL/TLS only for handling sensitive information, such as passwords or credit card numbers, you can opt to use SSL/TLS for all aspects of the Web server's operations simply by entering *HTTPS* rather than *HTTP* as the protocol. Note, however, that this will not work for Web servers that do not support SSL/TLS.

IP DATA AND POSTCARDS

Think of Internet traffic, which is composed of IP packets (that is, units of information transmitted from sender to destination network and station), as postcards. Postcards travel from a source to a destination, sometimes through multiple intermediaries, and *they can be read by anyone along the way.*

You'll know if you're using SSL/TLS because Internet Explorer will display a bright yellow lock at the bottom of the screen. You can also check the strength of the encryption key by positioning the mouse pointer over the lock; a ToolTip will appear and display the information, as shown in Figure 4-2. Double-clicking on the lock displays the Web server's SSL/TLS certificate.

Figure 4-2. *Looking at the SSL/TLS encryption strength in Internet Explorer.*

SSL/TLS is explained in this chapter in "SSL/TLS and Certificates," in Chapter 5, "Internet Information Services Security Overview," and in Chapter 9, "Practical Privacy, Integrity, Auditing, and Nonrepudiation."

> **WARNING** You might not see the lock icon if you are invoking Internet Explorer technology from something other than the Internet Explorer process. So be careful not to transfer confidential data over the Web unless you have no doubt that the channel is secured.
>
> In addition, you might not see the lock in Internet Explorer when HTML frames are used, because parts of the frameset might be using HTTP and other parts might be using HTTPS. In this case, the padlock is not shown even though the data is protected by SSL/TLS. However, if you right-click a frame and choose Properties from the context menu, you'll see that the page is using SSL/TLS.

CODE SAFETY AND MALICIOUS CONTENT

The race to produce more flexible and functional Web applications requires some degree of client-side code, so many Web sites include code that's executed in the browser. Examples of such code include the following:

■ Dynamic HTML

■ JavaScript

■ Microsoft Visual Basic, Scripting Edition (VBScript)

- Java

- ActiveX components

- PostScript

- Scripting code in word processing and spreadsheet documents

Client-side code serves two main purposes: The first is to offload work from the server. If work is performed at the client rather than at the server, the cost of a round-trip to the Web server is avoided. The second is to boost functionality. There are many things HTML simply cannot do; after all, HTML is a text layout language and nothing more.

Running client code carries risks, however. You might not be able to tell whether the code is malevolent or benign, and many vulnerabilities over the past few years relating to downloadable or mobile code have come to light. The threats include the following:

- Code that deletes data (data integrity threat)

- Code that copies confidential data and makes it available to other users (privacy or disclosure threat)

- Code that consumes all disk space or consumes CPU time (denial of service threat)

- Code that attempts to gain administrative access to the computer (elevation of privilege threat)

As a Web site developer, you should determine what capabilities are required by your applications and then choose the technology that most closely maps to those capabilities. In a way, it's a twist on the least privilege rule: use the technology with the fewest capabilities that gets the job done.

The threats based on security bugs are often fixed rapidly by the software manufacturer, but not all systems install the security patches in a timely manner. It is imperative that you stay abreast of security updates for all the products you use, regardless of the vendor. For example, *http://www.microsoft.com/security* has all the latest information about security in Microsoft products.

If your business needs require you to use technologies like Java and ActiveX, make sure you digitally sign the component. More information on signing code can be found at *http://msdn.microsoft.com/workshop/security/authcode/signfaq.asp*. Also note that you can selectively disable ActiveX components from running by setting the "kill bit" on the component. Refer to Knowledge Base article Q240797, "How to Stop an ActiveX Control from Running in Internet Explorer," at *http:// support.microsoft.com/support/kb/articles/Q240/7/97.asp* for more detail.

SECURITY ZONES

Security zones, introduced in Internet Explorer 4, are an easy way to administer security because they allow you to gather security settings into easy-to-manage groups. The security settings are enforced when you browse Web sites. The main tenet behind security zones is that some Web pages need to be handled with specific security restrictions depending on their host Web site, thereby matching security restrictions with Web page origin. In essence, zones are a form of security policy that is enforced when you browse certain classes of Web sites.

Another goal of zones is to reduce the number of times a user is prompted to make a security decision. If a user is asked to make numerous yes-no decisions, often the user will end up repeatedly hitting Yes out of frustration without really reflecting on the question being asked.

The security settings that can be assigned to the various zones are as follows:

- **Low**   Only the most trusted sites should run at this level because it performs the fewest security checks and rarely warns the user by providing a prompt.

- **Medium-Low**   This level is more secure than Low—unsigned active content is not downloaded—but it includes few prompts.

- **Medium**   This level is more secure than Medium-Low, and it includes more prompts, including prompts before potentially unsafe content is downloaded.

- **High**   This is the most secure but least functional (from the perspective of the person browsing the Web) level. Cookies are disabled, and many prompts are provided for the user.

- **Custom**   This level allows complete control over every security aspect, including ActiveX controls, cookies, file downloading, Java support, scripting language support, and authentication.

The zones and their default security settings included in Internet Explorer 5 are described in Table 4-1. For most users, the default security settings should be safe enough without sacrificing functionality.

Zone	Comments
Local Intranet	Any computer on a corporate intranet is in the Local Intranet zone. A corporate intranet computer is defined as any site that does not require access via a proxy site or that has no period in its URL (for example, *http://merlin*) or in its Universal Naming Convention (UNC) pathname (*merlin**data*). The default security level for Local Intranet is Medium-Low.
Trusted Sites	This zone includes sites explicitly trusted by the user—in other words, sites you believe to be benign and contain no content capable of damaging your system or invading your privacy. For example, if you trust your own corporate Web site, you might add it to the Trusted Sites zone. For extra safety, you can also require that all Web sites in this zone have an SSL/TLS connection. By default, no Web sites are included in this zone and the security level is Low.
Restricted Sites	This zone is the opposite of Trusted Sites. You should add sites you don't trust but might need access to and sites that could possibly damage your computer to this zone. By default, the zone has no sites and its security level is High.
My Computer	As the name implies, this zone's only member is your computer. You cannot configure this zone in Internet Explorer, but you can do so with the Internet Explorer Administration Kit (IEAK). Refer to the next section for information on the IEAK.
Internet	This zone includes all sites that are not on your intranet and not listed in any other zone, and it does not include your local computer. The default security level for this zone is Medium.

Table 4-1. *Internet Explorer zones and their default security level settings.*

The Internet Explorer Administration Kit

The IEAK is an administration tool for Internet Explorer that allows administrators to determine how Internet Explorer is configured. Some of the security features that can be enabled with the IEAK include the following:

- Administrator specification of what ActiveX controls are allowed to run on user's machines

- Choosing which software publishers to trust

- Automatic digital signing (using Authenticode) of controls

- Presetting and lockdown of the following security settings:

  ❑ Security zone settings

  ❑ Policy lockout—prevents users from changing a particular policy for a particular zone

  ❑ Domain lockout—prevents user from changing domain mapping (or site) to another zone

- Prepopulating and enforcing trusted certification authorities

- Locking down proxy settings

- Using content ratings through the Platform for Internet Content Selection (PICS)

You can find out more about the IEAK at *http://www.microsoft.com/ie/ieak.*

ZONES AND THE DOTLESS-IP ADDRESS DILEMMA

If your knowledge of TCP/IP addressing is excellent, you might be aware that an IP address can appear either as dotted notation, such as 158.23.111.15, or as a number with no dots. For example, the IP address 158.23.111.15 would be represented by the number 2652335887. Because no period appears in the address in this form, you might think that Internet Explorer would consider the site an intranet site.

If this were the case, it would create an interesting security vulnerability: a Web site could trick your browser into visiting a part of the site with malicious content by using an address format (such as *http://2652335887*) associated with intranets. Then the browser would run the content with fewer security measures. However, this is not the case in Internet Explorer 5. When browsing to a Web site with an address composed completely of numbers, the browser considers the Web site to be in the Internet security zone, even if the site is an intranet site.

You can calculate a dotless-IP address by taking a dotted-IP address—that is, an address in the form a.b.c.d—and using this formula:

Dotless-IP = (a x 16777216) + (b x 65536) + (c x 256) + d

So that you are not vulnerable to this kind of attack, make sure you update your browser if you are running Internet Explorer 4.0 or 4.01—the benefits of Internet Explorer 5.0 greatly outweigh the time it takes to perform the upgrade. Also, refer to Knowledge Base article Q168617, "Update Available for Dotless IP Address Security Issue," for more information on this matter.

Security Zones in Other Tools

Other Internet tools can use zones because support for zones is built into the *URL Moniker* dynamic-link library (DLL) called URLMon.dll, not the core Internet Explorer engine. (You can find more information about functionality in URLMon on the MSDN CDs or at *http://msdn.microsoft.com*.) For example, Microsoft Outlook 2000 uses zones to determine whether to run script and active content in HTML-formatted messages. You access these settings in Outlook 2000 like so:

1. Open Outlook 2000.

2. Choose Options from the Tools menu.

3. Click the Security tab.

You can now set the zone, as shown in Figure 4-3, in which e-mail will be opened; it's highly recommended that you choose the Restricted Sites zone. When you open an e-mail with dynamic content embedded in HTML-formatted text, the HTML will execute as though it came from a distrusted Web site.

More information about security zones can be found in Knowledge Base article Q174360, "How to Use Security Zones in Internet Explorer," at *http:// support.microsoft.com/support/kb/articles/Q174/3/60.ASP*.

SECURING E-MAIL CONTAINING HTML

It's very easy to send e-mail from a bogus source because many SMTP servers do not authenticate the sender first. For example, an attacker could send a fake e-mail to you from your manager. It's a common prank! A knowledgeable user will know to look at the SMTP headers to see that the user was not authenticated, but most e-mail readers hide the headers from you by default.

This can be an issue for e-mail readers that use HTML-formatted text. You might decide to trust e-mail from a specific location (because of your zones configuration), but an attacker could spoof a trusted address and send you a malicious HTML-based e-mail message that is a security threat to your system.

A way around this is to use digitally signed e-mail using technologies such as S/MIME (Secure/Multipurpose Internet Mail Extensions), which Microsoft Outlook 2000 supports. When you digitally sign an e-mail message, users can verify that the message was not tampered with and thus that the message came from you and not an imposter.

Figure 4-3. *Setting zones in Outlook 2000.*

SSL/TLS AND CERTIFICATES

Internet Explorer 5 supports the industry-standard privacy and data integrity proto-cols: Secure Sockets Layer and Transport Layer Security. Internet Explorer also sup-ports the Fortezza-enabled version of SSL.

Fortezza is a specification for hardware-based cryptography for use in the U.S. Department of Defense. It is used to transfer sensitive, but nonclassified, data. Fortezza enables secure SSL/TLS connections to Fortezza-enabled Web sites using Fortezza PCMCIA cards. IIS 5 also supports Fortezza; the TLS protocol currently does not.

You can determine which SSL/TLS protocols Internet Explorer supports by doing the following:

1. Open Internet Explorer.

2. Choose Internet Options from the Tools Menu.

3. Click the Advanced tab.

Scroll down the Security node.

You can now set which SSL/TLS protocols you want to support. In highly se-cure environments, you should enable SSL 3.0 and TLS 1.0 but disable SSL 2.0 and PCT 1.0, as shown in Figure 4-4.

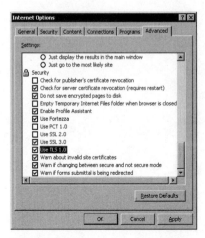

Figure 4-4.   *Setting SSL and TLS protocols in Internet Explorer 5.*

WHAT IS PCT?

Private Communication Technology (PCT) is a security technology akin to SSL and TLS. It was invented by Microsoft to address some of the weaknesses in the SSL2 protocol—namely, the situation in which an attacker could force SSL2 to "roll back" to a weaker set of cryptographic protocols (called *ciphersuites*). However, these issues were later remedied in SSL3 and TLS. Because of this, PCT is a deprecated protocol and should not be used.

Internet Explorer also supports X.509 client authentication certificates for strong authentication environments. Today, it's common that the certificate and associated private key be held in software or on a smartcard. Refer to Chapter 15, "An Introduction to Cryptography and Certificates in Windows 2000," for more information about certificates.

THE ROLE OF SCHANNEL.DLL

In Windows, you'll often hear of Schannel.dll in conjunction with SSL, PCT, and TLS. This DLL, an abbreviation for secure channel, performs all SSL/TLS functionality. The Windows Internet library, WinInet, also uses Schannel.dll to create secured channels between clients and servers.

COOKIE SECURITY

Cookies are small amounts of information written to your computer about you and your visits to Web pages. When your browser makes a request to a Web site, the browser checks its cookie file for any cookies matching the Web site. If a cookie is found, it is sent automatically by the browser as part of the HTTP headers to the Web server. Cookies are mainly used for custom pages, shopping carts, targeted advertising, and session maintenance.

Let's look at each in turn.

Custom Pages

Many news-oriented Web sites or Web portals allow you to maintain your favorite settings—for example, local news, space news, sports, business, and so on. This information is sent to the browser as a cookie that is sent back to the server the next time you visit it. The server then deciphers the cookie and displays the information you want.

Shopping Carts

If you visit a site that features a "shopping cart" of items you want to purchase, a cookie can keep track of what you put in the cart. If you need to leave and come back later, the cookie makes sure your shopping cart is as you left it.

Targeted Advertising

A little like tracking, cookies are maintained by an advertising company to determine which sites you visit and possibly what options you elect to use on each Web site.

Session Maintenance

Active Server Pages (ASP), the server scripting technology in Internet Information Services, uses cookies to maintain session information during the lifetime of a user's connection. This is necessary because HTTP is a stateless protocol. In other words, as far as the Web server is concerned, each connection is a new connection and the server retains no knowledge of previous requests.

ASP exposes a COM+ object called the Session object to ASP developers to maintain information about the user while the user is connected. For example, it's possible to easily create a shopping cart by using the Session object.

> **NOTE**   You can disable ASP's use of sessions, and therefore not require the use of cookies, by setting the following in your ASP pages:

```
<%@ EnableSessionState = False %>
```

Now that we've looked at the common cookie, let's look at how cookies can cause privacy and security issues.

One concern is that cookies are often written to the disk drive, and therefore a malicious Web site might be able to read sensitive information—such as passwords and credit card numbers—from the cookies stored on your machine by inserting client JavaScript code into the Web pages that read the cookie information.

There have been vulnerabilities in the past with cookie implementations leading to illicit access to cookie information. At the time of writing, however, there were no known issues with either Netscape Navigator or Internet Explorer.

COOKIES—A REALITY CHECK

It's rare that cookies contain sensitive data such as passwords and credit card information, but it's not impossible. Still, it's unlikely that an attacker accessing your cookies will gain anything of interest other than some of your surfing habits or preferences. Often, the cookie data is merely a pointer into a database held at the Web server—that kind of cookie data is useless to an attacker.

A cookie is merely a piece of text; it is not a program and cannot be used to harness a virus.

Because much Web site technology, including IIS, uses cookies to maintain session information, another cookie security concern is the possibility that a malicious user could sniff the connection between the Web server and the browser, take a note of the cookie being used, and then replay the cookie to access the Web server. In doing so, the attacker might get access to the legitimate client's data.

You can mitigate this risk either by prompting users to reauthenticate themselves at sensitive points in the data transfer or by switching to an SSL/TLS session to protect the data and the cookie.

SESSION STATE IN INTERNET INFORMATION SERVICES 5

Session state—such as what page the user is viewing, information entered or requested by the user, and the number of times a user has visited a particular Web page—in IIS 5 is maintained by using cookies that have a name such as *ASPSESSIONIDxxxxx=yyyy*, where *xxxx* is a set of letters that represents the IIS process handling the client request and *yyyy* is a random value used to identify the user session.

Viewing and Deleting Cookies

You can view cookies in Windows 2000 by performing the following steps:

1. Open Windows Explorer.

2. Navigate to the Documents And Settings folder.

3. Open the folder with your name on it. You might be denied access to other directories.

4. Open the Cookies folder.

In the Cookies folder, you'll see multiple text files, each of which is a cookie for a Web site you visited. The format of each file is *yourname@website.txt*, where *yourname* is your Windows 2000 account name and *website* is the name of the Web site the cookie came from. Because the security for this folder is controlled by access control lists (ACLs) if you're running NTFS, no one can access your cookies other than you and the computer's administrator. You can safely delete any of these files.

> **NOTE** Because cookies are stored on a per-user basis on the current machine and the security for the folder in which the cookies are stored is controlled by ACLs, cookies cannot be used if you move to another machine or log on as a different user.

Preventing Cookies and Prompting Before Cookies Are Downloaded

You can configure Internet Explorer to reject cookies, to prompt the user for a response regarding cookies, or to accept cookies based on the security zone the browser is using. For example, the Local Intranet zone enables cookies, but the Restricted Sites zone does not enable cookies whatsoever. You can configure the cookie settings when you define security zones for your browser.

A great resource for cookie information is the Cookie Central Web site at *http://www.cookiecentral.com*.

Now that we've covered some of the basics of browser security, let's turn our attention to the other end of the connection, the Web server and Internet Information Services.

## Chapter 5

Internet Information Services Security Overview

Internet Information Services (IIS) 5 is a mature, high-performance Microsoft Windows 2000–based Web server, which builds on the success of IIS 4, the most popular Web server for Microsoft Windows NT 4. In this chapter, we'll examine some of the security features of IIS 5 as well as some of the server's new functionality.

Because IIS is a Windows 2000 system service and relies heavily on the security functionality in Windows 2000, it's assumed in this chapter that you have read Chapter 3, "Windows 2000 Security Overview," or have a good working knowledge of Windows 2000 security.

We'll cover the following topics in this chapter:

■ Internet authentication

■ Web authentication protocol details

■ Anonymous access

■ Basic authentication

■ Digest authentication

- Integrated Windows authentication and the Negotiate protocol
- X.509 client certificate authentication
- Configuring SSL/TLS
- IIS authorization—the marriage of Windows 2000 security and the Web
- IIS process identities

A NEW FEATURE OF IIS 5—WEBDAV

Defined in RFC 2518 (*http://www.ietf.org/rfc/rfc2518.txt*), Web-based Distributed Authoring and Versioning (WebDAV) is a set of extensions to the HTTP 1.1 protocol that allows users to collaboratively edit and manage documents on Web servers. IIS 5, Microsoft Internet Explorer 5, and Microsoft Office 2000 support WebDAV.

You can find more information about WebDAV at the WebDAV Resources Web site (*http://www.webdav.org*) and at the Microsoft Developer Network (MSDN) Web site at *http://msdn.microsoft.com/standards/WebDAV.asp*.

INTERNET AUTHENTICATION

There are three types of Web access in a Web application, be it on the World Wide Web or on an intranet:

- Anonymous access
- Identified access
- Authenticated access

In the anonymous access scenario, you don't care who the user is—users have access to all the resources you want them to have access to and no more. A good example of this is simple Web presence; most Web sites use anonymous access for their home page and their marketing or sales material. For example, the vast majority of *www.microsoft.com* uses anonymous access, including its sales, marketing, and developer-related materials.

Identified access is for Web areas where you are providing personalized services—you are not giving users access to private data known only to the company and the user. For example, you have the option to customize the home page of The

Microsoft Network, *www.msn.com,* so that you can see your favorite stock quotes, news sources, leisure categories, and so on. This Web information is not confidential; it is customized.

In the authenticated access scenario, you need to know who the user is and the user has to have access to data that might be private, sensitive, or personal.

Notice that as you progress from anonymous to authenticated access there's a greater need to trust the user's credentials, as shown in Figure 5-1. For anonymous access, there's far less of a need to know who the user is; in fact, some might argue that you needn't care at all. For identified access, you need to know who the user is but only to the extent needed to provide a service or personalized but public content associated with that identity. With authenticated access, access is denied if you cannot confirm the credentials of the calling user.

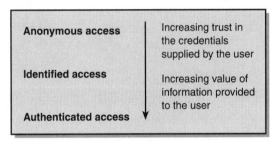

Figure 5-1. *Valuable information requires stronger credentials.*

Each of these scenarios depends on the degree to which you trust the credentials supplied by the user. Anonymous access requires no credentials, identified access uses weak credentials, and authenticated access requires strong credentials. The strength of the credentials required is related to the value or sensitivity of the data you are providing. This is not to say that sales and marketing information available to all users is not valuable, but it is not as valuable as projected sales and marketing information internal to the organization.

In the example shown in Figure 5-2, the public area of the fictitious Exploration Air Web site requires no authentication (anonymous access), and the internal part of the site requires either HTTP 1.1 Digest authentication or Integrated Windows authentication, both of which are covered later in this chapter. The directories used to serve the content should be controlled by access control lists (ACLs) according to who the users are. Notice the use of the Deny access control entry (ACE) for the anonymous user account on the internal directory in the figure. If the administrator accidentally sets anonymous access as a valid authentication scheme, the anonymous account will still be denied access to the site content because of this ACL setting.

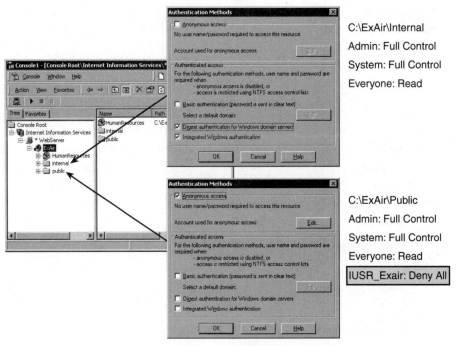

Figure 5-2. *Public data requires weak or no credentials; private or confidential data requires stronger credentials using authentication techniques.*

Authentication Protocols Supported by IIS 5

Before we look in depth at the authentication protocols supported by IIS 5, an overview of how Web authentication works is in order.

Web authentication protocol details

Web authentication requires multiple interactions between the Web browser and the Web server. The general steps, as shown in Figure 5-3, are as follows:

1. The browser requests data from the server by using an HTTP GET verb.

2. If the Web server requires the client to authenticate himself, it sends an HTTP 401 error back to the browser, along with a list of the authentication schemes it supports and data, often called a *challenge,* with which the client can resubmit the request. The challenges are sent as one or more WWW-Authenticate headers in the server's response.

3. The browser chooses an authentication scheme it supports and reconstructs the request to include a *response* to the challenge. The response is data based on the user's credentials and the challenge data sent by the server. The response is sent back as part of an Authorization header. Note

that Internet Explorer will always pick the first authentication scheme if given the option of choosing from multiple authentication schemes. For example, if Basic authentication is listed before Digest authentication, Internet Explorer will pick Basic.

4. The browser reissues the request including the response data.

5. The server authenticates the newly submitted data and, assuming all is well, sends the response, and the requested resource, back to the user, including an *HTTP 200 status code – no error* message.

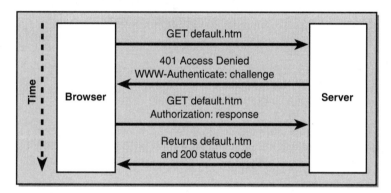

Figure 5-3. *Overview of Web authentication protocols data flow.*

IMPORTANT When the server sends an HTTP 401 error to the client, it sends a list of supported authentication protocols. Therefore, if your Web server supports authentication protocols A and B, you must be willing to accept credentials from the weakest protocol because the browser might understand (or choose) only the weaker protocol. If you're not willing to accept weak credentials, you should not select that protocol for your Web site.

As shipped, the Web server in IIS 5 supports the following authentication protocols:

■ Anonymous access

■ Basic

■ Digest

■ Integrated Windows

■ X.509 client certificates

Each of these is explained in detail in the following sections, so let's get started with the weakest of all the authentication schemes, anonymous access.

Anonymous access

Technically, anonymous access is not an authentication scheme because the calling user is never asked to present credentials such as a password. However, Windows 2000 requires that all users authenticate themselves before they access any resource. To this end, IIS provides a default user account called IUSR_*machinename* as the Anonymous User account for anonymous access. All anonymous access is performed in the context of this account.

The account is defined at setup time with a very strong password—comprising uppercase and lowercase letters, numbers, and punctuation—and can be changed by the administrator later, but you are not obliged to use this and only this account for anonymous access. In fact, you can set different user accounts to be used in different parts of your Web space, such as at a Web server, virtual directory, directory, and file levels.

You can change the account in the IIS administrative tool like so:

1. Right-click the My Computer icon on your desktop.

2. Choose Manage from the context menu.

3. Expand the Services And Applications node.

4. Click Internet Information Services.

5. Right-click the Web server, virtual directory, directory, or file in question.

6. Choose Properties from the context menu.

7. Click the Directory Security tab.

8. Click Edit in the Anonymous Access And Authentication Control box.

9. Make sure Anonymous Access is checked.

10. Click Edit.

11. Enter the account name and the account password. If the password box is grayed out, you need to clear the Allow IIS To Control Password check box first.

12. Click OK three times.

You can also set the anonymous account programmatically by using Active Directory Services Interface (ADSI). Refer to Chapter 13, "Security Administration with ADSI, WMI, and COM+," for an example.

IMPORTANT   It is imperative that the Anonymous User account be an account with few privileges, minimal group membership, and minimal access to resources.

Failure to configure the account this way will compromise the security of your Web site because all anonymous access will operate in the context of the anonymous account. You have been warned!

Why change the Anonymous User account?

It's useful to change the Anonymous User account if you host multiple Web sites. You can set up one Anonymous User account per Web site and set ACLs on the resources used by that Web site. For example, say you host *www.SiteA.com* and *www.SiteB.com*. You could then set the account for *www.SiteA.com* to be AnonA and the account for *www.SiteB.com* to be AnonB. The scenario would look like that in Figure 5-4.

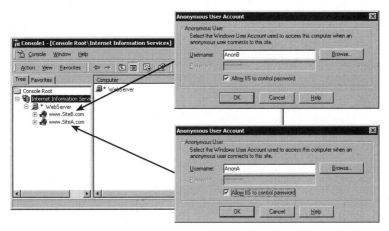

Figure 5-4. *Using different Anonymous User accounts for different Web sites.*

Privileges required when using the Anonymous User account

There has been much confusion about the Anonymous User account and anonymous access in IIS relating to which privileges are required for the account. The question is, "Does the Anonymous User account need network logon or interactive logon privileges?"

The answer is, it depends!

If you have the Allow IIS To Control Password option checked in the Anonymous User Account dialog box, the account must have the Access This Computer From The Network privilege; otherwise, the Log On Locally privilege is required. IIS will log the account on using different techniques, depending on the Allow IIS To Control Password setting, which is our next topic.

The Allow IIS To Control Password setting

If the Allow IIS To Control Password setting is checked, IIS calls a *subauthenticator* to validate the password. Subauthenticators are implemented as dynamic-link libraries (DLLs). A subauthentication DLL allows the authentication information stored in the Windows 2000 user account database (the Security Accounts Manager [SAM] or the Directory) to be augmented with other account validation capabilities.

For example, a server might supply a subauthentication DLL that validates a user's password via a different algorithm or specifies special workstation restrictions.

All of this can be accomplished using subauthentication DLLs without sacrificing the use of the Windows 2000 user account database and its administration tools.

IIS 5 supplies a subauthentication DLL called IISSUBA.DLL to verify that the password is correct and then informs Windows 2000 that the password is valid so that the user can log on. Note that this functionality is available in Internet Information Server 4 also.

Accounts authenticated using a subauthentication DLL are always network logons and thus must have the Access This Computer From The Network privilege.

IMPORTANT   Only administrators can add subauthenticators to the operating system.

For more information about subauthentication DLLs, refer to the MSDN CDs or to *http://msdn.microsoft.com*.

If Allow IIS To Control Password is not checked, IIS will log the account on using the Windows API *LogonUser* and pass in the name of the Anonymous User account as well as the password, both of which are stored in the IIS configuration store, the *metabase*. Hence, if the control password setting is not set, the anonymous account must have the Log On Locally privilege.

Basic authentication

Basic authentication is a simple authentication protocol defined as part of the HTTP 1.0 protocol defined in RFC 2617 (available at *http://www.ietf.org/rfc/rfc2617.txt*). Although virtually all Web servers and Web browsers support this protocol, it is extremely insecure because the password is in *cleartext* (also called *plaintext*), meaning it's passed over the network "in the clear." (Actually, it's not in the clear; it's base64-encoded, which is so trivial to decode that it might as well be cleartext!). Basic authentication works well through proxy servers and firewalls.

Basic authentication, as implemented in IIS 5, requires Windows 2000 accounts, either in the SAM or in Active Directory. This allows the Web site to use ACLs to determine access to resources. When a user connects to a Web site using Basic authentication, IIS gets the username and password from the HTTP Authorization header, calls the *LogonUser* API, and then impersonates the user.

By default, users accessing your Basic authentication Web server need the right to log on locally, although this can be changed in the IIS metabase by using ADSI. Refer to Chapter 13 for this method.

So, why change the logon type? The *LogonUser* API allows you to determine how the account is logged on. For example, the account can be logged on using log on locally, network, or batch privileges. Interactive logon is the default because it's the most flexible setting for most environments; it's not necessarily the most secure. Giving users this privilege allows them to log on to the Web server if they have physical access to the server.

The flexibility of a local logon is a legacy of Windows NT 4 and IIS 4. If an account is authenticated using NTLM or is logged on with network privileges, the account cannot access secured resources on another remote computer. While the issue of client delegation is resolved in Windows 2000 by using Kerberos, the only way to work around this in Windows NT with IIS 4 and Windows 2000 with IIS 5 in a non–Active Directory environment is to log the account on using log on locally privileges.

With log on locally privileges, information about the client, such as group membership and privileges, is stored so that the account can perform an offline logon if the server performing the logon cannot access a domain controller. The downside to storing this information is its effect on speed—it takes a certain amount of time to load and store the data.

Nevertheless, you can get the best of both worlds—speed and the ability to "hop" onto a remote server securely—by using the batch logon privilege. However, few user accounts have this privilege, so you must grant the privilege to the users in question.

The Network Logon With Cleartext password setting

Just to make things a little more interesting, there's another option! Once you give a user the network privilege—again, the Access This Computer From The Network privilege—you can allow the user to hop off the IIS server and onto a remote server by using a flag in the call to *LogonUser* that is new to Windows 2000: the Network Logon With Cleartext password setting. This is a new implementation in Windows 2000 of the network logon, a way of using the network privilege when calling *LogonUser*. This capability can be set only by using ADSI, as we'll describe in Chapter 13.

Table 5-1 outlines the advantages and drawbacks of each logon privilege when applied to Basic authentication.

Privilege	*Pros*	*Cons*
Local	User can perform a hop to a remote, secured server running Windows NT or Windows 2000.	Insecure—giving users this privilege allows them to log on to the Web server if they have physical access to it. Slower than other logon types because client information is cached.
Network	Secure—the user cannot log on to the server even with physical access to the server. Fast because no client data is cached.	User is unable to make a hop to a remote server.

Table 5-1. *Basic authentication and the effects of different privileges.*   *(continued)*

Table 5-1. *continued*

Privilege	Pros	Cons
Batch	User can make a hop to a remote server. Secure—the user cannot log on to the server even with physical access to the server. Fast because no client data is cached. (Note: future versions of Windows might support caching client data for batch logon.)	Very few accounts have this privilege by default.
Network with cleartext logon	Secure—the user cannot log on to the server even with physical access to the server. Fast because no client data is cached. User can make a hop to a remote server.	

Using Basic authentication with Active Directory

Basic authentication, when used on a system with Active Directory, offers two other features:

■ The ability to delegate identity

■ The use of user principal names (UPNs)

Let's look at both in turn.

By default, the account logging on to the Web server using Basic authentication must have the Log On Locally privilege, by which IIS can make requests for secured resources on a remote computer on behalf of the user. In other words, if Cheryl attempts to use a resource on a remote computer, the remote computer will see that Cheryl is performing the task. However, if the remote computer attempts to access a resource on another computer, the next computer won't see that Cheryl is making the request. In fact, the chances are good that the request will fail. This is the delegation problem, which Figure 5-5 shows more clearly. As you can see, there's a limit to how many times the user's credentials can be used to set up secure connections between computers running Windows NT or Windows 2000.

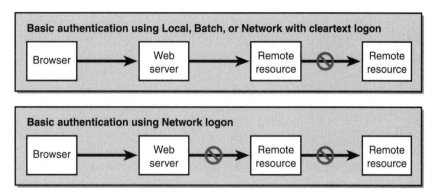

Figure 5-5. *The delegation effects of different logon schemes when used with Basic authentication.*

However, when Active Directory is used the delegation issue is solved because Windows 2000 uses Kerberos (which, as we know, is enabled when Active Directory is installed) to perform delegation. The net effect of this configuration is shown in Figure 5-6. In short, the delegation problem is solved when using Basic authentication and Active Directory.

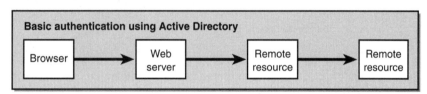

Figure 5-6. *The effect of using Basic authentication in an Active Directory environment.*

Another useful feature of Basic authentication when used in conjunction with accounts held in Active Directory is the ability to use UPNs—names in the form *user@domain.com.* The following must be true to use UPNs in conjunction with Basic authentication:

- The server on which IIS 5 is running must have access to Active Directory.

- The account must have a UPN. (By default, all accounts in Active Directory have a UPN.)

- The Basic domain name must be set to "\". This is used as an indicator to IIS to use UPN naming rather than classic Windows NT DOMAIN\Account naming.

As already discussed, users must have accounts in either the SAM or Windows 2000 Active Directory to access resources on IIS 5. If the user logs on and does not enter a domain name, it's assumed that the domain to be used for the account is the same domain in which the Web server is running. For example, if the Web server is located on a server on the Sales domain and Richard logs on using Basic authentication, he will log on with the *SALES\Richard* account unless he explicitly logs on with another account such as *DEVELOPMENT\Richard*. Setting Basic authentication to use a default domain of "\" tells IIS 5 to disregard any domain names and use a UPN instead. This is possible because a UPN has domain information built in to the name itself.

You can set the default domain to "\" by following these steps:

1. Right-click the My Computer icon on the desktop.

2. Choose Manage from the context menu.

3. Open the Services And Applications node.

4. Open the Internet Information Services node.

5. Right-click the Web site, virtual directory, directory, or file in question, and choose Properties from the context menu.

6. Click the Directory Security tab.

7. Click Edit in the Anonymous Access And Authentication Control box.

8. Enable Basic authentication.

9. Read the warning message, and select Yes if you want to continue using Basic authentication.

10. Click the Basic authentication Edit button.

11. Enter "\" (without the quotes) in the Domain Name box.

12. Click OK three times.

Figure 5-7 shows the domain name to enter in the Basic Authentication Domain dialog box in the Internet Service Manager administration tool so that UPN naming will work.

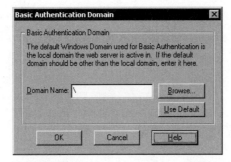

Figure 5-7. *Setting the domain name to support Windows 2000 UPNs.*

You can achieve the same result programmatically by using ADSI and the *DefaultLogonDomain* property. The following Windows Script code shows how to set Basic authentication on a virtual directory named *Private* and configure it to use UPNs:

```
' Authentication protocol constants.
AUTH_ANON = 1
AUTH_BASIC = 2
AUTH_WINDOWS = 4
AUTH_DIGEST = 16

Set oVdir = GetObject("IIS://localhost/W3SVC/1/Root/Private")

' You can use AUTH_DIGEST to use UPNs with
'  Digest authentication.
oVdir.AuthFlags = AUTH_BASIC
oVdir.DefaultLogonDomain = "\"
oVdir.SetInfo

Set oVdir = Nothing
```

> **NOTE** The "\" domain name also applies to Digest authentication. If you enter the domain name in the Basic authentication user interface or set it using ADSI, Digest authentication will support UPNs also. Digest authentication is discussed later in this chapter.

Figure 5-8 shows an example of entering a UPN into the Internet Explorer 5 dialog box that appears with Basic authentication.

Figure 5-8. *Entering a UPN into the Basic authentication dialog box.*

The danger of Basic authentication

It's no secret that Basic authentication is an insecure protocol. The password along with some other data sent to the Web server is encoded by base64; it's a trivial exercise for an attacker to determine the password. However, Basic authentication is still a feasible authentication protocol if used in conjunction with the Secure Sockets Layer/Transport Layer Security (SSL/TLS) protocol. If a virtual directory is configured to use SSL/TLS and Basic authentication, all transmitted data, including the username and password, is encrypted by SSL/TLS first. This makes it infeasible to determine the user's credentials.

> **NOTE**   It's commonly thought that using Basic authentication over SSL/TLS still yields some of the HTTP headers in cleartext and that Basic authentication occurs before SSL/TLS is used to encrypt the connection. This is incorrect. When IIS is configured to use any authentication scheme in conjunction with SSL/TLS, the SSL/TLS negotiation happens first and the secure channel is established, after which the authentication happens. Because the channel is now encrypted, the authentication data is secure, including the Basic authentication header information.

Note that some Web sites using SSL/TLS and Basic authentication make a serious security mistake. The site prompts you to enter your credentials using a channel secured by SSL/TLS, but after the site has authenticated the user account and password it no longer requires SSL/TLS on other parts of the Web property but still uses Basic authentication. The problem is that the browser continues to send the Basic authentication data—the username and password—to the Web site for every request in the clear. In fact, the Web browser will continue to do this until it is restarted. This problem is partially avoided if the Web site requires Basic authentication and uses realms. (See the following sidebar.) This will force the browser to prompt for new credentials because the user might have a different username and/or password in a different part of a Web server.

BASIC AUTHENTICATION AND REALMS

Basic authentication includes the notion of realms, a way of naming various portions of a Web site for security purposes. The user agent (usually a Web browser) is expected to temporarily cache a username and password for each realm used by the Web server. If the user attempts to access a realm and the browser does not have a cached copy of the username and password for that realm, it will prompt the user to enter a valid username and password. By default, the realm used in IIS is the name of the Web site.

You can set the realm only by setting the *Realm* ADSI property; setting realms is currently not a capability of the Internet Information Services tool. The following Windows Script code shows how to set a new realm named *PrivateData* on a virtual directory named *private* on the default Web site (Web site #1):

```
Set oVdir = GetObject("IIS://localhost/W3SVC/1/Root/Private")
oVdir.Realm = "PrivateData"
oVdir.SetInfo
Set oVdir = Nothing
```

Although Basic authentication is an old, insecure protocol, it's common on the Web today and supported by just about every Web browser and Web server vendor. Because of its serious security problems, use it only for access to low-value data unless SSL/TLS is first used to secure the connection.

Digest authentication

Digest authentication is a reasonably new authentication scheme that is part of the HTTP 1.1 protocol; like Basic authentication, it's defined in RFC 2617 at *http://www.ietf.org/ rfc/rfc2617.txt*. Also like Basic authentication, Digest authentication can work through proxy servers and firewalls.

HOW DIGEST AUTHENTICATION GOT ITS NAME

Digest authentication does not transmit the user's password to the server in cleartext; rather, it hashes information—such as the resource being accessed, the password, and the realm—and passes the request to the server. The process of hashing is often referred to as creating a digest, hence the name.

In case you really want to know, the default hash function for Digest authentication is the MD5 hash function developed by RSA Data Security. You can find out more about MD5 in RFC 1321 at *http://www.ietf.org/rfc/rfc1321.txt*; refer also to Chapter 15, "An Introduction to Cryptography and Certificates in Windows 2000," for further details about hashing and hash functions.

Digest authentication offers advantages over Basic authentication; most notably, the password does not travel from the browser to the server in cleartext. Digest authentication's biggest shortcoming at this point is browser and server support. Currently, Internet Explorer 5 and later is the only browser and IIS 5 is one of a very small number of Web servers supporting Digest authentication. The good news, however, is that Digest authentication is being considered for use by Internet protocols other than HTTP, such as LDAP (directory access), IMAP, POP3, SMTP (all e-mail), and ACAP (Application Configuration and Profile).

Setting up Digest authentication

For Digest authentication to work, the following must be true:

- The machine running Windows 2000 Server is in an Active Directory domain.

- IIS 5 is configured to use Digest authentication.

- A file called IISSUBA.DLL is installed on the domain controller; this is performed at Windows 2000 setup time.

> **NOTE** You might notice that this is the second time we've mentioned IISSUBA.DLL. This DLL performs work during anonymous access and Digest authentication.

■ All accounts logging on using Digest authentication are configured with the Store Password Using Reversible Encryption option enabled on their accounts. This option stores an encrypted copy of the account's cleartext password in Active Directory; this gives Digest authentication access to a cleartext copy of the account's password.

> **NOTE** Simply enabling the Store Password Using Reversible Encryption option does not store a user's password as cleartext in Active Directory. After setting this option, you must either force the user to change the password or set the password using the Active Directory administration tools. This will allow Windows 2000 to pick up the cleartext copy of the password and store it in Active Directory.

Figure 5-9 shows the setting on the user account object in Active Directory necessary to support Digest authentication.

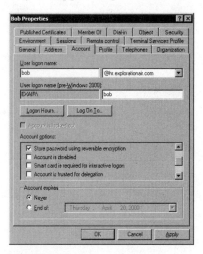

Figure 5-9. *Setting the Store Password Using Reversible Encryption option on a user account in Active Directory.*

Three Digest authentication caveats

You need to be aware of three issues with Digest authentication: one relates to the IIS 5 implementation of the protocol, one relates to using Digest authentication in conjunction with Basic authentication, and the last relates to the Digest authentication specification.

Caveat #1: The implementation of Digest authentication in IIS 5 suffers a drawback: the user's identity cannot leave the IIS 5 server. In other words, you cannot delegate identity to another computer. This is because the account is logged on using a subauthentication DLL and Windows 2000 does not trust accounts validated using subauthentication DLLs. There are plans to remedy this in a future version of Windows.

Caveat #2: If you opt to use Basic authentication and Digest authentication together—by selecting the two protocols on the Directory Security tab in the IIS administrative tool—Digest authentication is listed after Basic authentication in the set of WWW-Authenticate headers sent to the client. The client can then choose Basic authentication rather than Digest authentication. This is the case with Internet Explorer 5.

Caveat #3: The last issue relates to the overall authentication "strength" of Digest authentication. According to RFC 2617, "Both Digest and Basic authentication are very much at the weak end of the security strength spectrum." The main issue is that both protocols are subject to a *replay* attack. During a replay attack, an attacker listens, or *sniffs,* an initial transaction traveling from the client to the Web server and then uses the information to replay that transaction. Basic authentication is particularly weak because the password can be used to access other resources accessible only to the original user.

Digest authentication is susceptible to replay, but it's more robust because the attacker cannot use a GET verb to access any other resource other than the original resource requested by the user. The resource being demanded is hashed into the initial request, and it's infeasible to derive the hash unless the attacker knows the user's password.

STORING CLEARTEXT PASSWORDS IN ACTIVE DIRECTORY

As noted in "Setting up Digest authentication," Digest authentication requires cleartext user passwords to operate. Obviously, storing any form of cleartext password is a security risk, and that's why the Store Password Using Reversible Encryption option is disabled by default. If you opt to use Digest authentication, make sure the servers are well protected from attack.

You might be wondering why Active Directory doesn't just store a hash, or digest, of the passwords rather than the requisite cleartext password. First, the Store Password Using Reversible Encryption setting is not just used for Digest authentication; it can be used by other protocols, some of which might require the cleartext password. For example, Internet Authentication Server, which provides RADIUS support and is included with Windows 2000, uses this setting.

The second reason Active Directory needs to store cleartext passwords is that Digest authentication doesn't just hash the password. The password and other information, such as the realm, are hashed together before being sent from the client to the server. At the very least, the server would have to store hashes of all users and all possible realms. This is an unmanageable solution because you might change a realm name or add or delete a realm on your Web sites at any stage.

Integrated Windows authentication and the Negotiate protocol

In Internet Information Server 4, Integrated Windows authentication was referred to as Windows NT Challenge/Response authentication, which is also known as NT LAN Manager (or NTLM) authentication. This is the native authentication protocol in all Windows platforms prior to Windows 2000.

However, there's a twist on this in IIS 5, which we'll explain when we discuss the Negotiate protocol. For the moment, just keep in mind that Integrated Windows authentication is a superset of NTLM authentication.

NTLM authentication works especially well in an intranet environment where users have Windows accounts, because the browser attempts to use the current user's credentials from a domain logon. If those credentials are rejected, the Web server will send an HTTP 401 error back to the browser to prompt the user for a username and password so that the request can be made again.

The user is not prompted for a username and password for each HTTP request; rather, this will happen only when the cached credentials do not have sufficient permissions to access a specific page or file.

HTTP 401 ERRORS AND HTTP 403 ERRORS

It's important to make the distinction between these two HTTP errors. The 401 error means that the user account credentials are incorrect—perhaps the user entered an incorrect name or password or the Caps Lock key was down!

The 403 error means that the credentials are correct (in the nonanonymous case) but the account does not have access to the requested resource. Examples of this kind of error include ACL conflicts.

The default browser behavior for either error is to prompt the user to enter a username and password. However, prompting the user to enter a new username and password is somewhat troubling because the user is not told if the account credentials are at fault.

If you want to find out what the error was, hit the Esc key when the credentials dialog box pops up—you'll then see the error generated by the server.

With NTLM authentication, the user's password is not sent from the browser to the Web server. If a user has logged on as a domain user, the user won't have to be authenticated again when accessing a Web server configured to use NTLM authentication in that domain. Before Windows 2000, Windows NT used only the Windows NT Challenge/Response authentication protocol. However, Windows 2000 Server supports both NTLM and the Kerberos V5 authentication protocol, which is why IIS 5 no longer lists the Windows NT Challenge/Response authentication protocol in the Authentication Methods dialog box—the authentication scheme used can be Kerberos or NTLM.

Windows 2000, Internet Explorer 5, and IIS 5 all use the Negotiate protocol to determine whether NTLM or Kerberos authentication is to be used. The process works like this:

1. The client, using Internet Explorer 5 in Windows 2000, requests a resource from the IIS 5 server running on Windows 2000.

2. IIS sends an HTTP 401 error response including two WWW-Authenticate headers—one for Negotiate and one for NTLM—back to the browser.

3. Internet Explorer sees that an HTTP 401 error is raised and examines the response to see which WWW-Authenticate headers it understands. It will choose the first protocol it understands, Negotiate—the browser understands NTLM also, but Negotiate is listed first. Internet Explorer then makes a call to the client-side Negotiate Security Support Provider (SSP). The programmatic interface to SSP is called the Security Support Provider Interface (SSPI), which is a standard way to refer to the multiple authentication schemes in Windows.

   NOTE For more information on SSPs and SSPI, refer to the SSPI white paper at *http://www.microsoft.com/windows2000/library/howitworks/security/sspi2000.asp*, the MSDN CDs, or *http://msdn.microsoft.com* .

4. The Negotiate SSP gets appropriate data from the NTLM and Kerberos SSPs and builds up a response blob. The response has enough information to authenticate the client to the server and to determine whether NTLM or Kerberos will be used as the authentication protocol. We'll explain when Kerberos is used over NTLM shortly.

5. The client-side Negotiate SSP passes the blob to Internet Explorer.

6. Internet Explorer builds a new request, this time including the HTTP Authorization header and Negotiate information, and passes it to IIS.

7. The Web server takes the new request and passes the Negotiate blob into the server-side Negotiate SSP.

8. The Negotiate SSP determines whether Kerberos or NTLM is used.

    NOTE   Steps 6, 7, and 8 can be repeated multiple times if NTLM is chosen during the Negotiate phase. Don't be surprised if you see two HTTP 401 errors sent to the browser by IIS—this is by design for Integrated Windows authentication.

9. If all goes well, SSP returns a token to IIS and the Web server impersonates the user represented by the token and accesses the resource.

10. Access issues aside, IIS returns the requested data back to the client with an *HTTP 200 status code – no error* message.

    Figure 5-10 outlines the steps taken in this process.

CHALLENGE/RESPONSE MECHANISMS IN A NUTSHELL

Most challenge/response systems work in the following manner. Note that the user's password does not go across the network.

1. The client wants to access a resource on the server.

2. The server requires the client to authenticate herself.

3. The server sends a random value, the challenge, to the client.

4. The client hashes the random value and her password to create a response.

5. The client sends the response and her name to the server.

6. The server receives the response from the client.

7. The server performs the same hash operations as the client.

8. If the hash sent by the client is the same as the hash derived by the server, the chances are very good that the client is who she says she is.

    This system is more secure than sending a cleartext password across the network because only hashes, not passwords, travel across the network.

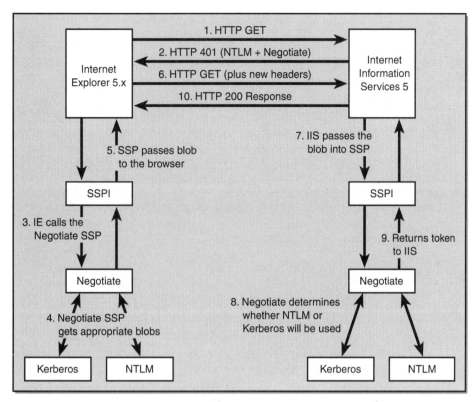

Figure 5-10. *The Negotiate SSP series of interactions.*

The reason for passing both an NTLM and Negotiate header back to the client is for maintaining backward compatibility. Versions of Internet Explorer prior to Internet Explorer 5 and versions of Windows prior to Windows 2000 do not recognize the Negotiate header, but they do recognize NTLM.

NTLM vs. Kerberos

So, the question remains: when does the Negotiate package use Kerberos, and when does it use NTLM? If the following criteria are true, Kerberos is used. If any one condition is not met, NTLM is used.

- The client is a Windows 2000 client using Internet Explorer 5 or later.

- The server is running Windows 2000 and IIS 5 or later.

- The client and the server are in the same Windows 2000 domain or in trusted domains.

- IIS 5 is configured to use Integrated Windows authentication.

- If you are accessing the Web server with a name other than the name of the server running Windows 2000, a new service principal name (SPN) must have been registered using the Setspn tool from the Windows 2000 Server Resource Kit. For example, if the Web server is responding to a Domain Name System (DNS) name of *www.exair.com* but the server (or servers) is named *webservers.development.exair.com*, you must register *www.exair.com*. SPNs and the Setspn tool are explained in detail in Chapter 14, "An Introduction to Kerberos Authentication in Windows 2000."

Kerberos's advantages over NTLM

Kerberos offers a number of significant advantages over NTLM, including the following:

- Kerberos can be faster than NTLM.

- Kerberos is more secure than NTLM.

- Kerberos authenticates the server and the client; NTLM authenticates the client only. Using NTLM, the client can't really know whether the server he or she is talking to is valid.

But here's the really good news about being authenticated using the Kerberos authentication protocol rather than NTLM: you can pass a client's identity from one computer to another. In other words, Kerberos solves the delegation problem. We discussed this in Chapter 3, "Windows 2000 Security Overview," and we'll discuss it in further detail in Chapter 10, "Building a Secure Solution," and Chapter 14.

X.509 client certificate authentication

Both IIS 4 and IIS 5 support using X.509 client certificates to authenticate users when used in conjunction with the SSL/TLS protocol. If you're unfamiliar with X.509 client certificates, first read Chapter 15, "An Introduction to Cryptography and Certificates in Windows 2000."

Authenticating the server

In short, SSL/TLS always uses certificates to authenticate the Web server. When a client connects to a Web server, the server's certificate is used to authenticate itself. So, let's take a moment to look at what happens in a normal SSL/TLS connection that does not use client authentication certificates.

When you connect to the *www.exair.com* Web site using SSL/TLS by typing *https://www.exair.com*, the browser compares the Web site's URL with the common name in the Web server's certificate. If the two are the same, the Web server is determined to be owned by Exploration Air and not, say, by a competitor. Note the use of *https* rather than *http*; this tells the browser to use SSL/TLS on TCP port 443 by default, rather than TCP port 80.

Actually, there are many more steps than just checking the name in the certificate. These checks include the following:

- A cryptographic check to determine that the Web site owns the private key associated with the public key in the certificate.

- A check that the name in the certificate is the same as the name of the Web site.

- A check that the issuer of the Web site's certificate is trusted.

- A check that the certificate has not expired.

- A check that the certificate has not been revoked. By default, this is not performed by Internet Explorer; it's performed by IIS.

- A check that the certificate has not been tampered with.

If any of these checks fail, a warning is displayed to the user and the connection might be dropped. If your browser informs you that something is possibly wrong with the certificate, it's recommended that you do not continue with the connection.

Authenticating the client

SSL/TLS includes an optional step: authenticating the client. As we've mentioned, when an SSL/TLS connection is established, the client authenticates the server by inspecting the Web server's certificate, after which the Web server can optionally ask the Web user to authenticate himself. After such a request, the browser will prompt the user to choose from a list of client certificates, as shown in Figure 5-11.

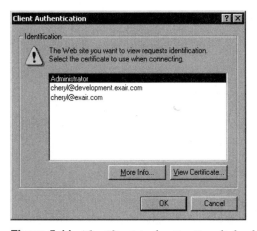

Figure 5-11. *The Client Authentication dialog box in Internet Explorer 5.*

When the Web server asks the client to authenticate himself, it sends a list of certificate authorities (CAs) it trusts to the client. For example, if the Web server trusts VeriSign and Thawte and the user has certificates from Thawte and Equifax, the browser will give the user the option to select the Thawte certificate only because that's the only certificate the Web server trusts.

> NOTE Internet Explorer remembers which certificate you selected for client authentication to a particular Web site. In Windows 2000, Internet Explorer credentials are remembered even if they failed to authenticate to the remote Web server. Therefore, if you select an invalid certificate, you'll need to close all open Internet Explorer windows and open a new browser window. You'll then be prompted to select a valid certificate for client authentication.

How IIS uses X.509 client certificates

IIS uses X.509 client certificates in one of four ways:

- It doesn't require them.
- It gives users the option of providing a certificate but does not require one.
- It requires a client certificate from the user.
- It requires a client certificate from the user and uses this to map to a Windows 2000 user account.

The first option is self-explanatory: the client is not given the option of presenting a certificate. The next two options are somewhat similar; the only difference is that the former option doesn't require the client to provide a certificate and the latter does. In both cases, if the client certificate is provided, its information is used to populate the Active Server Pages (ASP) *Request.ClientCertificate* collection. Using this data, you can make authentication and authorization decisions in ASP.

For example, the following ASP code will make an authorization decision based on the domain name of the user's e-mail address:

```
<%
    Dim strValidDomain, strEmail
    strValidDomain = "@exair.com"
    strEmail = Request.ClientCertificate("SubjectE")

    If InStr(strEmail, strValidDomain, 1) Then
        ' Certificate contains @exair.com in
        '  user's e-mail name.
        Response.Write("You have access!")
    End If
%>
```

In this example, the e-mail address *cheryl@exair.com* would be allowed access, but *cheryl@microsoft.com* would not.

You should be aware that simply checking a name or another entity in a certificate is insecure. An application should also check the issuer of the certificate. This is a cryptographic operation performed by IIS. If you don't check the issuer, you have no way of knowing that the certificate was issued by someone you trust, such as Thawte, VeriSign, or perhaps your own certification authority, and not by a bogus certification authority issuing certificates to all and sundry! Anyone could use, say, Microsoft Certificate Services to issue a certificate with a subject e-mail name of *cheryl@exair.com*, but if the Web server doesn't trust the issuer the connection will fail.

In the preceding example, the Exploration Air Web site trusts certificates issued by the Exploration Air User Certification Authority only. In IIS 5, you can configure which roots are trusted by the Web server by using a *certificate trust list (CTL)*. A CTL is a CryptoAPI 2.0 data structure containing a list of root certification authority certificates that have been deemed trustworthy by an administrator. You can set different CTLs on a per–Web site basis. CTLs can be managed at the Web site level, not for individual virtual directories, files, or any service other than the Web service.

THE ACTIVE SERVER PAGES *CLIENTCERTIFICATE* COLLECTION

As discussed, ASP exposes a collection of client certificate information through the *ClientCertificate* collection. This information includes the following:

- The raw certificate data using *Request.ClientCertificate("Certificate")*

- Client certificate issuer information (that is, who issued the certificate to the subject) using *Request.ClientCertificate("IssuerX")* where *X* is a subcode discussed below

- Client certificate subject information (that is, the principal using the certificate) using *Request.ClientCertificate("SubjectX")* where *X* is a subcode discussed below

- The certificate serial number using *Request.ClientCertificate("SerialNumber")*

- The certificate validity period using *Request.ClientCertificate("ValidFrom")* and *Request.ClientCertificate("ValidTo")*

When using the Issuer and Subject keys, you can also use subfields such as *C* for country, *CN* for common name, *O* for organization, and so on. Refer to the sidebar on X.500 Naming in Chapter 15 for more subfield options.

WARNING   If you perform many-to-one client certificate mapping, it's highly recommended that you have only one root CA certificate in the CTL so that the name matching is unambiguous.

If you do not set a CTL on a Web server, all client authentication certificates are considered valid.

You can add new CTLs to IIS 5 in two ways: using the CTL wizard from within the IIS tool or using the wizard from within the Global Policy tool. We'll look at the former simply because it's built into IIS, because Global Policy requires Active Directory, and because you cannot create CTLs by using local security policy. Refer to the Windows 2000 online help if you want to use Global Policy to define CTLs.

NOTE   It is recommended that you use the IIS tool to perform CTL manipulation of IIS-specific CTLs, because fewer steps are required than when using Global Policy.

You can create and edit CTLs from within the IIS tool by following these steps:

1. Right-click the My Computer icon on the desktop of the computer for which you have administrative privileges.

2. Choose Manage from the context menu.

3. Expand the Services And Application node.

4. Expand the Internet Information Services node.

5. Right-click the Web server in question.

6. Choose Properties from the context menu.

7. Click the Directory Security tab.

8. Click the Edit button in the Secure Communications box. If this option is grayed out, you have not yet selected a server certificate to use for SSL/ TLS communication.

9. Check the Enable Certificate Trust List option.

10. Click the New button to create a new CTL; this will invoke the CTL wizard. Or click Edit to edit an existing CTL.

You can now add and remove root CA certificates to the CTL. Any root CA certificate you add to a CTL assigned to a Web site is trusted by that Web site for client authentication certificates.

Figure 5-12 shows the CTL wizard being used from within the IIS tool.

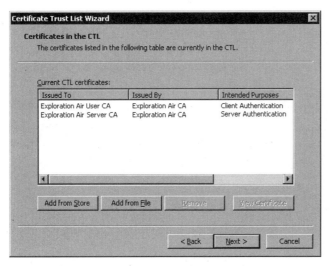

Figure 5-12. *Using the CTL wizard within IIS.*

By default, IIS 5 will check to see whether a client authentication certificate has been revoked. If so, it will return a 403.13 error: *Client certificate revoked.* If IIS cannot reach the location of the certificate revocation list (CRL) defined in the client authentication certificate—the CRL distribution point, or CDP—it will assume the worst: the CDP has been attacked and taken off line. Because of this, IIS will issue a 403.13 error even if the certificate has not been revoked, unless there is a current copy of the CRL cached by IIS indicating that the certificate has not been revoked.

Figure 5-13 shows the process more clearly.

ALTERNATE MEANS OF MANIPULATING CTLS

You can create and manipulate CTLs from languages such as C++ by using the CryptoAPI 2.0 certificate trust list functions, such as *CertAddCTLContextToStore*, *CertDeleteCTLContextFromStore*, and *CertFindCTLInStore*.

You can also use the MakeCTL and CertMgr tools included with the Microsoft Platform SDK to view, create, and manipulate CTLs.

Refer to the MSDN CDs or DVD, or to *http://msdn.microsoft.com* for further information on these functions and tools.

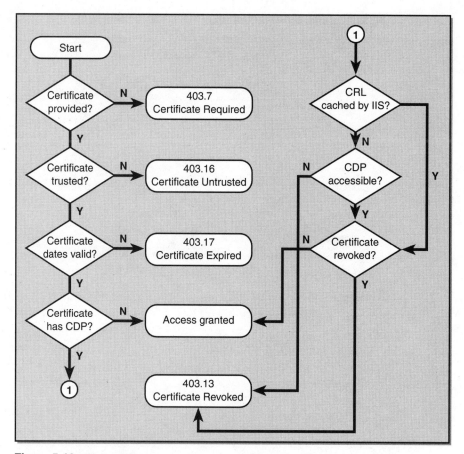

Figure 5-13. *The certificate revocation process performed by IIS 5.*

You can disable certificate revocation checking on each Web site by using ADSI; this is not configurable from the user interface. The following code shows how to disable CRL checking:

```
Set oWeb = GetObject("IIS://localhost/W3SVC/1")
oWeb.CertCheckMode = 1 ' 0 == check CRL; 1 == don't check CRL.
oWeb.SetInfo
Set oWeb = Nothing
```

Client certificate mapping

IIS 5 allows the Web site developer to use client authentication certificates as strong authentication credentials. This process is called *certificate mapping* because the certificate information is used to map to a Windows 2000 account, at which point the Web site user is accessing resources in the context of the mapped account.

IIS 4 provides a simple method to map client certificates, which IIS 5 also uses. However, it is Microsoft's intention to phase out this method in favor of the Active Directory mapping available in IIS 5, which is even easier to use. Let's look at both options.

WARNING The two mapping methods are mutually exclusive; you cannot mix them. Therefore, you should determine which method is right for your application before you start building it.

IIS mapping, also available in IIS 4, works in one of two modes: one-to-one mapping and many-to-one mapping. When using one-to-one mapping, IIS looks at the client certificate and, based on its entire contents, uses the certificate to log a user account onto the system. For example, you can say that certificate A maps to *cheryl@development.exair.com* and certificate B maps to *michael@development.exair.com*. This method is quite flexible because you can also say that certificate C and certificate D both map to *dev-team@development.exair.com*. The downside of this model is scalability: IIS needs to store a copy of each certificate used for mapping purposes, which limits the number of certificates to about 2000–3000.

NOTE Subject name information held in the certificate is not used to directly identify the client. Indeed, the certificate might reference *cheryl@development.exair.com*, but you might choose to map the certificate to *dev-team@development.exair.com*.

Many-to-one certificate mapping is based on rules. The administrator defines a series of certificate content rules and uses these rules to map to a Windows 2000 account. For example, the administrator might define a rule such that all client authentication certificates created by the Exploration Air User CA (that is, the only trusted root in this example) with an organization of ExAir (*O = ExAir*) and an organizational unit of Development (*OU = Development*) map to the *dev-team@development.exair.com* account.

The downside with both of the IIS 4 legacy certificate mapping methods is high administrative overhead: the administrator must enter the user account and the password of each account used in the mapping process. Further overhead is incurred because administrators often incorrectly enter passwords and usernames. Nonetheless, the many-to-one mapping method is supremely flexible.

NOTE IIS certificate mapping will work with or without Active Directory installed.

Let's look at an example of setting up IIS certificate mapping. We'll set up an IIS server to map all certificates that have the following properties:

- They are issued by the Exploration Air User CA.

- They have an organizational unit (OU) set to *Development*.

- They have an organization (O) set to *ExAir*.

This involves setting a CTL on the Web server in question that contains the Exploration Air User CA only, which satisfies requirement 1, and setting two rules to satisfy requirements 2 and 3. First we need to set up the CTL by performing the following steps; this is performed only once per Web site and is a Web site policy.

1. Right-click the My Computer icon on the desktop, and choose Manage from the context menu.

2. Expand the Services And Applications node, and then expand the Internet Information Services node.

3. Right-click the Web server (not the virtual directory or directory) you want to apply certificate mapping to.

4. Choose Properties from the context menu, and click the Directory Security tab.

5. Click Edit in the Secure Communications box. If this button is disabled, you have yet to assign a server certificate to the Web site. If this is the case, refer to the section later in this chapter on configuring SSL/TLS in IIS.

6. Select the Enable Certificate Trust List check box, and then click the New button.

7. When the CTL wizard comes up, click Next.

8. Click Add From Store to select the Exploration Air User CA certificate. At this stage, you will add the root certificates you trust.

    NOTE It is recommended that you have only one root certificate listed in the CTL when performing certificate mapping.

9. Click Next.

10. Enter a friendly name and description from the CTL—for example, *Client Certificate mapping trusted roots* and *Root certificates trusted for client certificate mapping*. Then click Next.

11. Click Finish.

Now that we have set the CTL, only client certificates issued by CAs listed in the CTL can be used on this Web site. This satisfies the first requirement. Figure 5-14 shows what the Secure Communications dialog box should look like after applying these settings. Figure 5-15 shows what the CTL dialog box looks like after you've added the Exploration Air root certificate.

Figure 5-14. *Requiring client certificates and using them for mapping.*

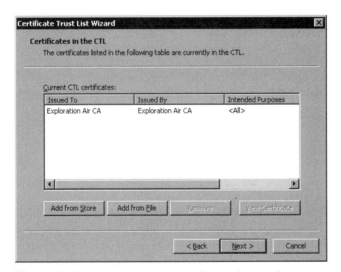

Figure 5-15. *Setting valid root certificates for certificate mapping using a CTL.*

To satisfy the other two requirements and set the rules, perform the following steps while still in the Secure Communications dialog box:

1. Select the Require Secure Channel (SSL) check box.

2. Select the Require Client Certificates radio button.

3. Select the Enable Client Certificate Mapping check box.

4. Click the Edit button in the Enable Client Certificate Mapping box.

5. Click the Many-to-1 tab.

6. Click Add.

7. Enter *ExAir Mapping Rules*.

8. Click Next.

9. Click New.

10. Select Subject in the Certificate Field combo box and O in the Sub Field combo box, type *ExAir* in the Criteria field, and click OK.

11. Once again, click New to enter the next rule.

12. Select Subject in the Certificate Field combo box and OU in the Sub Field combo box, enter *Development* in the Criteria field, and click OK.

13. Click Next.

14. Make sure the Accept This Certificate For Logon Authentication radio button is selected.

15. Click Browse, and select the account to which you want to map this set of rules. In our example, we're going to use the dev-team account.

16. Enter the password for the dev-team account.

17. Click Finish.

18. Reenter the password, and click OK.

19. Click OK.

Now when IIS sees a client certificate matching the criteria defined above, it will log on the dev-team account.

Figure 5-16 shows what the certificate mapping rules dialog box should look like after entering these rules.

IIS also provides a COM+ object to ASP applications for manipulating certificate mapping. Called *IIsCertMapper*, this object does exactly the same job as one-to-one certificate mapping, but it does so programmatically. The process is simple: you pass a client certificate to the object and provide the object with a username and a password. IIS will automatically attempt to log the user account on to the system when it encounters the client certificate at the start of the SSL/TLS connection. The user account making the call to this object must be a member of the administrator's group.

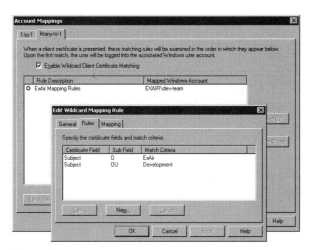

Figure 5-16. *A series of certificate mapping rules.*

The following, somewhat contrived, sample ASP code requires that IIS be configured to request a client certificate. It then uses the information provided by the user to create a certificate mapping. The data (username, password, and friendly mapping name) is passed to the ASP page as part of the HTTP query string; it could be passed as part of a forms POST instead.

```
<%
    ' Get the client certificate from the connection.
    Dim oCert
    oCert = Request.ClientCertificate("Certificate")

    If Len(oCert) Then
        Dim oMap
        Set oMap = _
            GetObject("IIS://localhost/w3svc/1/IIsCertMapper")

        Dim strUser, strPassword, strMappingName
        strUser = Request.QueryString("MapUser")
        strPassword = Request.QueryString("MapPassword")
        strMappingName = Request.QueryString("MapName")

        ' Create an account mapping based on the certificate.
        oMap.CreateMapping oCert, strUser, strPassword, _
            strMappingName, 1
        Response.Write "Done!"
    Else
        Response.Write "No Client Certificate received."
    End If
%>
```

Other security settings could be added to this code; for example, the administrator could add ACLs to the ASP page to make sure that only valid users can perform this task. In addition, a check could be made that the account name is derived from the certificate itself rather than the account name entered by the user. For example,

```
strUser = Request.ClientCertificate("SubjectE")
```

will get the e-mail name held in the client certificate and use it to create the mapping.

Now let's turn our attention to the new certificate mapping capability of IIS 5: Active Directory client certificate mapping, also called Windows Directory Service mapping. Active Directory client certificate mapping uses client certificate information held in Active Directory to map to a user account. For example, suppose that an account, *michael@development.exair.com*, has a client certificate associated with it in Active Directory. If IIS is configured to use Active Directory mapping, it will compare specific information held in the client certificate and presented during the SSL/TLS handshake phase with client certificate information in Active Directory. If Active Directory finds an account with the appropriate certificate information, it will automatically log the account on. Unlike the IIS client certificate mapping methods, there's no need to enter a password for the user account being mapped to.

So, how does it work? Active Directory client certificate mapping operates in two ways:

- An Active Directory lookup of the *Subject name* in the certificate finds the Active Directory user in the directory by that name. This is very fast.

- An Active Directory search of the *Subject Alternative Name* in the certificate finds a match for the user in Active Directory.

Once a match is found, by either method, the Local Security Authority Subsystem (LSASS.EXE) automatically maps the client certificate to the appropriate Windows 2000 account; no other administrative intervention is required.

Active Directory client certificate mapping is much easier to configure than IIS client certificate mapping simply because there's little administration overhead. Here are the requirements:

- Windows 2000 Active Directory is populated with user and associated client authentication certificates.

- IIS is configured to use Active Directory rather than IIS client certificate mapping.

SELECTING MULTIPLE AUTHENTICATION SCHEMES

In all versions of IIS, you can select more than one authentication scheme—for example, you could opt to use both Basic and Integrated Windows authentication. This is perfectly valid, but note that if you select more than one authentication scheme, the browser can use any of them. In this example, the browser can choose either Basic or Integrated Windows. According to the HTTP specification, it should select the strongest authentication protocol it understands, but don't rely on this. Internet Explorer, for example, chooses the first authentication protocol it understands.

Select the authentication protocols you are happy supporting. If you think Basic authentication is too weak for your application, do not enable it as an authentication option in IIS. Also, if you select anonymous access authentication and another scheme such as Basic authentication, IIS will try anonymous access first; if anonymous access fails because of an ACL conflict, it will try Basic authentication.

Client certificate mapping is a little different because it does not use a series of HTTP authentication headers to determine the client's identity; rather, it's part of the SSL/TLS handshake. Because of this, you need not select any authentication scheme when using client authentication certificates. If the certificate mapping fails, the connection simply fails.

Once Active Directory client certificate mapping is enabled, IIS will no longer use any other IIS-specific mapping rules you have configured. Note also that the client certificates used for both IIS and Active Directory client certificate mapping can be held in software or on smart cards.

To configure IIS to use client certificates held in Active Directory, perform the following steps:

1. Right-click the My Computer icon on the desktop.

2. Choose Manage from the context menu.

3. Expand the Services And Applications node.

4. Right-click the Internet Information Services node, and choose Properties from the context menu.

5. Select WWW Services Master Properties, and click the Edit button.

6. Click the Directory Security tab.

7. Select the Enable The Windows Directory Service Mapper check box, as shown in Figure 5-17.

Figure 5-17. *Enabling Active Directory client certificate mapping in IIS*

While we're on the subject of SSL/TLS and client authentication certificates, we should take a moment to look at how to configure SSL/TLS in IIS.

CONFIGURING SSL/TLS

As discussed, SSL/TLS is a set of cryptographic technologies that provides authentication, privacy, and data integrity. It's also the most common security protocol used on the Web today because it is well understood and requires virtually no extra work on behalf of your users. All you need to configure SSL/TLS is a server X.509 certificate from a certification authority.

To make the certificate manipulation process easier, IIS 5 introduced a certificate wizard specific to the Web that is considerably more straightforward to use than KeyRing (also called Key Manager) in IIS 4. In fact, the Web Server Certificate wizard was added to IIS 5 based on user feedback about KeyRing.

The process of setting up SSL/TLS might seem complex at first, but it's quite easy using the new wizard. At the highest level, the process is as follows:

1. Enroll for a server certificate with a certification authority (such as VeriSign or your own certificate authority using Microsoft Certificate Services).

2. Apply the certificate to the Web server in question.

3. Enable SSL/TLS on the appropriate virtual directories, directories, or files.

Installing a server certificate for use with SSL/TLS does not mean that SSL/TLS is enabled. In fact, the default is not to enable SSL/TLS because of the performance impact of the protocol.

IIS includes flexible SSL/TLS options. In Figure 5-18, a Web site is configured to use three SSL/TLS settings. The root of the Web site, *www.exair.com*, does not require SSL/TLS. However, because the certificate contains the name of the Web site, this is where the certificate is applied. You cannot set another certificate at another part of the Web space. The Marketing virtual directory also does not require SSL/TLS. The Secure and HighSecure virtual directories both require SSL/TLS, but the latter also requires stronger, 128-bit SSL/TLS.

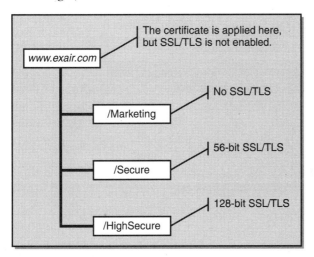

Figure 5-18. *Setting different SSL/TLS options on different parts of the Web space.*

NOTE   Once you install a server certificate on IIS, SSL/TLS can still be used even if you don't require that the protocol be used. When the certificate is installed, a user can enter *https://www.exair.com/marketing* to access the marketing part of the Exploration Air Web site using SSL/TLS even though the marketing virtual directory does not require SSL/TLS.

A Closer Look at Configuring SSL/TLS

Although the process of configuring SSL/TLS is quite easy using the new wizard, there are a couple of matters you should be aware of. In the following example, we're going to assume you're enrolling for a new certificate, because this process requires the most steps. To enroll for a new certificate for your Web site, perform the following steps:

1. Right-click the My Computer icon on the desktop.

2. Choose Manage from the context menu.

3. Expand the Services And Applications node, and then expand the Internet Information Services node.

4. Locate the Web server for which you want to get a certificate, and right-click it.

5. Choose Properties from the context menu.

6. Click the Directory Security tab.

7. Click the Server Certificate button. If this button is grayed out, you haven't right-clicked the Web server—instead, you've right-clicked a virtual directory, directory, or file. If this is the case, close the dialog box, and select the Web server.

8. Read the opening screen of the IIS Certificate wizard. It not only introduces you to the wizard but also informs you of the status of any enrollments you performed in the past.

   NOTE   Because the wizard knows the current state of the certificate request, it displays only the appropriate options and will warn you if you try to do something that might invalidate the request.

9. Click Next.

10. Select Create A New Certificate.

11. You have two options, as shown in Figure 5-19: Prepare The Request Now, But Send It Later and Send The Request Immediately To An Online Certification Authority. The first option is always available, and the latter is available only if the Web server has access to one or more Microsoft Certificate Services servers in a Windows 2000 domain configured to issue Web server certificates.

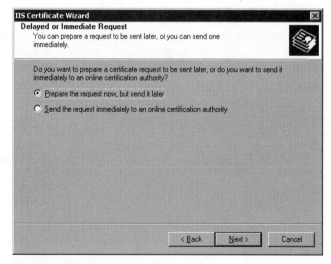

Figure 5-19. *The two certificate enrollment options in the IIS Certificate wizard.*

If you are running in an intranet environment and have configured a corporate public key solution, you'll probably want to select the first option. However, if you want to get a certificate from an external CA, such as VeriSign, you should select the second option. We'll assume you want to prepare the request now and send it later, so check the first option and click the Next button.

12. Enter the name of the Web site. The wizard will automatically extract the friendly name of the Web site defined when you initially configured the site. This property is not used in the certificate; it's just a friendly name to help the administrator.

13. Select the public key length of the certificate. Usually, this will be 2048 bytes for North American sites and 1024 bytes for other sites.

14. If you want to use a Server Gated Cryptography (SGC) certificate, check the SGC box.

    NOTE SGC is an extension of SSL/TLS that allows financial institutions with export versions of Windows 2000 Server to use 128-bit encryption. However, with new cryptographic export laws that allow much stronger encryption than previously available outside North America, this capability is no longer required.

15. Click Next.

16. Enter a valid organization (such as Exploration Air) and organization unit (such as Development Department). This information will go into the certificate, so make sure it's accurate.

17. Click Next.

18. Enter the name of the computer to be certified. It's imperative that you get this correct; failure to do so will later create problems in the user's browser. By default, the wizard will select either the NetBIOS or DNS name of the server. If the computer is to be used as an intranet server, you could use either name. If the server is to be placed on the Web, the name will be the name of the Web server as it appears on the Web. For example, the computer might have a NetBIOS name of *WebServer* and an internal DNS name of *webserver.explorationair.com*. However, because it's to be used as a Web server on the Internet, its Internet DNS name will be *www.exair.com*. This is the name you should enter into the Common Name edit box. This information will also go into the certificate; in fact, it's probably the most important information in the certificate.

19. Click Next.

20. Enter the country or region, the state or province, and the city in which you are located. This information will also be included in the certificate.

> **NOTE** When entering the state, enter the entire name of the state, not just its abbreviation. For example, if the company is in Washington State, enter Washington in the state field, not WA. If the company is in Queensland, Australia, enter Queensland, not QLD.

21. Click Next.

22. Enter the name of the text file that will contain the certificate request information. By default, the file name is C:\Certreq.txt. The file will look something like the following abridged sample, a base64-encoded text file. The certificate request is known as a PKCS #10 certificate request. You can find out more about PKCS #10 in Chapter 15.

```
-----BEGIN NEW CERTIFICATE REQUEST-----
MIID+DCCAuACAQAwXjEXMBUGA1UEAxMObWlrZWhvdy1sYXB0b3AxDDAKBgNVBAsT
A0R1djEOMAwGA1UEChMFRXhBaXIxCzAJBgNVBAcTA1JlMQswCQYDVQQIEwJXQTEL

      .
      . more
      .

LNihpipWqerGWnZAmSDtKmqnsOZsptlrTzIRMsSQSWmlmacTYExE0+6SPkyO2XeC
pEzrI08CBxrheiZYf14K2gm12A62AItLznxIwgV4H+qP7jqkC9KmiW9WDwhdHneA
3Dq1dsTlscfyhsFU
-----END NEW CERTIFICATE REQUEST-----
```

> **NOTE** You can view the contents of the certificate request from the command line by using the Certutil.exe tool included with Microsoft Certificate Services. Typing *certutil –v certreq.txt* displays the contents of the PKCS #10 request that will be sent to the certification authority.

23. Click Next. The wizard will display a summary of the information you entered. After reviewing the information, click Next to complete the wizard.

24. You can click the Click Here option to view a list of certification authorities that offer services for Microsoft products.

25. Click Finish.

The certificate request file can now be sent to a certification authority for processing. (A list of CAs is available at *http://backoffice.microsoft.com/securitypartners*.) Processing time will vary depending on the type of certificate you asked for and the policies of the CA.

> **IMPORTANT** The certificate request contains only the public key that will go into the certificate. The private key associated with the public key does not leave the computer on which the request was generated.

Once you receive the certificate response from the CA, you can continue the enrollment process by using the Web Server Certificate wizard. The response from the CA is a PKCS #7 package containing your certificate. You can find out more information about PKCS #7 in Chapter 15.

Continue the enrollment process by performing these steps:

1. Right-click the My Computer icon on the desktop.

2. Choose Manage from the context menu.

3. Expand the Services And Applications node and then the Internet Information Services node.

4. Locate the Web server you want the certificate for, and right-click it.

5. Choose Properties from the context menu.

6. Click the Directory Security tab.

7. Click the Server Certificate button. If this button is grayed out, you haven't right-clicked the Web server—you've right-clicked a virtual directory, directory, or file. In this case, close the dialog box and select the Web server.

8. Read the opening screen of the Web Server Certificate wizard. It should indicate that you have a pending certificate request, as shown in Figure 5-20.

Figure 5-20. *The Web Server Certificate wizard informing you that you have a pending certificate request.*

9. Click the Next button.

10. Select Process The Pending Request And Install The Certificate, and click the Next button.

11. Enter the path and file name of the file containing the CA's response. If necessary, use the Browse option to locate the file.

12. Click Next.

13. Look at the certificate overview, and click Next.

14. Click Finish.

A Web server certificate is now installed on the computer.

WHERE IS THE PRIVATE KEY HELD DURING A CERTIFICATE REQUEST?

When IIS makes a certificate request, the wizard creates a public and private key pair. The public key goes into the certificate request. The private key, along with other information about the certificate request, is held in a protected location called the REQUEST store.

You can look at the REQUEST store by performing these steps:

1. Click Start.

2. Choose Run, type *mmc /a*, and hit Return.

3. Choose Add/Remove Snap-in from the Console menu.

4. Click Add, and select Certificates from the list of available snap-ins.

5. Click Add.

6. Select Computer Account, click Next, and then click Finish.

7. Click Close, and then click OK.

8. Expand the Certificates node, and open the REQUEST node.

If you look inside the Certificates node, you'll see any pending certificate requests. Do not delete any pending certificate requests from this store unless you absolutely must. If you delete a pending certificate request, the private key associated with the certificate request will be deleted.

Now that you've applied your certificate to the Web site, you can go to appropriate virtual directories, directories, and files and enable SSL/TLS. It is not recommended that you require SSL/TLS at the root of a Web server unless all the content on the Web site is to be protected in transit from the Web server to the browser, which is highly unlikely.

You can check that the certificate is installed correctly by typing *https://servername* into your Web browser, where *servername* is the name of the Web site. If you see a lock icon appear on the Internet Explorer status bar, SSL/TLS is correctly installed. If you're using Netscape Navigator, you'll see that the broken key is now joined together or an open lock is now in the locked position, depending on the version of the browser.

If you want to find out a little more about the SSL/TLS connection, use the following ASP code:

```
<H2>SSL/TLS Information</H2>
<PRE>
SSL/TLS Connection?  <%= Request.ServerVariables("HTTPS") %>
Server Cert. Issuer
    <%= Request.ServerVariables("CERT_SERVER_ISSUER") %>
Server Cert. Subject
    <%= Request.ServerVariables("CERT_SERVER_SUBJECT") %>
Symmetric Key Size
    <%= Request.ServerVariables("HTTPS_KEYSIZE") %>
Public Key Size?
    <%= Request.ServerVariables("HTTPS_SECRETKEYSIZE") %>
</PRE>
```

SSL/TLS connection logging

You can determine which protocol is used during the SSL/TLS connection by looking at the Windows 2000 event logs. To do this, you must first modify the following Registry setting:

HKEY_LOCAL_MACHINE
  \System
    \CurrentControlSet
      \Control
        \SecurityProviders
          \SCHANNEL
            \EventLogging: REG_DWORD : 0

This entry is set to 0 by default, which means that no SSL/TLS events will be logged. To enable SSL/TLS event logging, set the entry to one of the values in Table 5-2 and reboot the computer. Note that these values can be ORed together.

Value	Description
1	Log errors
2	Log warnings
4	Log informational and success events

Table 5-2. *SSL/TLS logging options.*

NOTE   It's recommended that you set this Registry value to 7, which means all categories of SSL/TLS data are logged.

When an SSL/TLS connection is successfully negotiated, look in the System log for events that look like that shown in Figure 5-21.

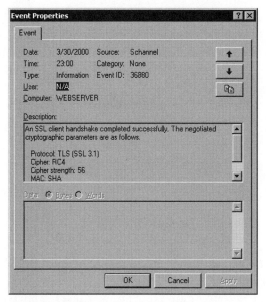

Figure 5-21. *A successfully negotiated TLS connection between a Web server and a Web browser.*

SSL/TLS is an easy-to-use technology, especially for your users. However, there are some scenarios that make it complex to administer, some of which are discussed in the following sections.

SSL/TLS and Multiple Web Sites

IIS can host hundreds of virtual Web servers on a single computer, but doing so can lead to interesting problems when using virtual hosting and SSL/TLS together. First, let's look at virtual hosting in detail.

IIS supports virtual Web sites in one of three ways:

■ By using multiple IP addresses, each having its own network card in the computer

■ By having each Web site listen on a different port but use the same IP address

■ By assigning multiple domain names and IP addresses to a single network card in the computer and using HTTP 1.1 Host headers to differentiate Web sites

For example, Figure 5-22 illustrates a server running Windows 2000 named
\\exair; hence, the computer has one default Web site named *http://exair*. In addition, Exploration Air's administrators have created three other virtual Web sites in IIS
for the Marketing, Development, and Human Resources departments named *http://
Marketing, http://Development*, and *http://HumanResources*, respectively.

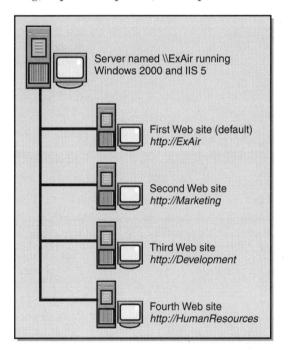

Server named \\ExAir running
Windows 2000 and IIS 5

First Web site (default)
http://ExAir

Second Web site
http://Marketing

Third Web site
http://Development

Fourth Web site
http://HumanResources

Figure 5-22. *A Windows 2000 server running IIS hosting one default Web site and
three virtual Web sites.*

In this example, the \\exair computer could have an IP address of 157.65.122.22
and each other Web site could listen on the same address but a different port, on a
different IP address and the same port, or on the same IP address and the same port
while using HTTP 1.1 Host headers to differentiate which server a client request is for.

Tables 5-3, 5-4, and 5-5 show the possible combinations.

Server	IP Address	HTTP Port	SSL/TLS Port	Host Header
Default (*http://exair*)	157.65.122.22	80	443	Not used
http://Marketing	157.65.122.22	81	444	Not used
http://Development	157.65.122.22	82	445	Not used
http://HumanResources	157.65.122.22	83	446	Not used

Table 5-3. *The \\exair server configured to use the same IP address but differing port numbers for each virtual Web site.*

Server	IP Address	HTTP Port	SSL/TLS Port	Host Header
Default (*http://exair*)	157.65.122.22	80	443	Not used
http://Marketing	157.65.122.23	80	443	Not used
http://Development	157.65.122.24	80	443	Not used
http://HumanResources	157.65.122.25	80	443	Not used

Table 5-4. *The \\exair server configured to use differing IP addresses but the same port numbers for each virtual Web site.*

Server	IP Address	HTTP Port	SSL/TLS Port	Host Header
Default (*http://exair*)	157.65.122.22	80	443	Exair or None
http://Marketing	157.65.122.22	80	443	Marketing
http://Development	157.65.122.22	80	443	Development
http://HumanResources	157.65.122.22	80	443	HumanResources

Table 5-5. *The \\exair server configured to use the same IP address and the same port numbers but different Host headers for each virtual Web site.*

Why SSL/TLS fails when using host headers

The first two scenarios, in which the IP addresses or port numbers differ, will work correctly with SSL/TLS. When IIS processes the request from the client, it uses the IP address and port number to look up which certificate and private key to use for the connection. When Host headers are used, the IP address and port number are the same for each Web site—the only differentiator is the Host header sent in the HTTP request. However, the client cannot send the HTTP data to the Web server until the SSL/TLS connection has been established, and the Web server can determine which certificate and private key to use to establish the secure connection based only on something that uniquely identifies the Web site. That something happens to be the Host header, and it hasn't been sent yet. It's a classic chicken and egg scenario.

In short, if you want to use SSL/TLS with multiple virtual Web sites, you need to use unique IP addresses or unique port numbers. Multiple Web sites with the same IP address and the same port number will fail.

SSL/TLS and Multiple Web Servers

It's quite common for multiple Web servers to act as a single instance. Various technologies are used to provide scalability and reliability in this scenario, but they do run into some interesting SSL/TLS problems. Figure 5-23 shows an example Web site—the first bank of servers are load-balanced servers, each of which responds to the same DNS name and can take an HTTP request and send the request to one or more clustered database servers.

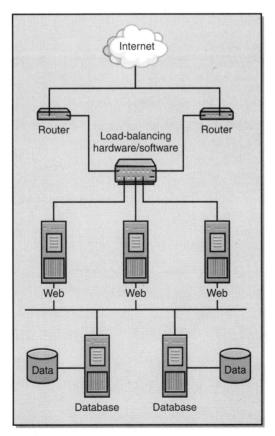

Figure 5-23. *Example Web site using load balancing and clustering.*

NOTE   Windows 2000 Advanced Server offers two node clusters, and Windows 2000 Datacenter Server provides four node clusters to provide redundancy and failover. Windows 2000 also supports network load balancing (NLB) to balance loads of up to 32 Windows 2000 Web servers.

Two problems, one concerning Web server certificates and the other SSL/TLS affinity, arise when SSL/TLS is required on a load-balanced Web site. The following sections described these problems.

Web server certificates

Each computer needs a certificate (and private key) that has the same common name (CN) as all the other Web servers. This might require that you have a unique certificate and key per server or that you get one certificate and replicate it (and the associated private key) for each computer in the Web farm. You should consult the appropriate licensing documentation issued by your certification authority before you copy the certificate and private key to each computer.

In IIS 5, you can replicate the certificate from one computer to another by following these steps:

1.   Click Start.

2.   Choose Run and type *mmc /a*.

3.   Choose Add/Remove Snap-in from the Console menu.

4.   Click Add, and select Certificates from the list of snap-ins.

5.   Click Add.

6.   Click the Computer Account option, and click Next.

7.   Click Finish.

8.   Click Close.

9.   Click OK.

10. Expand the Certificates (Local Computer) node.

11. Expand the Personal node, and click Certificates.

12. Right-click the appropriate certificate in the right pane.

13. Select All Tasks.

14. Choose Export.

15. Click Next when the Certificate Export wizard appears.

16. Click the Yes, Export The Private Key radio button.

NOTE You must be able to copy the private key to the other computer for SSL/TLS to work. If this option is disabled, the private key cannot be exported from the computer and the process will fail.

17. Click Personal Information Exchange – PKCS #12 (.PFX).

18. Enable the Include All Certificates In The Certification Path If Possible option.

19. Click Next.

20. Enable the Enable Strong Protection (Requires Internet Explorer 5, Windows NT 4 SP4 Or Above) option.

21. Enter and confirm a password to protect the exported certificate and private key.

22. Click Next.

23. Enter the name of the file you want to export.

24. Click Next, and then click Finish.

It's recommended that you copy the exported data to a floppy disk and delete the export file from the Web server.

You can import the key into each Web server by using the Web Server Certificate wizard. Once you've installed the private key and certificate on each computer in the Web farm, store the floppy disk in a highly secure area to prevent theft or duplication.

SSL/TLS affinity

SSL/TLS connections should be *affinitized*. For example, if a Web client connects to your Web site and has its request processed by the second server in the farm, subsequent requests should go to the same Web server. Otherwise, a new, expensive SSL/TLS connection must be established with another computer. Hence, determine whether this feature exists in your load-balancing software. The load-balancing software in Windows 2000 Server and Windows 2000 Advanced Server supports this capability.

Setting SSL/TLS Ciphers

In Windows 2000, you can configure which SSL and TLS cryptographic protocols (ciphers) are supported, as well as whether SSL2, SSL3, or TLS is used when establishing a secure channel between the Web server and the browser.

WARNING Do not change any of these settings without understanding the implications of the changes.

To choose which ciphers to allow, navigate to the following location in the Registry by using the Registry editor:

HKEY_LOCAL_MACHINE

    \System

        \CurrentControlSet

        \Control

            \SecurityProviders

                \SCHANNEL

                    \Ciphers

Figure 5-24 shows what this part of the Registry looks like.

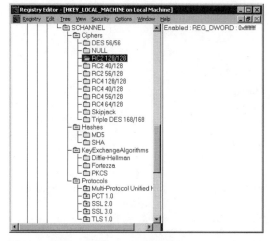

Figure 5-24. *Configuring SSL/TLS ciphers in the Registry.*

Each cipher has an Enabled value. If this value is set to 0, the cipher is disabled. If it's set to 0xffffffff, the cipher is enabled. You must reboot the computer for Registry changes to take effect.

NOTE Any SSL/TLS changes you make will affect all applications on the computer, not just IIS.

For further information on setting ciphers in Windows 2000, refer to the following Knowledge Base articles at *http://support.microsoft.com*:

- Article number Q216482, "How to Control the Ciphers for SSL and TLS"
- Article number Q241447, "How to Restrict the Use of Certain Ciphers in IIS5"

- Article number Q245030, "How to Restrict the Use of Cryptographic Algorithms and Protocols"

Let's look at another important aspect of Web security: authorization.

IIS Authorization—The Marriage of Windows 2000 Security and the Web

Windows 2000 uses access control lists to determine whether accounts are authorized to access resources. Because Internet Information Services is a service running on Windows 2000, and because it always authenticates and impersonates connections before accessing resources, it also uses ACLs. However, IIS also supports two other Web-specific authorization mechanisms: Web permissions and IP restrictions.

Web Permissions

Web permissions are a way of painting broad access permission to part of a Web space—for example, a Web site, virtual directory, directory, or file. They augment NTFS ACLs and can be used on non-NTFS volumes such as FAT disk partitions.

> **NOTE**   FAT partitions are not recommended for use on secure Web servers because FAT does not support ACLs.

You can configure Web permissions on a Web location by performing the following steps:

1. Open the Internet Information Services tool.

2. Right-click the Web location in question, and choose Properties from the context menu.

3. Click the Home Directory tab, Virtual Directory tab, Directory tab, or File tab, depending on the Web resource type you selected, as shown in Figure 5-25.

> **NOTE**   If NTFS file ACLs and Web permissions conflict, the most restrictive setting will be enforced. For example, if the Web permissions on a virtual directory are Read and Write but the ACLs on the files in the directory are Read-only, write operations will fail.

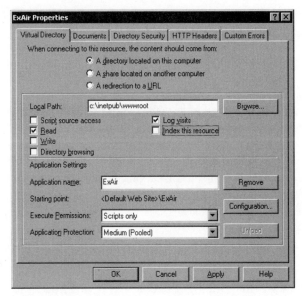

Figure 5-25. *The Web Permissions options for a virtual directory.*

Table 5-6 explains each IIS Web permission.

Permission	Comments
Script Source Access	This option is appropriate only when used in conjunction with the Read and/or Write permissions.
	Its primary use is to support the HTTP 1.1 WebDAV protocol, because when using WebDAV you might want to view the source of a document, not the results of a document.
Read	Data can be read or downloaded (depending on the content type).
Write	Data can be written to or files can be uploaded using the HTTP 1.1 PUT verb (depending on the content type).
Directory Browsing	If a user navigates to this virtual directory or directory and does not specify a resource, a listing of the directory contents will appear.
Execute Permissions: None	ASP files and executable files (batch files, .EXE files, .DLL files) will not run.
Execute Permissions: Scripts Only	ASP files will operate correctly, but executable files will not run.
Execute Permissions: Scripts and Executables	Both ASP files and executable files will run.

Table 5-6. *IIS 5 Web permissions.*

IP Address and Domain Name Restrictions

Another important IIS authorization mechanism is access restriction by IP address or DNS name. Using IP address and DNS name restrictions, you can grant access to all hosts other than those you specifically deny or make sure that no host has access other than those you specifically allow.

When controlling access by IP address, be aware that many Web users will be passing through a proxy server or a firewall. The incoming connection to your Web server will appear to have originated from the proxy server or firewall and not the client's computer.

If you're performing restrictions based on the domain name, IIS must perform a reverse DNS lookup. If the lookup fails—for example, because of a failure to access the DNS server—the request is refused. Also note that DNS lookups can be time-consuming and thus their use is discouraged on high-volume Web sites.

Perform the following steps to configure IP address and domain name restrictions:

- Open the IIS tool.
- Right-click the Web site, virtual directory, directory, or file in question.
- Choose Properties from the context menu.
- Select the appropriate security tab.
- Click Edit in the IP Address And Domain Name Restrictions box.

Accessing IP restrictions from ADSI

The *IIsIPSecurity* object is an ADSI object that you can use to set access permissions by IP address and domain address. The following Visual Basic ADSI code will set the IP restrictions on the default Web server such that it can accept only connections from the local computer (localhost):

```
' Get the IP settings.
Set oVDir = GetObject("IIS://localhost/W3SVC/1")
Set oIP = oVDir.IPSecurity

' Set the IP grant list to 127.0.0.1 with subnet mask
'   255.255.255.0.
Dim IPList(1)
IPList(1) = "127.0.0.1,255.255.255.0"
oIP.IPGrant = IPList

' Do not grant access by default.
oIP.GrantByDefault = 0
```

(continued)

```
' Write the information back to IIS and clean up.
oVDir.IPSecurity = oIP
oVDir.SetInfo
Set oIP = Nothing
Set oVDir = Nothing
```

This code yields the IP Address And Domain Name Restrictions dialog box in the IIS tool, as shown in Figure 5-26.

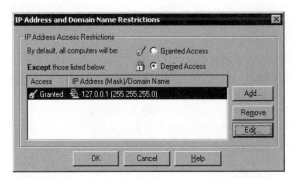

Figure 5-26. *Setting IP and domain name restrictions in the IIS tool.*

The Permissions Wizard

In the past, administering permissions was time-consuming and prone to error. To help alleviate this, Microsoft added the Permissions wizard to IIS 5. The purpose of this wizard is to set a known security baseline comprising authentication schemes, file access control lists, IP restrictions, and Web permissions. Running this tool on a Web server, virtual directory, or directory will set each of these mechanisms to a recommended minimum. From there, you can tweak the settings to meet your security requirements.

You access the wizard like so:

1. Right-click the Web server, virtual directory, or directory in question in the IIS tool.

2. Select All Tasks.

3. Choose Permissions Wizard, which will display the wizard, as shown in Figure 5-27.

4. Click Next.

Figure 5-27. *The IIS 5 Permissions wizard.*

The next screen offers two options, as shown in Figure 5-28: Inherit All Security Settings and Select New Security Settings From A Template. The first means "forget all the settings on this node; use the settings from the node above me." The second option steps you through some scenarios to derive security settings.

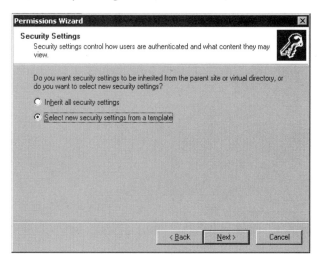

Figure 5-28. *Selecting security settings in the IIS 5 Permissions wizard.*

Assuming you want to set new security settings, let's continue with the process.

5. Click Select New Security Settings From A Template, and click Next.

6. Select the type of Web site scenario you want to use. Public Web Site is for Internet servers, and Secure Web Site requires that users authenticate themselves first.

7. Click Next.

8. It's recommended that you replace all current file ACLs with those recommended by the wizard, so select Replace All Directory And File Permissions (Recommended) and click Next.

9. Review the changes the wizard will make, and click Next.

10. Once the changes have taken effect, click Finish.

NOTE The Windows 2000 Resource Guide CD includes a tool called the Internet Information Services Permissions Wizard Template Maker that allows you to create your own custom templates for inclusion in the Permissions wizard.

IIS PROCESS IDENTITIES

The purpose of this section is to describe the identities Internet Information Services processes use when executing client requests. When IIS accepts a client request, it acts on behalf of a user account, as shown in Figure 5-29.

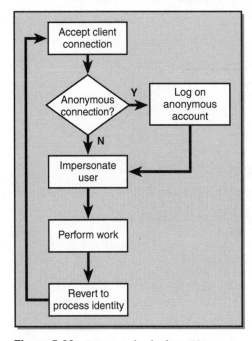

Figure 5-29. *Steps involved when IIS processes a client request.*

The core IIS process, InetInfo.exe, is a service that runs under the *LocalSystem* account, and it is this process that does the following:

1. Takes the client request

2. Impersonates the user

3. Performs the appropriate tasks

4. Finally, reverts to the process identity, which is *LocalSystem*

The entire process is shown in Figure 5-30.

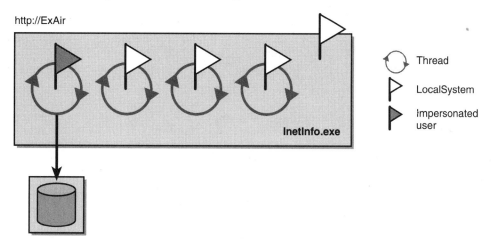

Figure 5-30. *A thread inside IIS running in a user context accessing a resource. All other threads are in the* LocalSystem *context waiting for work to arrive.*

Protection Levels

Here's a twist, however: for robustness reasons, IIS can be configured to run parts of the Web site in a separate process, so if the process crashes it doesn't crash the InetInfo.exe process. The processes in question, called DllHost.exe, are controlled by COM+. In IIS 4, the processes were called Mtx.exe and were controlled by Microsoft Transaction Server.

When a request is received by the Web server, it looks into the configuration store to look at the Application Protection settings for that part of the Web site's address space. You can configure the protection level of a Web site or a Web application by doing the following:

1. Open the IIS tool.

2. Right-click the Web server or Web application in question.

3. Choose Properties from the context menu.

4.   Click the Virtual Directory or Home Directory tab.

5.   Choose the application protection level from the Application Protection drop-down list.

Figure 5-31 shows what the options look like.

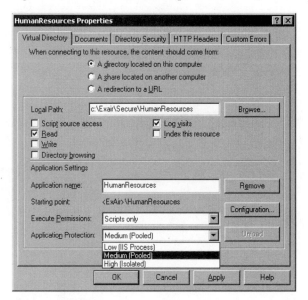

Figure 5-31.   *Choosing an Application Protection setting in the IIS tool.*

There are three levels of protection:

■   Low (IIS Process)

■   Medium (Pooled)

■   High (Isolated)

The default for all new Web sites is Medium (Pooled). Let's look at each setting in detail.

Low (IIS Process)

This is the way IIS ran prior to IIS 4; all requests are performed in the InetInfo.exe process. This is the fastest option, but it is also the least robust because a rogue application could crash the InetInfo.exe process.

Medium (Pooled)

This is a new option in IIS 5 and is the default setting for all new Web applications. In this model, all parts of the Web space marked as Medium (Pooled) run in the same process external to InetInfo.exe. As already mentioned, the process name is DllHost.exe and this process does not run as *LocalSystem* as InetInfo.exe does. Instead, DllHost.exe runs under the identity of an account controlled by IIS. By default, the identity is *IWAM_machinename*.

When the request is received, IIS (using COM+) checks to see if a process is running to handle the medium protection Web applications. If not, COM+ starts the process and IIS offloads the work to the new process. If the process is already running, IIS simply passes the work to the process.

The net effect, as shown in Figure 5-32, is that in a default installation of IIS two processes run: InetInfo.exe, running as *LocalSystem*, and an instance of DllHost.exe, running as *IWAM_machinename*.

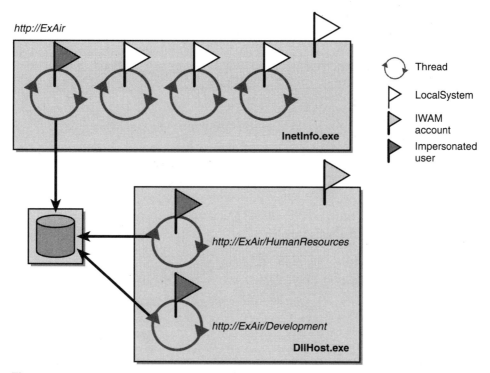

Figure 5-32. *A thread inside IIS running in a user context accessing a resource, and a thread in an instance of DllHost.exe doing likewise.*

This offers the best performance/robustness trade-off, because if a Web application crashes it might crash only the instance of DllHost.exe, not the InetInfo.exe process. However, all other Web applications running in the DllHost.exe process will stop functioning also. Nevertheless, when IIS receives a new client request, the Web server will automatically start a new instance of DllHost.exe.

High (Isolated)

This option, introduced in IIS 4 and shown in Figure 5-33, executes each Web application in its own instance of DllHost.exe that runs in the context of the *IWAM_machinename* account. In doing so, it offers the highest degree of robustness, but it's not as fast as Medium.

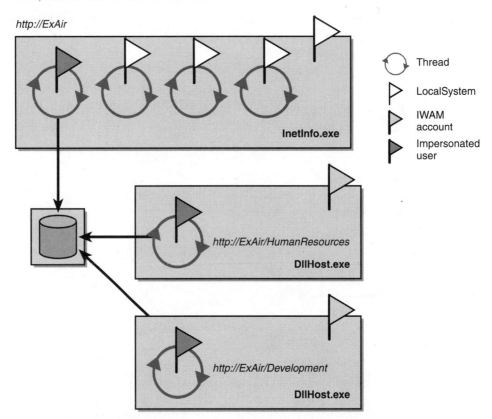

Figure 5-33. *A thread inside IIS running in a user context accessing a resource, and a thread in two separate instances of DllHost.exe doing likewise.*

Figure 5-34 shows a server running Windows 2000 and IIS with two instances of DllHost.exe running.

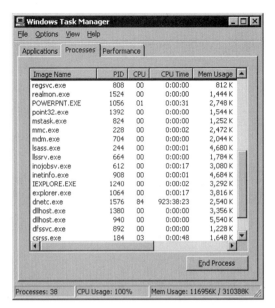

Figure 5-34. *Two DllHost.exe processes executing.*

Why Is the *IWAM_machinename* Account Needed?

As already discussed, IIS runs all Web applications marked as requiring Medium protection in one process named DllHost.exe. The process is created by COM+. Each Web application marked as requiring High protection runs in its own instance of DllHost.exe.

The processes are implemented as COM+ applications, and you can view these applications by using the Component Services tool as follows:

1. Click Programs on the Start menu.

2. Choose Component Services from the Administrative Tools menu.

3. Expand the Component Services node.

4. Expand the Computers node.

5. Expand the My Computer node.

6. Expand the COM+ Applications node.

You will see an application named IIS Out-Of-Process Pooled Applications. This is the COM+ application that will start when IIS processes any application marked for Medium protection. You'll also see a COM+ application for each Web application marked for High protection. The name of these COM+ applications is something like IIS-{Default Web Site//Root//HumanResources}. The first part of the name—in this case, Default Web Site—is the name of the Web site where the Web application resides, and the last part of the name—Root//HumanResources—is the name of the Web application. This is the application marked to run with High protection.

As you've probably determined by now, these COM+ application settings are created ahead of time when you create the Web application in the IIS tool, because COM+ must know the identity of the application ahead of time. You can verify this by performing these steps on the COM+ application in question:

1. Right-click the COM+ application—for example, IIS Out-Of-Process Pooled Applications.

2. Choose Properties from the context menu.

3. Click the Identity tab.

You'll see something like what's shown in Figure 5-35. As you can see, the process is marked to start under the *IWAM_machinename* account; this is set automatically by the IIS tool when the application is created.

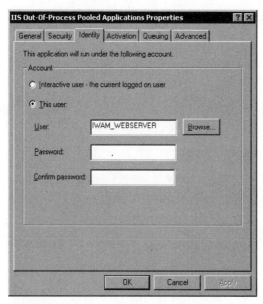

Figure 5-35. *COM+ application identity for Medium protection Web Applications.*

Changing the startup account

Using the COM+ Component Services tool, you can change the startup account of an IIS/COM+ application to another account. For example, you might want to run the application as This User—take another look at Figure 5-35—for debugging purposes.

However, there is a caveat. If you want to set the user account back to *IWAM_machinename*, you probably don't know the account's password, and failure to enter the correct password will result in failed Web requests. When this happens, the following two events are written to the system event log:

```
Event ID: 10004 Source: DCOM
Error: DCOM got error "Logon failure: unknown user name or
 bad password." and was unable to logon.

Event ID: 36 Source: W3SVC
Error: The server failed to load application '/LM/W3SVC/1/Root/
 HumanResources'. The error was 'The server
 process could not be started because the configured identity is
 incorrect.  Check the username and password.'
```

To correct this problem, run the SyncIwam.vbs utility in the InetPub/AdminScripts directory.

Protection Levels, ISAPI Applications, and ISAPI Filters

The Internet Server Application Programming Interface (ISAPI) is an API for writing high-performance applications in C or C++ for Web servers, including IIS.

ISAPI applications

ISAPI applications, also called ISAPI extensions, are implemented as DLLs and operate in a similar fashion to a CGI script: the Web server loads the file, the file performs its function, and the file then returns control to the Web server.

ISAPI applications run in the same security context as the impersonated user account and obey the same protection rules discussed earlier. Therefore, a Web application marked to run with High protection and using an ISAPI application will run the ISAPI application in a DllHost.exe process. The process will, by default, run as *IWAM_machinename*.

ISAPI filters

ISAPI filters, also implemented as DLLs, run in the InetInfo.exe process and respond to events such as authentication requests and logging events. ISAPI filters allow the Web developer to preprocess user requests and postprocess server responses. Because they run in the InetInfo.exe process, ISAPI filters always run in the same security context as the Web server, *LocalSystem*.

Protection Levels, Impersonation, and *RevertToSelf*

When a process starts in Windows 2000, it does so in a specific security context. For example, all default DllHost.exe processes run as *IWAM_machinename* and the InetInfo.exe process runs as *LocalSystem*.

A process can contain multiple threads, each of which will also be running in the same security context. When a client request is processed, IIS impersonates the client before performing the work; this involves changing the thread context from *IWAM_machinename* or *LocalSystem* to the user context. Once the work is completed, the thread drops back to the process context—in other words, *IWAM_machinename* or *LocalSystem*. This process is called *reverting to self*.

Some Web developers perform a dangerous trick, which we strongly discourage. When their Web application processes a client request, they call a function called *RevertToSelf*. At that point, the thread handling the client request is no longer impersonating the user. It is running as the identity of the process, and if the Web application is running with low protection it will revert to the InetInfo.exe identity, *LocalSystem*. Because this account is a highly privileged account, any security mistakes made while running in the *LocalSystem* context can be very serious indeed.

Calling *RevertToSelf* from a Medium or High protection Web application will revert to the *IWAM_machinename* account.

> **WARNING** Do not rely on being able to revert to the *LocalSystem* context. Microsoft has stated that it intends to remove this side effect in a future version of the Web server.

SUMMARY

Internet Information Services 5 offers a number of new security features over its predecessor—most notably, integration with Windows 2000 Active Directory for Kerberos, User Principal Names, client certificate mapping, and new wizards to help solve common security scenarios.

To thoroughly understand IIS, you must understand Windows 2000 security because IIS is a Windows 2000 service that leverages the security capabilities of the operating system.

IIS offers a full range of authentication protocols, from anonymous access to high-trust protocols such as X.509 authentication and Kerberos. It also offers seamless access to ACLs and integrates Web-specific permission techniques in the form of Web permissions and IP/DNS restrictions. Privacy and integrity are offered by SSL/TLS. It's important to review the range of technologies available to you before embarking on creating your Web-based solution, and Internet Information Services is rich in security features.

Chapter 6

SQL Server Security Overview

This overview of Microsoft SQL Server security will cover both SQL Server 7 and SQL Server 2000. Note that at the time of this writing SQL Server 2000 has not shipped, so some information regarding the new server might change slightly based on last-minute modifications. However, we'll identify information specific to SQL Server 2000—otherwise, all information applies equally well to SQL Server 7 and SQL Server 2000.

SQL Server 7 runs on Microsoft Windows 95, Windows 98, Microsoft Windows NT 4 (Service Pack 4 or later), and Windows 2000. SQL Server 2000 runs on Windows 98, Windows Me, Windows NT 4 (SP5 or later), and Windows 2000. Throughout this chapter, for both versions of SQL Server, we'll be describing features only as they run on Windows 2000. Do note that there is no such thing as integrated Windows security in Windows 9*x*, so if you want SQL Server to be secure you should be running it on Windows 2000.

SECURITY MODES

SQL Server relies on Windows 2000 to perform many functions, including security. SQL Server supports two authentication modes—integrated security and mixed security—which we'll discuss in the following sections.

Integrated Security Mode

For a secure installation, you should run SQL Server in integrated security mode. Integrated security means that SQL Server will use Windows 2000 authentication, which is implemented by calling the Security Support Provider Interface (SSPI). When a client attempts to connect to SQL Server over the network, SQL Server requests that Windows 2000 authenticate the client. Windows 2000 verifies the identity of the user, performing mutual authentication if necessary, and then allows a login to SQL Server to proceed, passing the access token to SQL Server. Mutual authentication is supported only on SQL Server 2000 using Kerberos authentication.

The authentication performed in integrated security mode is based entirely on Windows Security Account Manager (SAM) accounts or Windows 2000 Active Directory members. For each user you want to grant access to SQL Server, you must have a matching SAM or Active Directory user account. SQL Server understands Windows group membership, so you can add groups to SQL Server as well as individual user accounts.

Mixed Security Mode

SQL Server originally came to Microsoft under an agreement with Sybase, and some of the server's code and backward compatibility considerations stem from the original Sybase implementation. Mixed security mode is one of those considerations. Sybase implemented their own security system, and Microsoft SQL Server inherited this system. In earlier releases of SQL Server, mixed security mode was referred to as standard security, and it's still called that sometimes. In this mode, the client must specify a login ID and password other than the client's Windows 2000 credentials. This login ID and password are then passed to SQL Server, which verifies that the login exists and the password is correct for the specified login. This security mechanism is internal to SQL Server—no Windows security APIs are used.

In mixed security mode, logins for both integrated security mode and standard security are allowed. This means it's up to the client either to request a trusted connection or to request a nontrusted connection and specify login credentials for SQL Server. If a trusted connection request is specified, the user's Windows security credentials are used and the user isn't prompted further for security information, thus implementing the "single sign-on" mechanism for SQL Server.

> **NOTE** A *trusted* security connection is one where integrated security is used. A *nontrusted* connection is one that uses standard SQL Server security.

Mixed security mode is not recommended for secure applications. SQL Server's standard security mechanisms have not been enhanced for many releases and will be phased out. These mechanisms don't support even the simplest security strategies, such as enforcing minimum password length and not allowing blank passwords. Windows 2000 security is much stronger, so anyone interested in having SQL Server run securely should be running in integrated mode. Getting the hint?

An authentication troubleshooting tip

If your server is in integrated security mode, the client might not understand this and might believe there's a security hole in the server. Say the user starts a query tool and specifies some standard credentials, such as *sa* (for system administrator) and a random password (or no password at all). Upon successfully logging in to SQL Server, the user will immediately come to you and claim to have found a security hole. What's probably happened instead is that the user has been logged in with his or her Windows credentials.

Ask the user to run *select suser_sname* and see whether the results come back as *DOMAIN\Username*. If they do, a trusted connection was made by using the user's Windows credentials. You can perform this function with the SQL Server Query Analyzer. Figure 6-1 shows an example of the output you'll receive.

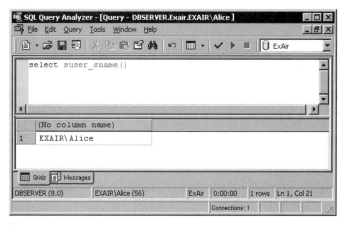

Figure 6-1. *Using SQL Server Query Analyzer to determine whether a connection is trusted.*

Setting the Security Mode of SQL Server

Follow these steps to set the mode of SQL Server security:

1. Start the SQL Server Enterprise Manager.

2. Drill down in the user interface to your instance of SQL Server.

3. Right-click your instance of SQL Server, and choose Properties from the context menu.

4. Click the Security tab, and then select either mixed security mode—that is, SQL Server And Windows NT/2000—or integrated security mode, Windows NT/2000 Only.

You'll need to stop and restart the SQL Server service (MSSQLServer by default) for the change to take effect. The following command line instructions will start and stop SQL Server:

```
net stop MSSQLServer
net start MSSQLServer
```

When you change the authentication scheme, you are changing the following Registry key: HKEY_LOCAL_MACHINE\Software\Microsoft\MSSQLServer\MSSQLServer\ LoginMode. The key's values are

- 0 or 2 - Mixed Security Mode
- 1 - Integrated Security Mode

This applies to SQL Server 7.0 and a default instance of SQL Server 2000. If you're using a named instance of SQL Server 2000, the Registry location will be HKEY_LOCAL_MACHINE\Software\Microsoft\Microsoft SQL Server\<InstanceName> \MSSQLServer\LoginMode and it will have the same values.

> **NOTE** A named instance is an instance that is distinct from the default instance. A default instance is one that looks (from a service name, Registry key, and so on) like an instance of SQL Server 6.5 or SQL Server 7. The named instance is compliant with the Windows 2000 application standards and can be connected to with a special name of the form *Servername\Instancename* instead of just *servername*. You can have only one default instance installed at any given time and any number of additional named instances installed at any time.

LOGINS, USERS, AND PERMISSIONS

As mentioned previously, we strongly recommend you run SQL Server in Windows integrated security mode. However, several valid security scenarios might lead you to use standard SQL Server security for logins. Therefore, we'll explain standard security exceptions when they come up, but for the most part we'll assume you're using the Windows integrated security mode.

Once you've set the security mode, it's time to examine the security architecture of SQL Server. In SQL Server 2000, a "prelogin" connection is made to SQL Server. This prelogin handshake occurs over UDP port 1434, and the connection returns information to the client, such as which instances of SQL Server are running on the machine and whether the machine is a cluster, as well as information required to establish a Kerberos delegable ticket to the server. It's at this point that the server will also attempt to negotiate Secure Sockets Layer/Transport Layer Security (SSL/TLS) encryption with the client. We'll examine that a bit later on.

NOTE Prelogin is a feature of SQL Server 2000. SQL Server 7 does not perform this step because it doesn't support multiple instances of the service on a single computer, nor does it support Kerberos delegation.

What happens next depends on what network library the client computer is using. If the client computer uses the Named Pipes or Multi-Protocol network libraries, the Windows Server service will validate the connection attempt via Windows security *before* it gets to SQL Server. This is true even if you're requesting a standard security login. If the reason you set up mixed security mode was that some users wouldn't otherwise be able to connect to the server, they'll get stopped here, usually with an error message stating that SQL Server is unavailable or does not exist. (However, if you turned on a network monitor, you'd see that they were getting system error 5, which means that access is denied.) The users will not be stopped if you use the TCP/IP network library, in which case Windows does not first validate socket connections because the Windows Sockets (Winsock) interprocess communication mechanism has no notion of secure connections. Rather, it relies on higher-level protocols to provide security services. Figure 6-2 shows the location of SQL Server and Winsock in the network protocol stack.

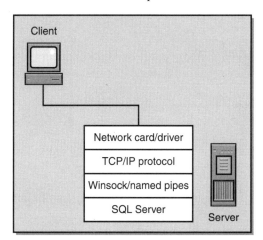

Figure 6-2. *Where SQL Server resides in the network protocol stack.*

Now that you've successfully presented some login credentials to SQL Server, we switch to the next phase of SQL Server authentication and authorization. SQL Server essentially has three "layers" of security that a client must negotiate successfully before it can retrieve data from the server. These are the login layer, the database user layer, and the permissions-checking layer.

As you can see from Figure 6-3, the preconnection sequence we examined above takes place. Once the proper handshake is established, your login credentials are presented to SQL Server. If you've chosen to use SQL Server standard security credentials, the login name is compared to the logins available in the *sysxlogins* system table in the *master* database. If a matching login name is found, the password you provided is encrypted within SQL Server and then compared to the stored password for that login. If they match, login access is granted.

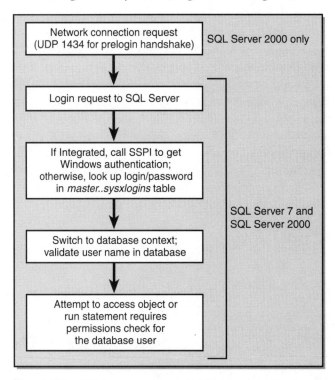

Figure 6-3. *SQL Server preconnection and connection sequence.*

If you're using Windows integrated mode, your credentials will be passed along to Windows by the SSPI. (SSPI was discussed in Chapter 5, "Internet Information Services Security Overview.") Windows will then return an access token—assuming that the credentials are correct and can connect to the computer—which includes information such as your primary security identifier (SID) and the SIDs of groups of which you are a member. SQL Server will then look for a matching SID in the *master* database's *sysxlogins* system table. SQL Server first looks for any entry that has denied you login to SQL Server. It looks through every SID in your access token so that any denial will always be honored. If no denial entry is found, SQL Server tries to find your primary SID. If that's not found, it'll look for any SID in your access token to allow you access to the server. If some matching entry is found, you will be successfully logged in to SQL Server—otherwise, your connection attempt will be denied.

At this point, your connection will switch to a database context. This switch can either be established as part of your login or specifically requested during the connection attempt. Put another way, your connection has moved from being validated by SQL Server to accessing a database. A login does not give you access to any database by default. Well, that's not completely true—SQL Server does include a guest database user account that has limited access rights, and the *master* and *tempdb* databases require that the guest user exist. Therefore, if you can't get anywhere else in SQL Server, you'll always be able to get into *master* and *tempdb*.

When you attempt to access a particular database, SQL Server will look for a database user ID entry that would allow you to connect to that database. You can gain access to a database in several ways, and we'll examine each of these later in this chapter. Next, you'll probably attempt to perform some action. When you do so, security permissions will be checked based on your database user ID. In general, security rights belong to database users, not to logins. Permissions are assigned separately to database users in each database and are enforced when an access attempt is made. We'll also go into permissions checking in detail a bit later.

NETWORK SECURITY OPTIONS

Now that we have an overview of how to get from the client to the server, it's a great time to start drilling down into the details of SQL Server security. The most logical place to start is the network. By default, everything except the user ID and password go across the network in cleartext. If you're concerned about security, and you must be to be reading this book, you'll probably want some way to encrypt the data flowing across your network. You can enable network encryption for all network traffic from the client computer to the server by using IPSec in Windows 2000. However, if you're encrypting only SQL Server traffic, you should use the mechanisms provided with SQL Server.

The Multi-Protocol Network Library

The Multi-Protocol network library uses Windows remote procedure call (RPC) support to communicate between the client and the server. However, what it does that's interesting from a security perspective is allow you to encrypt your data traffic to or from SQL Server.

To enable encryption at the server, you can check Enable Multi-Protocol Encryption in the server network utility or, when performing a custom setup, check the Enable Encryption option. Or you can create the key *RPCNetlib* in your Registry at *HKEY_LOCAL_MACHINE/Software/Microsoft/MSSQLServer/MSSQLServer/Client* and then add a value named *Security* of type *Reg_Sz* and set its string to *Encrypt*.

To enable encryption on the client side, edit the Registry on the client and add the same key just described, with the same value.

Note that the Multi-Protocol network library is supported to connect only to default instances of Microsoft SQL Server. It's being replaced with a new mechanism for enforcing network-level security for SQL Server: the Super Socket network library in SQL Server 2000.

The Super Socket Network Library

SQL Server 2000 introduces the Super Socket network library in an attempt to simplify how clients communicate with SQL Server. Essentially, SQL Server 2000 will communicate over TCP/IP sockets or named pipes, and the client can use either interface. However, from a security perspective, SQL Server 2000 offers something a bit more exciting: encryption of all network traffic, regardless of the network library being used under the covers.

If your server has a certificate that the client trusts, the network libraries will authenticate the server and negotiate an SSL/TLS connection between the client and the server. If you've set the client network utility option Enable Protocol Encryption, the client will attempt to use SSL/TLS. If it fails—because the server doesn't have a certificate, for instance—you won't be able to connect to the server.

On the server side, during setup there's an option to enforce encryption, and the same option exists in the server network utility: Require Protocol Encryption. If this option is set, all network traffic with that instance of SQL Server will be encrypted. If a client attempts to connect and the SSL/TLS handshake fails, the client will not be able to log in to SQL Server.

For databases handling sensitive data, you'll most likely want to enforce encryption of your data traffic. Good examples of such information include payroll, human resources, and medical data.

SQL SERVER LOGINS

As we said earlier, SQL Server 7 and SQL Server 2000 provide two login modes: integrated security mode in which Windows logins are allowed, and mixed security mode in which both Windows logins and SQL Server standard logins are allowed. Now let's examine the difference between each login type and how you can best exploit Windows 2000.

Standard Security Logins

As we stated before, SQL Server standard security logins have been around a long time. The implementation requires that a login name be passed, along with a password. The login name is compared to any existing logins in the *sysxlogins* table in the *master* database. Assuming a match is found, the password supplied by the client is then encrypted and compared to the encrypted password stored in the password column of the *sysxlogins* table. If a match is found, access is granted to SQL Server. Note that unlike in Windows NT or Windows 2000 passwords are not case sensitive, even if you set up SQL Server with a case-sensitive sort order.

SQL Server standard security logins are assigned SIDs within SQL Server. However, these are not valid Windows SIDs—they are 16-byte GUIDs that are used strictly within the SQL Server environment.

> **NOTE** What's a GUID? A GUID (globally unique identifier) is a 128-bit (16-byte) integer that is virtually guaranteed to be unique in the world across space and time.

Either a standard security login exists in the *sysxlogins* system table or it does not. Unlike in Windows NT or Windows 2000, the option to suspend or temporarily disable a SQL Server login does not exist. To add a SQL Server login, you can connect to SQL Server as a system administrator (that is, by using the *sa* login) and then run the following command:

```
exec sp_addlogin 'loginname', 'password'
```

The login name will be created, and the password you supplied will be encrypted and stored in the *sysxlogins* table. You can also add a login by using SQL Enterprise Manager. Note that the login name and password will cross the network unencrypted unless you've enabled a network encryption option, as previously discussed.

Although SQL Server standard security logins work fine, they're not the best security mechanism for a number of different reasons. They don't support even basic security options, such as password expiration, minimum password length, and retry lockout. Also, having more than one point of user account administration is expensive and error-prone. If you want any of these features, you should use Integrated Windows authentication, which we'll turn to now. SQL Server standard security is not being enhanced because Windows 2000 provides all the features needed for the best security integration and protection.

Integrated Windows Logins

As stated earlier, the preferred login mode is Windows NT/2000 integrated security mode. In either this mode or mixed security mode, integrated Windows logins are always allowed. An integrated Windows login receives the login credentials from the client's session with SQL Server and then uses SSPI in Windows to verify the user's identity. Windows returns an access token, which is used to determine access to SQL Server.

Even integrated Windows logins must first be registered with SQL Server. When both SQL Server 7.0 and SQL Server 2000 are installed, the local administrator's group is added as a login to SQL Server. You can then add any additional users or groups later.

When a login attempt is made using Windows integrated security, the access token is checked and all SIDs are checked. Then, a search is made through the *sysxlogins* table for a match with the Deny option set—that is, bit value *&1* in the *xstatus* column. If a match is made and the login right has been denied, the login attempt is refused. If no match is found, the user's primary SID is extracted from the access token and a search looks for a matching SID to gain access that way. If no match is found, all group SIDs are searched to allow access to SQL Server via Windows group membership. This is how members of the local administrators group are allowed to log in initially.

We must take a moment and say a bit more about the Deny option, since it's specific to Integrated Windows logins. An integrated login is in one of three states: granted (access allowed), denied (access prevented), or revoked (removing either of the two previous status options). A deny state for either the user or any group of which the user is a member will always take precedence. Denying login rights to "Everyone" will deny access to everyone regardless of any other right. If you want to remove a specific login right or remove a deny right, you use the *revoke* command. Each of these operations can be performed via the SQL Enterprise Manager interface, as shown in Figure 6-4.

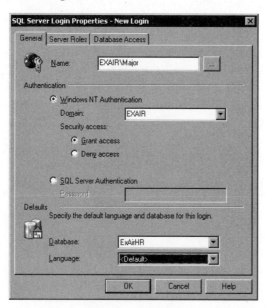

Figure 6-4. *Setting login information in SQL Enterprise Manager.*

You can also run the commands described in Table 6-1.

Request	*Command*
Grant login rights	*exec sp_grantlogin [mydomain\myuserorgroup]*
Deny login rights	*exec sp_denylogin [mydomain\myuserorgroup]*
Revoke an existing login or deny right	*exec sp_revokelogin [mydomain\myuserorgroup]*

Table 6-1. *Setting login information by using SQL.*

Since you can have access via either a group or individual account, which one will be selected when you log in? Well, you'll always get in with your own Windows SID if a matching row exists (and there are no Deny entries). However, there's no guaranteed order of selection for group SIDs—simply the first match is accepted. This is potentially important because some other settings, such as default database and default language, are set based on login.

Because both individual user accounts and groups are allowed, you can combine these in an effective fashion. For instance, you can create a domain group named SQL Server Accounting Logins in the EXAIR domain, add the appropriate Windows users to that group, and then grant access rights to SQL Server for that group. Start with this command:

```
exec sp_grantlogin [EXAIR\SQL Server Accounting Logins]
```

The command will add a row to the *sysxlogins* table for the SID of the SQL Server Accounting Logins group. At this point, any member of that group will be allowed to log in to SQL Server. Let's assume Michael is a member of that group but you need to deny him access to SQL Server but not revoke his group membership. Use this command to deny Michael login rights:

```
exec sp_denylogin [EXAIR\Michael]
```

This will add an additional row to *sysxlogins*, specific to Michael's SID, with the Deny flag set. Now, if Michael attempts to log in to SQL Server, he won't be allowed to log in. To allow Michael to log in again, you must revoke the Deny option (with *sp_revokelogin*) or explicitly grant login rights (with *sp_grantlogin*).

TROUBLESHOOTING TIP

When a user is unable to log in to SQL Server, look up his or her Windows group membership and verify no Deny entries apply in *sysxlogins*—that's usually the source of the problem.

Fixed Server Roles

In general, rights are always given to database users and not to SQL Server logins. Fixed server roles are one exception. Fixed server roles are a (fixed) set of rights that can be assigned to a SQL Server login. They are assigned to logins rather than database users because the rights assigned by these roles transcend a single database. An example of these rights is the ability to shut down SQL Server. You cannot alter the rights of each role. Fixed server roles include SysAdmin, ServerAdmin, SecurityAdmin, SetupAdmin, ProcessAdmin, DBCreator, DiskAdmin, and BulkAdmin. We'll describe these roles in the following sections. It's important to note that in addition to the rights we'll describe when describing the various roles, each role has the additional right to add other logins to itself.

SysAdmin

The SysAdmin fixed server role represents the system administrator. Logins who are members of this role have unlimited access to SQL Server. In most cases, they are literally above the permissions-checking systems. You should be paranoid about who you permit in the SysAdmin role.

By default, the *sa* standard security user is a member, as is the BUILTIN\ Administrators Local Administrators group. You can modify this list by using the Windows 2000 user/group administration tools, if you have the appropriate privilege. Make sure that the service accounts that you run SQL Server under, as well as the service account for the SQL Server Agent, are members of this role. You can set SQL Server and SQL Server Agent to run as *LocalSystem* because this account is a member of the Local Administrators group.

ServerAdmin

ServerAdmin role members have limited rights, including the ability to shut down SQL Server. They can shut down SQL Server only by using the SQL Server command *SQL SHUTDOWN* and are not granted the rights in Windows 2000 to stop SQL Server services. Members of this role can also reset configuration options for SQL Server and configure the full-text service.

SecurityAdmin

Members of the SecurityAdmin role can act as security administrators for SQL Server. They can grant, revoke, and deny integrated Windows logins, as well as add and remove standard security logins. They can also modify additional properties of logins, such as the default database and default language; add or remove linked server logins (that is, connections to remote SQL Server instances); and grant, revoke, or deny the create database permission, which is described in Table 6-2 (on page 181). SQL Server 2000 allows members of this role to reset the passwords of other standard security users also, except members of the SysAdmin role.

SetupAdmin

SetupAdmin role members can add, remove, and configure linked SQL Servers.

ProcessAdmin

ProcessAdmin members can terminate SQL Server processes by using the SQL *KILL* command. Typically, operations staff has this right so that they can terminate runaway queries, such as massive Cartesian joins.

DBCreator

Members of the DBCreator role can create, alter, or drop any database in SQL Server. They can also back up and restore databases as well as rename them.

DiskAdmin

DiskAdmin role members are allowed to run commands that were compatible with SQL Server 6.*x*. These include all SQL *DISK* commands, as well as the ability to add and remove backup devices, such as logical pointers to tape drives and backup locations.

BulkAdmin

The BulkAdmin role is new to SQL Server 2000. Members of this role are allowed to run the SQL *BULK INSERT* command. This allows a user to load a data file that the SQL Server service has rights to read into a table. The user must also have *INSERT* rights in the table into which they are loading the file. Since the *BULK INSERT* operation runs in the context of the SQL Server service, you must have membership in this role. In SQL Server 7, this role does not exist and the *BULK INSERT* command is restricted to SysAdmin role members only.

SQL SERVER DATABASE USERS

Once a database login has been successfully performed by any of the methods we've described, the connection to SQL Server must switch to the context of a database. When this is done, the login is mapped to a user context within each database. Note that a user context is database-specific, meaning that a single login can be represented as a different database user in each database. For example, *EXAIR\Richard* might be represented as *Richard* in one database but as *RichardW* in another. Without a database user mapping for a login, the user will not be able to use a database. Adding a login does not actually grant access to any particular database, except those databases with a guest user, explained on page 177.

Database users are stored in the *sysusers* system table in each database. A user is tracked within the database via either his or her SID—the same SID mentioned earlier for each SQL Server login—or a user ID (UID) value. There is one-to-one mapping between an SID and a UID within a database, but a UID is referenced in all database-level system tables for historic reasons.

To grant database access, use the *sp_grantdbaccess* system stored procedure or the SQL Enterprise Manager. You can grant access to a standard security login, a Windows NT/2000 group, or a Windows NT/2000 user. You can also revoke access with the *sp_revokedbaccess* system stored procedure. No Deny option exists for database users.

Now let's examine database access for each type of login.

Standard Security Users

We'll start with standard security users because they're the easiest to understand. The first parameter to the *sp_grantdbaccess* system stored procedure is the login name that you'd like to add to a database. For instance, to create a login named *Richard*, you would run this:

```
exec sp_grantdbaccess 'Richard'
```

The SID in the database will map to the SID of the login *Richard*.

Windows Groups and Users

We started with SQL Server logins because they're easy. Windows logins aren't that much harder to understand, but there's one catch—there's not necessarily a mapping of a login directly to a database user.

Let's start with the easy case. If the user *EXAIR\Michael* has been granted login rights to SQL Server and you want to give him access to a particular database, you'd run this:

```
exec sp_grantdbaccess [EXAIR\Michael]
```

There's a one-to-one mapping just as with standard security logins.

It gets interesting when you want to mix groups and users, which is probably the best way to work with security anyway. Let's say that you've granted login rights to *EXAIR\Domain Users* and you then want to grant just *EXAIR\Michael* access to the accounting database. You would run the same command:

```
exec sp_grantdbaccess [EXAIR\Michael]
```

Moreover, the entry generated in the *sysusers* table in the database is identical to the first *sp_grantdbaccess*. However, there's no one-to-one mapping back to any particular entry in *sysxlogins* since only the group had the right to log in. Because SQL Server has Michael's access token, it'll allow him to log in because of his group membership. When he tries to switch to this database, it'll recognize his primary SID and allow him in.

THE *SYSUSERS* TABLE AND DATABASE ACCESS

Not all entries in *sysusers* necessarily have database access. When you grant permissions, as examined below, you'll normally grant them to a database user. However, you can also grant them to a Windows user who doesn't necessarily have a database username. Say you've added *EXAIR\Domain Users* as both a login and a database user in the Accounting database. You now issue the following command:

```
grant create table to [EXAIR\Michael]
```

SQL Server will grant the *create table* right to Michael's account. When it doesn't find an entry for the user *EXAIR\Michael* in the *sysusers* table, SQL Server finds the SID for *EXAIR\Michael* and adds an entry to the table. However, the *HasDBAccess* flag in the *sysusers* table will be set to 0 (that is, no access). This means that the entry in the *sysusers* table is not there to allow database access for a specific database user. It's for some other purpose—in this case, to track permissions. Whether Michael has access to the database is up to you—either via some group membership that Michael has that gives him access to the database or via his user account in the database if the administrator specifically grants database access to *EXAIR\Michael* later.

Furthermore, if at some later point you explicitly grant Michael access to the database (via *sp_grantdbaccess*), all that will happen behind the scenes is that the row in *sysusers* will have the *HasDBAcess* flag reset from 0 to 1.

The dbo User

There are two special users in each database (potentially). The first of these is the dbo user, which exists in every database. It's the one and only true database owner, and it's always mapped back to a valid SQL Server login, since a SQL Server login must create a database. Ownership of a database can be reassigned, and doing so assigns a different login to the dbo user.

The Guest User

The other special database user is the guest user. Guest does what you'd think it does: it allows a valid SQL Server login to use a database, even if it wouldn't otherwise get database access. There's always a guest user in the *master* database—so that logins have some place to go when they first get created—and in the *tempdb* database—because even simple help procedures use *tempdb* to build the answers to some requests. You can't delete guest in these databases. In every other database in SQL Server, you can add guest by running *sp_grantdbaccess* for guest.

> **NOTE**   You'll find a row in *sysusers* for guest even if you haven't turned on the guest account for that database. The entry has the *HasDBAccess* flag set to zero, or no access. This is used to reserve the namespace for guest.

SQL SERVER DATABASE ROLES

Each SQL Server database can contain roles. Roles are similar to Windows groups, except that they are strictly internal to a particular database, unlike fixed server roles. There are three kinds of roles in a SQL Server database: fixed, user, and application. To add a user to a database role, run the *sp_addrolemember* command. For instance, to add *EXAIR\Michael* to the database *role db_owner*, you would run

```
exec sp_addrolemember 'db_owner', [EXAIR\Michael]
```

Role membership takes effect immediately; there's no need to restart SQL Server.

Fixed Database Roles

Fixed database roles are similar to fixed server roles—they provide a mechanism for convenient built-in groupings of rights to SQL Server users. There are nine fixed database roles, which the following sections describe. Unlike fixed server roles, members of each role don't have the ability to add other users to their roles, except where noted.

db_owner

Members of the db_owner role are, for the most part, equal to the database owner (that is, the dbo user). There are a few minor tasks that a dbo can do that a db_owner cannot—most of these commands are for backward compatibility with SQL Server 6.*x*. Otherwise, db_owner members can do any operation within a single database.

db_accessadmin

Members of the db_accessadmin role can grant and revoke access to the database.

db_securityadmin

Members of the db_securityadmin role are the other half of db_accessadmin role members from a security perspective—they can assign permissions (the *grant*, *revoke*, and *deny* statements examined on page 183) to users and roles within the database. They can also fully administer user-defined database roles and change ownership of database objects.

db_backupoperator

Members of the db_backupoperator role can back up a database and the transaction log as well as issue a *CHECKPOINT* command within the database.

db_ddladmin

Members of the db_ddladmin role can issue any data definition language (DDL) statements, such as *CREATE TABLE, CREATE VIEW*, and so on. They can also set full-text properties on tables and view index statistics.

db_datareader

The db_datareader role is a shortcut to grant select (read) permissions on all tables and views within a database.

db_datawriter

The db_datawriter role is a shortcut to grant insert, update, and delete permissions on all tables and views within a database.

db_denydatareader

Members of the db_denydatareader role are unable to select (read) any table or view in the database. Since the role is a deny role, it overrides any other rights you have granted. This role, along with db_denydatawriter, can be used when combined with db_backupoperator to give an operator the right to back up a database without being able to view the data within the database.

db_denydatawriter

The db_denydatawriter role prevents the user from issuing any *insert, update*, or *delete* commands against any table or view within the database.

User Database Roles

Besides the fixed database roles that come built in to each database, you're able to create your own roles in a database. You do this with the *sp_addrole* system stored procedure. For instance, to create a role named Payroll_Users, you would run

```
exec sp_addrole 'Payroll_Users'
```

This would add a new row to *sysusers* for the Payroll_Users role and assign it a SQL Server internal-use only SID (really a GUID, just as for SQL Server security logins).

To add a user to the role, use *sp_addrolemember*. To add Michael to this role, you would run

```
exec sp_addrolemember 'Payroll_Users', [EXAIR\Michael]
```

This adds a row to the *sysmembers* system table, reflecting Michael's membership in this role.

To drop the role from the database, you would run *sp_droprole*:

```
exec sp_droprole 'Payroll_Users'
```

Once this command is executed, the row in *sysusers* is deleted. All users who were in the role are simply removed from the role as it's being dropped.

The "Public" Role

Although, strictly speaking, Public isn't really a role, it's important to note it somewhere. Public is the equivalent of the Everyone group in Windows NT or Windows 2000. You can't remove someone from Public, and any grants to Public apply to everyone within the database. For example, if you deny Public insert permissions on a table, no one will be able to insert into that table, because "everyone" includes you! This is one of the frequent complaints of new security-conscious administrators.

Application Roles

Application roles group users together in a sense, like user-defined database roles; however, there is no such thing as membership in an Application role. Additionally, a password is assigned to an Application role. You create an Application role with the *sp_addapprole* system stored procedure. Application roles are also just entries in the *sysusers* table. When you add an application role, you must assign a password. For instance, to create a role named Payroll, you would run

```
exec sp_addapprole 'Payroll','MyHard$password@'
```

Where things veer off track is the way that Application roles are used. Ordinary roles simply take effect when you use a database. Application roles must be explicitly enabled. This is done with the *sp_setapprole* command:

```
exec sp_setapprole 'Payroll', {Encrypt N'MyHard$passw0rd@#}
```

When the Application role is enabled, all other permissions for the user are turned off within the database and only the permissions that have been specifically assigned to the role are enabled. The exception is that rights assigned to Public are still in effect, because the Application role is a member of the Public role.

The only way to turn off an Application role is to terminate your session with SQL Server.

So, why is this useful? Let's assume you've created a payroll application. You want to assign your users integrated Windows security, and you want them to be able to log in as themselves and switch to the payroll database when running your application. What you don't want them to be able to do is access payroll data outside of your application. So you add a login for the Windows group *EXAIR\Payroll_Admins* and add the group as a user to the payroll database. However, you don't assign any rights or role membership to the users. You grant all rights to the Payroll application role. Then, your application enables the application role with a call to *sp_setapprole*. All other rights are turned off in that SQL Server database, and your application essentially has the rights instead of the users having the rights directly. All activity is still audited with the user's real Windows login names, so you'll know who authorized that 15 percent raise but didn't share with you.

SQL Server Permissions

So, now you have a login to SQL Server. You've switched to a database context and established your identity within the database. What can you do? Well, not a whole lot—you need permissions to do everything within a database, unless you're a member of the *sysadmin* fixed server role. You can run three statements affecting persmissions: *grant* to give permissions to someone, *deny* to explicitly deny permissions, and *revoke* to remove a previous *grant* or *deny*. Two types of permissions exist: statement permissions, which give the rights to run particular statements, and object permissions, which give the rights to perform certain operations against a particular database object.

Permissions are cumulative, except for *deny*. A user can be associated with many types of permissions—those for themselves, those for each Windows group of which they are a member, and those for any SQL Server role of which they are a member. To find out a user's effective permissions, you need to add them all up. However, any *deny* is always preventative and always honored before any *allow*. So, if you have Select, Insert, Update, and Delete rights on a table because of group memberships but are individually denied (or any group of which you're a member is denied) Select on the table, you will be denied all access to the table.

Statement Permissions

Statement permissions give the database user the right to run a particular statement. There are no restrictions on how many times the user runs a particular statement. Upon running one of these statements—which are typically used to create objects—the user becomes the owner of the objects he or she created. The statement permissions that you can grant others the right to run are described in Table 6-2.

Permission	*Comments*
create database	Allows a user to create databases. This permission is valid in the *master* database only, so you must create a user account for a login in *master* for the target user and then run the *grant* statement for that user in the *master* database.
create table	Allows a user to create tables. This permission is valid in every database.
create view	Allows a user to create views. This permission is valid in every database.
create procedure	Allows a user to create stored procedures. This permission is valid in every database.

Table 6-2. *SQL Server statement permissions.* *(continued)*

Table 6-2. *continued*

Permission	Comments
create function (SQL Server 2000 only)	Allows a user to create user-defined functions. This permission is valid in every database.
create rule	Allows a user to create rules, mostly used for backward compatibility with SQL Server 6.x. This permission is valid in every database.
create default	Allows a user to create defaults—again, mostly for backward compatibility with SQL Server 6.x. This permission is valid in every database.
backup database	Allows a user to back up a database or a subset of files within the database. This permission is valid in every database.
backup log	Allows a user to back up the transaction log of a database. This permission is valid in every database.

Object Permissions

Object permissions allow you to grant access to specific database objects. By default, you can grant any permission available for objects that you create, including those described in Table 6-3.

Permission	Comments
select	Allows the user to read from a table or view
insert	Allows the user to add one or more rows of data to a table or view
update	Allows the user to modify one or more rows of data in a table or view
delete	Allows the user to remove one or more rows of data from a table or view
references	Allows the user to set a foreign key constraint against a table or to use schema binding against a function, view, or table
execute	Allows the user to run a stored procedure or user-defined function

Table 6-3. *SQL Server object permissions.*

Grant, Revoke, and Deny

Now that you know what kind of permissions there are to give, let's examine the three types of security statements: *grant*, *revoke*, and *deny*.

The *grant* statement

The *grant* statement is what you use to give a permission. To grant a statement permission, you'd issue something like this:

```
grant create table to [EXAIR\Michael]
```

To grant an object permission, you'd run something like

```
grant select on mytable to [EXAIR\Michael]
```

See the SQL Server Books Online for syntax and additional details for these statements.

The *deny* statement

The *deny* statement for permissions works much like a deny right does for integrated Windows logins. A deny is always preventative—any deny right will always override any grant. To deny rights, you'd run something like

```
deny create table to [EXAIR\Accounting]
```

or

```
deny insert on mytable to [EXAIR\Michael]
```

The *revoke* statement

The *revoke* statement takes away an existing *grant* or *deny* entry, much as it does with Windows integrated logins. You'd use it just like *grant* or *deny*. Here are some examples:

```
revoke create table from [EXAIR\Michael]
revoke select on mytable from [EXAIR\Michael]
```

Object Ownership Chains

Object ownership chains are an important security consideration in SQL Server databases. In a common scenario, you don't want to give direct access to your tables to users. This scenario is addressed to some extent by the application role concept. Another way to do this is to grant users access via only stored procedures, functions, and views. SQL Server makes this practical with object ownership chains. Each object in SQL Server has an owner—the user who created the object, just like in Windows 2000. Object ownership can be reassigned by *sysadmin*, *db_owner*, or *db_ddladmin*. If an object references another object and each object has the same object owner, no permissions check is made on the dependent object.

For example, if a view on a payroll table doesn't include the salary column, users can be granted select rights on the payroll view. They do not need select permissions on the payroll table as long as the object owner for both the payroll table and the payroll view are identical. Then you can grant access to the salary column to a subset of users or allow access via an application role only.

If at any point in the object ownership chain the object owner changes, a permissions check will be performed and the appropriate permissions will be checked. For example, if I create a stored procedure that inserts into the payroll table but the payroll table has a different object owner, anyone trying to execute the stored procedure will also have to have insert rights into the payroll table. You must consider this behavior when designing your database and object owners.

Run a Security Audit in SQL Server 2000

SQL Server 2000 introduces full audit capability via the SQL Server Profiler. You should enable auditing for SQL Server security events so that you know when key events happen. Turning on full auditing can create massive amounts of data, so you might want to limit your auditing to logins, administrative actions, and failed operations.

You can set up C2 audit mode with the following command:

```
exec sp_configure 'C2 Audit Mode', 1
go
reconfigure
go
```

Then restart the SQL Server service. When SQL Server is restarted, all permissions audits will be written to a file named in the form *audit_YYYYMMDDHHMMSS_ <SequenceNumber>*—for example, audit_200001071401000001_1.trc. *YYYYMMDDHHMMSS* is the time the file was created.

To turn off C2 audit mode, run the following commands:

```
exec sp_configure 'C2 Audit Mode',0
go
reconfigure
go
```

You can also use the SQL Server Profiler to perform a security audit with the user interface, as shown in Figure 6-5.

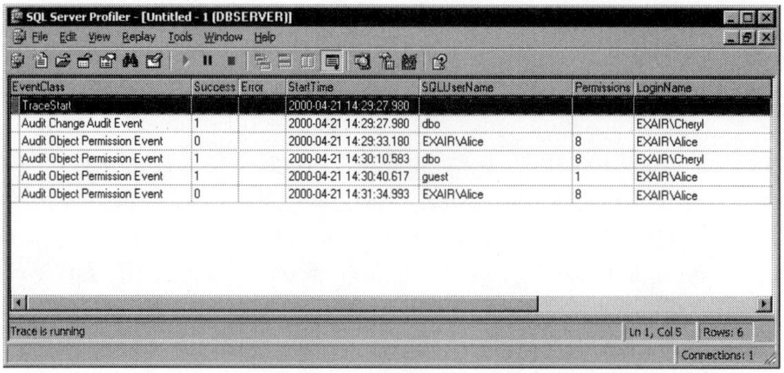

Figure 6-5. *Using the SQL Server Profiler to audit security events.*

If you want this *trace*—that is, the auditing of specified events—to run at all times, create a stored procedure that turns on the trace as you'd like to configure it and then set the stored procedure to be run at service startup. The example in the next section creates a stored procedure that monitors some auditing events and then sets the stored procedure to start the next time SQL Server is started. It also then immediately starts the stored procedure, which in turn starts the trace.

Please see SQL Server 2000 Books Online for details of which event numbers and columns are present in SQL Server.

Example audit stored procedure

The following is an example SQL stored procedure that will audit SQL Server even if the server is restarted. You'll notice that the *sp_trace_setevent* system stored procedure is used throughout; here's the syntax for *sp_trace_setevent*:

```
sp_trace_setevent [ @traceid = ] trace_id
    , [ @eventid = ] event_id
    , [ @columnid = ] column_id
    , [ @on = ] 'on' or 'off'
```

Table 6-4 describes the *sp_trace_setevent* arguments.

Argument	*Comments*
@traceid	The trace id assigned to the trace by the server.
@eventid	The event ID for the event—see SQL Server 2000 Books Online for the complete list.
@columnid	The column ID for the column you want to show—see SQL Server 2000 Books Online for the complete list.
@on	Turns on the column in the trace.
@off	Turns off the column in the trace.

Table 6-4. *The* sp_trace_setevnt *argument descriptions.*

Now for the example code:

```
use master
go
drop proc p_audittrace
go
create proc p_audittrace
with encryption
as

-- declare variables.
declare @traceid int -- The ID of the audit trace.
```

(continued)

```
-- Create the trace container, and
--  get trace id from the server.
exec sp_trace_create @traceid output,
-- Rollover file (2), shutdown server if audit can't be
--  maintained (4).
    6,
-- Location of the file - note it's a Unicode string,
--  hence the 'N'.
    N'd:\program files\microsoft sql server\mssql$sql2000\
        audit\myaudit',
-- Each file will reach 500 MB.
    500


-- Let's just add backup/restore (115), and object permissions
--  grants (103) add the backup/restore entry.
exec sp_trace_setevent @traceid, --trace number
    115, --login/logout
    27, -- the event class column
    1 -- turn it on

-- Turn on the subevent class (1=backup, 2=restore).
exec sp_trace_setevent @traceid, 115, 21, 1

-- Turn on the success/failure flag (1=success, 0=failed).
exec sp_trace_setevent @traceid, 115, 23, 1

-- Turn on the servername (i.e., this SQL server).
exec sp_trace_setevent @traceid, 115, 26, 1

-- Turn on the datetime (choose start time just because...).
exec sp_trace_setevent @traceid, 115, 14, 1

-- Turn on the appname field.
exec sp_trace_setevent @traceid, 115, 10, 1

-- Turn on the Windows NT username column.
exec sp_trace_setevent @traceid, 115, 6, 1

-- Turn on the server SPID column.
exec sp_trace_setevent @traceid, 115, 12, 1

-- Turn on the computername that the user's working at.
exec sp_trace_setevent @traceid, 115, 8, 1

-- Turn on the SID the login has.
exec sp_trace_setevent @traceid, 115, 43, 1

-- Turn on the login name
```

```
--  (will be different than Windows NT username if
--  standard security enabled).
exec sp_trace_setevent @traceid, 115, 42, 1

-- Turn on the database ID that the backup/restore
--  is running in.
exec sp_trace_setevent @traceid, 115, 3, 1

-- Turn on the name of the database as well.
exec sp_trace_setevent @traceid, 115, 35, 1

-- Turn on the database user name that's running
--  the command.
exec sp_trace_setevent @traceid, 115, 11, 1

-- Let's capture the text of the backup/restore
--  statements as well.
exec sp_trace_setevent @traceid, 115, 1, 1

-- Add the object permission grants.
exec sp_trace_setevent @traceid, --trace number
    103, --Login/logout.
    27, -- The event class column.
    1 -- Turn it on.

-- Turn on the subevent class (1=grant, 2=revoke,
--  3=deny).
exec sp_trace_setevent @traceid, 103, 21, 1

-- Turn on the success/failure flag (1=success,
--  0=failed).
exec sp_trace_setevent @traceid, 103, 23, 1

-- Turn on the servername (i.e., this SQL server).
exec sp_trace_setevent @traceid, 103, 26, 1

-- Turn on the datetime (choose start time just because...).

exec sp_trace_setevent @traceid, 103, 14, 1

-- Turn on the appname field.
exec sp_trace_setevent @traceid, 103, 10, 1

-- Turn on the Windows NT username column.
exec sp_trace_setevent @traceid, 103, 6, 1

-- Turn on the server SPID column.
exec sp_trace_setevent @traceid, 103, 12, 1
```

(continued)

```
-- Turn on the computername that the user's working at.
exec sp_trace_setevent @traceid, 103, 8, 1

-- Turn on the SID the login has.
exec sp_trace_setevent @traceid, 103, 43, 1

-- Turn on the login name
--   (will be different than Windows NT username
--   if standard security enabled).
exec sp_trace_setevent @traceid, 103, 42, 1

-- Turn on the database ID that the grant is run in.
exec sp_trace_setevent @traceid, 103, 3, 1

-- Turn on the name of the database as well.
exec sp_trace_setevent @traceid, 103, 35, 1

-- Turn on the database user name that's
--   running the command.
exec sp_trace_setevent @traceid, 103, 11, 1

-- Show the permissions type.
exec sp_trace_setevent @traceid, 103, 19, 1

-- Let's capture the text of the
--   grant/revoke/deny statements.
exec sp_trace_setevent @traceid, 103, 1, 1

-- Start the trace.
exec sp_trace_setstatus @traceid, 1

return
go

/* To mark this as startup so that it would run each
--   time the server starts, run the following command. */
exec sp_procoption 'p_audittrace', 'startup', 'true'

-- Start the trace now.
exec p_audittrace
```

SUMMARY

SQL Server 7 dramatically improved the integration of SQL Server with the Windows operating system. Windows integrated security provides secure authentication services, and SQL Server provides full discretionary access control. Permissions in SQL Server are assigned to database users, not to SQL Server logins. You use this mechanism to isolate applications and users among multiple databases while still using a single instance of SQL Server. Permissions in general are restrictive rather than permissive. Therefore, by default when you create a new object, no one but the creator can access the object. This is different from in Windows, where in general everyone on a machine has access to a file until you secure it.

SQL Server 2000 goes even further in integrating with Windows, allowing full integration with Windows 2000 features such as Kerberos and client delegation. SQL Server 2000 introduces full auditing capabilities, including an easy-to-use graphical interface for viewing and saving the audit logs. SQL Server 2000 also supports C2-style auditing for applications that must perform a full security audit. SQL Server 2000 also extends the protection provided by the server across the network. You can encrypt all communications with SQL Server without using IPSec in Windows 2000, via the SSL/TLS mechanisms and X.509 certificates.

These features and more provide you with a secure database platform that will continue to take advantage of the capabilities of future releases of Windows. SQL Server is inherently secure and can protect your data fully. You should take advantage of the Windows 2000 platform by installing SQL Server in a secure way (that is, into an NTFS partition) and using the Windows 2000 security features available to you, such as encrypting your data files with the Encrypted File System.

Chapter 7

COM+
Security Overview

This chapter introduces COM+ 1.0 security and focuses on the features most important in building secure Web applications. COM+ 1.0 is included in Microsoft Windows 2000 and represents a synthesis of COM and Microsoft Transaction Server (MTS). The COM+ 1.0 architecture is based on the model of providing *services* to application *components* that implement a number of *interfaces*. The COM+ 1.0 services include the following:

■ Automatic transactions

■ Resource pooling

■ Thread management (for example, synchronization)

■ Security

Interfaces are collections of method declarations and associated data types that represent units of functionality offered by a component. Note that the COM+ 1.0 notions of *component* and *interface* correspond to the notions of *class* and *interface* in modern object-oriented languages. It's also important to understand that COM+ 1.0 components are accessible using the standard COM protocols, both for in-memory and out-of-process—with Distributed COM (DCOM)—components.

COM+ 1.0 further groups components into COM+ 1.0 *applications,* which are the COM+ 1.0 units of deployment and administration. For the reader familiar with

MTS, the COM+ 1.0 *application* corresponds to the MTS *package*. Furthermore, note that COM+ 1.0 applications delineate the security boundaries where the COM+ 1.0 security service policies are applied. Figure 7-1 shows the configuration of a COM+ application.

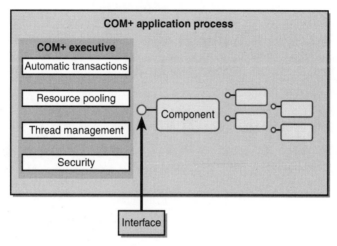

Figure 7-1. *COM+ 1.0 services, components, and interfaces.*

ARCHITECTURE

COM+ 1.0 security is articulated around the interaction between a client and a COM+ 1.0 application: a client performing a method call against one of the application components, as shown in Figure 7-2.

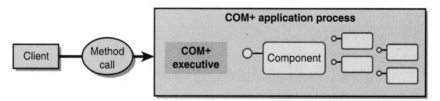

Figure 7-2. *A COM+ method call.*

Note that from a COM+ 1.0 perspective the application components are the objects of the client request—that is, the resources requiring protection.

To make component authorization meaningful, it is necessary to authenticate the client. Furthermore, the server identity might also need to be authenticated to alleviate client concerns. Finally, the method call itself requires protection against information disclosure and data tampering—the confidentiality and integrity protection that is paramount in a distributed setting when the method call is carried over DCOM.

The goal of COM+ 1.0 security is to provide mechanisms that address these concerns and simplify the programmer's task. As with the other COM+ 1.0 services, this is accomplished by providing a declarative model—to cover the proverbial 80 percent case—in which both authorization and authentication are configured.

To address more elaborate scenarios—for example, the delegation scenario in which the COM+ application needs to perform work under the client authority—this configuration paradigm is supplemented by programmatic controls to express the few idioms required to support those scenarios.

Authorization Overview

For authorization, applications control access with *roles,* which represent application-specific categories of principals. In COM+ 1.0, these principals are Windows 2000–authenticated principals. Protection is configured to restrict access to method calls or programmed to restrict access to private application resources. In addition, COM+ 1.0 supports the Windows 2000 impersonation-style access control when the application accesses resources on the client's behalf, as shown in Figure 7-3.

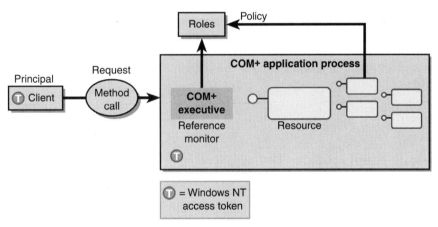

Figure 7-3. *COM+ 1.0 authorization overview.*

Now let's turn our attention to another critical aspect of security: authentication.

Authentication Overview

For authentication, COM+ 1.0 relies completely on Windows 2000. This means, as noted in the previous section, that COM+ 1.0 principals are Windows 2000 principals. In addition, COM+ 1.0 uses the authentication services provided by Windows 2000. This is accomplished through various mechanisms, such as the layering of DCOM over Microsoft remote procedure call (RPC), which in turn relies on the various Windows 2000 Security Support Providers (SSPs)—for example, Kerberos and NTLM—to offer authentication, confidentiality, and integrity services. Figure 7-4 gives an overview of COM+ 1.0 authentication.

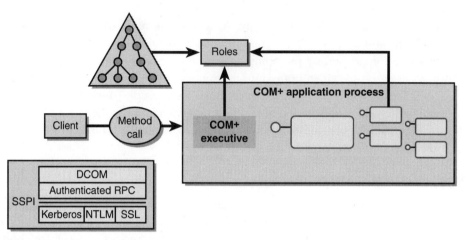

Figure 7-4. *COM+ 1.0 authentication overview.*

COM+ 1.0 provides a thin configuration layer that controls various authentication settings. This authentication control, as we'll see in "Configuring Authentication," can be applied administratively at various levels of configuration granularity and, in the rare cases in which it's needed, programmatically.

COM+ AUTHENTICATION

In this section, we describe in greater detail the relationship of COM+ 1.0 authentication to Windows 2000 authentication and the mechanisms that COM+ 1.0 offers to control authentication.

Client-Application Trust

COM+ 1.0 leverages Windows 2000 authentication mechanisms through integration with Microsoft RPC and the various Windows 2000 SSPs. Note, however, that different SSPs offer somewhat different levels of functionality. For example, Kerberos supports mutual authentication, but NTLM authenticates the client only, not the server. This makes the SSPs' support at the COM+ 1.0 level (through DCOM) not completely transparent. Therefore, although more extensive coverage might be provided in the near future, COM+ 1.0 in Windows 2000 supports only the Kerberos, NTLM, and Negotiate protocols.

This means that for a client and the COM+ 1.0 application to engage in an authenticated communication a trust path must exist between the client and the application domains. In the trivial case, both client and application are members of the same domain. In more elaborate scenarios, interdomain trust must exist between the client and application domains.

However, in many common cases, including the Web scenario that is the primary example in this book, the client identity is not a domain identity or, at least, cannot be directly authenticated as such. In that situation, the relationship between client and application is typically mediated by a Web server—that is, the client is a Web browser interacting over HTTP with logic hosted by the Web server, which in turn dispatches work to COM+ components. It's therefore possible to defer the job of authenticating and establishing a domain identity for the client to the Web server. Once this is accomplished, the Web server can impersonate the client in its interaction with the COM+ 1.0 application.

The COM Internet Services (CIS) and Simple Object Access Protocol (SOAP) (once it becomes available) can also be used to support those scenarios in which the Internet client needs to perform a direct method call against a COM+ application. See the discussions of CIS and SOAP later in this chapter in "Using DCOM over the Internet."

Configuring Authentication

Authentication configuration is provided to control the level of protection, including whether to authenticate, applied to method calls. Both client and application can set requirements for this control. At the outset of a conversation, the client and application engage in what can be thought of as a negotiation to determine the authentication/protection that will be applied to their interaction. The setting applied to method calls between client and application is the more stringent of the two. Figure 7-5 shows the authentication process between the client and the COM+ application.

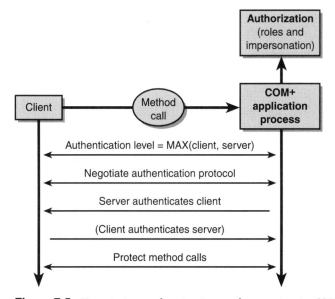

Figure 7-5. *Negotiating authentication and protection in COM+.*

For the client, the authentication configuration is machinewide. This is set by using the Default Authentication Level list box on the Default Properties tab of the My Computer object (the compmgmt.msc Microsoft Management Console [MMC] snap-in in Windows 2000), as shown in Figure 7-6. Note that this setting can be overridden programmatically by the client code.

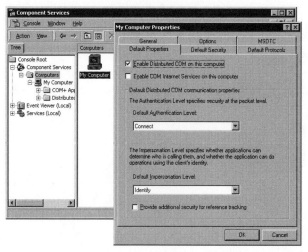

Figure 7-6. *Setting the default DCOM authentication properties.*

In addition to setting the default authentication level for clients, the default configuration also includes the following settings:

■ **Enable Distributed COM On This Computer** This setting controls whether crossmachine calls using DCOM are allowed from or to the computer. The default setting is selected, or enabled.

■ **Enable COM Internet Services On This Computer** This setting controls whether calls using CIS—see "COM Internet Services" later in this chapter—are allowed to the computer. The default setting is cleared, or disabled.

Each COM+ 1.0 application can independently configure its authentication controls. For the application, this setting applies both to the application when it acts as a server (that is, when it receives client calls) and when it acts as a client (when it originates calls to other applications). In the latter case, the authentication and protection level can also be overridden programmatically. Authentication is set with the Authentication Level For Calls list box on the Security tab of the application's Properties dialog box, as shown in Figure 7-7.

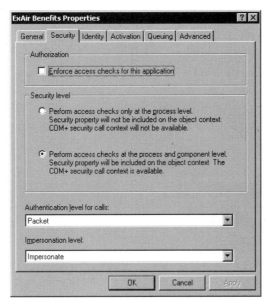

Figure 7-7. *Setting authentication requirements for a COM+ application.*

In addition to letting you set the authentication requirements for the COM+ application, the Security tab also exposes two coarse controls over *authorization*:

■ **Enforce Access Checks For This Application**   This is the top-level switch that allows you to control whether the COM+ security service will perform authorization checks for the application. The default setting is cleared, or unenforced. Note that even if the authorization checking is disabled, the client can still be required to pass the muster of authentication as determined by the authentication level.

■ **Security Level**   This property determines whether the application uses fine-grained role-based authorization or only coarse application-level access control. The default setting is to perform access checks at the process and component levels.

Authentication and protection levels

COM+ 1.0 supports the authentication and protection levels in Table 7-1. Note that these protection levels are cumulative—that is, each level offers its protection in addition to that offered by lower levels.

Setting	Comments
None	No authentication is required.
Connect	Authenticates only on the initial connection between the client and the application.
Call	This level is always promoted to Packet protection.
Packet	Verifies that the data received in the course of a call originated with the correct client.
Packet Integrity	Verifies that the method call data was not modified in transit.
Packet Privacy	Encrypts the call data to protect against on-the-wire disclosure.

Table 7-1. *COM+ authentication and protection levels.*

A note on library applications

A COM+ 1.0 library application is hosted by another process, and therefore its authentication and authorization settings are, by default, controlled by the hosting process. The hosting process security settings are configured either as a client or as an application, as described earlier.

In some situations requiring callbacks (for example, for notification), this setup can cause difficulties, especially when the hosting process is a client process that is subject to the broad machinewide security settings. In such a situation, callbacks often will fail to pass the muster of the security check and will therefore fail altogether. To handle this scenario, COM+ 1.0 provides a way for library applications to disable any automatic security check for their components. This is done by clearing the Enable Authentication check box on the Security tab of the library application. (Note that this check box appears for library applications only.) Obviously, this facility should be used with care.

Application Identity

A COM+ 1.0 application can be hosted either in its own process—such an application is known as a *server application*—or as a dynamic-link library (DLL) hosted in a caller process, in which case it's called a *library application*.

For a server application, it's necessary to configure a principal under whose identity the application will operate. This identity is the one that the client authenticates when using an authentication service, such as Kerberos, that supports mutual authentication. It's also the default identity used when the application acts as a client in the course of its work. We'll see later how an application can use impersonation to temporarily assume the identity of one of its clients while doing work on its behalf.

The application identity can be configured to be that of the currently logged user—also known as the *interactive user*—or a designated user, as shown in Figure 7-8.

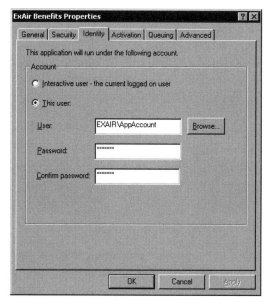

Figure 7-8. *Setting a COM+ server application identity.*

The interactive user setting is not suitable for a production situation since the application would require a user to be logged on in order to run. Furthermore, an application configured that way exposes the interactive user identity to misuse. This setting is therefore useful only in limited situations, such as in the course of developing a COM+ application.

Finally, note that COM+ 1.0 does not yet support running an application as a service or under the local system account. (The exception to this rule is the COM+ 1.0 System Application, which runs under the local system account.) There is, in fact, something to be said for this limitation because it prevents running application code with system-level privileges.

COM+ AUTHORIZATION

COM+ 1.0 authorization involves three main concerns:

- Protecting access to an application's method calls
- Protecting access to private application resources
- Protecting access to external resources that the application can use on behalf of the client

The first and second concerns are addressed by COM+ 1.0 roles with, as we'll see shortly, support for authorization driven by access control lists (ACLs). With the critical support provided by Windows 2000, COM+ 1.0 addresses the third concern, at the core of three-tier scenarios, with two important idioms:

■ The trusted application model, in which the application makes the access decision and accesses external resources under its own identity

■ The impersonation, or delegation, model, in which the application takes on the client identity while doing work on its behalf

Figure 7-9 illustrates these models.

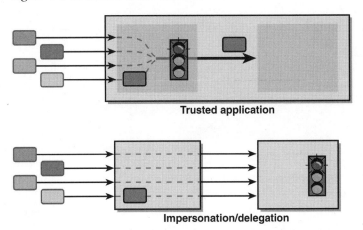

Figure 7-9. *The COM+ trusted application and impersonation/delegation models.*

COM+ Roles

COM+ roles are used to establish an authorization policy: determining whom to let in and with what authority. In constructing a policy, you're deciding who should be able to perform which actions and access which resources. Roles facilitate this by acting as an access control mechanism invoked whenever a user attempts to access any application resource. A role is essentially a list of users—more precisely, a grouping of users that share the same security privileges. When you assign a role to an application resource, you're granting access permission for that resource to whoever is a member of that role.

Therefore, you can define an extremely particular security privilege by declaring it as a role and then assigning the role to specific resources. This design is fulfilled when the application is deployed and system administrators populate the role with users and user groups. When the application runs, COM+ 1.0 will enforce the policy by carrying out role checks.

The fundamental asset you protect with roles is code: methods that can be called by clients of a COM+ application. With role-based security, the application protects resources by protecting the code accessing those resources. (Alternatively, as we'll discuss in a moment, in the impersonation/delegation model the application can simply act on the client's behalf with the client's authority.) Role membership is checked whenever a client attempts to call a method exposed by a component in an application. The call will succeed only if the caller is in a role assigned to the method being called.

It's often useful to configure role membership by using Microsoft Windows NT/ Windows 2000 groups, rather than individual users. Here are some reasons:

- If you have a large number of COM+ applications and roles, it might be possible to define a much smaller set of groups that can be mapped to the application roles. This can simplify administration dramatically for some organizations.

- For roles containing large numbers of users, performance will be improved by using a group to describe this membership. Group membership is determined at logon and added to the user's token, which can be more quickly checked against the small security descriptor representing the role.

- If applications are deployed across multiple machines, user authorization can be more easily administered for the network through Windows NT groups.

Controlling Access to Methods and Private Application Resources

Access to application methods is controlled through configuration, as described in the previous section. Access to private application resources is controlled programmatically either with roles or ACLs. Figure 7-10 illustrates both methods of accessing private application resources.

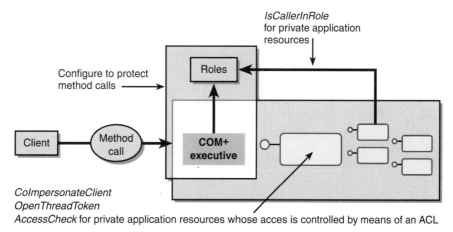

Figure 7-10. *Accessing methods and private application resources.*

Configuration

Roles are defined per application by using the Component Services snap-in, which is shown in Figure 7-11. The Roles folder in each application contains the roles defined for that application. Each role object, such as Administrator in the figure, contains a Users folder that contains Windows 2000 users and groups defining that role membership.

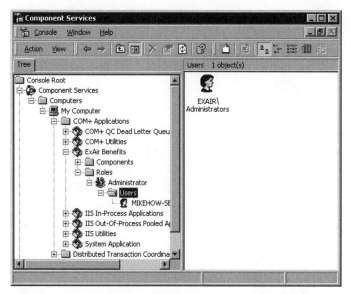

Figure 7-11. *Defining roles in the Component Services snap-in.*

Once a role has been defined, it can be used to enforce either coarse-grained access control to the entire application or fine-grained access control to the application's components, interfaces, and methods. One of these access control policy types is selected by setting the security level on the Security tab of the application's Properties page, as was shown in Figure 7-7 (on page 197). When fine-grained access control is selected, roles can be used to protect a method call by associating the role in the following ways:

- With a component to grant access to all methods offered by that component to the members of that role—using the Security tab of the component object's Properties dialog box

- With an interface to grant access to all methods of that interface to the members of that role—using the Security tab of the interface object's Properties dialog box

- With a method to grant access to the method to the members of that role—using the Security tab of the method object's Properties dialog box

Figure 7-12 shows a role being associated with an interface.

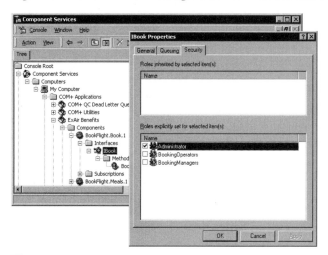

Figure 7-12. *Associating a role with an interface to protect that interface's methods.*

Note that a common source of trouble with the fine-grained security level is defining a role for an application without associating the role to a component, interface, or method. In this case, the user sometimes mistakenly expects that the members of the role will be granted access to all the application methods. This is not the case, and the result is denial of access even for those users who are members of that role. Again, with the fine-grained security level, roles at the application level are simply *defined* and are not used to directly grant access to the application components, interfaces, or methods.

In addition to role configuration, COM+ 1.0 offers other controls that affect authorization:

■ An application-level switch to turn access checking on or off for the entire application (the Enforce Access Checks For This Application check box on the Security tab of the application object's Properties dialog box, shown in Figure 7-7)

■ Component-level switches to turn access checking on or off for the methods of that component (the Enforce Component Level Access Checks check box on the Security tab of the component object's Properties dialog box, shown in Figure 7-13)

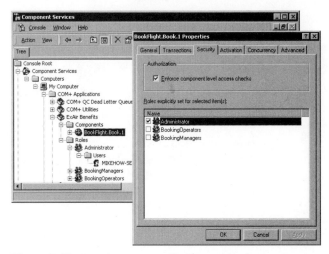

Figure 7-13. *Toggling access checking on a component.*

Programming

To control access to a private application resource, the application developer needs to gate access to that resource with a test of role membership, as shown here:

```
Dim objCallCtx As SecurityCallContext
⋮
' Get the security call context.
Set objCallCtx = GetSecurityCallContext();
⋮
' Perform the role check.
Allowed = objCallCtx.IsCallerInRole("<role name>");

' Act according to the result.
If (Allowed) Then
⋮
End If
```

Alternatively, in the case of resources protected by ACLs, COM+ 1.0 supports the following programming idiom, as demonstrated in C++:

```
// COM server impersonates client to obtain its token.
CoImpersonateClient();
// Obtain private object security descriptor.
MyStatus = GetObjectSD(Object, …, &SD); // Your own routine.
// Obtain client's token; revert to the server's identity.
Status = OpenThreadToken(…, &Token);
CoRevertToSelf();
// Perform access check.
Status = AccessCheck(SD, Token, DesiredAccess, GenericMapping,
    &PrivsUsed, &PrivLength, &GrantedAccess, &Allowed);
if (Allowed) {
⋮
}
```

Three-Tier Scenarios

Aside from the technical details of how to realize one or the other three-tier authorization models, it's important to understand some of the reasons underlying the choice of one or the other models.

It's useful to recall that meaningful security rests on a policy that defines "who can do what to what." Note that typical policies will make statements about both *subjects,* the principals attempting access, and *objects,* the resources that are the target of that access. Here are some sample policy statements:

- Administrators can do everything. Everyone else can only read.

- Managers can perform financial operations less than $X. Clerks can perform financial operations less than $Y.

- A manager can access only her employees' personnel data.

Each of these statements expresses access that depends in varying degrees on both the subjects and objects of the underlying operation. For instance, the first statement is very much centered on the subject—administrator vs. everyone—but the third one concerns a subtle relationship between subject and object, manager and data. These observations are somewhat simplistic, but they do offer some insight as to how to approach the problem of defining access policy and how, as we will see, this characterization affects the choice of a three-tier authorization model (or any authorization model for that matter).

The trusted application model

The trusted application authorization model is characterized by the fact that the application enforces the access control policy and accesses external resources under its own identity. In other words, the application is trusted by the external resource managers—for example, Microsoft SQL Server—to make the proper access decisions.

This model is most applicable when the overall application policy primarily concerns subjects performing the various application requests. This is the case because the subject security information is readily available to the application and because information about external resources is not essential to access control.

The strength of this model is its simple implementation and scalability because the application performs all secondary access under its own identity. Resources that are subject to per-identity constraints can be efficiently managed because the single application identity does all the work. This makes connection pooling viable because connection pooling does not work well with many authenticated connections using different identities.

Finally, note that this model requires careful design and implementation so that flaws cannot be exploited by the client to gain access through the trusted application to resources that the client is not entitled to access directly. In other words, it's essential to this model that the application live up to its title of "trusted."

The impersonation/delegation model

The impersonation/delegation model consists of the application taking on the client's identity during the course of work performed on the client's behalf. Figure 7-14 illustrates the COM+ impersonation/delegation model.

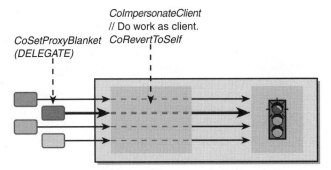

Figure 7-14. *The COM+ impersonation/delegation model.*

This model is useful when the application access policy expresses statements about the objects of a client's request. This is, for example, the case for access policies centered on data.

The implementation of this model requires the delegation capabilities of Kerberos, which will be autoselected by COM+, if possible.

The disadvantages of this model are its relative complexity and its reduced scalability compared with the trusted application model. Issues related to scaling include the following:

■   Two authentications required per request: client-application and application–external resource manager. Note that this cost is mitigated for clients making several calls, because the Kerberos authentication protocol will make use of cached credentials.

■   Expensive (late) access-failure—that is, the resource manager (for example, the file system) might fail a request that the COM+ 1.0 application has let through.

■   The defeat of resource pooling, such as connection pooling.

Configuration

For delegation to work, the following client-side requirements must be met:

■   The client must have an account in Active Directory.

■   The client user identity must not be marked as sensitive in Active Directory.

- The client must allow its identity to be delegated. You can configure a client to allow its identity to be delegated by one of the following methods:

    ❑ Set the machinewide impersonation level setting for simple clients or for each COM+ 1.0 application.

    ❑ Set the impersonation level programmatically using *CoSetProxyBlanket*.

- On the server side, the Windows 2000 server must be marked as trusted for delegation in Active Directory.

Programming

As noted in the previous section, the client might want to explicitly allow its identity to be delegated for use by the application through a call to *CoSetProxyBlanket*. On the application side, the following programming form is used for the application to perform work under the client's identity:

```
⋮
// COM server impersonates client.
CoImpersonateClient();
// Do work as the client.
⋮
// Revert to server's own identity once we are done.
CoRevertToSelf();
⋮
```

You'll need to use the following code declarations if you want to use *CoImpersonateClient* and *CoRevertToSelf* in your Visual Basic components:

```
Public Declare Function CoImpersonateClient _
    Lib "ole32.dll" () As Long
Public Declare Function CoRevertToSelf _
    Lib "ole32.dll" () As Long
```

The following example code shows how to use these functions in a Visual Basic method call:

```
' ' ' ' ' ' ' ' ' ' ' ' ' ' ' ' ' ' ' ' ' ' ' ' ' ' ' ' ' ' ' ' ' ' ' ' ' ' ' ' ' ' ' ' ' ' ' ' ' ' ' ' ' ' '
' This function is an example only. It is not
' recommended that you:
' (a) return large database result sets from COM+ processes
' (b) pass arbitrary SQL queries and execute them
'      without checking the query syntax first
' ' ' ' ' ' ' ' ' ' ' ' ' ' ' ' ' ' ' ' ' ' ' ' ' ' ' ' ' ' ' ' ' ' ' ' ' ' ' ' ' ' ' ' ' ' ' ' ' ' ' ' ' ' '
Public Function GenericQuery(ByVal ConnectionString As String, _
                    ByVal QueryString As String) _
                    As ADODB.Recordset
```

(continued)

```
Dim hr As Long
Dim rs As ADODB.Recordset
Dim conn As ADODB.Connection

On Error GoTo ErrorHandler

hr = CoImpersonateClient

'Open the connection to the database.
Set conn = New ADODB.Connection
conn.Open ConnectionString
conn.CursorLocation = adUseClient

'Execute the query.
Set rs = conn.Execute(QueryString)

Set GenericQuery = rs

hr = CoRevertToSelf

Exit Function

ErrorHandler:

    If Not conn Is Nothing Then
        Set conn = Nothing
    End If
    hr = CoRevertToSelf
    Err.Raise Err.Number, Err.Description
End Function
```

A Note on cloaking

Until Windows 2000, the behavior of COM—and, by extension, that of MTS because it is built on COM—was anomalous with respect to impersonation. In particular, if an impersonating thread (that is, one carrying the security context of a caller) made a COM call, the security context associated with the call was the security context of the process, not the impersonated security context. This problem is rectified in Windows 2000, but to prevent compatibility problems with existing applications, COM+ 1.0 introduces a way to control this behavior through a capability called *cloaking*. When cloaking is disabled, the impersonation behavior is the old one—calls to COM and COM+ 1.0 components are carried out in the security context of the process. If cloaking is enabled, calls to COM and COM+ 1.0 components are carried out in the impersonated security context, provided one exists, of course. Figure 7-15 illustrates impersonation with and without cloaking. Cloaking is controlled programmatically and enabled by default for COM+ 1.0 applications.

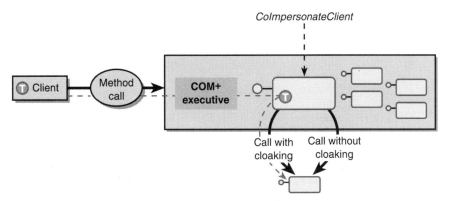

Figure 7-15. *Impersonation with and without cloaking.*

Call context

COM+ 1.0 provides a mechanism that enables you to retrieve security information regarding all upstream callers in the chain of calls to your components. This information is available only when the security level is set to fine-grained access control. The data carried in the call context is formed by COM+ 1.0 from call information supplied by the authentication service on every call. This information is then packaged by COM+ 1.0 and sent along the call chain, as shown in Figure 7-16.

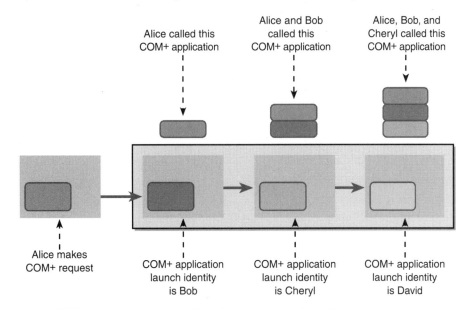

Figure 7-16. *Collecting call security information with the call context.*

Note that the trustworthiness of the call context information is based on

- The authentication service for the information related to the direct call
- The upstream identities for the information related to upstream calls
- The fact that call data is authenticated

Thus, it's important to use the call context information carefully. This facility is particularly useful for detailed logging in an environment in which the application logic is distributed among several COM+ 1.0 applications that trust one another. You can access security call context information by using the *ISecurityCallContext* interface.

DEBUGGING TIPS

COM+ 1.0 logs access failures in two places: the system log and the application log. Activation failures are logged in the system log. When the failure is related to security reasons, the description reports some of the user details. Note that the event source is reported as DCOM, even though the component being activated is hosted in a COM+ 1.0 application, because it's the DCOM activation services that activate COM+ 1.0 components. Figure 7-17 shows an example.

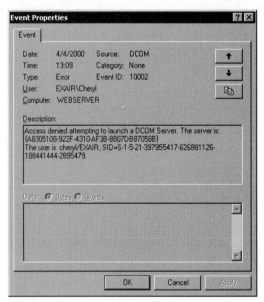

Figure 7-17. *An activation failure event.*

For failures on calls, COM+ 1.0 reports events in the application log. In this case, the event source is noted as COM+. The event description for the failed call includes the details described in Table 7-2.

Figure 7-18 shows an example of a call failure event recorded in the Windows 2000 event log.

Field name	*Comments*
Application Id	The GUID (globally unique identifier) for the COM+ application hosting the targeted component.
CLSID	The CLSID (class identifier) of the targeted component.
IID	The IID (interface identifier) of the targeted interface.
Method #	The method number (vtable slot) of the targeted method.
Caller Information	Security information about the call.
Svc	The authentication service used for the call. This is an integer identifying one of the following services:

Authentication Service ID	*Service*
0	None
10	Windows NT—that is, local or NTLM
16	Kerberos

Lvl	The authentication and protection level, as described in Table 7.1, which ranges from 0 (None) to 6 (Packet Privacy).
Imp	The impersonation level: 1 (Identify), 2 (Impersonate), or 3 (Delegate).

Table 7-2. *Call failure event details.*

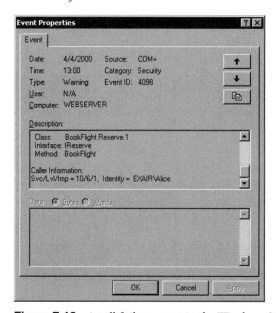

Figure 7-18. *A call failure event in the Windows 2000 event log.*

USING DCOM OVER THE INTERNET

Although the use of DCOM between a desktop client and a COM+ 1.0 application (or generic DCOM server) is rare over the Internet today, the use of DCOM in a demilitarized zone (DMZ) setting, in which the requirements are substantially similar to firewall issues, is much more common. Therefore, the scenario we'll examine here is Internet Information Services (IIS) running in a DMZ interacting with a COM+ 1.0 application within the corporate firewall, as shown in Figure 7-19.

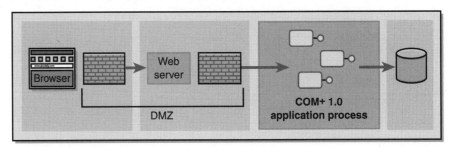

Figure 7-19. *COM+ in a DMZ scenario.*

COM Internet Services

COM Internet Services (CIS) introduces support for a new DCOM transport protocol called the Tunneling Transmission Control Protocol (TCP), which allows DCOM to operate over TCP port 80. This allows a client and a server to communicate in the presence of most proxy servers and firewalls, thereby enabling a new class of COM-based Internet scenarios.

A DCOM transport protocol

In many Internet situations, the network connectivity between a client and a server is subject to a number of restrictions:

■ A proxy server that filters outbound network traffic might control the client's ability to send information over the Internet. This is often the case for applications running in a corporate environment, but it can also apply to applications run by a user connecting to the Internet through an ISP.

■ A firewall often controls incoming Internet traffic and defines which combinations of network ports, packets, and protocols are accepted to protect the server (or client) network environment.

In practice, the net effect of such restrictions is that a client and a server will probably have a very narrow set of protocol and port combinations available to carry out a conversation. Because DCOM dynamically selects network ports in a range (1024–65535) in which Internet-to-intranet network traffic is typically not allowed, it's not possible to reliably use the existing DCOM transport protocols over the Internet, although they are perfectly suitable for intranets. Moreover, firewalls are often set up to restrict access to port 135, upon which DCOM depends for a variety of services.

The Tunneling TCP protocol introduces a special handshake at the beginning of each DCOM connection that allows the connection to pass through most firewalls and proxies. After this handshake, the wire protocol is simply DCOM over TCP. This means that the protocol is transparent to both client and server. Neither the client code nor the server code needs to be modified to use CIS. Also, all the DCOM-over-TCP protocol services are available—including DCOM security and lifetime management (that is, "pinging") services.

Tunneling TCP protocol overview

The Tunneling TCP protocol is illustrated in Figure 7-20 and proceeds as follows:

1. If the client configuration indicates that HTTP traffic to the server should be routed through a proxy, the client DCOM run-time environment establishes a TCP/IP connection to that proxy. It then sends the *HTTP CONNECT* method to the proxy, requesting connection to port 80 on *<server host>*.

2. The proxy establishes a TCP/IP connection with *<server host>*. Note that this assumes that the proxy is configured to enable the *HTTP CONNECT* method on the port connected by the client. This port configuration on the proxy is sometimes referred to as *enabling SSL tunneling*.

3. If the client configuration does not use a proxy, the DCOM run-time environment establishes a TCP/IP connection to port 80 on *<server host>*. After this step, whether or not the client uses a proxy, the client has a connection to port 80 on *<server host>*, which is perhaps mediated by a proxy. The client now sends the *RPC_CONNECT* command to the server, requesting connection to the DCOM server on *<server host>*.

4. In response to the *RPC_CONNECT*, the server RPC run-time environment— implemented in part by an ISAPI filter/extension pair—establishes a local connection to the DCOM server.

5. Client and server have now established a mediated TCP/IP connection and engage in a DCOM-over-TCP conversation.

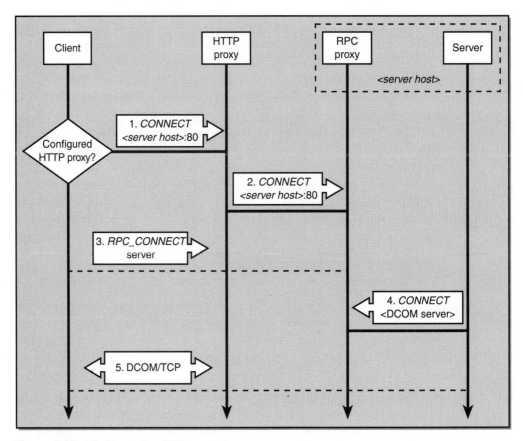

Figure 7-20. *The Tunneling TCP protocol.*

For more information regarding CIS, refer to *http://msdn.microsoft.com/library/backgrnd/html/cis.htm.*

A Tunneling TCP protocol limitation

The Tunneling TCP protocol has the following requirements:

■ It requires that IIS 4 or later be installed on the server-side machine hosting CIS-accessible COM objects, because part of CIS functionality is implemented using an ISAPI filter.

■ Because Tunneling TCP consists of non-HTTP traffic after the initial handshake, CIS requires that proxy servers and firewalls permit such traffic over a port opened to HTTP.

Note that because of these requirements, CIS does not support callbacks. For example, your applications cannot perform notifications by using the connection point or advise sink mechanisms. However, if the CIS client can function as a CIS server, nothing prevents the client from receiving DCOM calls—including callbacks.

Simple Object Access Protocol

The Simple Object Access Protocol (SOAP) is a proposed standard defining a protocol for accessing objects over the Internet. While products supporting SOAP were not yet available at the time of this writing, we expect them to become available shortly.

SOAP defines an RPC mechanism using HTTP as the transport and XML documents for encoding request and responses. The primary objective of SOAP is to provide an object invocation mechanism built on Internet standards. In particular, one of the important design goals of SOAP is that it be usable over today's World Wide Web infrastructure, specifically with regard to the use of proxies and firewalls.

For details about the SOAP protocol, visit *http://msdn.microsoft.com* and search for SOAP.

Chapter 8

Practical Authentication and Authorization

This chapter discusses pragmatic authentication and authorization from an application design point of view. As we described in Chapter 1, "Security 101," authentication is the process of verifying the identity of a principal, such as a user or a computer. Authorization is the process of confirming that an authenticated principal is allowed predetermined access to one or more resources. For example, one user might be allowed read and write access to a file, and another might be allowed read access only. Sometimes authorization is referred to as access control. However, we'll make an important distinction between the two: authorization determines whether an authenticated principal has access to a resource, and access control determines access based on conditions not directly related to the principal. For example, access control consideration might include time-of-day information—you might prohibit access to resources between midnight and 3 A.M.

The subjects we'll cover in this chapter include the following:

- Where to perform authentication and authorization

- A security best practice

- Application vs. operating system identity flow
- Relative Internet Information Services (IIS) authentication performance
- Example authentication and authorization scenarios
- Microsoft Passport
- A warning about passwords and custom authentication

WHERE TO PERFORM AUTHENTICATION AND AUTHORIZATION

Where you have your security system perform authentication and authorization is an important issue because of the numerous ramifications of these decisions. In our example application architecture defined in Chapter 2, "A Process for Building Secure Web Applications," there are three possible locations at which to perform authentication and authorization:

- At the Web server, in which case IIS is the gatekeeper
- In the COM+ business components—COM+ is the gatekeeper
- In the Microsoft SQL Server database—SQL Server is the gatekeeper

A gatekeeper is a service that controls access to resources. Note that before deciding where authentication and authorization will occur you need to determine whether the user's identity originates from the Web server and whether the identity is application level or operating system level. We'll discuss these issues in "Application vs. Operating System Identity Flow," later in this chapter.

A Security Best Practice

A well-known security best practice is the leveraging of as much of the operating system's security capabilities as possible rather than the creation of your own. There are two reasons for doing this:

- Operating system security code is usually better tested and more secure than custom security code.
- The possibility of back-end servers, such as database servers and file servers, being attacked is minimized by operating system security.

Take a look at Figure 8-1. In this scenario, authentication and authorization is performed at the back-end database server. Regardless of how an attacker attempts to access the data, he will be denied access because the database server performs access checks.

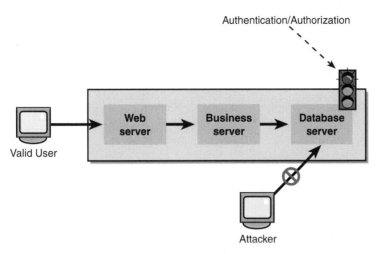

Figure 8-1. *An attacker is denied access to a database server that performs access checks.*

In the next, less secure example, shown in Figure 8-2, the access checks are performed by the server in front of the database server—for example, a COM+ business rules server. Because the database server assumes that all connections come from the COM+ server and that the COM+ server performs the appropriate checks, an attacker might be able to bypass the COM+ server and access the database directly.

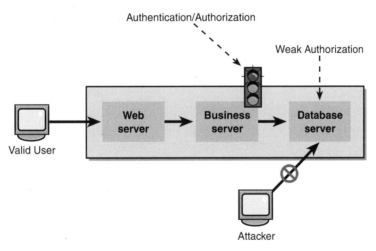

Figure 8-2. *An attacker accesses a database server that relies on other servers to provide security services.*

Here's an example of the less secure scenario that the authors have seen on more than one occasion: an intranet solution using an IIS server configured to utilize Integrated Windows authentication is built from Active Server Pages (ASP) pages querying a SQL Server database. The SQL Server database is configured to use standard security, rather than Windows authentication, and queries are made to SQL Server by passing the username as part of an SQL query.

The username is used to provide "authentication"—if the user account does not appear in the database *User* tables, the user is not granted access. "Authorization" is determined by evaluating which records the user account can access also based on their entry in the *User* table. The SQL code generated by the ASP pages and sent to SQL Server looks like this:

```
strUser = Request.ServerVariables("AUTH_USER")
strSQL = "SELECT Project.ProjectID, Project.ProjectName, " & _
        "Status.Comment, User.UserName " & _
        "FROM Project, User, UserProject, Status " & _
        "WHERE User.UserName = '" & strUser & "'" & _
        "   AND UserProject.UserID = User.UserID " & _
        "   AND UserProject.ProjectID = Project.ProjectID " & _
        "   AND Status.StatusID = Project.StatusID"
```

Notice how the first part of the *WHERE* clause adds the username to the SQL query.

> **NOTE**   Note another security mistake in this SQL statement. The *strUser* variable is fed directly into the SQL string without checking its validity. Although the chance of a rogue value being used is slim, it's still good practice to check the validity of all external data before using it as part of an SQL statement. You can find more information on how to do this in Chapter 12, "Securing Against Attack."

The pertinent aspects of the data model in this example of weakened security are shown in Figure 8-3.

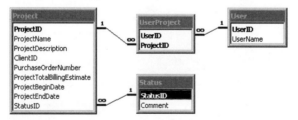

Figure 8-3. *Part of a data model of a database containing sensitive project information.*

In this case, the user account, gathered from IIS when the user is authenticated, is used to build up an SQL statement. When SQL Server receives the statement, it returns sensitive project status information available only to that user, because authorization is determined by row membership in the *UserProject* table.

The big security weakness in this example is the fact that SQL Server resides on the same network as the IIS server and hence can be accessed directly through the use of data access techniques such as open database connectivity (ODBC) and OLE DB. (OLE DB is a strategic system-level programming interface to data. Whereas

ODBC was created to access relational databases, OLE DB was designed for relational and nonrelational information sources.) Through such access, a user can bypass all authentication and authorization checks made by IIS. For example, an attacker could build up an SQL string from, say, Microsoft Excel and, using ODBC, request and receive sensitive information. Assuming that IIS, which the user has just bypassed, is performing authentication, SQL Server performs no authentication steps of its own.

You can fix this problem a couple of different ways. First, you can place the SQL Server computer on a private network and make it accessible from the IIS server only. You do this by adding a second network card to the Web server, using a private subnet between the two servers, and disabling routing on the Web server computer. Figure 8-4 shows this scenario.

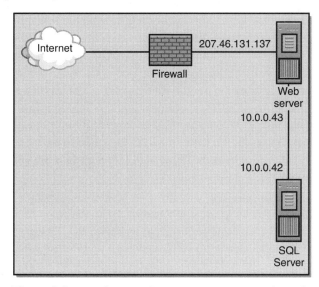

Figure 8-4. *A Web server that contains two network cards: one listening on IP address 207.46.131.137 for Internet traffic, and the other using IP address 10.0.0.43 for communicating with SQL Server.*

Second, you can use Internet Protocol Security (IPSec) and configure the SQL Server computer to allow communication between only the Web server and any administration servers.

Finally, you can perform security checks in the database rather than assume that the Web server is performing all the work.

The moral of this story? Perform operating system–level authentication and authorization in the database servers, if possible. This will require that you flow the user's identity from the Web server through the middle COM+ layers to the back-end data sources. Until Microsoft Windows 2000, this was a problem because the Windows NT Challenge/Response authentication protocol does not support delegation. (Delegation was discussed in Chapter 3, "Windows 2000 Security Overview," and will be covered in more detail in Chapter 10, "Building a Secure Solution.") However, Windows 2000 supports Kerberos authentication, and Kerberos supports delegation.

You might choose not to use operating system–level identity flow if you can trust the resilience of the servers behind the Web server and rely solely on identity information gathered by the Web server. Nevertheless, you should make sure those COM+ servers and SQL Server servers are well protected and you trust the people administering them.

APPLICATION VS. OPERATING SYSTEM IDENTITY FLOW

Application-level identity flow is the carrying of identity from tier to tier (that is, server to server) as arguments to functions, method calls, or parts of an SQL query string. With operating system–level identity flow, the carrying of identity is automatic and part of any communication from the Web server to the COM+ object and finally to SQL Server. Of course, the operating system must support flowing identity. Microsoft Windows NT 4 supports identity flow in a limited fashion: once a server has authenticated a connection, the server cannot make a call to another server in an authenticated manner. As far as the remote server is concerned, the connection is anonymous and can be denied access. Windows 2000 supports the capability fully through Kerberos authentication delegation.

> NOTE   The anonymous account in Windows NT and Windows 2000 is not the same as the IIS anonymous account. Windows NT and Windows 2000 use a specific account called NT AUTHORITY\ANONYMOUS LOGON with a well-known SID: S-1-5-7. The IIS anonymous account is a real Windows account—IUSR_*machinename*, by default—used by the Web server to mimic anonymous Web access. The Windows anonymous account is used when an identity cannot be authenticated.

RELATIVE IIS AUTHENTICATION PERFORMANCE

Before we move on to various authentication scenarios and their relative strengths, let's turn our attention to the relative performance of the various authentication protocols offered by IIS. The statistics given in Table 8-1 stem from a scenario performed on a Pentium III Xeon server running at 450 MHz with 128 MB of main memory. The Web server is also running Active Directory. The scenario was 10,000 user accounts held in Active Directory and 1000 accounts being used at random—no connections were reused. Also note that in further tests no noticeable performance degradation occurred as the number of user accounts increased, nor was there any degradation as more virtual Web sites were added to IIS.

Authentication Protocol	Performance
Anonymous	860 requests per second
Basic	780 requests per second
NTLM	99 requests per second
Digest	96 requests per second
Negotiate (using Kerberos)	55 requests per second

Table 8-1. *IIS authentication protocol performance.*

Table 8-2 shows the performance for certificate-based authentication protocols. In each case, the Secure Sockets Layer/Transport Layer Security (SSL/TLS) protocol was TLS using 56-bit RC4, SHA-1 hash, and 512-bit RSA key exchange. There were no other authentication protocols used. Note that you should allow approximately 1 KB of memory per connected user account authenticated by IIS.

Authentication Protocol	Performance
Anonymous access requiring a client certificate (that is, no mapping)	35 requests per second
Client certificate required and using Active Directory certificate mapper	23 requests per second
Client certificate required and using IIS certificate mapper	2 requests per second

Table 8-2. *SSL/TLS-based IIS authentication protocol performance.*

EXAMPLE AUTHENTICATION AND AUTHORIZATION SCENARIOS

Let's look at some common identity flow scenarios and the authentication and authorization implications of each.

The Complete Delegation Scenario

This first example is new with Windows 2000: the user accesses the Web server, which authenticates the user using Integrated Windows or Basic authentication. Authorization is performed when the user accesses Web pages or other objects (such as writing to files) or invokes components by virtue of access control list (ACL) checks on the files.

The Web server accesses remote COM+ applications configured to delegate the calling users. COM+ authorization includes checks of launch permissions and method roles, and code-based access checks through the use of the *IsCallerInRole* method. For more on these checks, see Chapter 7, "COM+ Security Overview."

Finally, the COM+ application impersonates the user and then calls SQL Server by using OLE DB. SQL Server is configured to use Windows security, rather than standard security, and the database connections from COM+ to SQL Server have the *Trusted_Connection* connection option set—that is, each connection uses the calling client's identity rather than the COM+ launch account identity. This assumes that the COM+ component is impersonating the original caller. If a COM+ component does not impersonate the user, the request to SQL Server has the identity of the process used to launch the COM+ application.

For example, the following OLE DB connection string will connect to a computer named DBServer, open the ExAir database in SQL Server, and use the calling user's identity:

```
Provider=SQLoledb;Server=DBServer;
 catalog=ExAir;Trusted_Connection=Yes
```

This is in contrast to a connection like the following one, which uses an embedded username and password:

```
Provider=SQLoledb;Server=DBServer;
 catalog=ExAir;uid=DBUser;pwd=!611M
```

If you specify a username and password for a trusted connection, the username and password are ignored.

NOTE Go on, admit it—how many of your Web pages make connections to a SQL Server database using the following connection string?

Provider=SQLoledb;Server=DBServer;catalog=ExAir;uid=sa;pwd=

We see a lot of these in ASP pages, where a Web developer uses the SQL Server system administrator account (that is, sa) to access SQL Server data and leaves the password blank. This is a very bad thing; do not do this. Do not use sa to connect to a SQL Server, because sa is an administrative account with special privileges in SQL Server. It is not a generic data access account.

While we're on the subject, never leave the sa password blank. Give it a strong password. Refer to Appendix B, "Strong Passwords," for details on what makes a password strong.

The Web application might or might not include specific authorization at the Web server other than ACL checks performed by the Web server itself. However, at the very least, we need to flow identity from the Web server to COM+ objects and SQL Server and determine whether we're going to perform extra authentication and authorization steps along the way.

There's one important note about all this. When any access is made from one computer to another, Windows 2000 attempts to authenticate the connection first. For example, when an ASP page in IIS launches the COM+ component on a remote server, Windows 2000 attempts to authenticate the user before access to the remote server is granted. If access is granted, the COM+ application starts up and then attempts to query SQL Server on another computer. Windows 2000 will authenticate this new connection before access to SQL Server is granted.

Here are the steps taken, assuming no authentication or authorization failures occur:

1. The client accesses the Web server, which is configured to use Integrated Windows or Basic authentication.

2. The Web server authenticates the client.

3. The Web server loads the ASP page.

4. The ASP page invokes a COM+ application on a remote computer.

5. A new authenticated connection is attempted between the Web server and the COM+ server. In doing so, the server hosting the COM+ application authenticates the initial user.

6. COM+ checks whether the user can launch the COM+ application and then checks (as the calls are made) whether the user can make method calls.

7. A method in the COM+ application impersonates the original caller.

8. The same COM+ method call sends a query to SQL Server over a trusted connection. The computer hosting SQL Server verifies that the user can access this computer.

9. SQL Server then checks whether the user has access permission to the database and then to each table accessed or stored procedure used.

As you can see, this process is a little involved, but it is, by far, the most secure scenario. At no point can an attacker get around any system, because each part of the application performs its own authentication and authorization and all use the same user account database, Active Directory in Windows 2000, and the same authentication mechanism, Kerberos.

Notice that both Integrated Windows authentication and Basic authentication are listed as possible authentication modes capable of supporting this scenario. Integrated Windows authentication as a choice is easy to explain: it natively uses Kerberos, and Kerberos supports delegation. But why Basic authentication? Basic authentication is a special case because when IIS calls *LogonUser* to authenticate and log the user account on to the system, the call primes the Kerberos Security Support Provider (SSP) with the user's credentials in case Kerberos is required later. Hence, the scenario works with Basic authentication and any browser that supports Basic authentication, even if the user is accessing the Web server from across the Internet. Of course, we hope you're using SSL/TLS to protect the username and password!

Figure 8-5 shows where authentication and authorization are performed in the complete delegation scenario. We'll explain the setup and configuration of this scenario in Chapter 10.

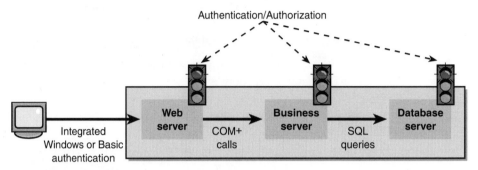

Figure 8-5. *Where authentication and authorization checks occur in a full delegation scenario using Kerberos.*

A caveat regarding the complete delegation scenario

From a security perspective, the complete delegation scenario is an excellent approach: there's one set of user accounts at any point in the system, and you can deny access to a user or group. However, you should keep in mind that in this scenario database connection pooling is defeated when authenticated connections are used between the COM+ applications and SQL Server.

Database connection pooling enables an application to use any unused connection from a pool of connections that do not need to be reestablished for each use. Once a connection has been created and placed in a pool, an application can reuse that connection without performing the complete connection process. The main benefit of connection pooling is improved performance. Connection pooling is defeated when authenticated connections are used because it requires that all connections in the pool have the same identity associated with them. This is so that any user at any point can pick up any established connection. And, by definition, an established connection has already been authenticated. We'll elaborate on this issue in Chapter 10.

IIS, COM+, and SQL Server as Gatekeepers

In this scenario, IIS performs authentication and possibly authorization and passes the user's identity as an application-level variable to COM+ or SQL Server. At each step, COM+ or SQL Server can perform application-level authentication or authorization. By "application-level," we mean performed in user-written code rather than provided by an element of the operating system, such as ACLs in Windows 2000.

For example, a Web application might gather the user's identity by using Basic authentication and then authenticate the user against Windows 2000. Windows 2000 checks that the username and password are correct, as well as other logon rights, such as whether the user is allowed to log on at the current time. At this stage, we're using the operating system security services—Windows 2000, not an application, determines that the username and password are valid.

Assuming the authentication step succeeds, the ASP *Request.ServerVariables("AUTH_USER")* variable contains the name of the user and *Request.ServerVariables("AUTH_PASSWORD")* contains the user's password. This works for Basic authentication only because Basic is the one authentication scheme that passes the password in the clear to the Web server.

> **WARNING** Make sure to use SSL/TLS if you're using Basic authentication. Usernames and passwords are subject to disclosure otherwise.

The user credential data is then passed to COM+ business objects, which in turn pass the username and possibly the password on to SQL Server. Using application logic rather than operating system security, the COM+ applications and SQL Server can make authorization decisions. You're assuming that Windows 2000 and IIS have performed valid authentication steps that lead IIS to fill in the *AUTH_USER* and *AUTH_PASSWORD* server variables. Figure 8-6 shows the flow of user identity from the Web server to COM+ and SQL Server.

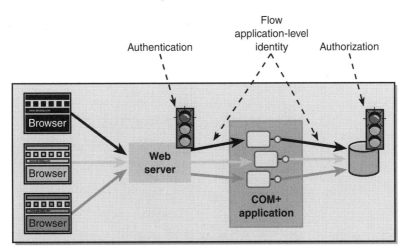

Figure 8-6. *User identity flows from the Web server to COM+ and SQL Server as arguments to method calls and SQL queries.*

Sample banking ASP code in IIS looks like this:

```
<% Option Explicit %>

<%
    Dim strTellerName, strTellerPassword, strAccount,
    Dim strType, lAmount, iRet

    strTellerName = Request.ServerVariables("AUTH_USER")
    strTellerPassword = Request.ServerVariables("AUTH_PASSWORD")
    strAccount = Request.Form("Account")
    strType = Request.Form("Type")
    lAmount = Request.Form("Amount")

    ' Create the business object.
    ' Note there is no need to use Server.CreateObject in IIS 5;
    '  CreateObject will suffice.
    Dim oBusinessObject
    Set oBusinessObject = CreateObject("Bank.Funds")

    oBusinessObject.Withdraw strTellerName, _
                             strTellerPassword, _
                             strAccount, _
                             strType, _
                             lAmount
%>
```

In this example, the ASP code gets the username and password from IIS and various account data from a posted form; invokes a COM+ business banking object written in Microsoft Visual Basic on a remote server (by using a COM+ application proxy); and then passes the user's credentials, the bank client's account number and account type, and a value to withdraw from the account. The Visual Basic code, which in turn calls a SQL Server stored procedure, might look something like this:

```
Sub Withdraw(ByVal strTellerName As String, _
             ByVal strTellerPassword As String, _
             ByVal strAccount As String, _
             ByVal strType As String, _
             ByVal lAmount As Long)
    Dim oRS As New ADODB.Recordset
    Dim strSQL As String
    Dim strConnect As String

    strConnect = "Provider=SQLoledb; " & _
                 "Server=FINANCES; " & _
                 "Initial Catalog=bank; " & _
                 "UID=bankid; pwd="
```

```
' Build up call to spWithdraw stored procedure.
strSQL = "{call spWithdraw('" & strTellerName & "', " & _
                    "'" & strTellerPassword & "', " & _
                    "'" & strAccount & "', " & _
                    "'" & strType & "', " & _
                    Str(lAmount) & ") }"
```

```
oRS.Open strSQL, strConnect
```

```
Set oRS = Nothing
```

Note how we are no longer using a trusted connection between the COM+ application and SQL Server. Instead, the Visual Basic COM+ application uses a predetermined account named *bankid* that has no password to make the connection. The following code then calls a SQL Server stored procedure, which performs the real work and makes the decision about whether the teller can make the withdrawal for the client:

```
CREATE PROCEDURE spWithdraw(@tname char(64),
                            @tpassword char(20),
                            @acc char(10),
                            @acctype char(10),
                            @amount money ) AS
if (select count(*) from tellers
    where tellername = @tname
        and tellerpassword = @tpassword
        and limit >= @amount) >= 1
begin
    update accounts
        set balance = balance - @amount
    where account = @acc
        and accounttype = @acctype
        and balance >= @amount
end
```

From an implementation perspective, this common authentication and authorization example is organized as shown in Figure 8-7.

The SQL UPDATE will occur only if all of the following are true:

■ The teller is authorized to withdraw from the account.

■ The account and suffix exist.

■ The client has the funds.

In other words, the SQL UPDATE performs application-level authorization.

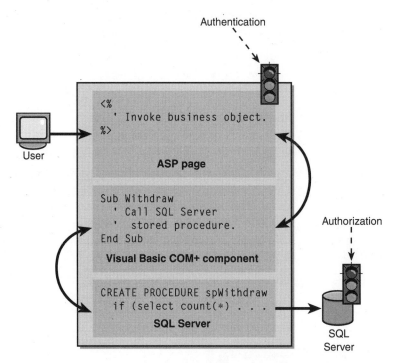

Figure 8-7. *The Web server authenticates the user and passes the user's credentials as arguments to various middle-tier and back-end services.*

The downside to this scenario is simple: it's insecure! It's easy to call the stored procedure, directly pass in the name of a teller, and bypass the authentication step performed by IIS, as described earlier in this chapter.

NOTE One of the reasons for the scenario's insecurity is an attacker's ability to try thousands of passwords by creating a simple application that calls the stored procedure directly and changes the password for each new request. Because SQL Server does not know that the second argument to the stored procedure is a password, it cannot perform bad-password lockout as Windows 2000 does. Such an attack will fail if Windows 2000 accounts are used throughout the application.

This scenario is secure enough for systems in which the data is noncritical or the COM+ and SQL Server servers are adequately protected from attack should the attacker bypass the security steps performed by the Web server. However, be sure to avoid a mistake that's commonly made when creating this security solution: adding a SQL Server username and password in the ASP code or COM+ component code.

For example, an ASP page with a line of code like the following one is dangerous:

```
<%
    oDB.Open "{call spGetPlaneMaintenanceRecords}", _
    "Provider=SQLoledb; " & _
    "server=DBServer;initial catalog=ExAirMaintenance; " & _
    "uid=EngineeringAccount;pwd=$#D0n+Tell;network=dbmssocn", _
    0, 1
%>
```

Here are the problems this code creates:

■ Providing a username and password to SQL Server works only with SQL Server's legacy authentication scheme, standard security. However, Microsoft recommends that SQL Server use integrated security (Windows NT Security) rather than standard security.

■ The application will no longer work if the password is changed in SQL Server.

■ The application will not work if the username or password is not correct in the ASP or Visual Basic code.

■ If a nonauthorized user gains access to the ASP or Visual Basic source code, that user also gains access to the "secret" SQL Server username and password. The most common cause of this type of vulnerability is incorrect ACLs on the ASP files.

   NOTE Another common cause of ASP source code disclosure is the inclusion of sample software on the Web site's production servers. For example, IIS 4 included sample code to view other ASP source code as part of a complex demonstration. Clearly, this should not be included on a production Web site.

Adding authorization to IIS

Notice that SQL Server performs all authorization in this example by calling a stored procedure that determines access. However, sometimes you'll want to add a greater degree of authorization to the application. Of a number of ways to do this, the most common is to use Windows 2000 ACLs on files used by IIS.

For example, while writing this book, the authors set up a Web site for document reviewers to use to access the latest versions of manuscripts. Access to all other parts of the Web site was open, but access to the manuscripts was restricted to a list of trusted people. To achieve this, we used two ACLs. All normal files had the following ACL:

■ Everyone (Read)

■ Administrators (Full Control)

■ SYSTEM (Full Control)

The ACL for the manuscripts was as follows:

- Reviewers (Read)
- Administrators (Full Control)
- SYSTEM (Full Control)

Reviewers is a local group containing the list of user accounts trusted to review the manuscripts.

ACLS ON FILES

It's generally considered good practice to use groups rather than individual user accounts when setting ACLs. Use local groups when you need to add a number of users to an ACL on a resource. To do this, perform the following steps:

1. Create a local group by using the Local User and Groups Microsoft Management Console (MMC) tool.

2. Add users to the local group.

3. Give the local group the appropriate access to the resource in question.

It's easier to maintain local groups rather than individual accounts. Imagine having 1000 resources, each with an ACL like the following:

- Everyone (Read)
- Squirt (Full Control)
- Major (Full Control)
- Cheryl (Full Control)
- Administrators (Full Control)

A year or so later, it's decided that Frodo also has full control of all resources. You now need to go to all 1000 resources and change the ACLs. A painful task indeed. Instead, it would be better to have an ACL like the following one on the resources in question:

- Everyone (Read)
- Trusted People (Full Control)
- Administrators (Full Control)

Trusted People is a local group containing the Cheryl, Major, and Squirt accounts. Add Frodo to the Trusted People local group, and you don't need to change any ACLs on any resources.

Finally, don't set ACLs on files. Set them on directories and use ACL inheritance—it's easier to manage!

Alternate Web authentication schemes

You'll notice that the sample banking ASP code shown earlier uses the *Request.Server-Variables("AUTH_USER")* variable. This will work with the following authentication schemes only:

- Basic authentication
- Integrated Windows authentication (NTLM or Kerberos)
- Digest authentication
- Certificate mapping

The variable is an empty string if you use Anonymous authentication.

All these mechanisms, described in detail in Chapter 5, "Internet Information Services Security Overview," use real Windows 2000 accounts. Sometimes, however, you might want to use alternate authentication schemes, such as cookie-based or forms-based authentication. These methods usually use a database, such as SQL Server, to perform a lookup of the username and password; if the username and password are valid, access is granted.

Forms-based authentication

Forms-based authentication requires the user to visit a login page and enter credentials, such as a username or identification number and a secret (such as a password) known to the Web site and the user. Usually, this step is performed over an SSL/TLS connection so that the information is encrypted and kept confidential. The credentials are then used as a lookup in the SQL database. For example, the following statement returns zero if a user whose identity is *Mike* and password is **7Y!2kJ* is not found in the *user* table:

```
select count(*) from user where id='Mike' and pwd='*7Y!2kJ'
```

Once the user has been authenticated, the server creates a special *session key* unique to that session; it then adds the session key to the query string used by the browser on all subsequent requests so that the user does not need to be reauthenticated.

TAKE CARE WHEN PROCESSING STRONG PASSWORDS WITH SQL

Be careful when processing usernames and passwords. Well-chosen passwords will likely include either quotation marks or single quotes. (Refer to Appendix B for more information on well-chosen passwords.) However, processing such passwords by using SQL in, say, Visual Basic or ASP code might cause an error. For example, say that the password is *1Auckland'* and you use the following to build the SQL string:

```
strSQL = "select count(*) from accounts " & _
         "where id = '" & strUser & "' " & _
         "pwd = '" & strPassword & "'"
```

The following string results:

```
select count(*) from accounts
    where id='mike' and pwd='1Auckland''
```

The two single quotes at the end of the string make this is an invalid SQL statement that will fail when SQL Server is asked to process it.

To avoid this problem, use the *Replace* function in the Visual Basic or ASP code to replace all instances of a single quote with two single quotes, thereby creating a valid SQL statement. Another method is to pass the data to a SQL Server stored procedure and use the SQL *REPLACE* function to perform the same task.

Session keys

The session key is often derived from the following items: username, password, random number, and timestamp. The random number is maintained by the server and is usually renewed on a regular basis or at each new session.

> **NOTE** Do not be tempted to use random number functions built into programming languages or programming language libraries, such as *Rnd* in Visual Basic, *rand* in C/C++, and *Math.random* in Microsoft JScript. Most of these use mathematical formulae to derive their numbers. Although seemingly random, the values are predictable because they are derived using mathematical functions. This book's companion CD includes a COM+ object called *CryptUtil.Random* that generates better random numbers by using the Microsoft CryptoAPI (CAPI) tools.

The timestamp reduces the useful lifetime of the key. This means that the key is useless if someone manages to discover the key a few days or, possibly, hours after the session has finished.

To derive a session key, use the following algorithm

```
R ":" T ":" HEX(HASH(R ":" T ":" U ":" P))
```

where

- *R* is a random number, often called a *nonce*.

- ":" is the colon character.

- *T* is a timestamp.

- *HASH* is a hash function, such as MD5 or SHA-1.

- *U* is the user's identification or name.

- *P* is the password.

- *HEX* is a function that converts a binary data stream to a stream made of hexadecimal numbers (0–9 and A–F inclusive). You could also use base64 encoding, which converts a binary data stream to a stream made up of alphanumeric and punctuation characters. The Multipurpose Internet Mail Extensions (MIME) specification, RFC 1341, defines base64 encoding as a way to encode binary information for transmission in e-mail. Note that base64 encoding is not the same as UNIX uuencode encoding.

WHAT ARE HASH FUNCTIONS?

Hash functions, also called *digest functions,* are cryptographic algorithms that produce a different output, called a *message digest,* for each unique data. Identical data has the same message digest, but if even one of the bits of a document changes the message digest changes. Message digests are usually 128 bits or 160 bits in length, depending on the algorithm used. For example MD5, created by RSA Data Security, Inc., creates a 128-bit digest, and SHA-1, developed by the National Institute of Standards and Technology (NIST) and the National Security Agency (NSA), creates a 160-bit digest.

Not only is it impossible to determine the original data by knowing just the digest, it is also infeasible to determine data that will match any given hash. A good analogy is your thumbprint. Your thumbprint uniquely identifies you, but it does not reveal anything about you.

NOTE Once you've determined the session key to send back to the client, there's no need to use SSL/TLS. SSL/TLS need only be used when the user enters a username and password or when other sensitive data that should be encrypted is sent from the client to the server or vice versa. The reason is that the session key does not include the user's password.

The random number R must be expressed as cleartext as well as used in the hash if the server is to maintain no state for the user's connection; otherwise, the server won't know how to rederive the hash if it no longer has the nonce. Because the nonce is exposed as cleartext, it's often called a *salt*. Its main purpose is to make sure that two people with the same name and password who log on at the same time don't get the same hash. Because the random number changes for each connection, the hash changes also.

NOTE Another use for salts is to prevent *dictionary attacks,* in which an attacker who has generated and stored hashes for every word in the dictionary manages to access your database file and rapidly compare password hashes rather than calculating hashes on the fly, which is a much slower process. If you add 80 bits of random salt, the attacker needs to pregenerate and store hashes for every word in the dictionary for each value of the random salt. For a 90,000 word dictionary, this is 90,000 hashes versus 90,000 x 2 ^ 80 hashes, or 108,803,323,765,317,000,000,000,000,000 hashes. Using a small amount of salt renders a dictionary attack infeasible.

The main purpose of T is to add a useful lifetime to the session key. For example, you might determine that a session is valid for no more than thirty minutes and, after that, a user must reauthenticate. Because the timestamp is in cleartext, the server can check it, and because the timestamp added to the hash, it's difficult to forge. It's usually better to add the timestamp as some form of numeric value rather than as a string representation of the date and time—that way you are not affected by any regional date formats. For example, you could use the following code to get the value of a date and time if you are using VBScript in an ASP page:

```
<%
    Dim dTimeStamp
    dTimeStamp = CDbl(Now)
%>
```

This will encode the current date and time as a double-precision floating-point number. For example, 24-Nov-1999 6:03:46 PM becomes 36488.7526157407, and the latter number is then included in the session key. You can check that the session key has not expired with the following ASP code:

```
<%
    ' Maximum session time is 30 minutes (30 x 60 seconds).
    Dim MAX_SESSION_TIME
    MAX_SESSION_TIME = 30 * 60
    If DateDiff("s", dTimeStamp, Now) > MAX_SESSION_TIME Then
        ' Session is too old.
        ' Redirect to login page.
        Response.Redirect("login.asp")
    Else
        ' Normal processing.
    End If
%>
```

The same code fragments in JScript look like this:

```
<%
    var dt = new Date();
    var dTimeStamp = dt.valueOf();
%>
```

The timestamp in this case is not a double; rather, it's expressed in milliseconds elapsed since January 1, 1970 UTC. For example, 15-Apr-2000, 8:13:38 PM Pacific Daylight Time becomes 955854818666. The following JScript code will verify that the time is within the valid range:

```
<%
    // Maximum session time is 30 minutes.
    //   (30 x 60000 milliseconds).
    var MAX_SESSION_TIME = 30 * 60 * 1000;
    var dtNow = new Date();
    var dNow = dtNow.valueOf();
    if (dNow - dTimeStamp > MAX_SESSION_TIME) {
        // Redirect to logon page.
    } else {
        // All ok.
    }
%>
```

Note that it is assumed that *dTimeStamp* contains the timestamp held in the session key and is parsed out of the query string elsewhere in the server-side ASP code.

So, what does one of these session keys look like? Here's an example of what one might look like using the Visual Basic code defined above:

```
01E28172AAB99182:36488.7526157407:49EC8175911A9FE709EAB6EA
```

You can get the query string by using *Request.QueryString* inside your ASP code and parse out the session key by using a regular expression. In Visual Basic, use the following syntax:

```
Dim strQueryString, regExp
set regExp = New RegExp

strQueryString = Request.QueryString

regExp.Pattern = ":(.*):"
Set colMatches = regExp.Execute(strQueryString)
dTimeStamp = colMatches.item(0)
```

The same expression in JScript looks like this:

```
var regExp = /:(.*):/;
var strQueryString = Request.QueryString;
regExp.exec(strQueryString);
var dTimeStamp = RegExp.$1;
```

Now back to the session itself. The first series of hexadecimal numbers before the first colon is a 128-bit random number. The number before the second colon is the timestamp and the final series of hex digits is the hex-encoded 160-bit result of the SHA-1 hash of the random number, timestamp, username, and password. For an attacker to reconstruct a valid hash, she must know

- The random number maintained by the server
- The timestamp
- The username
- The user's password

This is certainly not a perfect authentication scheme—and it's in no way as good as the authentication schemes in Windows 2000—but it might be good enough for noncritical environments, such as those providing access to subscriptions or real-time stock updates. The scheme's weakness stems from it being subject to replay. In other words, an attacker sniffing the connection between your computer and the server might learn the session key and use it to access the data without needing the password because the session key is used to gain access.

To minimize this risk, reduce the useful lifetime of the session key in your ASP code. For example, if the key is valid for only 15 minutes, an attacker can use the key for at most 15 minutes, after which time he must know the password to get a new session key. However, remember that the key is valid for only 15 minutes for the rightful user also, so try to balance usability and security.

Don't Use IP Addresses
for Authentication Purposes

Why don't we use the IP address of the client in the hash too? That way no one could use the session key unless they also had the client's IP address. The session key algorithm would look like this:

```
R ":" T ":" HEX(HASH(R ":" T ":" U ":" P ":" IP))
```

So why wouldn't this work? The Web server knows the IP address the connection is coming from; it's available in the *Request.ServerVariables ("REMOTE_ADDR")* variable. Think about it for a moment, and then read on!

The client IP address can be transient; it can change between requests. Imagine that your client is located behind a bank of proxy servers. She connects to your site and logs in, and you build a session key that includes the client's IP address. Right? Well, no! The IP address is the IP address of the proxy server. The next connection from the client might not come through the first proxy server; it might come through another proxy server that has a different IP address, and therefore the hash will no longer be valid.

Because forms-based authentication does not use real Windows 2000 accounts, there's no way to flow real operating system identity from the Web server to COM+ and SQL Server. Instead, the data must be sent as arguments to COM+ methods or properties and SQL statements. This can pose a risk if the connections between the computers are open to network sniffing or other forms of interception.

> **NOTE** Microsoft Commerce Server 2000 and Microsoft Site Server Membership and Personalization use forms-based authentication and map the user's identity to one or more groups by using low-level Windows 2000 security functions. They perform this by adding groups to a preset proxy user account token. Group membership information is held in the Membership Lightweight Directory Access Protocol (LDAP) Directory.

Making Basic authentication look like forms-based authentication

You can also use Basic authentication and leverage Windows 2000 user accounts without the Basic authentication dialog box appearing! You can do this in two ways: by using the XMLHTTP object or by using some little-known URL syntax.

The first method involves the Extensible Markup Language (XML) support built into Microsoft Internet Explorer 5.0 and later. This will not work with any other browser. Your code can prompt the user to enter the username (*strUser*) and password (*strPwd*) and then pass the information to the client-side JScript code shown on the next page in Internet Explorer.

```
<script>
    var xmlHTTP = new ActiveXObject("Microsoft.XMLHTTP");
    xmlHTTP.open("get","http://www.exair.com/logon", & _
        false, strUser,strPwd);
    xmlHTTP.send("xmlDoc");
    document.write (xmlHTTP.responseText);
</script>
```

When the user's browser attempts to access *http://www.exair.com/logon*, which is configured to require Basic authentication, the XML object model attempts to handle the authentication phases for the user without Internet Explorer having to display the logon dialog box. Plus, so long as the Basic authentication realm does not change, Internet Explorer will continue to send the correct credentials to the Web server at *www.exair.com* and there'll be no need to use the XML again. You can find out more about this technology by searching for XMLHttpRequest at *http://msdn.microsoft.com/xml*.

The second method involves a little-known, but valid, URL format:

```
http://username:password@webserver
```

This is defined in RFC 1738, "Uniform Resource Locators (URL)," at *ftp://ftp.isi.edu/ in-notes/rfc1738.txt*. The most relevant text, from "3.1. Common Internet Scheme Syntax," reads like so:

> While the syntax for the rest of the URL may vary depending on the particular scheme selected, URL schemes that involve the direct use of an IP-based protocol to a specified host on the Internet use a common syntax for the scheme-specific data:
>
> //<user>:<password>@<host>:<port>/<url-path>
>
> Some or all of the parts "<user>:<password>@", ":<password>", ":<port>", and "/<url-path>" may be excluded. The scheme specific data start with a double slash "//" to indicate that it complies with the common Internet scheme syntax. The different components obey the following rules:
>
> | | |
> |---|---|
> | User | An optional username. Some schemes (e.g., ftp) allow the specification of a username. |
> | Password | An optional password. If present, it follows the username separated from it by a colon. |
>
> The username (and password, if present) is followed by a commercial at-sign "@". Within the user and password field, any ":", "@", or "/" must be encoded.
>
> Note that an empty username or password is different than no username or password; there is no way to specify a password without specifying a username. E.g., <URL:ftp://@host.com/> has an empty username and no password, <URL:ftp://host.com/> has no username, while <URL:ftp:// foo:@host.com/> has a username of "foo" and an empty password.

For example, Cheryl's browser might gather her credentials and then use them to build up the following URL by using client-side JScript:

```
https://cheryl:password@www.exair.com/logon
```

There are limitations on what characters can be used in the URL. For example, DOMAIN\Account syntax will fail because the \ character is invalid. You can alleviate this issue by encoding the \ character as *%2F* in the URL. (*2F* is the hexadecimal value of the \ ASCII character.) If Cheryl wanted to include her domain information in the above syntax, she would have to enter

```
https://EXAIR%2Fcheryl:password@www.exair.com/logon
```

> **NOTE** Note the use of *https* rather than *http* at the start of the URL. Because a valid username and password is provided in the URL, it will be in cleartext as it is sent to the server. Hence, a secure SSL/TLS session must be used to prevent attackers from determining the username and password.

This URL format does not display the username and password in the Web browser's URL field when accessing Web sites. Please also note that this method has been tested in Internet Explorer 5 and Netscape Navigator 4.7, but that there's no guarantee it will work in any other browser.

Cookie-based authentication

Cookie-based authentication is similar in principle to forms-based authentication, but the session key is sent as a cookie rather than in a query string. The biggest barrier to using cookies is the fact that some users disable cookie usage in their browsers, thereby ruling out this form of authentication for those users. Cookie-based authentication is most often used for low-security sites, such as those providing online subscriptions. For example, Dow Jones Interactive (*http://www.djinteractive.com*) uses this authentication, as do many newspaper Web sites.

The server will check whether you have the appropriate cookie set when you access the Web site for the first time. If the cookie is not there, is invalid, or has expired, you'll be directed to enter a username and password on a form. Assuming the username and password are correct, the server-side ASP code will build a new cookie that's stored on the client computer.

ASP can read cookies by using the *Request.Cookies* collection and can create or modify a cookie by using the *Response.Cookies* collection. You can make a cookie expire at a specified date by using the *Expires* property. For example, *Response.Cookies("Subscription").Expires = "September 3, 2001"* will make the cookie related to subscription expire on September 3, 2001; at that time the client will need to pay some more money to continue the subscription. However, this is not a secure mechanism because the expiration date can easily be changed in the cookie. If you want to enforce secure cookie expiration, you should build a field into the cookie that contains a hash of the date and some other data known only to the server.

As with forms-based authentication, identity flows at the application level and not as operating system identity.

DON'T RELY ON THE HTTP REFERER HEADER

The HTTP Referer—yes, the word is misspelled, but the name has stuck!—header is sent by a browser indicating which Web page linked to your page. Some misguided Web sites use this header as a means of authentication.

For example, the authors have seen commercial software that includes a page named post.cgi that takes user input from a form, newad.html, but only if the post came from newad.html. The CGI script, post.cgi, queries the Referer header—if it equals newad.html, the data must have come from newad.html and nothing else, right? No.

The header in question is just that, an HTTP header and nothing more, and it can easily be faked. The following simple Perl script shows how to get around this simple authentication scheme:

```perl
#!/usr/bin/perl
# Perl 'headers'
use HTTP::Request::Common qw(POST GET);
use HTTP::Headers;
use LWP::UserAgent;

# URL to send fake post
$url = 'http://webserver/photoads/cgi-bin/post.cgi';
# build up a new post with 16,000 letter 'A's as the comment
$ua = LWP::UserAgent->new();
$req = POST $url,[ Name => 'Mikey', Comments => 'A' x 16000];

# fill in the referer header
$req->header(Referer => 'photoads/newad.html');

# send the request to the application
$res = $ua->request($req);
```

In short, do not use the Referer header for anything but analysis; it's too easy to spoof to be used for authentication means.

Cryptography required in ASP to perform custom authentication

Custom authentication mechanisms using forms and cookies require cryptography. While all Windows platforms have built-in support for cryptographic functions through the CryptoAPI, little of this is directly available to ASP programmers. CAPI supports key storage and retrieval, encryption, decryption, hashing, certificates, and more.

You can use CAPI from ASP by writing a C++ COM+ component—you could use Visual Basic, but CAPI is very low-level and C++ is a better language for that task—or you can use a prebuilt component such as AspEncrypt from Persits Software.

The following example ASP code uses AspEncrypt and could be used to perform the session key derivation described earlier:

```
<%
    ' Create the Persits COM+ crypto component.
    Set oCM = Server.CreateObject("Persits.CryptoManager")
    Set oContext = oCM.OpenContext("WebAppContainer", True)

    ' Create SHA Hash object.
    Set hHash = oContext.CreateHash

    ' Constants used when creating random numbers.
    Const FORMAT_HEX = 0
    Const FORMAT_BASE64 = 1
    Const FORMAT_ASCII = 2

    ' Initialize random number variable.
    Dim oRnd, iRnd
    Set oRnd = Server.CreateObject("CryptUtil.Random")
    iRnd = oRnd.GenRandom(32,FORMAT_ASCII)
    Set oRnd = Nothing

    dTimeStamp = CDbl(Now)
    strUserName = strUserName ' Taken from form post.
    strPwd = strPwd ' Taken from form post.

    ' Build up the text to be hashed.
    strHashValue = iRnd & ":" & _
        dTimeStamp & ":" & _
        strUserName & ":" & _
        strPwd

    ' Derive the hash and get the hex result.
    hHash.Reset
    hHash.AddText strHashValue
    strHashValue = hHash.Value.Hex

    ' Build up the session key including the
    '  cleartext and the hash.
    strKey = iRnd & ":" & _
        dTimeStamp & ":" & _
        strHashValue
%>
```

Note the use of the *CryptUtil.Random* component—this is a C++ COM+ component written by one of the authors and included with the source code on the companion CD. More information about AspEncrypt can be found at *http://www.persits.com*.

Microsoft Passport

If all of this cryptography makes you a bit dizzy and you realize that you're really in the business of selling goods and services rather than building security infrastructure, you might want to consider using Microsoft Passport. Microsoft Passport is a single-sign-in technology for multiple Web sites. Once a Passport user has logged on to Passport, he can access any other Passport-enabled Web site without being prompted to enter credentials.

Importantly, you can access certain information about the user without prompting the user for it—this does not include credit card information, in which case the user will be asked if it's satisfactory for the data to be accessed. For example, assume you need to know the user's location to customize the user's experience of your site. If the user has already logged on to Passport, either through the Microsoft Passport site at *www.passport.com* or another Passport-enabled site, and then accesses your site, she will not be prompted to enter her Passport information again and you will gain access to her information without having her fill out another annoying form! The information is available to you as a service of Passport.

At the time of this writing, there were over 55 million Passport users worldwide and in excess of 200 Web sites. You can get more information about Microsoft Passport at *http://www.passport.com*.

A WARNING ABOUT CUSTOM AUTHENTICATION AND PASSWORDS

If you're designing your own authentication schemes, you probably don't need to store the user's password in your account database; rather, you could store just the hash of the password. When the user passes his username and password to you, you hash the password and compare it with the hash held in the database. If the two hashes are the same, the user is authentic.

The reason for doing this is simple: if your user account database is compromised, the attacker will not get the passwords. The best she'll get is the hashes, and it's much harder to determine a password knowing only its hash. An attacker cannot log on knowing only the hash.

To make life a little more difficult, you could also store a random salt with each user determined at account inception. Just invoke the *CryptUtil.Random* component, and call the *GenRandom* method. Store this random salt value in the database along with the account information, hash the password and the salt together, and store that in the database. Hence, two users with the same password will have different hashes because of the influence of the salt on the hash.

When a user logs on, you take the username and use that to query for the hash and salt in the database. Hash the user-provided password with the salt held in the database, and if the hashes match you can be confident that the password provided by the user is the correct one.

Here's some pseudocode to perform these steps:

```
StrUser = Request.Form("User")
StrPassword = Request.Form("Pwd")
SELECT SaltedPassword, Salt
    FROM user WHERE UserName = strUser
strSaltedPassword = HASH(StrPassword, Salt)
if strHash == strSaltedPassword then
    // Allow access.
else
    // Access denied.
end if
```

SUMMARY

Authentication and authorization are mandatory processes for any secure Web application, and it's commonplace to use alternate security techniques such as cookies or forms to achieve Web-based solutions. However, you should always leverage the operating system's capabilities wherever possible. Failure to do so can lead to vulnerabilities that might be exploited by attackers.

This chapter discussed some ways you can perform your own authentication and authorization by using cryptographic means. If you decide to develop your own security mechanisms, be sure to protect your COM+ and database servers from attack and seriously consider not storing user's passwords in the database. In a world where privacy issues are becoming daily headline news, it's imperative that you take steps to protect your clients. Not only is the protection of communication between the client and your Web server important, but the data you hold about your clients must also be protected from attack. Privacy and its associated topics are the subject of the next chapter.

## Chapter 9

Practical Privacy, Integrity, Auditing, and Nonrepudiation

In this chapter, we'll discuss privacy, integrity, and auditing from an application design point of view. We'll also touch on some of the technical, design, and legal aspects of nonrepudiation. More specifically, the subjects covered in this chapter include the following:

- Privacy and integrity overview
- Where privacy and integrity issues occur
- Mitigating privacy and integrity threats
- End-to-end security protocols
- The Secure Sockets Layer/Transport Layer Security (SSL/TLS) protocol

■ Protecting persistent data

■ Problems with persistent data privacy and integrity

■ Obfuscating ASP code

■ Securing log files against attack

■ An introduction to nonrepudiation

PRIVACY AND INTEGRITY OVERVIEW

Privacy should be an incredibly important consideration for you; it is for your users. Just about all privacy breaches on the Web are jumped upon by the media to fuel the argument that commerce on the Internet is dangerous and should be avoided. It's an incredibly sensitive subject, and, to complicate matters, it's even difficult to reach a consensus on the definition of privacy! Quite fortunately, adding privacy technologies to your application is simple, and most privacy problems are easy to remedy.

Like privacy, integrity is also of paramount importance: changed or deleted data can lead to wasted time while data is rebuilt or restored from backups or, worse, the integrity attack might go unnoticed and decisions might be made based on incorrect data.

PRIVACY STATEMENTS

It's recommended that your Web site include a privacy statement to let users know what data you collect about them and how you intend to use it. For example, it's common to include a privacy policy link at the bottom of a Web site's home page.

You can get information on privacy policy and privacy statements at the TRUSTe Web site at *www.truste.com* or from the Better Business Bureau at *www.bbbonline.com*. The TRUSTe Web site includes an excellent wizard to help you form the basis of a privacy statement.

Note that a law was passed in April 2000 in the United States requiring all Web sites that ask for certain information about children under age 13 to receive permission from parents to gather the information. The rules are part of the 1998 Children's Online Privacy Protection Act, and there are stiff fines for violators. Refer to *http://www.ftc.gov/bcp/conline/edcams/kidzprivacy* for further details.

Finally, if you offer a privacy statement, it's crucial that you adhere to it!

Ensuring privacy is all about mitigating information disclosure threats (the *I* in the STRIDE model, first described in Chapter 2, "A Process for Building Secure Web Applications"); integrity issues involve tampering with data threats (the *T* in the STRIDE model). We discussed some of the approaches used to mitigate these threats in Chapter 2, including the following for mitigating information disclosure threats:

- Using strong access control mechanisms

- Performing correct file canonicalization

- Limiting specific file operations

- Employing end-to-end encrypted data transfer protocols

- Not storing secrets of any kind in configuration files, unless you're using secure encryption mechanisms

You can use the following methods to mitigate data-tampering threats:

- Using strong access control mechanisms

- Requiring hashes and digital signatures on resources

- Employing end-to-end tamper-resistant data transfer protocols

---

WHAT IS CANONICALIZATION?

Canonicalization is a way to reduce a name to its canonical—meaning, in this case, standard or recognized—form or forms. For example, in Microsoft Windows 2000, a username can appear in one of two forms: user principal name (for example, *cheryl@development.explorationair.com*) or Security Account Manager (SAM) name (for example, *EXAIR\Cheryl*).

Other canonical name variations include those for server names: you can use a Domain Name System (DNS) name (for example, *webserver. explorationair.com*), a NetBIOS name (such as \\webserver), or an IP address (such as 172.0.0.42). In NTFS, a filename can take the long form, such as ThisIsALongFileName.doc, or the FAT 8.3 filename, such as ThisIs~1.doc. If you make decisions based on the name of something, it's important that you use a canonical representation of the name. You can choose which canonical form to use for each type of name, but you must be consistent.

You'll notice that privacy and integrity issues are often deeply intertwined. If an attacker has illicit access to data, he might also be able to modify the data. For example, compare the following access control lists (ACLs) used to protect a file. The first ACL allows every user to have read access:

- Administrators (Full Control)
- System (Full Control)
- Everyone (Read)

The next ACL allows every user to have read and write access to the file:

- Administrators (Full Control)
- System (Full Control)
- Everyone (Read & Write)

The first ACL could lead to an information disclosure threat if other security mechanisms fail—the last access control entry (ACE) in the ACL allows all users to have read access to the resource. The second ACL is much more troublesome; it could yield a data-tampering threat because the last ACE allows all users read and write access to the resource. As you can see, a single ACE can change the vulnerability from a privacy issue to a privacy and integrity issue.

You can mitigate this by replacing the Everyone ACE with a Windows 2000 group ACE and adding trusted users to the new group. If you do this, only users known to you will have access to the resource. The new ACL looks like this:

- Administrators (Full Control)
- System (Full Control)
- WebAuthors (Read & Write)

The moral of the story is to use appropriate ACLs on protected resources.

WHERE PRIVACY AND INTEGRITY ISSUES OCCUR

Figure 9-1 shows a high-level view of an Internet infrastructure and the many points in a Web application at which privacy and integrity threats can arise. We'll look at each of these points in more detail in the following sections.

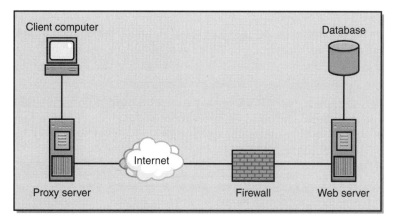

Figure 9-1. *Locations where privacy and integrity issues may arise in a Web application.*

Privacy and Integrity Issues on Client Computers

Privacy and integrity issues at the client are often overlooked. In the case of a Microsoft Windows NT or Windows 2000 desktop used by one person in a secure environment, these issues might not be crucial because a Windows NT or Windows 2000 desktop can be locked if the owner desires, preventing a malicious user from accessing or modifying data. However, if the computer is connected to the Internet, malicious Web sites might attempt to attack the computer. And in many documented cases Web browsers have had privacy-related bugs which could, in theory, have led to an invasion of the user's privacy through the malicious accessing of cookie files and the browsing of history data. Integrity issues are less common, but not improbable.

Privacy threats also exist in a kiosk or shared workstation environment. Rather than the attack coming across a network or modem connection, the attack comes from another user of the shared computer, if that user can access private data cached by software on the computer. Examples of shared computer scenarios include the following:

- Library computers shared by library members

- An engineering workshop's shop floor computer shared by many engineers

- An airport computer allowing users to access their Internet-based e-mail

The first type of threat possible in the client computer scenario is an information disclosure threat, whereby a user sees which Web sites another user visited and possibly the data the user entered and viewed, such as stock trades, usernames, passwords, e-mail, and bank account information. The second threat is a little more insidious. If a user leaves the browser open and has used an authentication scheme while accessing a Web server, the user's credentials might have been cached by the browser. Using the same browser, an attacker could navigate to a Web site visited by the first user. Because the browser has cached the credential information, it might not prompt the attacker to reenter a username and password. The attacker now has access to the previous user's data and could possibly modify the data.

In most circumstances, caching is useful because it provides users with a fast browsing experience and reduces network bandwidth requirements. However, when dealing with sensitive information, it's important to realize that under certain circumstances, caching can be dangerous.

Privacy and Integrity Issues at the Proxy Server

A proxy server is used by companies as a gateway to the Internet. Rather than linking directly to the Internet, users make Internet requests to the proxy server, which in turn accesses the data on the Internet. This has two major benefits:

- The Web site does not know which user made the request; as far it is concerned the request came from the proxy server. This can help maintain privacy because the user's internal IP addresses are not disclosed to Web servers.

- Most proxy servers cache frequently accessed Web pages. This capability increases throughput because cached Web pages are loaded quickly into the browser.

As in the previous section, however, the caching of information is also a source of threats. An attacker who has access to the proxy server also has access to user's data cached by the proxy and thus can view the data and possibly change it.

Proxy servers also log information about users as they browse the Internet. Any user who has access to these logs can determine your browsing habits. This might not seem like a big privacy issue, but it is. Imagine a manager who believes one of her employees is looking for another job ordering the engineer in charge of the proxy servers to provide her with the proxy server logs. Analyzing the logs, the manager can determine whether the employee has been searching career-oriented Web sites.

Privacy and Integrity Issues on the Internet

As information flows between Web clients and Web servers, the data passes through numerous routers, switches, bridges, and other computers. It's possible for an attacker or a malicious administrator to access confidential data or modify data as it passes through these devices. This also applies to e-mail messages. Often, e-mail messages are stored in multiple e-mail servers before arriving at the final destination.

Figure 9-2 outlines where privacy and integrity threats occur as data travels across an insecure network such as the Internet.

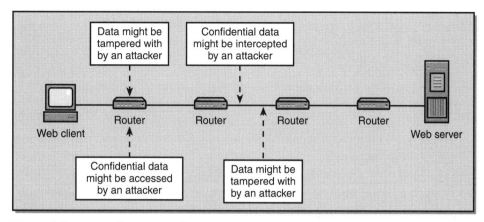

Figure 9-2. *Points of privacy and integrity vulnerability across the Internet.*

A NOTE ON ANONYMOUS ACCESS

Even though your personal identity might not be known to a Web site, much about you, such as the Web pages you visit, is known and stored in logs. Most notably, your IP address is logged by the Web site. Many Web sites do not use the logs' statistics for anything more than tuning the site's performance, tweaking content, and sometimes troubleshooting, but logs do provide long electronic trails of events on a Web site.

Note that if your IP address is that of a proxy server or an address assigned to you by an ISP, the IP address can still be traced back to you. Admittedly, it's not easy to do this and might require a search warrant, but take our word for it, the pieces are easy to put together. If you came through an ISP, the ISP has the date and time you dialed up as well as the timeframe within which you "leased" the IP address from the ISP. If your connection is through a proxy server, the proxy server's IP address will appear in your IP packets, but your real IP address will appear in the proxy server's log. Once again, it's easy to trace back to you.

Special servers called *anonymizing proxies* do provide greater protection for users by hiding their IP addresses; a user connects to the anonymizing proxy and the proxy connects to the requested Web server. However, once again, this is not foolproof because the anonymizing proxy knows your IP address. One popular proxy, by the way, is Anonymizer.com at *www.anonymizer.com*, which also provides anonymous e-mail.

In short, true anonymity is incredibly difficult to achieve on the Web.

Privacy and Integrity Issues at the Firewall

The firewall resides near the Web server and is used to filter network traffic before it reaches the Web server. Normally, a firewall is well configured and secure, but not always! Sometimes administrators can make errors that leave the firewall prone to attack.

Security threats at firewalls include information disclosure and tampering with data—specifically, the firewall's filtering rules. If an attacker accesses these rules, he might be able to determine weaknesses in the network infrastructure. For example, if the attacker determines that certain IP addresses are not filtered by the firewall, possibly because of administrative oversight, he can use these addresses in forged IP packets to attack the network. If the attacker can change the filtering rules, he can leave the network vulnerable to further attack.

Privacy and Integrity Issues at the Web Server

As a Web site designer, you need to keep your Web site application design private and secure from malicious alteration. For example, regarding privacy, if you include confidential data in some Active Server Pages (ASP) pages and an attacker can access the source code to the Web page, she will gain access to the confidential information. It's unfortunate, but many ASP pages include Microsoft SQL Server usernames and passwords in database connection strings, thereby endangering the database if an attacker gains access to the ASP page.

> **IMPORTANT**   As a Web application developer, you should not put private information such as a query string in any URL, even if you are sending the data when using SSL/TLS. It's possible that such data will be logged by the Web server. If the logs are compromised, an attacker will have access to confidential data.

Regarding integrity threats, obviously you don't want attackers manipulating your Web site's home page to include whatever messages the attacker wants to leave. Defacing home pages is a common pastime amongst *script-kiddies*. Script-kiddies are attackers with some technical skill who use scripts downloaded from the Internet to search for and attack vulnerable computers. Most commonly, vulnerable computers are computers that have not been updated to remedy a security problem.

Privacy and Integrity Issues at the Database

Privacy and integrity issues abound at the database, simply because all the information about the Web site resides here. For example, in the case of our Exploration Air example, when users make airline bookings, the flight and customer information resides in the database. If the database were compromised, the attacker could gain access to other users' information, such as address and credit card information, or to the airline's Web-based sales information. Alternatively, an attacker could tamper with client information, changing credit card information, addresses, and so on. It's imperative that the database be protected from information disclosure and integrity attacks.

THE CD UNIVERSE ATTACK

In late 1999, CD Universe (*www.cduniverse.com*) had a major privacy breach of their customer database because of a vulnerability in the company's payment-processing software. The attacker managed to get a list of thousands of CD Universe clients, the clients' addresses, and, most importantly, their credit card information.

One of the authors of this book had bought merchandise from CD Universe and was notified of the attack quickly by the vendor. The company also went one step further and notified the credit card–issuing banks, which then contacted their clients to offer replacement cards. The breach was a serious inconvenience for CD Universe customers because thousands of credit cards had to be canceled and reissued.

MITIGATING PRIVACY AND INTEGRITY THREATS

Having described some points of vulnerability in a Web application, now we'll take a look at technologies that can be used to mitigate the threats. As you might have noticed, two major categories of issues exist:

- Threats to the privacy and integrity of data that travels to and from the client (that is, the end-to-end scenario)

- Threats to the privacy and integrity of persistent data, or protection of data when held in persistent storage, such as on disk or in databases

The following sections discuss countermeasures to these threats.

End-to-End Security Protocols

In the end-to-end scenario, data must be secured as it flows from the client to the server and back. Using an end-to-end security protocol can mitigate privacy risks because the data is encrypted while it passes through intermediate servers and routers. Integrity risks are mitigated by using cryptographic hash functions that detect changes in the data. Usually, data traveling between the client and server is secured because a secure channel is negotiated at communication start and data then flows across the secured channel. Sometimes, the encryption key used to encrypt the channel is renegotiated at regular intervals to provide extra security.

End-to-end protocols are common on the Internet today. Example protocols include the following: SSL/TLS, IP Security (IPSec), PPTP, and L2TP. PPTP and L2TP are used for virtual private network (VPN) scenarios and are beyond the scope of this book. IPSec is a secure implementation of the IP protocol that supports authentication, privacy, and integrity. However, the most common protocol by far is SSL/TLS, which is our next subject.

The Secure Sockets Layer/Transport Layer Security protocol

SSL—also referred to by its name ratified by the Internet Engineering Task Force (IETF), TLS—is a security protocol providing authentication and protection against eavesdropping (privacy) and data tampering (integrity). Authentication is provided by X.509 certificates and proof of possession of the associated private key. Privacy is provided through data encryption. Integrity is provided by hash functions and Message Authentication Codes (MACs).

The main threats that SSL/TLS helps alleviate are

- Identity spoofing (by providing strong authentication)
- Information disclosure (by encrypting the communication channel)
- Data tampering (by providing message integrity codes)

How SSL/TLS works

A number of steps occur when an SSL/TLS session is established between the client and server. Figure 9-3 shows the main high-level negotiation stages. The figure's purpose is not to show every byte of each phase of the protocol; rather, it's to help you gain an understanding of why the stages occur. The figure assumes that the Web server is not configured to request a client authentication certificate.

For SSL/TLS to work, the Web server requires a certificate and private key. A core premise of SSL/TLS is that a certificate owner must prove that it owns the private key associated with the certificate. In other words, the authentication credential is the private key used in conjunction with the certificate. Having a certificate and private key allows the client to verify that the server is the server it claims to be. Once this trust is established, the two parties can agree on a key to use for encrypting data. This is an incredibly important step because you need to be sure of the identity of the server before you can have a private communication!

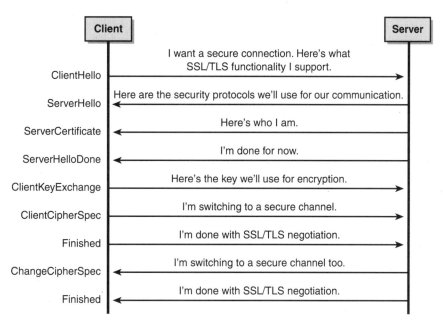

Figure 9-3. *High-level view of the SSL/TLS handshake process.*

The difference between SSL and TLS

SSL was invented by Netscape and became a de facto standard because the browsers and Web servers made by both Microsoft and Netscape included the technology, which lowered the entry barrier for Web sites and users alike. As e-commerce became widespread in the mid-to-late 1990s, the need for a secure means of transferring user and credit card information across the Web became paramount. E-commerce acted as the main catalyst of SSL's popularity. Two main versions of SSL exist: version 2 and version 3. SSL version 3 is much preferred over SSL version 2 because it fixes many more security weaknesses. The technical differences between the versions are beyond the scope of this book.

In 1996, the IETF decided to standardize the SSL protocol and in doing so renamed it Transport Layer Security. The current version is TLS version 1. Internally, the version number is 3.1 because TLS is a minor enhancement of the SSL protocol. Effectively, TLS is SSL 3.1. TLS is now an IETF standard, RFC 2246.

SSL/TLS port numbers

The standard port for HTTP traffic over SSL/TLS, otherwise known as HTTPS, is 443. However, SSL/TLS is not restricted to protecting HTTP data; SSL/TLS can be used to protect other Internet protocols. Some standard Internet protocols and their port numbers when using SSL/TLS include those shown in Table 9-1.

Protocol	Port	Description
HTTPS	443	HTTP over SSL/TLS
SMTPS	465	SMTP (e-mail) over SSL/TLS
NNTPS	563	NNTP (news) over SSL/TLS
LDAPS	636	LDAP (directory access) over SSL/TLS
POP3S	995	POP (e-mail) over SSL/TLS
IRCS	994	IRC (chat) over SSL/TLS
IMAPS	993	IMAP (e-mail) over SSL/TLS
FTPS	990	FTP (file transfer) over SSL/TLS

Table 9-1. *Common SSL/TLS-enabled protocols.*

Web browsers know to use port 443 rather than port 80 when you type *https://www.exair.com* rather than *http://www.exair.com* and will attempt to set up an SSL/TLS session with the server; the connection will fail if the server is not configured to use SSL/TLS.

> **NOTE** It's worthwhile to add a small lock icon to your secured Web pages, just in case the lock symbol in the browser is not visible. You might also want to include a comment explaining how your users can confirm the security of the Web page in their browser. If they're using Microsoft Internet Explorer, they can right-click the page and select Properties from the context menu. If they're using Netscape Navigator, they can click the lock icon in the status bar.

SSL/TLS performance

Owing to the cryptography required by SSL/TLS, the protocol can significantly degrade performance on your Web application. Table 9-2 gives you an idea of the performance characteristics of the various protocols. The test machine was a one-processor Pentium III Xeon running at 450 MHz. The requests/second figure is for new connections; once the connection is established, the throughput increases dramatically.

It might surprise you to learn that the implementation of SSL/TLS in Windows 2000 is slightly faster if the key size is 128-bit, rather than 40-bit or 56-bit, because of the way SSL/TLS implements keys. All keys are 128-bit; however, in situations where the key must be less that 128-bit, say 56-bit, the key is split into a 56-bit key and a 72-bit salt. Keeping track of this takes time; it's quicker to use a 128-bit key with no salt. The number of connections per second drops off dramatically if you increase the exchange key size from 512-bit to 1024-bit. Expect to see about a five times decrease. RSA is extremely slow in software, and as the key size grows the performance of RSA degrades rapidly.

Protocol	Cipher	Hash	Key Exchange	Requests/Second
PCT	40-bit RC4	MD5	512-bit RSA	108
SSL2	40-bit RC4	MD5	512-bit RSA	77
SSL3	56-bit RC4	SHA-1	512-bit RSA	83
TLS	56-bit RC4	SHA-1	512-bit RSA	90

Table 9-2. *Relative PCT, SSL2, SSL3, and TLS performance.*

With all this in mind, you should use SSL/TLS only where it is needed. The next section introduces some ways to reduce the impact of using SSL/TLS on your Web site.

SSL/TLS best practices

The problem with SSL/TLS is the performance overhead required when establishing new connections. A new connection consumes a great deal of CPU time because of the complex cryptographic public key operations required. Once the connection is established, however, encryption overhead is much smaller. To increase the speed of your Web site running SSL/TLS, follow these simple rules:

1. Keep the SSL/TLS portion of your Web site to a minimum.

   As already noted, you probably don't want to require SSL/TLS on all parts of your Web site, because most pages hold nonprivate information, such as marketing, sales, and technical documents that anyone can view. Use SSL/TLS only if you're sending confidential or sensitive data to your users—all other parts of your Web site should not require a secured connection. Details about enabling SSL/TLS on certain parts of the Web site are discussed in Chapter 5, "Internet Information Services Security Overview."

2. Keep the SSL/TLS pages simple.

   All content on pages requiring SSL/TLS, no matter the pages' size, must be encrypted, including images. Therefore, you should keep the number of images on secured pages to a minimum and keep the pages themselves simple. If you must use images, try to keep them small by using high JPEG compression and keeping the color depth low—don't use a 16 million–color palette for an image that requires only 256 colors.

   Some Web developers make the mistake of putting images in a directory that does not require SSL/TLS and referencing them from the pages requiring SSL/TLS. This sometimes causes browser warnings because the browser sees a combination of secure and insecure data. It's recommended that you don't do this—it's likely to confuse your users.

3. Reuse cached SSL/TLS connections.

Establishing a new SSL/TLS connection takes approximately five times as long as reconnecting using a cached SSL/TLS connection. The default time-out for such a connection is five minutes, raised from two minutes in Windows NT 4. You can extend the cache lifetime by setting the *ServerCacheTime* Registry subkey, as shown next. The value is measured in milliseconds—for example, 300,000 is five minutes.

HKEY_LOCAL_MACHINE
  \System
    \CurrentControlSet
     \Control
      \SecurityProviders
       \SCHANNEL
        ServerCacheTimeout: REG_DWORD : 300000

Consider the setting you choose carefully: if you make the time-out too long, the system might start consuming memory while it caches stale SSL/TLS connections.

4. Use cryptographic hardware accelerators.

Compared to many other Web servers, Internet Information Services (IIS) is extremely fast at handling new SSL/TLS connections. For example, on a 500-MHz Pentium III–class computer, IIS 5 can handle over 60 new SSL/TLS connections per second. Although this might not seem high, it compares extremely well with another Web server that performs approximately 10 SSL/TLS connections per second on similar hardware. However, IIS is capable of exceeding 1000 anonymous, non-SSL/TLS connections per second. To increase Web server throughput, you can use special hardware accelerators from companies such as nCipher (*www.ncipher.com*) or Compaq (*www.atalla.com*). These devices offload the complex and slow public key operations and perform the work in custom-made hardware. Depending on the hardware used, you might not see an increase in the number of SSL/TLS connections per second, but you'll always see a drop in CPU time when establishing new connections.

NOTE   If you're a cryptographic hardware vendor, Microsoft has provided a simple way to offload some of the most CPU-intensive work, modular exponentiation, to your hardware: the *OffloadModExpo* function. You can provide a dynamic-link library (DLL) that exports this function and passes the work to your hardware. For more information, refer to the *OffloadModExpo* function in Microsoft Developer Network (MSDN).

SSL/TLS and client access licenses

In IIS 5, each concurrent, unique authenticated connection and each unique SSL/TLS connection consumes a client access license (CAL). By default, the number of CALs is the same as the number of Windows server CALs. For example, if your Windows 2000 server has 250 server CALs, your Web site can accept any number of anonymous connections up to 250 SSL/TLS connections and 250 authenticated connections.

> **NOTE** Actually, it's a little more complex than this. One CAL enables four concurrent connections from one machine to accommodate framesets.

An unlimited Internet license is also available, which allows any number of simultaneous SSL/TLS and authentication connections for a Web server on the Internet. Refer to Knowledge Base article Q253239 at *http://support.microsoft.com/support/kb/articles/ Q253/2/39.asp* for further details about IIS 5 and CALs, and refer to "Windows 2000 Client Access Licensing Overview" at *http://www.microsoft.com/windows2000/guide/ server/pricing/model.asp* for more information regarding client access licenses.

A little-known fact about SSL/TLS in Windows

The following information technically doesn't relate to privacy or integrity; it concerns using SSL/TLS for authentication. SSL/TLS can support wildcards in the common name of the server certificate. For example, when you connect to *www.explorationair.com*, the common name in the certificate will read *www.explorationair.com* also. It's possible to use a wildcard certificate that applies to multiple Web sites maintained, in this example, by Exploration Air. For example, *development.explorationair.com* is in the explorationair.com domain. The common name in the certificate could read **.explorationair.com*, and the certificate might be used at *www.explorationair.com*, *development.explorationair.com*, and various other Web sites under the explorationair.com domain.

However, by default, this functionality is disabled in Windows 2000 and requires an updated system DLL. You can get information about the update from Knowledge Base article Q257873, "Error Message: The Name on the Security Certificate Does Not Match the Name of the Site," at *http://support.microsoft.com*.

Note the following restrictions on how wildcards work in certificates:

■ Wildcards must be situated in the leftmost part of the DNS name. For example, **.explorationair.com* is valid; *development.*.explorationair.com* is invalid.

■ Wildcards cannot be applied to high-level DNS components such as .com or .net. For example, **.explorationair.com* is valid, and **.com* is invalid.

■ The number of components in the DNS names must be the same. For example, **.explorationair.com* will support *www.explorationair.com* and *development.explorationair.com*—both of which consist of three name components—but not *www.development.explorationair.com*.

Figure 9-4 shows the certificate details when the default Web page on *https:// webserver.explorationair.com* is being accessed. The screen shot was taken while the site was being developed and has no content other than the default page warning the site administrator that the site contains no content. Note how the name in the certificate is **.explorationair.com*, because this is a valid way of representing *webserver.explorationair.com*.

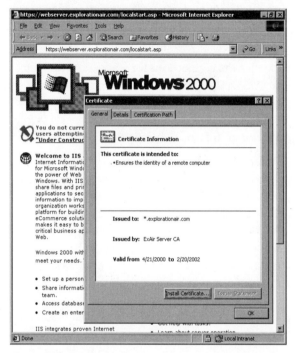

Figure 9-4. *Using a wildcard server certificate in IIS 5.*

IP Security

IPSec is a secure version of IP, hence the name. We've already covered the basics of IPSec in Chapter 3, "Windows 2000 Security Overview." IPSec provides privacy through encryption of the data channel between the two computers and provides integrity checking by using cryptographic hash functions.

Although SSL/TLS and IPSec might appear to solve similar problems, they have numerous differences, as described in the next section, that will determine which protocol you should use for securing your servers and your users.

When to use SSL/TLS and when to use IPSec

The decision to use SSL/TLS or IPSec is partly based on the protocol differences. The big variations between SSL/TLS and IPSec are as follows:

- IPSec secures all IP traffic between computers. SSL/TLS secures only specific protocol traffic, such as HTTP or LDAP.

- You have no choice over what is protected when using IPSec—everything is protected. With SSL/TLS, you can secure just the parts of your application that require security, such as logon Web pages or credit card entry information. This means that, overall, SSL/TLS is less CPU-intensive than IPSec.

- Software using SSL/TLS must have built-in support for the protocol. IPSec is transparent to applications.

- Because IPSec is transparent to applications and SSL/TLS is not, and because SSL/TLS requires applications to have innate knowledge of the protocol, IPSec can be used to secure otherwise insecure protocols such as FTP and Telnet.

- SSL/TLS relies solely on X.509 certificates for authentication. IPSec uses X.509 certificates, Kerberos, or shared secrets (passwords) for authentication.

- IPSec does not authenticate users; it authenticates computers. SSL/TLS can authenticate users by using client authentication certificates.

- SSL/TLS is built into most Web browsers and most Web servers, making it easy to deploy. IPSec is not built into many operating systems.

- Because of the point raised in the previous bullet, SSL/TLS is well deployed on the Internet. IPSec is relatively new.

Figure 9-5 shows the location of SSL/TLS and IPSec in the TCP/IP protocol stack.

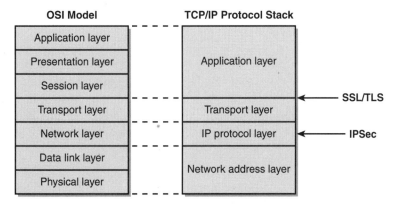

Figure 9-5. *SSL/TLS and IPSec in the TCP/IP protocol stack.*

If you configure your public Web site to require IPSec authentication, privacy, and integrity, chances are good that few users will be able to connect because IPSec is not a common protocol on the Internet at the time of writing. However, there's no doubt this will change over time. If you want to protect sensitive data in transit to and from your Web site, you will need to use SSL/TLS.

If you have a campuswide intranet solution or any environment in which you have control over the client configuration, IPSec is a viable protocol. Indeed, it's probably a good idea to use IPSec because as the population of your user base grows, the population of possible attackers increases also. IPSec mitigates the privacy and disclosure risks by encrypting all data between hosts, including operating system logon data, directory updates, and application traffic.

If you have a business-to-business extranet or a virtual private network (VPN), you should consider using IPSec because all data is protected. SSL/TLS is not designed to work in such an environment; it's designed to protect specific protocols. You can choose between IPSec transport mode between computers—that is, complete end-to-end security at the cost of more complex administration—or L2TP/IPSec tunnels between VPN gateway servers—that is, full security over the Internet and a less complex configuration, at the cost of traffic being exposed on the internal networks at either end of the tunnel. Also, vendors have achieved the greatest interoperability so far in their L2TP/IPSec implementations.

Note that if you have IPSec configured for privacy, you might not need to use SSL/TLS on the Web server unless you use client authentication certificates to require the client to authenticate himself or herself.

A Web server can use both IPSec and SSL/TLS protocols if the server computer has multiple network cards. For example, the Internet-facing network card in a Web server could use SSL/TLS for sensitive Web traffic, and the inner network card could use IPSec to communicate with a server that has a SQL Server database installed. The database server is also configured to use IPSec. In this configuration, only the Web server can communicate with SQL Server.

Figure 9-6 shows a similar scenario, but in this case the scenario includes a management computer also using IPSec. The Web server has three network cards: one listening to unencrypted and SSL/TLS traffic from the Internet, one for management communication, and one for bidirectional communication with the database server. The last two network cards are configured to use IPSec and to communicate with only the management server or the database server.

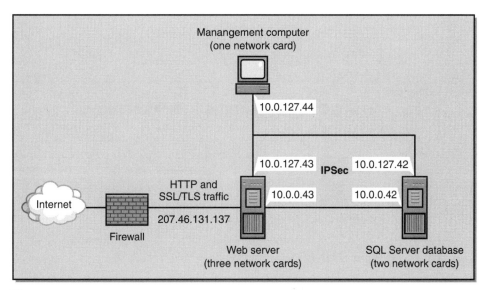

Figure 9-6. *A configuration that uses SSL/TLS and IPSec. IPSec is used for authentication and, optionally, privacy between the Web server, management server, and database server.*

An issue SSL/TLS and IPSec do not resolve

Getting data securely from the client to the server and vice versa is only half the challenge. What happens to data once it arrives at the server? Some of the data is short-lived and might not be stored on disk. Other data, however, such as credit card, address, and password information, is often stored in databases, where information disclosure and data-tampering threats cannot be ignored. Although SSL/TLS and IPSec do a good job of securing information as it travels from the client to the server and back, they do not secure the data once it is persisted to a database at the Web site.

THE SET PROTOCOL

One protocol, Secure Electronics Transactions (SET), designed by VISA and MasterCard, addresses the issue of storing credit card information. Simply put, when this protocol is used, the Web server never learns the credit card details; only the bank involved knows the credit card information. However, SET has not become a popular protocol because it's difficult to implement and it's extremely CPU-intensive.

You can get more information on the SET protocol at *http://www.setco.org*.

It's imperative that sensitive data be stored securely because of these threats to data stored in databases; data might be disclosed or modified if the database is compromised. Protecting persistent data from attack is our next subject.

VALID CREDIT CARD NUMBERS FOR TESTING

When testing your Web application, don't use real credit card numbers! Use the following credit card numbers to test your application's credit card privacy; these credit card numbers validate correctly but are not in circulation.

American Express: 3111-1111-1111-1117

Discover: 6111-1111-1111-1116

MasterCard: 5111-1111-1111-1118

Visa: 4111-1111-1111-1111

Persistent Data Protection

The persistent data case relates to static data often stored in databases or files. Examples of this include a Web site storing credit card information in its SQL Server database and password information in a browser cache. Storing confidential data in a browser cache or storing user accounts and cleartext passwords in databases is commonplace in many Web applications, and, as we've said repeatedly, doing so creates a huge security vulnerability. One more time: if the Web browser is accessed by another user or if the Web server or database server is compromised, your users' information might be disclosed or modified.

Let's look at both situations: client persistent data security and server persistent data security.

Securing client persistent data

The biggest issue facing Web browsers is caching. Caching is the process whereby a Web browser will store a previously received document, such as an HTML page or JPEG image, with the aim of reusing that document to increase efficiency. In most circumstances, caching is useful and is widely used to provide users with a fast browsing experience. However, when dealing with sensitive information, it's important to realize that under certain circumstances caching is not desirable. For example, if a Web application accepts credit card details and then presents a screen confirming those credit card details back to the user, the browser might cache that document. The cached document is then stored on the hard disk, potentially providing a malicious user with a local file containing the credit card details. For this reason, you need to consider the desirability of caching when working with sensitive data.

The factors determining the desirability of caching are

- The security of the computers upon which the browsers will be installed

- The type of users browsing on a shared computer

- The sensitivity of the information presented by the Web pages with regard to the environment in which the computer is used

If the browser is on a secure computer in a secure environment where only trusted individuals have access to the computer, caching might be acceptable—for example, on a bank computer that employs appropriate security techniques and that can be operated by trusted bank employees only. For a computer in an insecure environment where nontrusted individuals have access, avoid caching. For example, if a Web site is accessible to users at PCs in cybercafes or kiosks, caching confidential or personal information is undesirable.

The following three sections describe techniques for securing sensitive client information; we've presented the techniques in order of decreasing effectiveness.

Avoid sending pages that display sensitive information

The best possible way of preventing documents that contain sensitive information from being cached is to not send such documents to the user. Rather than sending complete credit card details to the user, just send the last four digits, the name on the card, and the expiration date. Also, any errors generated when filling in an HTML form should not result in sensitive information being echoed back to the user in the error response. For instance, suppose a form gathers details regarding a credit card the user holds. If a validation check fails because the card number was not correctly formatted, the correctly entered details should not be sent back to the user along with the error message highlighting the incorrect credit card number. Only point out the error.

There are two possible drawbacks to this solution:

- **Reduced ease of use**   It is possible that the design and usability of some online forms will be less polished if sensitive information cannot be echoed back to the user. Address this issue by spending some more time on user interface design and by informing users of the benefits of this security approach.

- **Increased application logic complexity**   When designing a form that does not echo back all user details, it is sometimes necessary to provide logic through which the application can remember all the information. This is technically feasible, but it adds extra complexity to the application.

The technique of avoiding sending sensitive information to the user's browser should be used as widely as possible to help ensure that secure information is never cached.

Prevent sensitive data caching

To prevent a document received by a browser from being written to the cache, make sure the page contains the appropriate HTML tags. Unfortunately, only HTTP 1.1 supports a directive to instruct a browser not to cache a file. HTTP 1.0 provides no support for instructing a browser not cache a file. In response to this issue, some browsers based upon the HTTP 1.0 standard implement various nonstandard techniques to instruct the browser not to cache pages. Because Internet Explorer 5 supports HTTP 1.1, it can be instructed not to cache data. Internet Explorer 4 supports a technique utilizing HTTP 1.0 commands over an SSL/TLS connection to instruct the browser not to cache documents.

Techniques to prevent caching are covered in the section "Anticaching techniques," which appears below.

Avoid displaying previously cached data

If a browser has previously cached some information, perhaps because it did not respect or understand a caching directive, it's important to ensure that the information is not revealed to users of the browser, who may or may not be the user who requested the sensitive information. Both HTTP 1.0 and HTTP 1.1 support techniques for informing a browser of the appropriate time in which to keep a cached item before considering it to be expired or stale. When a user requests a cached page that is considered expired, the browser will contact the server to request the document rather than display the cached version.

You can reduce the chance of cached information being displayed by ensuring that all documents are marked as "expiring immediately." Documents marked as expiring immediately will not be displayed by a browser that respects the expiration information, but the documents might be held in the local hard disk's cache for a short period. During this time, the files are still vulnerable to attack. For this reason, this technique is the least desirable anticaching technique.

> **NOTE**   Internet Explorer 5 does not refresh pages when the Forward and Back buttons are used. Pages are always pulled from the cache. The behavior of Forward and Back was changed to conform with the HTTP 1.1 specification.

Techniques for marking documents as expired are discussed in the next section.

Anticaching techniques

To ensure minimal caching of sensitive information, use the following techniques on pages that display sensitive information:

■ **Use SSL/TLS.**   Ensure that all documents and images that include sensitive information are delivered using the SSL/TLS protocol. This will prevent proxy servers and firewalls from caching the data. By default, Internet Explorer 4 and Internet Explorer 5 will not cache pages accessed when SSL/TLS is used.

■ **Set caching directives.**   Add the following lines of code to the top of all ASP pages dealing with sensitive information:

```
<%
     Response.AddHeader "Pragma", "no-cache"
     Response.Expires = -1
     Response.Cache-Control = "no-store"
%>
```

Table 9-3 details the effects of the directives in the preceding code.

Cache Header	*Comments*
Pragma:no-cache	Instructs HTTP 1.0 proxy servers to not cache the Web page. Internet Explorer will not cache a Web page accessed using SSL/TLS when this header is in effect.
Response.Expires	Instructs browsers that do cache pages to request a new page from the Web server rather than use a cached copy.
Cache-Control:no-store	Instructs Internet Explorer 5 not to cache the Web page, even when using the Back and Forward buttons. This option instructs HTTP 1.1 proxy servers to not cache the Web page.

Table 9-3. *HTTP headers that prevent browser caching.*

NOTE   It's recommended that you do not use Cache-Control:private, because this directive specifies that information can be cached on a per-user basis. Including this directive might override the no-cache directive.

Internet Explorer and AutoComplete

Internet Explorer 5 provides a feature called AutoComplete that saves users from repeatedly typing frequently requested details into HTML forms. The AutoComplete feature saves previous entries you've made for Web addresses, forms, and passwords. Later, when you type information in one of these fields, AutoComplete suggests possible matches. However, if a user accesses a Web site, enters a password, and opts to save the password by using AutoComplete, another user using the same machine and same user identity could navigate to the same Web site and the password might be automatically filled in by the browser.

You can disable this capability by performing these steps:

1. Open Internet Explorer.

2. Choose Internet Options from the Tools menu to display the Internet Options dialog box.

3. Click the Content tab.

4. Click the AutoComplete button.

5. Disable the options you don't want to support.

6. Click OK, and then click OK again.

Figure 9-7 shows the AutoComplete Settings dialog box.

Figure 9-7. *Configuring AutoComplete settings in Internet Explorer 5.*

As a Web site developer, you can force sensitive form fields or an entire form to disregard AutoComplete by setting the *AUTOCOMPLETE* attribute to *Off*. The following HTML code shows the attribute:

```
<FORM method=POST action="submit.asp" AUTOCOMPLETE="OFF">
```

Disable AutoComplete on per-field basis like so:

```
<input type="text" name="txtCreditCard" value=""
 size="16" maxlength="16" AUTOCOMPLETE="OFF">
```

Privacy issues with Basic and Digest authentication

When a user first connects to a Web server that requires Basic or Digest authentication, the user is presented with a dialog box in which to enter credentials. From that point on, the Web browser automatically sends the appropriate credentials to the Web server so that the user does not have to reenter them. The security threat is simple: as long as the browser is not shut down, it will continue to send the user's credentials to the Web server. Hence, a malicious user could navigate to the Web site and use the first user's credentials without entering them!

The best way to counter this threat is to close the browser, but you can offer another solution to this in Internet Explorer by creating a COM+ control that contains code like the following and calling it from client-side Microsoft Visual Basic, Scripting Edition (VBScript) or JScript:

```
STDMETHODIMP CInternetStuff::EndSession() {
    HRESULT hr = S_OK;
    DWORD   dwError = 0;

    // End the session.
    if (!InternetSetOption(NULL,
        INTERNET_OPTION_END_BROWSER_SESSION, NULL, 0)) {
        dwError=::GetLastError();
        hr=HRESULT_FROM_WIN32(dwError);
    }
    return (hr);
}
```

Refer to Knowledge Base article Q195192, "HOWTO: Clear Logon Credentials to Force Reauthentication," for further details on this functionality.

Now let's turn our attention to the other side of the Web connection, the server.

Securing server persistent data

Because they hold so much juicy data, your Web and database servers must be protected from privacy and integrity attacks. Data held in files or in the Registry on the server must be secured using appropriate ACLs. For extremely sensitive data, you should consider the Encrypting File System (EFS). With EFS, only an entity that holds a decryption key can decrypt the encrypted files, and the chances are slim that an attacker will have such a key. For example, SQL Server accesses its database files as the identity used to start SQL Server, not as the calling user. If you use EFS to encrypt database files, you must do so as the identity used to start SQL Server. From then on, only SQL Server can access the data files—every other attempt to access the database files by an attacker will fail unless the attacker can log on as the account used to start SQL Server.

Storing passwords at the server

It is the authors' contention that end users want a high degree of privacy and security as they browse the Web and purchase services and items. To that end, some users employ a startling array of passwords and user accounts to access personalized areas of their favorite Web sites. Unfortunately, many people forget their passwords and as a result use only one password for multiple Web sites, which is definitely a problem. If a Web site is successfully attacked and the user's password is disclosed, chances are good that the password can be used elsewhere on secure Web sites frequented by the user. Another serious problem is the case of a rogue Web site administrator. If he can access a user's password, he might attempt to access other Web resources by using the user's credentials.

You should counter these particular threats by storing a hash of the password rather than the cleartext password at the server. When a user connects and enters her password, your application can derive the hash of the password and compare the hashes. If the site is compromised, the attacker will get the hashes, not the passwords, and it's infeasible to determine a password knowing only the hash. We covered the concepts of storing hashes and salting hashes in Chapter 8, "Practical Authentication and Authorization."

This solution creates a usability issue, however. As we've already mentioned, users forget their passwords. To remedy this, many Web sites store the password and a *password hint* question. Either you click a button on the Web site to get your password e-mailed to you or you ask the Web site to give you the password hint. Hopefully, the hint is good enough for you to remember your password. For example, if your password is "S1riu$" and your hint is "a canine star," will you think of stars in the constellation Canis Major rather than Lassie, the canine film star? Password hinting isn't such a bad idea, so long as the cleartext version of the password is not maintained by the server. (It's also dangerous to send cleartext passwords in e-mail to the user. The e-mail could easily be read as it travels from the Web site to the user.) Also, make sure to avoid obvious hints—never use a hint like "capital city of England."

While we're on the subject of hints, please do not ask for the maiden name of a user's mother. This is virtually public information and of little security benefit.

> **NOTE** A cursory query by the authors for the exact phrase "password hint" in a popular search engine found over 42,000 Web sites that support a password-hinting feature.

A solution to storing cleartext passwords

Just say no to maintaining cleartext passwords unless you absolutely need to keep the passwords for alternate authentication purposes other than the initial logon to the Web site. If you must store cleartext passwords, offer your clients a service: sending their passwords to them in secure, encrypted e-mail, by using Secure/Multipurpose Internet Mail Extensions (S/MIME). For you to be able to do this, the client must have a client authentication certificate or an e-mail certificate, which can be obtained from many certification authorities, such as VeriSign (*www.verisign.com*) or Thawte Consulting (*www.thawte.com*).

The process works like this:

1. When the user signs up to use the service provided by your Web site, you can offer the option to provide secure password notification in the event the user forgets the password. This could also be an option on the user's account maintenance pages.

2. Selecting this option links the user to a page explaining that you require a client authentication certificate from the user. The certificate will be stored by the Web site in a secure database. However, there's nothing to fear because a certificate is public information. The user is then given the option of continuing or returning to the original page.

3. If the user chooses to continue, the link goes to a virtual directory that requires a client authentication certificate issued by one or more certificate authorities (CAs) you trust.

4. The user's browser prompts the user to select a client authentication certificate.

5. When the user selects the certificate and the rest of the SSL/TLS negotiation completes, the ASP page will have access to the client's certificate through the *Request.ClientCertificate("Certificate")* information.

6. The ASP page writes the client authentication certificate into the database alongside the user's information.

When the user notifies the Web site that she has lost her password, the following process occurs:

1. The user's password and client authentication certificate are retrieved from the database.

2. Using COM+ components such as AspEncrypt and AspEmail from Persits Software (*www.persits.com*), you construct a S/MIME message addressed to the e-mail name in the user's certificate and encrypted using the public key in the user's certificate. Because the user receiving the e-mail is the only person with the associated private key, only that user can decrypt the message.

The following sample ASP code will build an S/MIME response containing the user's password. It's assumed that the password and client certificate have already been retrieved from the database.

```
<%
    ' strPassword and blobCert
    '   already taken from the database.

    ' Instantiate various COM+ components.
    Set oMail = Server.CreateObject("Persits.MailSender")
    Set oCM = Server.CreateObject("Persits.CryptoManager")
    Set oContext = CM.OpenContext("emailcontainer", True )

    ' Extract e-mail name from the certificate.
```

(continued)

```
    Set certClient = oCM.ImportCertFromBlob(blobCert)
    strEmail = certClient.Subject("E")

    If strEmail <> "" Then
        Set oMsg = oContext.CreateMessage(CBool(0))

        ' Associate certificate with message.
        oMsg.AddRecipientCert certClient

        ' Build and send the encrypted message.
        oMail.Host = "mail.exair.com"
        oMail.Subject = "ExAir Password"
        oMail.From = "accounts@exair.com"
        oMail.FromName = "User Accounts"
        oMail.AddAddress = strEmail
        oMail.Body = "Your secret password is " & strPassword
        oMail.SendEncrypted Msg

        Response.Write "Message successfully sent to " & Email
    Else
        Response.Write "Certificate does not contain an" & _
            " Email address."
        Response.Write "Message Not Sent."
    End If
%>
```

This simple piece of code will send a secure e-mail message to the recipient. Because the e-mail cannot be decrypted by an attacker, the user's password is secure.

While we're on the subject of ASP code, let's turn our attention to a way of mitigating a threat on the mind of all security-conscious Web developers: illicit access to Web source code.

Obfuscating ASP code

A risk faced by all Web servers is an unforeseen information disclosure vulnerability that yields access to the server-side code, such as ASP or CGI, to the wrong people. For example, incorrectly set ACLs might allow an attacker to read the contents of your ASP applications when they should not be able to. Because of this, you should never store passwords, usernames, or other private information in server-side code. Including such information should be deemed a major security risk, and appropriate risk mitigation plans should be put in place in case the script is accessed by an attacker.

One such way to alleviate, but not fully mitigate, this risk is to use *script encoding*. Script encoding is a feature of the Microsoft script engines, including VBScript and JScript. The Microsoft Script Encoder, *Screnc.exe*, is a command line tool that enables ASP developers to encode their script so that other users cannot view or modify their source. Note that this encoding prevents only casual viewing of your code; it will not prevent a determined hacker from accessing the code. For example, the following two code samples from the Exploration Air example query a SQL Server database to get flight timetables; the code in the first sample is not encoded and the code in the second is. If an attacker accessed the cleartext ASP code, he would learn the name of the database server, DBServer.ExplorationAir.com. He could then use this information to probe for vulnerabilities that gain access to the database server.

First, here is the cleartext version:

```
<%
    ' Copyright (c) 1999-2000, Exploration Air. All rights reserved.

    ' **Start Encode**
    ' Open the database connection to get flight timetable.
    ' Only valid users can do this, based on permissions in
    '   SQL Server.
    Dim oDB
    Set oDB = Server.CreateObject("ADODB.RecordSet")
    oDB.Open "{call spCurrentTimeTable}", _
        "Provider=SQLoledb;" & _
        "server=DBServer.ExplorationAir.com;" & _
        "initial catalog=ExAir;" & _
        "Trusted_Connection=Yes", _
        0, 1

    ' Hoist the variables from the loop to increase performance.
    Dim fldFrom, fldTo, fldDepartTime, fldArriveTime
    Set fldFrom = oDB("fldFrom")
    Set fldTo   = oDB("fldTo")
    Set fldDepartTime = oDB("fldDepartTime")
    Set fldArriveTime = oDB("fldArriveTime")

    Response.Write "<TABLE>"
    Do while Not oDB.EOF
        Response.Write "<TR>"
        Response.Write "<TD>" & Trim(fldFrom) & "</TD>"
        Response.Write "<TD>" & Trim(fldTo) & "</TD>"
        Response.Write "<TD>" & Trim(fldDepartTime) & "</TD>"
        Response.Write "<TD>" & Trim(fldArriveTime) & "</TD>"
        Response.Write "</TR>"
        oDB.MoveNext
    Loop
    Response.Write "</TABLE>"

    oDB.Close
    Set oDB = Nothing
%>
```

And this is the abbreviated encoded version:

```
<%@ LANGUAGE = VBScript.Encode %><%
    ' Copyright (c) 1999-2000, Exploration Air.
    ' All rights reserved.

    '**Start Encode**#@~^TgQAAA==@#@&dv,ra+x,Y4nP9l0l(1dn,m
    U+1YkKU~YKPT+OPWsbo4Y,Oks+OC(V+@#@&iB~rsHP-mVbNP!/q./,m
    Cx,NG~DtkkSP(1/a[~WPa+.:rdkkGxk~kPj}dP?n.7+.@#@&7Gkh,
    WGA@#@&dUnY,W9A,'~jqD\q.R;D+mOnr(L3mO`E)Gr9Ac]+1W.[U+YEb
    @#@&7WG$cr21x,J1l^sPkw/EMDnUDKksnKm4V·NE~,{@#@&7d~EhDG\b
    ⋮
    0s[:WP~x,Dd`rW^NPKJ*@#@&i?fOP6V[fvwC.DKksnP,'PMdcJ6V9fn
    wC.DKr:@E#@#@&7jeYPWs9b.Db-fKrs+,P',DkcJ6V[bMDr-9KksnJ*
    @#@&@#@&7I5/aWU/n /nRq.bYn,J@!zKzAd3@*r@#@&@#@&dG9~RZ^G
    /3P@#@&7j+DPKf$Px~WOtbUo@#@&hy0BAA==^#~@%>
```

The overhead of performing the decoding phase is minimal because the appropriate script engine decodes the encoded script file when IIS loads the file for the first time. IIS then caches the decoded script, and there's no longer a performance penalty.

You can find out more about script encoding at *http://msdn.microsoft.com/scripting*.

AUDITING

Auditing is one of the cornerstones of any secure application. Frankly, without auditing, you have no idea what's going on from a security standpoint. Auditing serves two main purposes:

- Provides the ability to determine whether, how, and when you were attacked and what was attacked

- Provides the ability to troubleshoot security issues

The second bullet point is the subject of an entire chapter, Chapter 11, "Troubleshooting Secure Solutions." The rest of this section deals with the security implications of auditing and describes some best practices.

Windows 2000 includes many different types of log files, such as the Web server logs, Windows 2000 event logs, SQL Server logs, and perhaps logs from firewalls, proxy servers, and intrusion detection software. We'll refer to this entire group as the audit logs. An audit log records events in chronological order such that the details that lead up to the event can be determined at a later date. It is this point that makes audit logs interesting for forensics.

Securing Log Files Against Attack

Because audit logs contain so much important and potentially sensitive information, you must secure them from attack—most notably, from tampering—and back them up regularly. You can achieve the first goal by using appropriate ACLs. For example, the three log files that make up the Windows 2000 event logs—AppEvent.evt, SecEvent.evt, and SysEvent.evt in \WINNT\System32\config—have an ACL like this:

- SYSTEM (Full Control)

- Administrators (Full Control)

No user but an administrator can read or modify the log files.

The SQL Server logs have similar ACLs. However, the IIS logs inherit ACLs from the parent directory. Make sure the IIS log ACLs are similar to the ACLs on the SQL Server logs. The IIS audit logs reside at \WINNT\System32\LogFiles.

Audit log files are a precious resource, and backing up audit logs is paramount. You should have a rigorous backup plan and back up to tape or a write-once medium, such as a writable CD-ROM. One of the authors employs a Windows Script Host (WSH) script that runs four times a day as a task under the control of the Windows Task Scheduler. The script drives NTBackup.exe with command line arguments. Here is the script:

```
Option Explicit

' Build up the name of the backup file
'   from the date and time.
Dim dDate, strYear, strMonth, strDay, strHour, strName
dDate = Now
strYear = DatePart("yyyy", dDate)
strMonth = DatePart("m", dDate)
strDay = DatePart("d", dDate)
strHour = DatePart("h", dDate)

if strMonth < 10 Then strMonth = "0" & strMonth
if strDay < 10 Then strDay = "0" & strDay
if strHour < 10 Then strHour = "0" & strHour

' Filename is LogBackup-YYYYMMDD-HH.bkf.
strName = "LogBackup-" & _
          strYear & _
          strMonth & _
          strDay & "-" & _
          strHour & ".bkf"
```

(continued)

```
' Build up the backup command line.
' We will also back up the system state information.
Dim strShell
strShell = "ntbackup backup systemstate "
strShell = strShell & _
    """c:\LogBack\LogBackup.bks"" /J ""LogBack"" /F & _
    ""c:\LogBackup\" & _
    strName & """ /L:f /M incremental"

' Run the backup.
dim sh
Set sh = WScript.CreateObject("Wscript.shell")
sh.Run strShell, 1, 1

' Move the file to a secure remote server.
sh.Run "cmd.exe /c move *.bkf \\BackupServer\Logs", 1, 1
```

The script and the temporary copy of the backed-up log files reside in a strongly ACLd directory—only administrators have read access—called C:\LogBackup. The contents of the LogBackup.bks file determine which files are backed up. In this case, the file references these three directories:

- C:\Winnt\System32\LogFiles (Web server audit files)

- C:\Winnt\System32\Config (Windows 2000 audit files)

- C:\MSSQL7\LOG (SQL Server log files)

NOTE You can define your own .bks file by running NTBackup.exe, selecting the directories you are interested in, and saving the resulting .bks file.

Finally, the script moves the backup file to another well-protected server. The share named Logs is ACLd such that administrators have write-only access, and the directory to which Logs points is ACLd such that only administrators have read access. To protect the computer even more, only administrators have the Logon Locally and Logon Across The Network logon rights. No other users can access the computer, and there are no other local accounts on the server.

Refer to the Windows 2000 online help for details about using NTBackup.exe and the meaning of the command line options. Chapter 12, "Securing Against Attack," has guidelines about what you should audit for in IIS, SQL Server, and Windows.

WINDOWS SCRIPT HOST LOGGING

Using WSH, you can write your own custom events to the Windows 2000 event log. This JScript code will write an audit failure event to the security log:

```
var oWsh = new ActiveXObject("WScript.Shell");
oWsh.LogEvent(16, _
    "Unable to log the user onto the application.");
```

The same script written in Visual Basic is

```
oWsh = CreateObject("WScript.Shell")
oWsh.LogEvent(16, _
    "Unable to log the user onto the application.")
```

The first argument is the event type. Possible values are 0 (success), 1 (error), 2 (warning), 4 (information), 8 (audit success), and 16 (audit failure). Note that this code will not necessarily work in ASP because the user might not have the privilege to write to the event log.

AN INTRODUCTION TO NONREPUDIATION

In the digital world, nonrepudiation is a combination of technology, policy, and law that prevents a principal involved in a transaction from falsely refuting having participated in the transaction. Nonrepudiation is plentiful in the material world, and you're probably familiar with it without recognizing it.

For example, say that you order a book from a mail order company and receive the goods three days later. When you accept the merchandise, you're asked to sign and date a receipt by the delivery company. Two months later, you decide to telephone the mail order book company and ask them to credit your credit card because you haven't received the book yet. Of course, it's all a lie! You're trying to repudiate, or go back on, your side of the financial transaction and swindle the book company. However, the book company can prove that you received the books; they have a receipt signed by you. The book company has just performed nonrepudiation of delivery. Nonrepudiation of delivery is designed to protect the message or merchandise sender.

Another principle form of nonrepudiation is nonrepudiation of origin, or the ability to prove the origin of a message or merchandise. This form of nonrepudiation is designed to protect the recipient.

A More Formal Definition of Nonrepudiation

The ITU-T (formally CCITT) X.813 *Information Technology – Open Systems Interconnection – Security frameworks in open systems: Nonrepudiation* framework specification defines nonrepudiation as follows:

> The goal of Nonrepudiation service is to collect, maintain, make available and validate irrefutable evidence concerning a claimed event or action in order to resolve disputes about the occurrence or nonoccurrence of the event or action. The Nonrepudiation service can be applied in a number of different contexts and situations. The service can apply to the generation of data, the storage of data, or the transmission of data. Nonrepudiation involves the generation of evidence that can be used to prove that some kind of event or action has taken place, so that this event or action cannot be repudiated later.
>
> In an OSI environment the Nonrepudiation service has two forms:
>
> - Nonrepudiation with proof of origin, which is used to counter false denial by a sender that the data or its contents has been sent.
>
> - Nonrepudiation with proof of delivery, which is used to counter false denial by a recipient that the data or its contents (i.e., the information that the data represents) has been received.

The ITU-T definition of nonrepudiation is dry but precise. If you have more than a passing interest in the subject, you can get a copy of this document from the ITU Web site at *http://www.itu.int/itudoc/itu-t/rec/x/x500up/x813.html*.

Why Nonrepudiation?

Nonrepudiation is essential in commerce, including electronic commerce, because it protects both the seller and the consumer from fraudulent behavior by the other party. The idea of two or more parties agreeing on something (that is, goods or services) and carrying out the agreement is critical.

Imagine applying for a mortgage over the Internet in real time. You know that interest rates are fluctuating; they may go up half a percent or down half a percent. Of course, you don't know which way they'll go, and a poor decision could leave you paying dearly in mortgage interest repayments. So, you decide to lock in the current rate rather than risk rates going up. The lender receives your request but does not inform you of the receipt. The lender might then decide to accept your request if interest rates fall or ignore your request if rates go up because the lender will be able to charge higher loan fees. On the other hand, you might decide to renege on your request if interest rates go down, stating that it wasn't you who sent the request. Today, this type of scenario must often be resolved in a court of law, where both parties present enough evidence to sway the judge to one view or the other. In other words, nonrepudiation helps people avoid such conflicts.

To put this in perspective, let's recap the two major nonrepudiation categories and look at what techniques make up the various forms of nonrepudiation. The following sections explain nonrepudiation of origin and nonrepudiation of delivery. In the examples in these sections, Alice is the recipient and Bob is the sender or origin.

Nonrepudiation of origin

Nonrepudiation of origin helps mitigate the following disputes:

- Alice claims to have received a message from Bob, but Bob claims he did not send it.

- Alice and Bob agree that Alice received a message from Bob, but they disagree on the contents of the message.

- Alice and Bob agree that Alice received a message from Bob at a particular time, but they disagree on the time and date the message was sent.

Various evidence helps support nonrepudiation of origin, including the evidence in the following list. Note that the more evidence Alice has, the easier it is for her to prove that Bob sent the message.

- The message sender's identity—in this case, Bob

- The message content

- The time the message sender sent the message

- The message recipient's identity—in this case, Alice

Nonrepudiation of delivery

Nonrepudiation of delivery helps mitigate the following disputes:

- Bob claims to have sent a message to Alice, but Alice claims she did not receive it.

- Bob and Alice agree that Bob sent a message to Alice, but they disagree on the contents of the message.

- Bob and Alice agree that Bob sent a message to Alice, but they disagree on the time and date the message was sent.

Various evidence helps support nonrepudiation of delivery, including the evidence in the following list. In this case, the more evidence Bob has, the easier it is for him to prove that Alice received the message.

- The message recipient's identity

- The message content

- The time the message recipient received the message

- The message sender's identity

NOTE   It's important to note that nonrepudiation requires that the party disputing the transaction have as much evidence as possible to support their claim.

Using Technology to Support Nonrepudiation

This section looks at the different aspects of nonrepudiation and how technology can be used to provide nonrepudiation. We'll look at the following topics:

- Proving a message's origin

- Proving that the contents of a message have not been tampered with

- Proving the date and time the message was sent or received

Proving a message's origin

The most common and understood way to prove a message's origin is with digital signatures. Because the sender is the only subject that has access to the private key used to sign the message, the message must have come from the sender. The evidence provided by your being the possessor of a private key is directly proportional to the protection provided by the private key. If more than one person has access to the private key, the value of the key as evidence is substantially reduced. Refer to Chapter 15, "An Introduction to Cryptography and Certificates in Windows 2000," for details about digital signatures.

NOTE   An excellent summary of digital signature legislation in the United States and around the world can be found at the Web site of the law firm McBride Baker and Cole: *http://www.mbc.com/ecommerce*.

Technologies such as MACs cannot be used to provide nonrepudiation, because MACs require that the sender and the recipient know the key that was used to derive the MAC. Hence, either party could fraudulently create the message and claim that the other originated the message. The same applies to SSL/TLS, because both parties know the session key used to encrypt the channel.

Proving that the contents of a message have not been tampered with

As with proving the origin of a message, digital signatures can be used to determine whether a message has been tampered with. This is because the message hash is signed with the sender's private key. If the message is changed by an attacker, the hash must be recomputed and signed with the original sender's private key.

Proving the date and time the message was sent or received

Digital signatures allow you to verify who created the message and check whether the message was altered, but they do not address the time at which the document was created. To accomplish this, *timestamps* are used. The question is, who attests to the time? It's normal to use a third party, trusted by all parties in the transaction, to perform the timestamp operation, and it's the timestamp service's job to verify that the document existed at a particular time.

In the nonelectronic world, this task is often performed by a notary. A notary usually verifies the identity of the document creator, signs the document with a seal, and dates it. The notary often records the use of the seal in a logbook also. In the event that the validity of the document is called into question, the document's creator can prove the document did indeed exist at a specific date and time because it was notarized by a trusted third party. On the Internet, a third-party company—akin to a notary—takes information about documents sent by the originator, timestamps the documents, and archives the information about the documents in case a dispute arises.

> **NOTE** The seminal work on timestamping is "How To Time-Stamp a Digital Document" by S. Haber and W.S. Stornetta. A timestamping and notary company named Surety has a copy on the paper on its Web site, *www.surety.com.*

THE ROLE OF THIRD-PARTY TRUST

The more paranoid reader might ask, "Well, how do you know the sender and the trusted third party are not in some form of alliance against the recipient?" Quite simply, you don't! However, let's look at it from another perspective. Imagine that the third party is not so trustworthy after all. Given that the third party is in the business of trust, violating that trust would soon put them out of business.

Nonrepudiation in Your Web Application

If your Web application creates some kind of contract between you and a client, chances are you'll need to have a policy to determine how you handle repudiation disputes. For example, you might decide that requests for goods and services worth over, say, $10,000 must be digitally signed, and requests worth over $100,000 must be digitally signed and timestamped by a third party.

> **NOTE**   If you plan to ask your users to digitally sign their requests, you'll have to explain what you mean. Few people know what it means to digitally sign a document. To make the process easier for the user, you can also include an ActiveX control on your Web site that performs the task by using CryptoAPI functions such as *CryptSignMessage*.

There's no end to the kind of services you can offer to protect both yourself and your clients from nonrepudiation threats. You might determine that your concept of nonrepudiation of delivery is to e-mail the client a confirmation number. Confirmation of origin is determined by the client's use of his or her password to make the purchase.

Please note: The authors are not lawyers. If you plan to include nonrepudiation services as part of your Web application, we urge you to get legal advice first to make sure that the services you provide are legal and can be used in the case of a repudiation dispute.

SUMMARY

This chapter has dealt with some of the most important aspects of security in electronic commerce and the digital economy: privacy, integrity, auditing, and nonrepudiation. You'll notice that we covered nonrepudiation at the end of this chapter and the previous chapter, which covered authentication and authorization. That was by design. Nonrepudiation requires all the other supporting technologies to be effective.

We discussed many of the trade-offs you'll have to make when performing authentication and authorization, as well as some best practices if you decide to create or augment your own security services. Make sure you perform security due diligence when creating your own services. In our experience of reviewing many Web-based products, we've seen that custom-written security mechanisms are often vulnerable to attack.

You have many security tools and technologies to choose from. This and the previous chapter should help you decide which are appropriate for your application and where you need to add functionality to accommodate your business' security requirements. In the next chapter, we return to our main example and build the canonical end-to-end delegation solution using Kerberos authentication; we'll also show how to adjust the solution to meet your requirements.

Part III

In Practice

Chapter 10

Building a Secure Solution

In Part II, "Technologies and Trade-Offs," we looked at some of the technologies used to build secure solutions as well as some of the trade-offs required to solve real business problems. Now let's turn our attention to the steps required to build a comprehensive solution that uses end-to-end Kerberos authentication and Microsoft Windows 2000 access control mechanisms throughout. This solution, based on the Exploration Air example discussed in Chapter 2, "A Process for Building Secure Web Applications," can be used as the basis for your own security solution. Once you have this example running, you can apply many of the trade-offs discussed in Chapter 8, "Practical Authentication and Authorization," and Chapter 9, "Practical Privacy, Integrity, Auditing, and Nonrepudiation," to map more closely to your requirements.

The chapter is divided into three major sections:

- Putting together a secure solution

- Speed vs. security trade-offs

- Configuration checklists

We assume in this chapter that you have a certain level of administration knowledge for Microsoft Windows 2000. You must know how to install Windows 2000 and how to set up Active Directory, Dynamic Host Configuration Protocol (DHCP), Domain Name System (DNS), and Windows Internet Naming Service (WINS).

You can learn more about Windows 2000 network administration in the *Microsoft Windows 2000 Server Resource Kit* (Microsoft Press, 2000) or by referring to the Windows 2000 online help and taking a look at the checklists concerning DHCP, DNS, and WINS. Finally, we also assume you understand how to install Microsoft SQL Server and perform basic SQL Server administration.

Before looking at the steps required to configure the security solution, let's look at the overall application model, which we determined in Chapter 2 and which is shown in Figure 10-1.

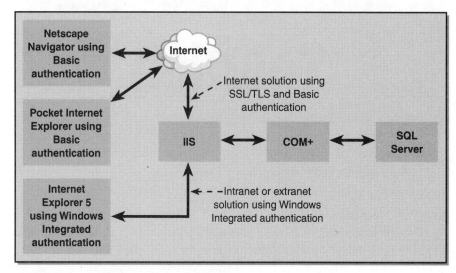

Figure 10-1. *A high-level view of the solution.*

Figure 10-2 shows a more detailed view of this model.

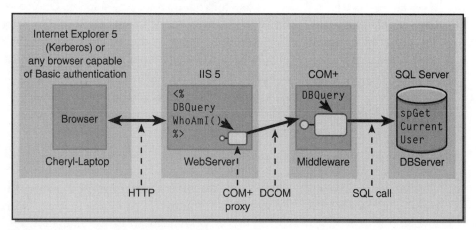

Figure 10-2. *A more detailed view of the solution.*

In this solution, the browser can be either Microsoft Internet Explorer 5 (or later) using Windows Integrated authentication or virtually any other browser supporting Basic authentication and Secure Sockets Layer/Transport Layer Security (SSL/TLS). These browsers will allow Kerberos identity to pass to the back-end database, SQL Server.

PUTTING TOGETHER A SECURE SOLUTION

In this section, we'll go over the steps required to put together the end-to-end Kerberos solution. The process might seem complex, but it isn't too bad. To make things a little easier, we've included checklists at the end of the this chapter; also, Chapter 11, "Troubleshooting Secure Solutions," discusses troubleshooting in detail.

NOTE   The companion CD includes a series of scripts that will automate some of the steps described in this chapter. The scripts are located in the end2end directory, beneath which is a series of subdirectories, one for each computer in the sample scenario. Not only do the scripts reduce the time it takes to configure the application, they also show you how you can use scripts for security administration, thereby augmenting the scripts described in Chapter 13, "Security Administration with ADSI, WMI, and COM+."

Figures 10-3, 10-4, and 10-5 show the results you should ultimately see in the browser when the solution is configured correctly. Note that it doesn't really matter what client operating system is being used, so long as the browser supports Basic or Kerberos authentication and the user has an account in Active Directory. Figure 10-3 illustrates Internet Explorer 5 running on Windows 2000 showing Alice's delegated identity, Figure 10-4 illustrates Internet Explorer running on a Pocket PC showing Alice's delegated identity, and Figure 10-5 illustrates Netscape Navigator running on Red Hat Linux 6.2 showing Alice's delegated identity.

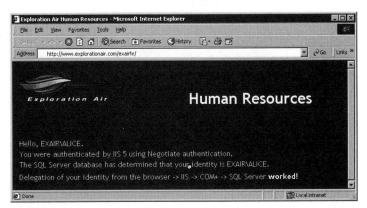

Figure 10-3. *Internet Explorer 5 showing Alice's delegated identity using Kerberos authentication.*

The first reference to the user's name, shown in the browser, is the name determined by Internet Information Services (IIS) when the user is authenticated; the second reference is the user's name determined by SQL Server. If the two identities are the same, delegation is working correctly.

Figure 10-4. *Pocket Internet Explorer on a Pocket PC showing Alice's delegated identity using Basic authentication.*

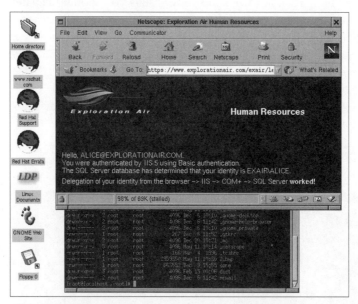

Figure 10-5. *Netscape Navigator running on Red Hat Linux 6.2 and GNOME showing Alice's delegated identity using Basic authentication.*

To build the example application with the least number of steps, we'll approach the task like so: configure the computers, the domain, the user accounts, and, finally, the application. Let's look at each step in detail. Technically, there are other ways to build the application, but this is the most straightforward.

Configure the Computers

The first step is to set aside four computers and install the appropriate operating systems onto each. To make this exercise easier, keep the machine names the same as outlined in this chapter. We'll use four computers, configured as described in Table 10-1.

Computer NetBIOS Name	Operating System	IP Address	Comments
Cheryl-Laptop	Windows 2000 Professional	Determined by DHCP	This could be any operating system, so long as the browser can perform Basic authentication. The easiest solution is to use Internet Explorer 5 and Windows Integrated authentication.
WebServer	Windows 2000 Server or Advanced Server	Determined by DHCP	The Web server is IIS 5 configured to run Windows Integrated authentication or Basic authentication over SSL/TLS.
Middleware	Windows 2000 Server or Advanced Server	Determined by DHCP	This server is configured to run one or more COM+ applications.
DBServer	Windows 2000 Server or Advanced Server	172.10.10.42	This server runs SQL Server, and, for the purposes of our demonstration, it is also the Windows 2000 domain controller, the DNS server, the DHCP server, and the WINS server.

Table 10-1. *High-level configuration of the four computers used in our example.*

Make sure you install IIS on the WebServer computer and DNS, DHCP, and WINS on DBServer.

Note that the IP addresses for all the computers, other than DBServer, are determined using DHCP because DBServer is the DHCP server. Once the computers are configured, you should be able to get IP addresses on reboot or by typing *ipconfig /release* and then *ipconfig /renew* at the command line.

CHECKPOINT   Before continuing, check that you can ping all machines by using their IP addresses. If you can't, either DHCP is configured incorrectly or the computers are not configured to request an IP address from a DHCP server.

Now it's time to configure the domain settings.

Configure the Domain

On DBServer, which is the domain controller, run Dcpromo.exe and set up the computer as the domain controller for a new domain. When prompted, create a new domain tree and create a new forest of domain trees. The full DNS name for the domain is *explorationair.com*, and the NetBIOS name for the domain is *EXAIR*. If you are prompted to install a DNS server, do so.

Once the dcpromo tool has installed Active Directory and you've rebooted the server, you'll need to add the other computers, Cheryl-Laptop, Middleware, and WebServer, to the domain. You can do this with the Active Directory Users And Computers Microsoft Management Console (MMC) snap-in.

CHECKPOINT   Before continuing, make sure you can ping all computers by using their NetBIOS and DNS names. You have a name resolution problem with the WINS server if NetBIOS name resolution fails or the DNS server if DNS name resolution fails.

CHECKPOINT   Double-check that the *net view* command displays all shares on each computer. The computers might not have any shares, but you should not get any access denied errors.

With the Active Directory Users And Computers MMC snap-in, verify that WebServer and Middleware are both configured as Trusted For Delegation. Double-click the computer in question, and select the Trusted For Delegation check box. There's no need to do this for Cheryl-Laptop or DBServer because neither is delegating identity. You can use the SetDelg.js script on the companion CD to configure this option if you don't want to use the administrative tools. Figure 10-6 shows the Trust Computer For Delegation option.

Finally, Kerberos authentication is time-sensitive, so make sure the time is set correctly across all computers in the domain. You can achieve this by using the *net time* command. Times are synchronized correctly in Windows 2000 domains, but it's worth double-checking.

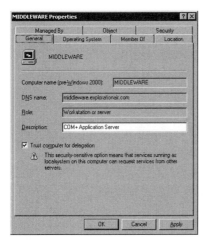

Figure 10-6. *The Trust Computer For Delegation option in the Active Directory Users And Computers MMC snap-in.*

Configure the Users

Now we need to add the sample users. All the users are domain accounts; none are local accounts, because Kerberos authentication works with domain accounts only. Think about it. For delegation to work, the accounts must be known on all computers, and only domain accounts are known on all computers. You can add users by using the Active Directory Users And Computers MMC snap-in, or the sample script AddUsers.js on the companion CD will automatically add the users for you. The settings for each account are described in Table 10-2.

Account	*Password*	*Trusted for Delegation?*	*Sensitive?*	*Password expires?*
Alice	y14c&yWbR-A	No	No	Yes
Bob	y14c&yWbR-B	No	Yes	Yes
Cheryl	y14c&yWbR-C	No	No	Yes
AppAccount	y14c&yWbR-Z	Yes	No	No

Table 10-2. *Sample domain user accounts and their settings.*

NOTE Obviously, it's not a good idea to print passwords in a book! The passwords in Table 10-2 are intended as examples that are somewhat easy to remember. The phrase to remember for the passwords is, "Your ideas are clever and you will be rewarded." Refer to Appendix B, "Strong Passwords," in the companion CD's electronic book to see how we derived the passwords in Table 10-2. (For those of you who really need to know, the quote comes from a fortune cookie I got at a Chinese restaurant. It's currently taped to my laptop!)

You can look at the various Windows 2000 user account settings in Figures 3-12 and 3-13 (on pages 70 and 71) in Chapter 3, "Windows 2000 Security Overview."

Alice, Bob, and Cheryl are normal user accounts. AppAccount is used as the process identity for IIS and the COM+ application. The account is marked as Trusted For Delegation because the IIS Web application process and the COM+ application must pass the caller's identity to another process or another computer. Give Alice, Bob, and Cheryl the rights to log on to Cheryl-Laptop. This step is not performed by the sample script.

Configure the Application

Three major parts of the application need configuring: the Web application that resides on WebServer, the COM+ application that resides on Middleware (and partially on WebServer), and the database that resides in SQL Server on DBServer. Let's focus on each.

The Web application

The Web application comprises a small number of Active Server Pages (ASP) pages that reside in a High Protection (Isolated) Web application—this is very important—named ExAirHR (Exploration Air Human Resources). Under the ExAirHR root lies another directory named Legacy. Legacy and ExAirHR use the same physical directory, C:\inetpub\wwwroot\exairhr, but ExAirHR requires Windows Integrated authentication and Legacy requires Basic authentication. The companion CD includes a tool named ExAirConfig.vbs that creates and configures these settings in IIS. You might need to adjust this script slightly if you installed IIS on a drive other than the C drive. The CD also contains all the ExAirHR Web application content in two files: default.asp and exair_logo.gif. Default.asp is simple: it merely calls a COM+ component on the Middleware server and presents the user with some information about the call. The most important information is the identity of the user as determined by SQL Server. If this identity matches the identity of the user accessing IIS, delegation has worked.

> **IMPORTANT**   You can't use the Web server code just yet. You need to wait until the COM+ application and SQL Server database are configured.

> **NOTE**   Actually, IIS does not call the COM+ application directly; instead, it calls a COM+ proxy, which in turn calls the COM+ application. We'll cover the steps required to configure the COM+ application later in this chapter in "The COM+ application."

A client using Internet Explorer 5 or later can browse to *HTTP://WebServer/ExAirHR*. Other browsers that do not support Kerberos can browse to *HTTP://WebServer/ExAirHR/Legacy* or *HTTPS://WebServer/ExAirHR/Legacy*, depending on whether you require SSL/TLS.

NOTE If you plan to perform Basic authentication on the Internet, you must use SSL/TLS to protect the username and password in transit to the Web server.

Now that we've created the Web application content, we need to configure the Web application startup identity and set it to delegate callers' identities. By default, the process handling the client request will start as *IWAM_machinename*. However, this account is not trusted for delegation. We could give the *IWAM_machinename* account this capability, but that would mean every out-of-process application started by IIS could pass clients' identities to a remote computer. This is not a good idea; only specific applications that require this capability should execute using accounts with this setting. Failure to heed this advice could lead to security vulnerabilities.

We will therefore set our Web application to run as the AppAccount identity. You might remember that earlier we set this account to be trusted for delegation. You set the IIS application identity with the Component Services tool. Navigate to the IIS-{Default Web Site//Root/ExAirHR} COM+ application, as shown in Figure 10-7, set the Impersonation Level to the Delegate option and the process Account to *EXAIR\AppAccount*, and set the AppAccount password.

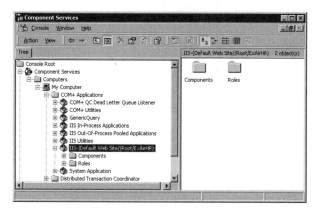

Figure 10-7. *Navigating to the correct IIS out-of-process Web application by using the Component Services tool.*

The two settings for the Web application in the Component Services tool are shown in Figures 10-8 and 10-9.

To make sure all settings are configured correctly and nothing is cached by IIS, enter *net stop iisadmin /y* and then *net start w3svc* at the command line. This will start and stop the Web server.

More configuration is necessary at the Web server: configuring a COM+ proxy to communicate with the COM+ application on Middleware. To install the proxy, you must install the COM+ component first, which is our next subject.

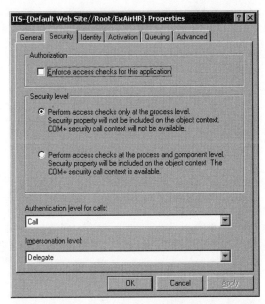

Figure 10-8. *Setting the IIS application Impersonation Level to Delegate.*

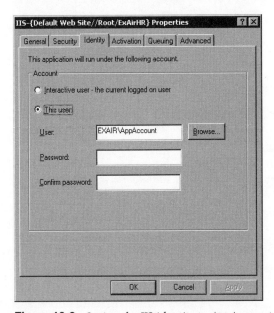

Figure 10-9. *Setting the IIS identity to AppAccount.*

The COM+ application

First we install the COM+ application on the Middleware server, and then we copy the COM+ proxy to WebServer. A COM+ proxy is a set of files containing registration information that allows a client to remotely access a COM+ server application. When run on a client computer, an application proxy file writes information about the server application—including CLSIDs, ProgIDs, the remote server name, and marshaling information—to the client computer. The client can then remotely access the server application. You can use the Component Services administrative tool to export a COM+ application proxy and simply run the resulting file on the client computer to set up the proxy.

The COM+ application is implemented as a dynamic-link library (DLL) written in Microsoft Visual Basic 6.0. The source code and binary files are included on the companion CD. The main file is named DBQuery.dll.

The general process for configuring the COM+ application used in our example is as follows:

1. Add a new COM+ application to the COM+ catalog.

2. Configure the security settings for the COM+ application.

3. Configure the security settings for the Middleware computer.

4. Export the COM+ application proxy.

5. Import the COM+ application proxy into WebServer.

The first step is the same for any COM+ application—we need to create a new, but empty, COM+ application, like so:

1. Start the Component Services tool.

2. Navigate to Computers, My Computer, and then COM+ Applications.

3. Right-click COM+ Applications, and click New; then click Application.

4. Click Next when the COM Application Install Wizard starts.

5. Click Create An Empty Application.

6. Enter the name of the application, ExAirHR, and make sure that Server Application is selected. Click Next.

7. Select the This User check box, and enter the application identity: EXAIR\AppAccount. The password is y14c&yWbR-Z.

8. Click Next, and then click Finish.

The next step is to add COM+ roles to the application. To keep things simple, we'll allow all users to access the component.

1. Select and right-click the Roles node under the ExAirHR application.

2. Click New, and then click Role.

3. Enter Everyone, and click OK.

4. Right-click the Users node.

5. Click New, and then click User.

6. Double-click Everyone in the Select Users And Groups dialog box; click OK.

Now you need to add the DBQuery.dll component to the COM+ application:

1. Select and right-click the Components node under ExAirHR application.

2. Click New, and then click Component.

3. Click Next when the COM Component Install Wizard starts.

4. Click Install New Component(s).

5. Locate the DBQuery.dll, and select it by clicking Open.

6. Click Next, and then click Finish.

Now we need to set up some security settings on the application. Most notably, we need to enforce security checks, make the application support delegation, and allow everyone to launch this application.

1. Select and right-click the ExAirHR application; then choose Properties from the context menu.

2. Click the Security tab.

3. Select the Enforce Access Checks For This Application check box.

4. Choose Delegate from the Impersonation Level drop-down list box.

5. Click OK.

6. Right-click the DBQuery.GenericQuery component, and choose Properties from the context menu.

7. Click the Security tab.

8. Select the Enforce Component Level Access Checks check box.

9. Select the Everyone Role check box.

10. Click OK.

You also need to set the ACLs on the DBQuery.dll file so as to allow Everyone execute access.

The last step is to export the COM+ application proxy and load it onto the IIS server, WebServer:

1. Select and right-click the ExAirHR application; then choose Export from the context menu.

2. Click Next when the COM Application Export Wizard starts.

3. Enter the name and location of the application file to be created. In this example, we'll save the file to the temporary directory and name the proxy ExAirHR.

4. Click the Application Proxy option button.

5. Click Next, and then click Finish.

Figure 10-10 shows what the COM Application Export wizard looks like.

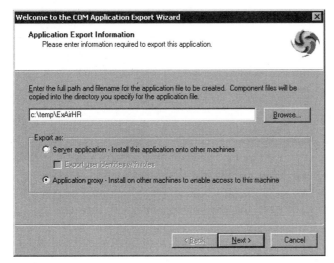

Figure 10-10. *Exporting a COM+ Application proxy by using the COM Application Export wizard.*

The Component Services tool has now created two files: a Windows Installer package named ExAirHR.msi and a Cabinet file named ExAirHR.msi.cab. Copy these files to a directory on the WebServer computer, and double-click ExAirHR.msi from the shell. When you double-click this file, you'll see the application proxy being automatically installed on the computer, as shown in Figure 10-11.

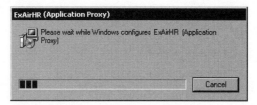

Figure 10-11. *Installing a COM+ proxy on another computer.*

At last, the COM+ application is installed on the Middleware server and the COM+ proxy is installed on the WebServer.

CHECKPOINT   You should be able to invoke the COM+ component at the Middleware server from the same server with the following simple VBScript code:

```
Set o = CreateObject("DBQuery.GenericQuery")
```

It won't do much, but you should see the ExAirHR COM+ application ball spin in the Component Services tool, showing that the component is activated. Stop the ball by right-clicking it and selecting Shut Down from the context menu. If all goes well, run the same code from WebServer. If you get no errors and the ball is spinning, give yourself a pat on the back. If things don't go so well, refer to the Middleware Server Settings checklist at the end of this chapter.

Now let's turn our attention to the final piece of this solution: the database.

The database application

Configuring SQL Server requires a small number of steps. First, the database server must be installed onto DBServer, and then you must create and populate a database with both data and a stored procedure. Next, you need to add logins to SQL Server and give the logins access to the database that was just created.

Regarding the installation of SQL Server, as we mentioned earlier we'll assume you know how to do this. Please make sure that you install the Named Pipes network library and make SQL Server run as LocalSystem.

IMPORTANT   Do not make SQL Server run as a non-LocalSystem account for this demonstration. If you do, you'll need to register a service principal name (SPN) for SQL Server. You can find out more about SPNs in Chapter 14, "An Introduction to Kerberos Authentication in Windows 2000."

Also make sure that SQL Server is configured to use Windows Integrated authentication rather than mixed authentication. Note that Windows Integrated authentication is the default configuration in SQL Server 2000. To check or set authentication in SQL Server, perform the following steps:

1. Open the SQL Server Enterprise Manager.

2. Right-click the database server in question—in this case, DBSERVER.

3. Choose Properties from the context menu, and click the Security tab.

4. Check the appropriate authentication radio button.

Once the database server is running, you need to create a database named ExAirHR. The most important part of the new database is a stored procedure named *spGetCurrentUser*. The syntax for this stored procedure is

```
CREATE PROCEDURE spGetCurrentUser AS
    select SUSER_SNAME()
GO
```

SUSER_SNAME() returns the user's login name. Feel free to add other tables if you want, but for the moment we're going to create only this stored procedure.

Next you need to add logins to the SQL Server database. We'll add only one login—EXAIR\Alice—who is permitted access to SQL Server, and the default database for her account is *ExAirHR*. Once the login is added, make Alice a valid user for the *ExAirHR* database:

1. Right-click the database in question—in this case, *ExAirHR*.

2. Select New from the context menu, and then select Database User.

3. Select the Login Name and assign any appropriate role memberships. By default, all users in this example should be in the public role. The resulting dialog box will look like what's shown in Figure 10-12.

Figure 10-12. *Adding users to a database.*

Now add the execute permission to the *spGetCurrentUser* stored procedure. To do so, right-click the stored procedure, choose Properties from the context menu, and then click the Permissions button. Figure 10-13 shows what the permissions for *spGetCurrentUser* should look like.

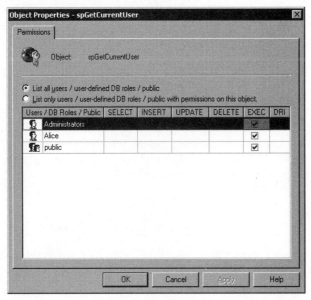

Figure 10-13. *Permissions for the spGetCurrentUser stored procedure.*

We've included a SQL script name ExAirHR.sql on the companion CD. You can load this into Query Analyzer to automate the setup of the database, including the data structures, the stored procedures, and the logins.

CHECKPOINT Before continuing, open the Query Analyzer and execute spGetCurrentUser. It should return one row of data containing your username.

All Done!

You should be all done now. You can test the application by opening the Web browser on Cheryl-Laptop and browsing to *http://webserver/ExAirHR*. If all goes well, you should see something like what's shown in Figure 10-5 (on page 290). If you decide to run SQL Server Profiler on DBServer, you should see something like what's shown in Figure 10-14.

Figure 10-14. *Using SQL Server Profiler to watch Alice's identity delegated to SQL Server.*

Look at the NT User Name column; it says *Alice*. This shows that Alice's identity flowed from the browser to the Web server to a COM+ application and finally to SQL Server.

DELEGATION IN SQL SERVER 7 AND SQL SERVER 2000

SQL Server 7 cannot delegate identity; however, SQL Server 2000 is aware of Kerberos and can delegate identity. Because of this, if a solution uses SQL Server 7, it must be the last server in the chain of Web, application, and database servers. Refer to Chapter 6 for more information about delegation in SQL Server 2000.

If things don't go well and you get some errors, refer to the configuration checklists at the end of this chapter, and then refer to the next chapter.

SPEED VS. SECURITY TRADE-OFFS

The example application we outlined in the previous section is secure and uses Kerberos authentication throughout. Only one set of authentication and authorization procedures is followed—all security policy is performed and enforced by the operating system, not by custom security code. There are times, however, when you might not want to use such a solution; or perhaps you'll supplement this base example with your own schemes. Note that you can gain some performance benefit from not using authenticated connections throughout, most notably in the areas of database connection pooling and the cost of delegating, which we'll look at next.

Database and Connection Pooling

We've already alluded to connection pooling previously in this book. Essentially, authenticated connections to a database defeat connection pooling. But you can relax the authentication requirements a little to prevent this. Rather than impersonating the user in the COM+ application before accessing the SQL Server database, the component identifies the user and uses that identity as an argument to a SQL statement or stored procedure to access SQL Server. Using this model, you need allow only one account access to SQL Server, and the COM+ application identity and connection pooling works!

Figure 10-15 shows the two scenarios. The first scenario is the complete end-to-end impersonation and delegation model. The COM+ request to SQL Server is performed only after impersonating Alice. In the second scenario, Alice is not impersonated; rather, the COM+ application identifies Alice and uses her name as an argument to a SQL Server request. In this case, SQL Server thinks that the COM+ application process, AppAccount, is making the call. Because of the single user account between COM+ and SQL Server, database connection pooling works.

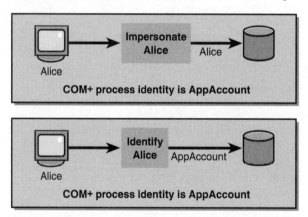

Figure 10-15. *Impersonating vs. identifying a user before making a SQL Server call determines whether database connection pooling works.*

The Cost of Identifying, Impersonation, and Delegation

Delegating a user account is much more expensive time wise than impersonating or identifying a user. However, speed differences are difficult to quantify owing to the numerous contributing factors. Nevertheless, you can expect delegation to be twice as costly as not delegating. Impersonating and identifying the user occur at the same speed, and impersonating or identifying is negligibly slower than an anonymous connection. This doesn't mean delegation is slow. It's not; it's just relatively slower than impersonation.

In Web sites with extremely high throughput, you might consider impersonation over delegation; but of course, delegation won't work! At least you have the option!

CONFIGURATION CHECKLISTS

The following checklists detail some settings that must be applied to make the end-to-end Kerberos example operational. If things have not gone as they should, consult these checklists to verify that the settings are configured correctly.

Client Settings

There is very little to configure at the client. We purposefully designed the application that way to reduce administrative costs. Check that the following is true:

- Client operating system is Windows 2000 Professional.

- Client computer is a member of the domain.

- The browser is either Internet Explorer 5 or later (for Kerberos authentication to work) or another browser capable of Basic authentication (for Basic authentication).

Web Server Settings

Check that the following is true for delegation to work correctly with IIS 5. Many of these settings are configured automatically by the ExAirConfig.vbs script, which is included on the companion CD.

- Server operating system is Windows 2000 Server or Windows 2000 Advanced Server.

- Server is a member of the domain.

- Server is configured as Trusted For Delegation in the Active Directory Users And Computers tool.

- Web server is configured to run the ExAirHR Web application with High (Isolated) application protection.

- The COM+ application process, named IIS-{Default Web Site//Root/ExAirHR}, handling the ExAirHR Web application is marked to execute as the App-Account identity. You can set this in the Component Services tool.

- The COM+ application process handling the ExAirHR Web application must be configured to use delegation. This is the Impersonation Level setting on the COM+ application in the Component Services tool.

- The ExAirHR COM+ application proxy is loaded.

- The ExAirHR Web application is marked as requiring Windows Integrated authentication, and the ExAirHR Legacy virtual directory is marked as requiring Basic authentication and, optionally, SSL/TLS.

Middleware Server Settings

Check that the following is true for delegation to work correctly with the COM+ component's interaction with SQL Server on the DBServer computer:

- Server operating system is Windows 2000 Server or Windows 2000 Advanced Server.

- Server is a member of the domain.

- Server is configured as Trusted For Delegation in the Active Directory Users And Computers tool.

- The ExAirHR COM+ application is installed.

- There is an Everyone role that contains the Everyone group.

- The ExAirHR COM+ application is configured to support delegation.

- The ExAirHR COM+ application is configured to require access checks.

- The DBQuery.GenericQuery COM+ component enforces component-level access checks, and the Everyone role has access to the component and its methods.

- The ACLs on DBQuery.dll must allow Everyone execute access.

- For debugging purposes, you might want to set the Minutes Until Idle Shutdown option to 0 in the Advanced options of the application properties. As soon as a request has finished, the application will unload, making it easier to build a new version if an update is required. It also gives you great feedback as to when the application is starting and stopping.

Database Server Settings

Check that the following is true for security to work correctly with SQL Server 7 or SQL Server 2000 on the DBServer computer. Remember that SQL Server must be configured so that it can accept a trusted connection from the COM+ component on the Middleware computer.

- Server operating system is Windows 2000 Server or Windows 2000 Advanced Server.

- Server is a member of the domain.

- There is no need to make this computer trusted for delegation.

- SQL Server 7 or SQL Server 2000 is installed.

- SQL Server is configured to run as LocalSystem, and it uses the Named Pipes network library. If you want to use SQL Server 2000 and want to change the example application such that you can delegate the client's identity out of SQL Server 2000, you must use the Super Socket network library.

- SQL Server is configured to support Windows Integrated authentication, not mixed authentication.

- The ExAirHR database is loaded.

- The Alice and Administrator accounts are valid logins to SQL Server, and the default database for each is ExAirHR.

- The Alice and Administrator accounts are valid database users.

- Alice and the Administrator have execute permission on the *spGetCurrentUser* stored procedure.

## Chapter 11

Troubleshooting Secure Solutions

Every security solution requires some degree of debugging, and the goal of this chapter is to make it much easier to find a solution to your debugging issues.

The chapter is divided into four parts:

■ Tools and logs available to you

■ The art of reading a Windows 2000 logon event

■ The art of reading an Internet Information Services (IIS) log entry

■ Problems and solutions

TOOLS AND LOGS AVAILABLE TO YOU

Microsoft Windows 2000, COM+, IIS, and Microsoft SQL Server all record various security-related information to log files. It's imperative that you use these logs and appropriate logging and analysis tools to help resolve your issues. Failure to use these tools will lead to wasted time and much frustration.

Using MMC to Its Fullest

The Microsoft Management Console (MMC) allows you to add administration tools to a single administration console. Using this functionality, you can create tools customized for security. For example, one of the authors created an administration tool that has the following snap-ins installed:

- Event Viewer

- Custom view of the Event Viewer, filtering success and failed logon and logoff events in the security log

- Custom view of the Event Viewer, filtering COM+ events in the application log

- Custom view of the Event Viewer, filtering Distributed COM (DCOM) events in the system log

- Custom view of the Event Viewer, filtering SQL Server events in the application log

- A Web page with a URL that points to the SQL Server log files

- A Web page with a URL that points to the IIS log files

The tool is shown in Figure 11-1.

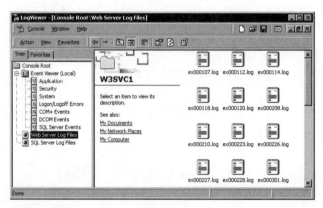

Figure 11-1. *The author's LogViewer tool, which is a collection of Event Viewer views and log file locations in MMC.*

You can create the tool by performing these steps:

1. Click Start, and then click Run.

2. Type *mmc.exe*, and press Enter.

3. Choose Add/Remove Snap-in from the Console menu.

4. Click Add.

5. Scroll and select the Event Viewer snap-in, and click Add.

6. Click Finish, click Close, and then click OK.

Next, we need to add a custom Logon/Logoff view of the Security log:

1. Right-click the Security log, and choose New Log View from the context menu.

2. Press F2, and type *Logon/Logoff Errors*. Then press Enter.

3. Right-click Logon/Logoff Errors, and choose Properties from the context menu.

4. Click the Filter tab.

5. Select the Information, Warning, and Error check boxes. Make sure that the Success Audit and Failure Audit event types are selected.

6. Select Security in the Event Source drop-down list box.

7. Select Logon/Logoff in the Category drop-down list box, and click OK.

To create a custom view for COM+ events, DCOM events, and SQL Server events, repeat these steps but use the options shown in Table 11-1. Note that in each case the event types are not changed; use the default settings.

View Name	*Event Log*	*Event Source*	*Category*
COM+ events	Application	COM+	All
DCOM events	System	DCOM	All
SQL Server events	Application	MSSQLServer	All

Table 11-1. *Custom Event Viewer views.*

Now we need to add the SQL Server log view and the Web server log view. To do so, perform these steps:

1. Choose Add/Remove Snap-in from the Console menu.

2. Click Add.

3. Scroll to the Link To Web Address snap-in, and click Add.

4. Enter the URL location of the SQL Server log files. By default, it is *file:// c:\mssql7\log* for SQL Server 7 and *file://c:\Program Files\Microsoft SQL Server\MSSQL\log* for SQL Server 2000.

5. Click Next, and type *SQL Server Log Files*.

6. Click Finish.

7. Highlight Link To Web Address, and click Add.

8. Enter the URL location of the Web Server log files. By default, it is *file://c:\winnt\system32\logfiles\w3svc1*.

9. Click Next, and type *Web Server Log Files*.

10. Click Finish.

11. Click Close and then OK.

Finally, save the log viewer settings by performing these steps:

1. Choose Save As from the Console menu.

2. Enter the filename—for example, *LogViewer.msc*.

3. Click Save.

> **NOTE** You can also add extra event log snap-ins that point to each server. For example, if you have five servers—ServerA through ServerE—you can open the Security Event Logs on each machine from a single MMC instance. It makes cross-referencing distributed security much easier.

Other Helpful Tools

You can use a number of other tools to troubleshoot problems. Some are part of Windows 2000, and others are in included in the *Microsoft Windows 2000 Server Resource Kit*. Table 11-2 gives a brief overview of each tool.

Tool	Location	Comments
IPSecMon	Windows 2000	IPSecMon displays the active security associations between computers. It's useful to help diagnose Internet Protocol Security (IPSec) failures.
SQL Server Profiler	SQL Server	SQL Server Profiler monitors events produced through SQL Server. It's useful to determine which user account is accessing SQL Server and which queries are being used.
Network Monitor	Windows 2000	Network Monitor captures and displays network data packets received and sent by a computer running Windows 2000. Network administrators can use Network Monitor to detect and troubleshoot networking problems. Network Monitor identifies many protocols, including HTTP, SMB, TPC, UDP, IP, RPC, and many more.

Table 11-2. *Useful tools to aid in security troubleshooting.*

Tool	Location	Comments
ElogDmp	Resource Kit	ElogDmp displays any of the Windows 2000 logs. When used in conjunction with the Windows 2000 *FindStr* command, it allows you to query for specific event log entries.
CyberSafe Log Analyst	Resource Kit	CyberSafe Log Analyst is an MMC snap-in that analyzes the Windows 2000 Security Event Log. The tool allows you to organize and interpret a computer's Security Event Log, providing more effective, systemwide user activity analysis.
Dumpel	Resource Kit	Dump Event Log is a command line tool that dumps an event log for a local or remote system into a tab-separated text file. When used in conjunction with the *FindStr* command, it's useful for finding that elusive "needle-in-the-haystack" information in a large log.
RPings and RPingc	Resource Kit	This tool confirms remote procedure call (RPC) connectivity between RPC servers and clients on a network. RPC Ping checks to see if RPC services are responding to RPC requests from client computers. It is very handy if you suspect an RPC or DCOM connection is failing due to RPC/DCOM configuration settings.
RPCdump	Resource Kit	This command line tool queries RPC endpoints for status information.
		RPC Dump interrogates the endpoint mapper database to obtain a list of every registered endpoint. Optionally, the tool pings each endpoint to determine whether the service that registered the endpoint is listening.
		This tool can help to isolate network troubles involving RPC.
ShowGrps	Resource Kit	This command line tool shows the groups to which a user belongs. It's useful if you don't have immediate access to Windows 2000 administration tools.

(continued)

Table 11-2. *continued*

Tool	Location	Comments
WhoAmI	Resource Kit	This tool, discussed in detail in Chapter 3 ("Windows 2000 Security Overview") displays information about the current user and optionally extra information from the user's token such as group membership and privileges.
W3Who	Resource Kit	W3Who is an Internet Server Application Programming Interface (ISAPI) application that works within an IIS Web page to display information about the calling user and the configuration of the Web server. It is somewhat similar in principle to WhoAmI.

THE VALUE OF TIME

If you're going to be analyzing multiple log files from multiple computers, you should synchronize the time on each computer; otherwise, hunting down issues will be much harder because log entries will have differing date stamps. If you're running a Windows 2000 environment with a Windows 2000–based domain controller and computers running Windows 2000 in the same domain, the Windows Time Service synchronizes time automatically. If your client computers are not running Windows 2000, you can use either the *net time* command or a tool that synchronizes with the domain controller by using the Simple Network Time Protocol (SNTP).

A Little-Known Troubleshooting Trick

It's often useful to determine the identities processes are using, especially when dealing with complex access denied errors. One tool for doing this is Plist.exe in the *Microsoft Windows 2000 Server Resource Kit*. Another method is to use Terminal Server. When Terminal Server is installed, it adds a process identity option to the Task Manager tool, as shown in Figure 11-2. You can enable this option from the View menu.

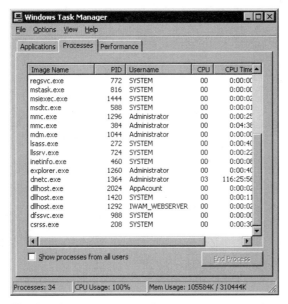

Figure 11-2. *Task Manager displaying process identities when Terminal Server is installed.*

THE ART OF READING A WINDOWS 2000 LOGON EVENT

Because connections in Windows 2000 are authenticated, you need to understand how to read logon events. The purpose of this section is to explain the different variables that make up a logon event.

Logon/Logoff Audit Settings

Microsoft Windows NT includes only one audit category for logon and logoff. Windows 2000 introduces a second. The two categories—Logon/Logoff and Account Logon—are explained in the following sections.

Audit account logon events (Logon/Logoff category)

This event category, available in all versions of Windows NT and Windows 2000, indicates that an account logged on or off or made a network connection to the computer. In other words, the audit event is triggered on the computer where the logon occurs. The Logon/Logoff category is important because it provides the most information when using IIS, SQL Server, and COM+.

The most significant events in the Logon/Logoff category are

- Logon/Logoff event 529 (logon failure)

- Logon/Logoff event 528 (logon success)

- Logon/Logoff event 540 (network logon success)

The following sections show these events, and Table 11-3 explains each of the fields in the events.

Logon/Logoff event 529 (logon failure)

```
Event Type:      Failure Audit
Event Source:    Security
Event Category:  Logon/Logoff
Event ID:        529
Date:            9/3/1999
Time:            8:57:21 PM
User:            NT AUTHORITY\SYSTEM
Computer:        CHERYL-LAPTOP
Description:
Logon Failure:
    Reason:          Unknown user name or bad password
    User Name:       Administrator
    Domain:          CHERYL-LAPTOP
    Logon Type:      2
    Logon Process:   seclogon
    Authentication Package: Negotiate
    Workstation Name: CHERYL-LAPTOP
```

Logon/Logoff event 528 (logon success)
and Logon/Logoff event 540 (network logon success)

```
Event Type:      Success Audit
Event Source:    Security
Event Category:  Logon/Logoff
Event ID:        540
Date:            1/23/2000
Time:            5:41:39 PM
User:            EXAIR\Cheryl
Computer:        CHERYL-LAPTOP
Description:
Successful Network Logon:
    User Name:       cheryl
    Domain:          EXAIR
    Logon ID:        (0x0,0x17872A8)
    Logon Type:      3
    Logon Process:   Kerberos
    Authentication Package: Kerberos
    Workstation Name:
```

Field	*Comments*
Event Type, Source, Category, and ID; Date; and Time	All self-explanatory.
User	The user account performing the logon.
	For example, this might be NT AUTHORITY\SYSTEM, which is the *LocalSystem* account used to start many Windows 2000 services.
Computer	The computer on which the event occurred.
Reason	Applies to logon failures only; it's the reason the account failed to log on.
User Name	The name of the user account attempting to log on.
Domain	The domain of the user account attempting to log on.
Logon Type	A numeric value indicating the type of logon attempted. Possible values are
	■ 2 - Interactive (interactively logged on)
	■ 3 - Network (accessed system via network)
	■ 4 - Batch (started as a batch job)
	■ 5 - Service (a Windows service started by service controller)
	■ 6 - Proxy (proxy logon; not used in Windows NT or Windows 2000)
	■ 7 - Unlock (unlock workstation)
	■ 8 - NetworkCleartext (network logon with cleartext credentials)
	■ 9 - NewCredentials (used by RunAs when the /netonly option is used)
Logon Process	The process performing the logon. The following are some example logon processes:
	■ Advapi (triggered by a call to *LogonUser*; LogonUser calls LsaLogonUser, and one of the arguments to *LsaLogonUser, OriginName*, identifies the origin of the logon attempt)
	■ User32 (normal Windows 2000 logon using *WinLogon*)
	■ SCMgr (Service Control Manager started a service)
	■ KsecDD (network connections to the SMB server— for example, when you use a *NET USE* command)

Table 11-3. *Success and failure logon fields.* *(continued)*

Table 11-3. *continued*

Field	Comments
Logon Process *(continued)*	■ Kerberos (the Kerberos Security Support Provider [SSP])
	■ NtlmSsp (the NTLM SSP)
	■ Seclogon (Secondary Logon—that is, the *RunAs* command)
	■ IIS (IIS performed the logon; generated when logging on the *IUSR_machinename* account or when using Digest or Basic authentication)
Authentication Package	The security package called to attempt to log on the account. An authentication package is a dynamic-link library (DLL) that analyzes logon data and determines whether to authenticate an account.
	Most common examples are
	■ Kerberos
	■ Negotiate
	■ NTLM
	■ MICROSOFT_AUTHENTICATION_PACKAGE_ V1_0 (also called MSV1_0; authenticates users in the SAM database, supports pass-through authentication to accounts in trusted domains, and supports subauthentication packages)
Workstation Name	Workstation name, if known, used by the principal during logon.

Audit account logon events (Account Logon category)

This event category indicates that an account logged on or off and that the computer was used to validate the account. In this case, the audit event is triggered on the computer where the account resides. Many Kerberos-related events, such as ticket issuing, are logged when this audit category is enabled.

The following sections show two often-seen account logon failure events.

Account Logon event 676 (logon failure): Authentication Ticket Request Failed

```
Event Type:     Failure Audit
Event Source:   Security
Event Category: Account Logon
Event ID:       676
```

```
Date:            5/11/2000
Time:            8:47:01 PM
User:            NT AUTHORITY\SYSTEM
Computer:        DBSERVER
Description:
Authentication Ticket Request Failed:
    User Name:  Major
    Supplied Realm Name:    EXPLORATIONAIR.COM
    Service Name:    krbtgt/EXPLORATIONAIR.COM
    Ticket Options:   0x40810010
    Failure Code:     6
    Client Address:   172.100.100.12
```

> **NOTE** What is the NT AUTHORITY\SYSTEM account? This account is usually referred to as *LocalSystem*; it's the account under which most services run. You'll see many references to this account in the Security Event Log.

Event 676 signifies that Major could not get an initial ticket granting ticket (TGT) from the Key Distribution Center (KDC). The most important part of the event is the failure code. These codes are the same as the MIT Kerberos codes. Table 11-4 describes some of the most common failure codes; a full list can be found in the main Kerberos Request For Comments: RFC 1510.

Failure Code	Comments
6	Client not found in the Kerberos database.
7	Server not found in the Kerberos database. This generally indicates a service principal name (SPN) has not been registered for the service.
23	Password has expired.
32	Ticket has expired.
33	Ticket not yet valid.
34	Request is a replay. Someone is trying to play back a Kerberos client's response; you are possibly being attacked.
37	Clock skew too great. Kerberos is time-critical; make sure all clocks are synchronized.

Table 11-4. *Some common Kerberos failure codes.*

Account Logon event 681 (logon failure) with a large number for the error code

You might sometimes see an error like the following. The problem is that the error code is virtually useless.

```
Event Type:      Failure Audit
Event Source:    Security
Event Category:  Account Logon
Event ID:        681
Date:            5/11/2000
Time:            8:47:01 PM
User:            NT AUTHORITY\SYSTEM
Computer:        DBSERVER
Description:
The logon to account: Major
 by: MICROSOFT_AUTHENTICATION_PACKAGE_V1_0
 from workstation: WEBSERVER
failed. The error code was: 3221225572
```

Table 11-5 describes some of the more common error codes.

Error Code (Decimal)	Error Code (Hex)	Comments
3221225572	0xC0000064	The specified user does not exist.
3221225570	0xC0000062	The name provided is not a properly formed account name.
3221225569	0xC0000061	A required privilege is not held by the client.
3221225578	0xC000006A	When trying to update a password, this return status indicates that the value provided as the current password is not correct.
3221225580	0xC000006C	When trying to update a password, this status indicates that some password update rule has been violated. For example, the password might not meet length criteria.
3221225585	0xC0000071	The user account's password has expired.
3221225586	0xC0000072	The referenced account is currently disabled.

Table 11-5. *Example Account Logon error codes.*

If you correlate the previous two security failure events—Major's request for an initial TGT failing with error 6 (Client not found in the Kerberos database) when he attempted to log on and a generic logon failure occurring with error 3221225572 (The specified user does not exist)—it's plain to see what the error is: Major isn't a valid account!

Now let's look at the next most important log type: the IIS log.

THE ART OF READING AN IIS LOG ENTRY

The standard Web server log format is named the W3C Extended log format. By default, these text log files can be found in %winnt%\system32\LogFiles\W3SVC*x*, where *x* is the Web site instance. For example, the default Web site is W3SVC1. The format for this log file is defined at the World Wide Web Consortium (W3C) Web site at *http://www.w3.org/TR/WD-logfile*.

Let's analyze a sample log file entry. First notice that each log file starts with the following line:

```
#Fields: date time c-ip cs-username s-ip s-port cs-method
 cs-uri-stem cs-uri-query sc-status sc-win32-status
 cs(User-Agent)
```

This indicates the fields used in the log file from this point on. You'll notice that some fields start with a prefix. Possible prefixes are

- **c** Client

- **s** Server

- **cs** Client to server

- **sc** Server to client

- **sr** Server to remote server (used by proxy servers)

- **rs** Remote server to server (used by proxy servers)

A log file could change fields, and this is reflected in the field heading. Table 11-6 describes these fields.

Field	Example	Comments
date	2000-04-25	Date of the request in Universal Coordinated Time (UTC).
time	14:20:03	Time of the request (UTC).
c-ip	172.100.100.13	Client IP address.
cs-username	EXAIR/Squirt	Client's name—a "–" value means anonymous or unidentified.
s-ip	157.42.12.122	Server IP address.
s-port	80	Server port number on which the request was received—another common value is 443 for Secure Sockets Layer/Transport Layer Security (SSL/TLS).

Table 11-6. *W3C extended log file components.* *(continued)*

Table 11-6. *continued*

Field	Example	Comments
cs-method	GET	HTTP method used to perform the request.
cs-uri-stem	/ExAirHR/ Default.asp	Stem portion of a Uniform Resource Identifier (URI).
cs-uri-query	-	Query portion of a URI. Note that this is often filled in by IIS when an error occurs and thus can be a goldmine of information.
sc-status	401	HTTP status—for example, 200 (OK) and 401 (unauthorized).
sc-win32-status	5	Win32 status—for example, 0 (no error) and 5 (access denied). This is not enabled by default; you can enable it using the IIS administration tool.
cs(User-Agent)	Mozilla/4.0+ (compatible;+ MSIE+5.01;+ Windows+NT+5.0)	The browser user-agent string.

PROBLEMS AND SOLUTIONS

Now that you have an understanding of how to read Windows 2000 Security Event Logs and IIS logs, we'll turn to the main content of this chapter: common security issues, where to look to verify an issue, and how to resolve an issue. This section uses the work performed in Chapter 10, "Building a Secure Solution," as the example. Each problem looks at two categories of information: symptoms/evidence and causes/ resolution.

Permission denied: 'CreateObject' When Launching a COM+ Component

In this scenario, the browser returns an error such as this:

```
Microsoft VBScript Runtime (0x800A0046)
Permission denied: 'CreateObject'
```

Figure 11-3 shows the entry that will appear in the event log on the server that attempted to instantiate the COM+ application.

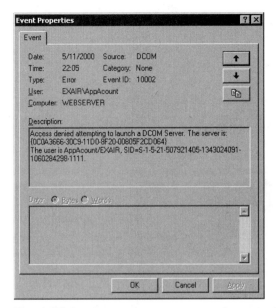

Figure 11-3. *The Windows 2000 system log entry showing a failed DCOM event.*

The following error, somewhat similar to the error returned in the browser, will appear in the IIS logs:

```
2000-05-12 05:05:26 172.100.100.13 EXAIR\Squirt 172.100.100.12 80
 GET /exairhr/Default.asp |15|800a0046|Permission_denied:
 _'CreateObject' 500 0 Mozilla/4.0+(compatible;+MSIE+5.01;
 +Windows+NT+5.0)
```

Causes and resolution

The problem occurs when you have no roles defined on the COM+ application or when you have defined roles but the caller is not a member of one of the roles. The simple remedy is to assign roles to your application and add the calling user to one of those roles that can launch the application.

Permission denied: but COM+ Application Ball Spins

On the surface, this seems like a very weird error. There's no SQL Server activity, but we can tell the COM+ application is activated because the ball in the Component Services tool is spinning. Furthermore, no COM+ or DCOM errors appear in the audit logs. The only evidence you'll see if you're auditing for failed object access and you place an audit access control entry (ACE) on the COM+ object in question (DBQuery.dll in our example) is shown in Figure 11-4.

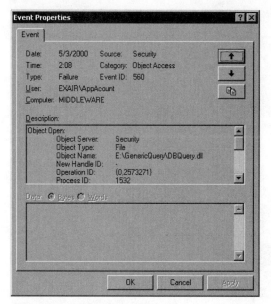

Figure 11-4. *A Windows 2000 Security Log Entry showing a failed object access.*

Causes and resolution

The DLL's access control list (ACL) is too restrictive and access was denied while COM+ attempted to load the DLL into the COM+ application. The COM+ ball is spinning because the COM+ application has started, but it hasn't loaded the DLL. The remedy is to loosen the ACL on the offending file so that the account can load the file. In this case, the account will be AppAccount because the COM+ application starts as this identity.

Login Failed for user '(NULL)'. Reason: Not associated with a trusted SQL Server connection

This error message will sometimes appear in the browser and in the SQL Server 7 log files, but the Web server and the COM+ application will be running correctly and reporting no error.

Causes and resolution

Something is causing SQL Server 7 to be unable to set up an authenticated connection with the client. This often occurs with sockets—a flaw in the SQL Server 7 socket network library prevents Kerberos mutual authentication from working correctly. You'll most likely see an error like this in the Windows 2000 Security Event Log, as shown in Figure 11-5, if you're auditing for failed Account Logon entries.

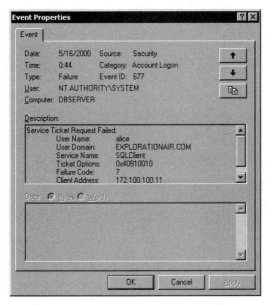

Figure 11-5. *A Windows 2000 Security Event Log entry showing that the SQL Server 7 socket network library is failing Kerberos authentication.*

You can rectify this problem in SQL Server 7 by disabling the socket network library and using the Named Pipes network library instead. Microsoft is aware of the problem and is working to rectify it. Note that SQL Server 2000 client network libraries do not suffer from this problem.

You can set network libraries in SQL Server by using the Server Network Utility included with SQL Server. You can perform a similar function at the COM+ component server (or any server performing data access with SQL Server) by using the Client Network Utility. Also, make sure you are not overriding the network provider in the Active Server Pages (ASP) page or COM+ component. For example, remove *network=dbmssocn* if you see it in the database connection string, because it overrides the database connection to use sockets.

Error: [DBNMPNTW] Access Denied.
80004005 Microsoft OLE-DB Provider for SQL Server.

This error appears in the browser; the error is a little insidious because no errors are written to any logs.

Causes and resolution

The most common security cause for the error is the IIS process handling the client request not being marked as running out of process or, if it is, not being marked as requesting delegation. Check that the Web application is running with High Protection

(Isolated) mode and that the COM+ application handling the out-of-process IIS application is not starting up as *IWAM_machinename* but as *AppAccount*. Finally, check that the COM+ application is marked to use delegation rather than impersonation. Normally, the name of the application looks something like IIS-{Default Web Site// Root/ExAirHR}.

Error: Login failed for user 'EXAIR\Alice'.
80040E4D Microsoft OLE DB Provider for SQL Server

You see this error in the browser, but everything appears to be fine in IIS—there are no IIS errors and the COM+ application ball is spinning, showing that COM+ services have started to process the user's request.

The SQL Server logs will contain the following line:

```
2000-05-03 00:09:08.58 logon     Login failed for
 user 'EXAIR\Alice'.
```

Windows 2000 will show a similar error coming from SQL Server in the application log. Windows 2000 will also show that the user has successfully logged on to the computer, as shown in Figure 11-6, but a SQL Server trace will show the request failing, as shown in Figure 11-7.

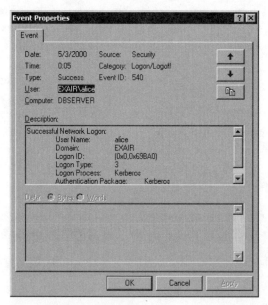

Figure 11-6. *A Windows 2000 Security Event Log entry showing the user successfully authenticated.*

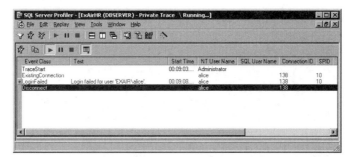

Figure 11-7. *SQL Server trace showing EXAIR/Alice failing to access SQL Server.*

Causes and resolution

This is common: you forgot to add the user as a valid logon to SQL Server, or you denied the user logon to the database server. The remedy is either to add the account as a SQL Server login or, if it exists, to allow the user to access the database server.

Error: Login failed for user 'EXAIR\AppAccount'. 80040E4D Microsoft OLE DB Provider for SQL Server

This is a slight twist on the previous error, but instead of the user account calling the Web application (for example, Alice), the error says that the COM+ process identity cannot access SQL Server.

Causes and resolution

We can almost guarantee that you'll come across this error at some stage. The error occurs when you forget to impersonate the client in the COM+ application. Call *CoImpersonateClient* before the database requests, and call *CoRevertToSelf* after the request is made.

Error: EXECUTE permission denied on object 'spGetCurrentUser', database 'ExAirHR', owner 'dbo'. 80040E09 Microsoft OLE DB Provider for SQL Server

You'll see this kind of error on many objects in SQL Server, especially tables and stored procedures.

Causes and resolution

In this case, a user does not have execute privilege to the *spGetCurrentUser* stored procedure. The remedy is simple: make sure the appropriate users have the appropriate privileges on the requested objects, such as stored procedures and tables. Figure 11-8 shows the Permissions dialog box on the *spGetCurrentUser* stored procedure. Permissions are a property of the object in question.

Figure 11-8. *The Permissions dialog box on the* spGetCurrentUser *stored procedure.*

Empty Client Certificate Dialog Box in Internet Explorer

You access a Web server that requires a client authentication certificate. However, when the dialog box is displayed to prompt you to choose a client authentication certificate, the dialog box is empty.

Causes and resolution

This is a common problem caused by one of two things: you have no client authentication certificates, or you have no client certificates trusted by the Web server. The second scenario is common if you've issued your clients' certificates by using Microsoft Certificate Services but IIS does not trust the root certificate of your certificate authority (CA).

Rectify this situation by opening the Certificate MMC snap-in and managing the Computer Account. You'll need to add the root CA certificate if it is not listed under the Trusted Root Certificate Authorities node. Also note that you can define a certificate trust list (CTL) in IIS that restricts the root CA certificates trusted by the Web server, so you'll need to check there too.

USING WFETCH

You can use WFetch, included on the companion CD, to help solve the Empty Client Certificate Dialog Box problem. WFetch allows you to choose from a list of client authentication certificates: one has expired, one is valid and trusted, one has no revocation information, one is revoked, and the last has expired. By looking at the results sent back by the server, you can better determine the cause of the problem.

> **NOTE** A new feature in Microsoft Internet Explorer 5.5 does away with the empty dialog box problem altogether. If the new security zone option called Don't Prompt For Client Certificate Selection When No Certificates Or Only One Certificate Exists is enabled, the dialog box will not appear if no client authentication certificate exists; you'll see a Web server error instead. If one client certificate exists, that will be used automatically.

Username Reported by SQL Server Is Different from Username Returned by IIS

You've configured your Web server to use Basic authentication and user principal names (UPNs)—that is, you've set the default domain to '\'—such as *major@explorationair.com* rather than SAM-compatible names such as *EXAIR\Major*. However, when you delegate the client identity to SQL Server, SQL Server says the user account is a SAM-compatible name.

Causes and resolution

SQL Server always returns SAM-compatible names from SQL stored procedures such as *SUSER_SNAME*. However, you can translate a user or computer name to another name format by using a new function in Windows 2000 called *TranslateName*. We've included a sample application and its C++ source code, called TranslateName, on the companion CD—the application performs similar Active Directory lookups from the command line.

Prompted to Enter Credentials When Using DNS Name as Web Server Name

You access an IIS server that requires Windows Integrated authentication, and you are prompted to enter your credentials. However, if you access the same site by using its NetBIOS name, you are not prompted to enter them.

The IIS logs should show a 401 HTTP status code (unauthorized), and if you're logging the Win32 error code you'll see a 5 error (access denied). If you hit the escape key when the credentials dialog box appears, you'll see a 401.2 error in the browser.

Causes and resolution

Internet Explorer is behaving correctly. When you access a Web site by using a DNS name, Internet Explorer assumes the site is on the Internet. Because of this, the browser will not use your Windows credentials when the Web server sends a 401 status back to the browser; instead, it will prompt you to enter your credentials.

You can get around this by adding the Web server's DNS name to the list of intranet sites known to Internet Explorer:

1. Open Internet Explorer.

2. Select Internet Options from the Tools menu.

3. Click the Security tab, and then click the Local Intranet option.

4. Click Sites, and then click Advanced.

5. Enter the DNS names of the Web sites on your intranet. Note that you can enter wildcards, as shown in Figure 11-9.

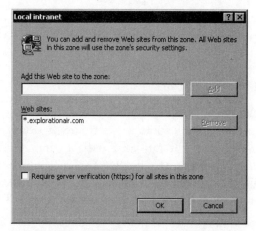

Figure 11-9. *Configuring Internet Explorer 5 to allow DNS names on an intranet.*

Security Alert While Using SSL/TLS

You access a Web site that requires SSL/TLS, but you see the Internet Explorer alert dialog box shown in Figure 11-10.

Figure 11-10. *Internet Explorer 5 warning the user about an SSL/TLS certificate problem.*

Causes and resolution

This error occurs in three situations: the name of the Web site you entered is the not the same as the name in the server certificate, the certificate has expired, or you don't trust the issuer of the server's certificate. The second and third scenarios are reasonably straightforward to resolve. The first issue, the name mismatch, is a little more complex because a computer can have many names. For example, it can have a DNS name (*www.explorationair.com*), a NetBIOS name (\\WebServer), and an IP address (172.100.100.13). Because of this, it's important that you choose the name that goes in the certificate to reflect the most common name used by your clients.

> **IMPORTANT** The current version of Pocket Internet Explorer does not support server certificates signed using SHA-1. By default, server certificates created by Microsoft Certificate Services use SHA-1. You should use MD5-based signatures instead (determined at Certificate Services installation time) if you use Pocket PC and SSL/TLS connections.

401.2 – Unauthorized Error When You Know You Have Access to the Resource

This is not a very common scenario: IIS is configured to use Windows Integrated authentication and you are a valid user—you must be, you just logged on to your workstation—but when using Internet Explorer you keep getting this error rather than being prompted to enter your credentials.

Causes and resolution

You probably have Internet Explorer configured to always use anonymous connections in the intranet zone. You can verify this by performing these steps:

1. Open Internet Explorer.

2. Choose Internet Options from the Tools menu.

3. Click the Security tab, and then click the Local Intranet option.

4. Click Custom Level, and scroll to the bottom of the Settings list box. If the dialog box looks like that shown in Figure 11-11, any form of authentication will fail. Click the Automatic Logon Only In Intranet Zone option button.

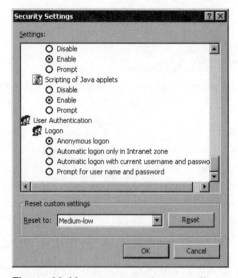

Figure 11-11. *Internet Explorer 5 will use not authentication schemes as long as the Anonymous Logon option is checked.*

401.3 – Unauthorized Error or Administrator Asked to Enter Username/Password

You're logged on to your desktop as an administrator, but each time you attempt to access a resource that has an ACL allowing administrators full control, you are prompted to enter your username, domain, and password or you get a 401.3 Access Denied By ACL On Resource error.

The main sources of forensics are the Windows 2000 logs and the IIS logs. If you're auditing for failed object access and place an audit ACE on the file in question, you'll see the entry shown in Figure 11-12. Note how the *IUSR_machinename* account is accessing the resource rather than the administrator.

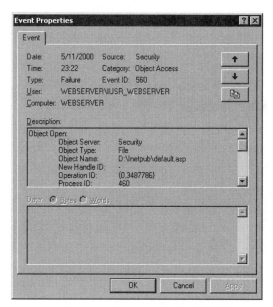

Figure 11-12. *A Windows 2000 Security Event Log entry showing a failed object access.*

Now look at the following IIS log entry. Note first the lack of a user account—the "-" before the IP address indicates no user (in other words, an anonymous user). And note the two errors: 401 (HTTP not authorized) and 5 (Win32 access denied error).

```
2000-05-12 06:13:35 172.100.100.40 - 172.100.100.12 80
GET /ExAirHR/ - 401 5 Mozilla/4.0+(compatible;+MSIE+5.01;
+Windows+NT+5.0)
```

Causes and resolution

This is very common; you have anonymous access enabled in IIS and no other authentication scheme. Because of this, the administrator account is essentially lost. IIS uses the *IUSR_machinename* account instead, and this account does not have access to the resource. Rectify the problem by choosing another authentication scheme in IIS or changing the file ACL.

401.4 – *Authorization Denied* by Filter While Using Digest Authentication

A user attempts to log on to an IIS server configured to require Digest authentication using Internet Explorer 5. However, the user is prompted to enter credentials, and the user receives a 401.4 error. The Windows 2000 Security Event Log will show a logon failure (that is, Logon/Logoff event 529) for the account attempting to log on.

Causes and resolution

The user does not have a plaintext password set in Active Directory. Get the user to change the password while the option is set.

403.13 – *Client Certificate Revoked* When You Know the Client Certificate Is Not Revoked

You access a Web page that requires a client authentication certificate. However, you're told that the client authentication certificate is revoked, and you're certain the certificate has not been revoked.

Causes and resolution

There are two causes for this: either your client authentication certificate has indeed been revoked (regardless of what you think) or your certificate has a certificate revocation list distribution point (CDP) that IIS cannot reach. If IIS cannot reach the CDP, it assumes someone has attacked the CDP and issues the error.

Look at the client certificate—you can view the certificate by using the Internet Options option on the Tools menu, clicking the Content tab, and clicking the Certificates button—and see what the CDP is. From the Web server, ping the location of the CDP and see whether you can retrieve the certificate revocation list.

Figure 11-13 shows a CDP in a certificate issued by Microsoft Certificate Services. Note that two CDP access protocols are listed: LDAP (Lightweight Directory Access Protocol) and HTTP. If both of these fail to resolve, IIS will reject the client request.

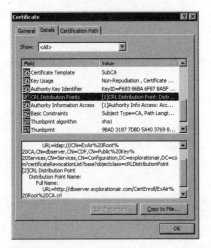

Figure 11-13. *A certificate and its CDP.*

> **NOTE**   You can add different CDPs to certificates issued by Microsoft Certificates Services. Access this functionality by following these steps: open the Certification Authority snap-in, right-click the CA, select Properties from the context menu, click Policy Module, click Configure, and click X.509 Extensions.

403.15 – Forbidden: Client Access Licenses Exceeded

When connecting to IIS, you receive this error message. You also see the following in the Windows 2000 application log:

```
Event ID: 27
Source W3SVC
Description: The server was unable to
 acquire a license for a SSL connection.
```

Causes and resolution

Either the number of authenticated users connected to the Web server has exceeded the number of client access licenses (CALs) or the number of SSL/TLS connections has exceeded the number of CALs. Another possibility: if the License Logging Service is stopped, only 10 concurrent authenticated or SSL/TLS connections will be permitted.

You can rectify this situation by purchasing more CALs.

Chapter 12

Securing Against Attack

At last, you've built your Web application and it's time to go live on the Web. Now the fun really starts! The Web has often been referred to as the "Wild, Wild Web," and for good reason—many people on the Web want to attack or access your computer without your sanction.

IMPORTANT   This chapter describes some of the procedures hackers use to attack servers and includes source code for mounting such attacks. We thought it best to show you what real hackers do to real servers so that you can better understand how to protect yourself. We in no way condone hacking into computer systems. To paraphrase Sun Tzu in *The Art of War,* "Know your enemy."

Much of the inspiration for this chapter comes from Farmer and Venema's classic paper, "Improving the Security of Your Site by Breaking into It." While this is an old, UNIX-centric paper, it focuses on what hackers do to attempt to break into systems. With these ideas and concepts in mind, you can increase the security of your network.

It's also important to note that little of this material is new. If you were to surf the Web long enough, you'd find all of this material. We decided to gather the key information into one chapter to save you the time and effort.

This chapter covers the following topics:

■   Why people attack Web servers

- How people attack Web servers
- Some common attacks
- How to detect whether you're under attack
- User input attacks
- What to do if you're under attack

WHY PEOPLE ATTACK WEB SERVERS

The complete answer to why people attack Web servers will probably never be known, but it's clear that few attacks are performed with malicious intent; most are made by people who want a little intellectual challenge. Of course, this doesn't mean that you can let your guard down. Even if only an extremely small percentage of people want to hack into your server, that's still a lot of people!

The following three factors generally hold true for people who attack servers:

- They have the motivation.
- They have a personal justification.
- They have opportunity.

Let's take a moment to look at each factor in detail.

Motivation

People who really want to do harm, especially those who attempt to deface a company's Web site, probably dislike the company because of its perceived environmental transgressions, its stance on a political issue, something the company said, or any of a myriad of other reasons. Remember, we're dealing with humans. Humans have emotions, and emotions can lead to irrational or antisocial behavior.

Attacks from within a company are most commonly initiated by a disgruntled employee. Don't overlook the possibility of attack from the inside.

The most likely reason for a disclosure attack (in which company secrets or documents are accessed) is industrial espionage. Your Web site might actually be an entry point into your corporate network!

> **NOTE** A study conducted by Michael G. Kessler & Associates, a New York–based security firm, found that theft of proprietary information from U.S. companies was committed by the following parties:
>
> - Employees: 35 percent
> - Outside hackers: 28 percent

- Other U.S. companies: 18 percent

- Foreign corporations: 11 percent

- Foreign governments: 8 percent

For more information, go to *www.apbnews.com/newscenter/internetcrime/2000/ 01/04/comptheft0104_01.html.*

Justification

A person who's motivated to mount an attack must justify her actions. For example, a discontented employee (or former employee) might rationalize destroying your Web site by thinking that her actions are minimal compared to the mental anguish she's endured because of some action taken by the company (such as firing her).

Opportunity

Finally, the attacker must find the right time to make the assault. Unfortunately, for computers on the Web this could be any time because the Web is open for business 24 hours a day. While you're sleeping, an attack might be coming from the other side of the world.

HOW PEOPLE ATTACK WEB SERVERS

The majority of attacks on Web sites aren't attacks at all—they're "scans" that probe to see what applications the site uses. Sometimes people are just being nosy and don't mean any harm. But from time to time, a scan might be a precursor to an attack. Let's take an in-depth look at how people attack servers.

Step 1: Find a Host to Attack

Most attackers choose sites with known vulnerabilities, but some attackers might choose a host at random using a host scan. A host scan is a program that "pings" a series of Internet addresses to see what's alive. The *Ping* command helps verify IP-level connectivity by sending a small packet of data to the host and waiting for a response; a response indicates that the host is running.

The following program, which we wrote using the Perl programming language, checks for running hosts. The program pings a series of IP addresses. If an address is up, the program performs a reverse Domain Name System (DNS) lookup to get the DNS name.

```
use strict;        # Similar to Visual Basic's strict option.
use Socket;        # Socket support.
use Net::Ping;     # Ping support.
```

(continued)

339

```
# A subnet to check.
my $subnet = "207.46.171.*";

# Make sure subnet format is correct and parse out octets.
if ($host =~ /(\d+)\.(\d+)\.(\d+)\.\*/)) {
    my $i;
    for ($i=0 ; $i < 254; $i++)  {
        ping ($1,$2,$3,$i);
    }
}


##################################################
# Ping.
# Pings the host with only 1 byte using ICMP.
sub ping {
    my ($a, $b, $c, $d) = @_;
    print " Attempting to ping $name ($a.$b.$c.$d) -> ";

    # Replace with TCP or UDP if target drops ICMP packets.
    my $p = Net::Ping->new("ICMP");
    my $ok = $p->ping("$a.$b.$c.$d");
    $p->close();

    if (!defined $ok)  {
        print "failed (host/ip invalid)\n";
    } elsif (!$ok) {
        print "failed (host unreachable)\n";
    } else {
    # Attempt to resolve the IP address.
        my $name = gethostbyaddr(pack('C4',$a,$b,$c,$d), PF_INET);
        print "$name\n";
    }
}
```

The following is an example of output from the program:

```
Attempting to ping 207.46.171.194 -> failed (host/ip invalid)
Attempting to ping 207.46.171.195 -> failed (host/ip invalid)
Attempting to ping 207.46.171.196 -> www.exair.com
Attempting to ping 207.46.171.197 -> secure.exair.com
Attempting to ping 207.46.171.198 -> failed (host/ip invalid)
Attempting to ping 207.46.171.199 -> failed (host/ip invalid)
Attempting to ping 207.46.171.200 -> failed (host/ip invalid)
```

As you can see, two hosts are running, *www.exair.com* and *secure.exair.com*. Now we can see what software they're running.

Step 2: Scan for Open Ports

Internet servers such as Web, mail, and Telnet servers listen on TCP or UDP ports. For example, by default a Web server listens on TCP port 80. Therefore, when you type *http://www.microsoft.com* in your Web browser, it knows to connect to TCP 80 on a server called *www.microsoft.com*.

> **NOTE** You can force the browser to use another port if the server is listening on another port—say, port 81. To do so, you type *http://www.exair.com:81*.

We know that the server at 207.46.171.196 (*www.exair.com*) is up, so let's perform a port scan on it. There are many ways to perform a port scan. The easiest way is to simply attempt to open the port at the server. If the port is open, a service (or a daemon, in UNIX terms) is listening.

For example, the following Perl and Microsoft Visual Basic, Scripting Edition (VBScript) code attempts to open TCP port 80 on 207.46.171.196:

Perl code:

```
# Set up socket and attempt connection.
socket(SERVER, PF_INET, SOCK_STREAM, getprotobyname('tcp'));
my $ip = pack('C4',207,46,171,196);
my $paddr = sockaddr_in(80,$ip);

if (connect(SERVER,$paddr)) {
    print "CONNECTED.";
} else {
    print "failed.";
}

close(SERVER);
```

VBScript code:

```
Set o = CreateObject("MSWinsock.Winsock")
o.Protocol = 0
o.Connect "207.46.171.196", 80

WScript.Sleep 2000

If o.State = 9 Then WScript.Echo "failed."
If o.State = 7 Then WScript.Echo "CONNECTED."

o.Close
```

Many tools are available for scanning a series of well-known ports to see whether they're open. The following is the output of a scan of *www.exair.com* at IP address 207.46.171.196.

NOTE   When you scan a DNS name, you might see many IP addresses. This is quite normal because it enables a simple form of load balancing called DNS-Round-Robin. For example, two physical Web servers might exist—one with an IP address of 207.46.196.4 and the other with an IP address of 207.46.196.5—and both might have the DNS name *www.advworks.com*. When a user types *www.advworks.com* in a browser, either Web server might be accessed.

```
SCAN - A Simple Port Scanner v1.01.12 (mikehow@microsoft.com)

Attempting to ping www.exair.com using ICMP -> SUCCEEDED

   21/TCP FTP                   at 207.46.171.196 CONNECTED.
 'Microsoft FTP Service (Version 5.0).'
   23/TCP TELNET                at 207.46.171.196 CONNECTED.
   25/TCP SMTP                  at 207.46.171.196 failed.
   53/UDP DNS                   at 207.46.171.196 failed.
   80/TCP HTTP                  at 207.46.171.196 CONNECTED.
 'Microsoft-IIS/5.0'
  110/TCP POP3                  at 207.46.171.196 failed.
  119/TCP NNTP                  at 207.46.171.196 failed.
  135/TCP RPC-DHCPMANAGER       at 207.46.171.196 failed.
  137/UDP NETBIOS-NAME-SERVICE  at 207.46.171.196 failed.
  138/UDP NETBIOS-BROWSE        at 207.46.171.196 failed.
  139/TCP NETBIOS-SESSION       at 207.46.171.196 failed.
  389/TCP LDAP                  at 207.46.171.196 CONNECTED.
  443/TCP HTTPS                 at 207.46.171.196 CONNECTED.
 1433/TCP SQLSERVER             at 207.46.171.196 failed.
 8080/TCP SOCKS                 at 207.46.171.196 failed.

Done...
```

Now we know a great deal more about *www.exair.com*. We know that the following services are running:

- File Transfer Protocol Server (FTP)
- Telnet Server
- Hypertext Transfer Protocol Server (HTTP, or Web Server)

- Lightweight Directory Access Protocol (LDAP) Server

- Secure Hypertext Transfer Protocol Server (HTTPS or SSL/TLS Web Server)

You'll also notice that we know what products the FTP and Web servers are—Microsoft FTP Server 5 and Microsoft Internet Information Services (IIS) 5. We got the Web server information by issuing a *GET / HTTP\1.0* request to the server and looking at the response, which includes the server type. The FTP server information was even easier to get. You just wait for the 220 status code, which includes the name of the server.

You can try this yourself without any code by using a Telnet client:

1. Type *telnet www.exair.com 80* at the command line to open TCP port 80 at *www.exair.com*.

2. In the telnet client, type *GET / HTTP\1.0* and press Return or Enter twice. You should see a message similar to this:

```
GET / HTTP\1.0

HTTP/1.0 400 Bad Request
Server: Microsoft-IIS/5.0
Date: Sun, 03 Sep 2000 04:53:33 GMT
Content-Type: text/html
Content-Length: 87

<html>.. .. .. .. </html>

Connection to host lost.
```

It doesn't really matter what data is returned. All you're interested in is the Web server type in the *Server:* header.

Once an attacker knows what ports are open and what services are running, he can start mounting an attack. For example, the attacker can easily search the Web to check for any known vulnerabilities in one of the services running on the computer and use this information to attempt an attack on the site.

A note on port-scanning strategies

By far the easiest way for a would-be assailant to scan for open ports is to use a simple TCP *connect*; it's also the fastest way. The good news for Web site operators is that this scanning method is the easiest to detect. Any good intrusion detection tool (covered later in this chapter) will warn you when it sees a series of sockets being opened and closed in rapid succession.

However, most attackers use other port scanning techniques that are more difficult—but not impossible—to detect. A common method is the half-open technique. To understand how this works, you need to understand how a TCP connection is made.

When a client wants to open a connection to a remote host, it constructs an IP packet that includes a flag called the SYN (synchronization) bit set to 1. The packet is then sent to the remote host. If the remote host is listening to the port specified in the IP packet, it sends a packet back to the client with both the SYN and the ACK (acknowledge) bits set to 1. Finally, the client sends another packet to the host with only the ACK flag set, and communication begins. This is often referred to as the TCP three-way handshake and is shown in Figure 12-1.

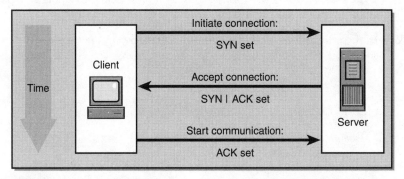

Figure 12-1. *The TCP three-way handshake.*

You can easily look at the TCP handshake by using a protocol analyzer such as the Microsoft Network Monitor included with Microsoft Windows 2000. Figure 12-2 shows part of the initial sequence when a Telnet client opens a connection to a Telnet server.

That's enough of the low-level TCP stuff for the moment. The point of all of this is that a common way to perform port scanning is to perform a SYN scan. In other words, you perform only the first part of the TCP handshake. If a SYN | ACK comes back, the server is listening on that port. The server should send back a reset (RST) if the port is not open. The SYN scan mechanism is more difficult to detect than a full *connect*, but most good intrusion detection tools will pick it up easily.

There are many other ways to scan for open ports. For details, see the online hacking magazine *Phrack* at

http://phrack.infonexus.com/search.phtml?view&article=p51-11.

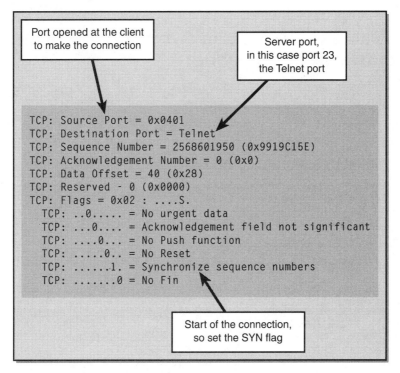

Port opened at the client
to make the connection

Server port,
in this case port 23,
the Telnet port

```
TCP: Source Port = 0x0401
TCP: Destination Port = Telnet
TCP: Sequence Number = 2568601950 (0x9919C15E)
TCP: Acknowledgement Number = 0 (0x0)
TCP: Data Offset = 40 (0x28)
TCP: Reserved - 0 (0x0000)
TCP: Flags = 0x02 : ....S.
  TCP: ..0..... = No urgent data
  TCP: ...0.... = Acknowledgement field not significant
  TCP: ....0... = No Push function
  TCP: .....0.. = No Reset
  TCP: ......1. = Synchronize sequence numbers
  TCP: .......0 = No Fin
```

Start of the connection,
so set the SYN flag

Figure 12-2. *An initial TCP packet used to connect to a Telnet server.*

Step 3: Gather Other Information

Once the attacker knows which ports are open, he might want to gather more details about the server before launching an attack. There are a few ways of gathering data (including user information and server information) about a computer running Microsoft Windows NT or Windows 2000. Most require TCP port 139 to be open. You can prevent this data gathering by shutting down the port (as described later).

Gathering user information

By default, Windows NT 3.1 and later don't require an authenticated connection to enumerate users and groups; you can use a NULL session (anonymous) connection. Therefore, it's a good idea to disable support for anonymous connections to secure computers on the Internet. (For a checklist on securing a Windows 2000 Internet server, see Appendix F, "Secure Web Server Checklist," in the electronic version of this book on the companion CD.)

CHECKING TO SEE WHETHER YOUR SYSTEM ALLOWS ANONYMOUS CONNECTIONS

You can run a simple test on any server running Windows NT or Windows 2000 to see whether it supports anonymous connections. Type the following at the command prompt:

```
net use \\myserver\ipc$ "" /u: ""
```

You're vulnerable to anonymous information gathering if you see The Command Completed Successfully.

You can disable this support in Windows NT by taking these steps:

1. In the Regedt32 tool, open *HKEY_LOCAL_MACHINE\SYSTEM\CurrentControlSet\Control\LSA*.

2. Choose Add Value from the Edit menu.

3. Enter the following information in the Add Key dialog box:
   Value name: *RestrictAnonymous*
   Data type: *REG_DWORD*
   Value: *1*

4. Exit the Registry editor, and reboot your computer.

You can disable this support in Windows 2000 by taking these steps:

1. In the Local Security Policy tool (or the Domain Policy tool if you're using a domain), select Local Policies (or Domain Policies).

2. Select Security Options.

3. Double-click Additional Restrictions For Anonymous Connections, and choose No Access Without Explicit Anonymous Permissions.

4. Close the policy tool. (There's no need to reboot.)

The following sample C++ code displays a list of users on a remote computer:

```cpp
void EnumUsers(LPWSTR wszServer) {
    const DWORD dwLevel = 1;
    const DWORD MAX_ENTRIES = 100;
    DWORD dwIndex = 0;
    DWORD dwEntryCount;

    wprintf(L"EnumUsers on %s\n\n",wszServer);
```

```
NET_API_STATUS err = ERROR_MORE_DATA;
while (err == ERROR_MORE_DATA) {
    char *pUsers;
    err = NetQueryDisplayInformation(
                wszServer,
                dwLevel,
                dwIndex,
                MAX_ENTRIES,
                MAX_ENTRIES * 2,
                &dwEntryCount,
                (LPVOID *)&pUsers);

    if (err != NERR_Success && err != ERROR_MORE_DATA)
        Error(err); // Error function is elsewhere.

    for (DWORD i=0; i < dwEntryCount; i++) {
        NET_DISPLAY_USER *pStart =
            (NET_DISPLAY_USER*)pUsers;
        NET_DISPLAY_USER pUser = pStart[i];

        wprintf(L"Name : %s\n", pUser.usri1_name);

        if (lstrlen(pUser.usri1_full_name))
            wprintf(L" %s\n", pUser.usri1_full_name);
        if (lstrlen(pUser.usri1_comment))
            wprintf(L" %s\n", pUser.usri1_comment);
        wprintf(L" RID: %d\n", pUser.usri1_user_id);

        if (pUser.usri1_flags & UF_ACCOUNTDISABLE)
            wprintf(L" Account is disabled\n");
        if (pUser.usri1_flags & UF_LOCKOUT)
            wprintf(L" Account is locked out\n");

        wprintf(L"\n");

        dwIndex = pUser.usri1_next_index;
    }

    NetApiBufferFree(pUsers);
}
}
```

Note that you must use Unicode when you compile this code using a C++ compiler because the Windows NT and Windows 2000 *NetXXXXX* APIs require Unicode strings.

Here's an example of output from this code:

```
EnumUsers on exair

Name : Administrator
 Built-in account for administering the computer/domain
 RID: 500

Name : Guest
 Built-in account for guest access to the computer/domain
 RID: 501
 Account is disabled

Name : exair
 Dummy account for development
 RID: 1037

Name : test
 RID: 1035
```

Gathering server information

A tool in the *Microsoft Windows 2000 Server Resource Kit* called Srvinfo.exe displays information about a remote server such as disk space, services, and networking information. As you can see in the following abbreviated sample output from the tool, it can give you a great deal of information:

```
Server Name: exair
Security: Users
NT Type: NT Member Server - Enterprise
Version: 5.0
Build: 2195
Current Type: Multiprocessor Free
Product Name: Microsoft Windows 2000
Registered Owner: IS
Registered Organization: ExAir
ProductID: 50292-170-1133541-11117a
Original Install Date: Wed Feb 16 02:11:04 2000
Domain: EXAIRCORP
PDC: \\EXAIRDC
Hotfixes:
    [Q147222]:
    [LastRan]: Wed Feb 16 02:31:18 2000

Services:
    [Running]    Alerter
    [Stopped]    Application Management
    [Running]    Computer Browser
    [Stopped]    Indexing Service
    [Stopped]    ClipBook
```

```
[Running]   Insight Host Agents
[Running]   Insight Server Agents
[Running]   Insight Storage Agents
[Running]   Distributed File System
[Running]   DHCP Client
[Stopped]   Logical Disk Manager Administrative Service
[Running]   Logical Disk Manager
[Running]   DNS Client
[Running]   Event Log
[Running]   COM+ Event System
[Stopped]   Fax Service
[Stopped]   IMDB Server
[Stopped]   Intersite Messaging
[Stopped]   Kerberos Key Distribution Center
[Running]   Server
[Running]   Workstation
[Stopped]   License Logging Service
[Running]   TCP/IP NetBIOS Helper Service
[Running]   Messenger
[Stopped]   NetMeeting Remote Desktop Sharing
[Running]   Distributed Transaction Coordinator
[Stopped]   Windows Installer
[Stopped]   Network DDE
[Stopped]   Network DDE DSDM
```

Another useful tool is nbtstat.exe, which comes with Windows 2000. This diagnostic command displays protocol statistics and current TCP/IP connections using NBT (NetBIOS over TCP/IP). Here's some sample output from nbtstat:

```
C:\>nbtstat -A 207.46.171.196 -n

Node IpAddress: [207.46.171.196] Scope Id: []

        NetBIOS Local Name Table

    Name              Type         Status

    ---------------------------------------------

    EXAIR            <00>  UNIQUE     Registered

    EXAIR-DOM        <00>  GROUP      Registered

    EXAIR            <03>  UNIQUE     Registered

    EXAIR            <20>  UNIQUE     Registered

    EXAIR-DOM        <1E>  GROUP      Registered
```

(continued)

```
INet~Services    <1C>   GROUP      Registered

IS~EXAIR         <30>   UNIQUE     Registered
```

Using this data, you can find out a great deal about the server. The NetBIOS naming convention allows for 16 characters in a NetBIOS name. The sixteenth character is a NetBIOS suffix, which identifies functionality installed on the registered device. Table 12-1 lists the NetBIOS suffixes used by Windows NT and Windows 2000. They're listed in hexadecimal format because many of them are unprintable otherwise.

NetBIOS Name	Suffix (Hex Format)	Type	Service
<computername>	00	U	Workstation Service
<computername>	01	U	Messenger Service
<__MSBROWSE__>	01	G	Master Browser
<computername>	03	U	Messenger Service
<computername>	06	U	RAS Server Service
<computername>	1F	U	NetDDE Service
<computername>	20	U	File Server Service
<computername>	21	U	RAS Client Service
<computername>	22	U	Microsoft Exchange Interchange
<computername>	23	U	Microsoft Exchange Store
<computername>	24	U	Microsoft Exchange Directory
<computername>	30	U	Modem Sharing Server Service
<computername>	31	U	Modem Sharing Client Service
<computername>	43	U	SMS Clients Remote Control
<computername>	44	U	SMS Remote Control Tool
<computername>	45	U	SMS Clients Remote Chat
<computername>	46	U	SMS Clients Remote Transfer
<computername>	4C	U	DEC Pathworks TCPIP
<computername>	52	U	DEC Pathworks TCPIP
<computername>	87	U	Microsoft Exchange MTA
<computername>	6A	U	Microsoft Exchange IMC
<computername>	BE	U	Network Monitor Agent
<computername>	BF	U	Network Monitor Application
<username>	03	U	Messenger Service
<domain>	00	G	Domain Name
<domain>	1B	U	Domain Master Browser
<domain>	1C	G	Domain Controllers

Table 12-1. *NetBIOS suffixes.*

NetBIOS Name	Suffix (Hex Format)	Type	Service
<domain>	1D	U	Master Browser
<domain>	1E	G	Browser Service Elections
<INet~Services>	1C	G	IIS
<IS~computer name>	00	U	IIS
<computername>	2B	U	Lotus Notes Server Service
IRISMULTICAST	2F	G	Lotus Notes
IRISNAMESERVER	33	G	Lotus Notes

Using this table, you can see that the server being probed has the following functionality:

- It's running the Workstation Service (<00> Unique)

- It's running in the EXAIR-DOM domain (<00> Group)

- It's running the Messenger Service (<03> Unique)

- It's running the File Server Service (<20> Unique)

- It's a domain controller in the EXAIR-DOM (<1E> Group)

- It's running IIS (<1C> and <30>)

NetBIOS name types describe the functionality of the registration, as shown in Table 12-2.

NetBIOS Name Type	Comments
Unique (U)	The name might have only one IP address assigned to it. On a network device, multiple occurrences of a single name might appear to be registered. The suffix might be the only unique character in the name.
Group (G)	A normal group. The name is unique but might exist with many IP addresses. Windows Internet Naming Service (WINS) responds to a name query on a group name with the limited broadcast address (255.255.255.255).
Multihomed (M)	The name is unique, but due to multiple network interfaces on the same computer, this configuration is necessary to permit the registration. The maximum number of addresses is 25.

Table 12-2. *NetBIOS name types.*

While nbtstat can supply a great deal of information about a server, other tools can probe for vulnerabilities and gather additional data:

- Legion (*rhino9.ml.org*), which scans multiple machines for unprotected shares on a computer running Windows.

- DumpAcl (*www.somarsoft.com*), which displays a remote computer's user, group, and permissions information.

- L0phtcrack (note the zero) (*www.l0pht.com*), which attempts to guess passwords for Windows user accounts.

- NetCat (*www.l0pht.com*), an all-around useful IP tool.

- Teleport (*www.tenmax.com*), which queries a Web site looking for key words. This tool can also copy a Web site or portions of a site to your computer.

- Grinder (*hackersclub.com*), which quickly scans a series of IP addresses to look for Web server version information.

- Whois database (Web interface at *www.networksolutions.com/cgi-bin/whois/whois*, Whois client [WS_Ping ProPack] at *www.ipswitch.com*, and Geektools at *www.geektools.com/cgi-bin/proxy.cgi*), which can obtain a great deal of information about a Web site by using only an IP address or DNS name. (You must use only the second-level domain name—for example, *microsoft.com*, not *www.microsoft.com*.)

- NSLookup (included with Windows 2000), a diagnostic tool that finds DNS information held on DNS name servers.

Attackers often spend quite a bit of time gathering information, like a burglar who "cases" a building before attempting to break in.

Step 4: Attack!

The next phase is the attack. As described in Chapter 2, "A Process for Building Secure Web Applications," there are six kinds of attacks based on the STRIDE vulnerability model: spoofing user identity, tampering with data, repudiability, information disclosure, denial of service (DoS), and elevation of privilege. The DoS attack is probably the easiest to perform and is less technically sophisticated than the other types. The problem with DoS attacks is that they can easily be launched from scripts written in Perl or executable programs written in C or C++. This code can be downloaded by "script kiddies" (people who understand security and low-level TCP/IP details and like to mount random attacks) or by people with little or no technical security experience who want to cause a little mayhem on the Web.

The evolution of many hacks goes like this:

1. A hacker finds a vulnerability in an application.

2. He writes some code to automate an attack.

3. He posts the code to various Web sites with a description of the attack.

4. A script kiddie finds a site that she wants to attack and performs a scan to determine what services are used on the site.

5. She uses a search engine to search the Internet for the words "vulnerability" and "security" and the name of the application she wants to attack.

6. She goes to a site that explains the vulnerabilities, common administration errors, or configuration errors in the specific version of the application.

7. She uses the hacker's code to mount an attack.

It's all too easy to mount this kind of automated attack. This is why you must stay on top of security-related fixes from vendors.

Although some other attack categories are scripted, they tend to be more technically challenging. A common data-tampering attack is one that defaces a Web site's home page. This usually involves exploiting a vulnerability in the Web server or operating system to give the hacker a high-privileged account—hence it's also an elevation of privilege attack—such as administrator or, in the UNIX world, root.

SOME COMMON ATTACKS

From August to October, 1999, the Windows 2000 security team hosted a server running Windows 2000 on the Internet to test its security. During that time, the server was attacked over 600,000 times. Happily, no Web pages were altered, no user accounts were changed, and none of the secrets liberally scattered around the server were found. We did, however, learn a great deal about how people attack Web sites. Before we look at some of the attacks detected on the Web site, let's discuss manual creation of IP packets because so many attacks rely on this capability.

Creating IP Packets

Normally, when your computer communicates with another computer using the TCP/IP protocol suite, the packets of data are "well formed"—that is, they comply with the appropriate Internet Engineering Task Force (IETF) standards. When a developer writes a program, he usually uses *sockets* to communicate using TCP/IP. You saw examples of using sockets in Perl and VBScript earlier in this chapter.

Many attacks involve a bogus packet (or packets) that's crafted to cause problems at the destination host. Creating these packets is quite a complex task and requires a good understanding of the TCP/IP protocol suite. Essentially, the attacker builds a packet in memory and then sends the packet to the destination host. This opens a special socket called a *raw socket*. It's raw in that the operating system doesn't attempt to modify the data as it's sent from the client host.

Many, if not all, TCP/IP attacks *spoof* the source host address or set a false source address so that the attack is essentially anonymous, or at best very difficult to trace. A good source of information about how to protect against such attacks is in RFC 2267, "Network Ingress Filtering: Defeating Denial of Service Attacks which Employ IP Source Address Spoofing."

The following is a C++ code fragment, sans error checking code, that creates a LAND-style (discussed later) TCP and IP header on an Intel-based computer:

```cpp
// IP header.
struct iphdr {
    uchar       version : 4;     // IP version.
    uchar       ihl : 4;         // Header length.
    ushort      len;             // Packet length.
    ushort      id;              // Packet ID.
    ushort      frag_offset;     // Fragment offset.
    uchar       ttl;             // Time to Live.
    uchar       protocol;        // Protocol (TCP, UDP, ICMP, etc.).
    ushort      checksum;        // Checksum.
    ulong       saddr;           // Source address.
    ulong       daddr;           // Destination address.
};

// TCP header.
struct tcphdr {
    ushort      source_port;     // Source port.
    ushort      dest_port;       // Destination port.
    ulong       seq;             // Sequence number.
    ulong       ack;             // Acknowledgment sequence number.
    uchar       unused1 : 4;
    uchar       offset : 4;      // Data offset.
    uchar       flags;           // Flags (SYN, ACK, etc.).
    ushort      window;          // Window.
    ushort      checksum;        // Checksum.
    ushort      urgent_ptr;      // Urgent.
};

// TCP flags.
enum {TH_FIN = 0x1,  TH_SYN = 0x2,  TH_RST = 0x4,
    TH_PUSH = 0x8, TH_ACK = 0x10, TH_URG = 0x20};
```

```
// Get the address of the target host (172.91.11.2).
struct sock_addr sin;
ZeroMemory(&sin, sizeof(sin));
sin.sin_family = AF_INET;
struct hostent *host = gethostbyname("172.91.11.2");
CopyMemory(&sin.sin_addr, host->h_addr, host->h_length);

// Get the port (80).
sin.sin_port = htons(80);

// Build the IP header.
// Note that the source and destination addresses are the same;
// this is the essence of the LAND attack.
struct iphdr ip;
ZeroMemory(&ip, sizeof(ip));
ip.version = 4;
ip.ihl = sizeof(strust iphdr) / 4;

// LAND attack has no body; it's just a bogus header,
// hence the length is just the size of IP and TCP headers.
ip.len = htons(sizeof(struct iphdr) + sizeof (struct tcphdr));
ip.id = htons(0xF1C);
ip.ttl = 255;
ip.protocol = IP_TCP;
ip.saddr = sin.sin_addr.s_addr; // Source address is "spoofed."
ip.daddr = sin.sin_addr.s_addr;

// Build up the TCP header.
// Note that the source and destination ports are the same;
// this is the essence of the LAND attack.
struct tcphdr tcp;
ZeroMemory(&tcp, sizeof(tcp));
tcp.source_port = sin.sin_port;
tcp.dest_port = sin.sin_port;
tcp.seq = htonl(0xF1C);
tcp.offset = sizeof(struct tcphdr) / 4;
tcp.flags = TH_SYN; // The first part of the handshake - SYN.
tcp.window = htons(2048);
tcp.checksum = checksum(); // Checksum is calculated.

int sock = socket(AF_INET, SOCK_RAW, 255);
sendto(sock, ...);
closesocket(sock);
```

As mentioned earlier, this is only a fraction of the code used to create a LAND attack; note that the source and destination host IP addresses are the same and the source and destination ports are the same, too.

```
// From the IP header.
ip.saddr = sin.sin_addr.s_addr; // Source address is "spoofed."
ip.daddr = sin.sin_addr.s_addr;

// From the TCP header.
tcp.source_port = sin.sin_port;
tcp.dest_port = sin.sin_port;
```

We hope that you now have an understanding of how raw sockets are created and the danger they can pose. Now let's look at some of the attacks observed at the Windows 2000 security test site, *www.windows2000test.com.*

LAND (DoS)

In this type of attack, a TCP SYN packet is sent with the source IP address and port number that match the destination IP address and port. This causes some TCP implementations to go into a loop until the machine crashes. Because the source IP address is spoofed, the attack is anonymous. The simplest way to prevent this kind of attack is to configure your router or firewall to block all incoming packets that contain your company's subnet addresses as the source address.

Smurf (DoS)

A smurf attack uses Internet Control Message Protocol (ICMP) echo request (ping) packets that are created with the victim's address as the source address. The packets are sent to a broadcast address that causes a large number of responses to the victim when each host on the subnet replies. This is often referred to as *attack amplification.*

Computers running Windows do not respond to broadcast pings, but this doesn't mean that they're invulnerable to smurf attacks. Rather, they won't participate in an attack. The easiest way to lessen the possibility of smurf attacks is to configure your router or firewall to disallow ICMP echo requests into your internal network.

The following Perl script pings an entire subnet with a broadcast ICMP packet. You can see the results of the broadcast in a network sniffer such as Microsoft Network Monitor. Notice that no computers running Windows reply to the broadcast.

```
@ip = (157,59,133,100);  ' Enter your IP address.
@mask = (255,255,252,0); ' Enter your subnet mask.

$subnet = (($ip[0] | ~$mask[0]) & 0xFF) . '.' .
          (($ip[1] | ~$mask[1]) & 0xFF) . '.' .
          (($ip[2] | ~$mask[2]) & 0xFF) . '.' .
          (($ip[3] | ~$mask[3]) & 0xFF);

`ping $subnet >&2`; # backticks (`) around the call to ping.
```

SYN Flood (DoS)

As discussed previously, a TCP/IP connection begins with an IP packet containing some data, and the SYN flag set to 1. When the server receives this packet, it allocates some memory and sends a SYN | ACK to the client. If the connection fails, the server tries again, possibly increasing the time to wait for the client to respond. A SYN flood attack uses fake, or spoofed, source IP addresses so that the server will never connect to the client. By sending numerous such SYN packets to a server, it uses up memory. Eventually, valid connections can no longer connect to the host—or worse, the server crashes. Windows 2000 has a number of internal heuristics to reduce the chance of this kind of attack succeeding.

Teardrop (DoS)

This attack requires a specially crafted set of IP packets that appear to be fragmented when they arrive at the server. The resulting reconstituted packet is invalid and causes the server to crash. Other variations of the teardrop attack include SynDrop, Bonk, Nestea, and NewTear. Windows 2000 is not vulnerable to this kind of attack.

HTTP ".." (Information Disclosure)

Some Web servers include server-side code to view sample applications, and this code allows the inclusion of ".." in the name of the file to examine. However, the same code can be used to download other files. For example, *http://www.exair.com/ samples/showcode.asp?file=./../../boot.ini* might download the boot.ini file. You should configure IIS 5 to not support the use of ".." in the filename, as shown in Figure 12-3.

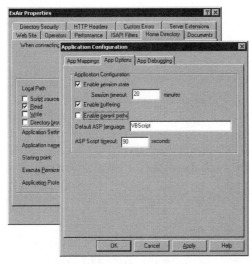

Figure 12-3. *Enabling or disabling parent paths in the IIS administration tool.*

Posting HTML or Script to the Web Server (Varies)

This is a common way to attack Web servers that accept user input because some Web site designers treat all user input as valid, well-formed data, even though it often isn't. This type of attack is covered later in this chapter in the section "User Input Attacks."

HTTP "::$DATA" (Information Disclosure)

The Windows NT File System (NTFS) supports multiple data streams, so a physical file can contain many units of data, each with a unique name. The default data stream, also called $DATA, is used when you don't define the name of the stream. Hence, file.asp is the same as file.asp::$DATA. IIS knows that a file ending in .asp is to be processed by the Active Server Pages engine (asp.dll). However, an older version of IIS doesn't recognize the extension .asp::$DATA, so it opens the file and returns the text of the file to the browser. The text in this case is the source code of the ASP file! The version of Internet Information Services included with Windows 2000 isn't susceptible to this kind of attack.

Windows NULL Session and Windows Remote Registry Access (Information Disclosure)

By itself, a Windows NULL session doesn't necessarily indicate that a machine is under attack. It might simply mean that this computer and another one are communicating anonymously. However, a Windows NULL session in conjunction with an attempt to remotely open the Registry might indicate that an attack is under way because account enumeration and the gathering of certain server information require a NULL session. (This was covered in detail earlier in this chapter.)

IP Fragmentation (DoS)

Quite often, IP packets are broken up into fragments as they're transmitted over the Internet and then reassembled at the destination. Some older routers block packets based on data in the first fragment's TCP header and then pass the remaining fragments unchecked. Some IP fragmentation attacks rely on specially crafted IP packets that overwrite parts of the TCP header when the packets are reassembled. This can trick the router into thinking that the packet is for an allowed port when in fact it should be blocked.

Ping Flood (DoS)

This is a very simple attack that saturates the network with ICMP echo requests (pings). The simple fix is to prevent these packets at the firewall or router.

Trace Route (Probe/Information Disclosure)

This isn't really an attack, but a precursor to a possible attack. A hacker uses the Tracert tool to determine the route taken by IP packets from your client to a destination; this tool can also be used to determine the makeup of a network. The former case is benign; the latter might be of concern. Often, the host prior to the Web server is a router or a firewall. If so, the hacker might simply perform a port scan on it and attempt to attack the router or firewall. People frequently lock down the Web site but fail to properly secure the router in front of it. The following is a sample fictitious trace route from Seattle, Washington, to Zambia in central Africa:

```
D:\>tracert mang.bnet.zm
Tracing route to mang.bnet.zm [196.7.240.10] over a maximum of 30 hops:
  1    180 ms    190 ms    191 ms  sdn-ar-
003waseat004t.dial.net [178.191.230.2]
  2    161 ms    180 ms    180 ms  sdn-hr-
003waseat004t.dial.net [178.191.230.1]
  3    220 ms    160 ms    171 ms  sdn-pnc2-sea-5-1-
T1.dial.net [217.143.225.105]
  4    331 ms    190 ms    200 ms  sl-bb3-sea-1-0.link.net [217.143.223.173]
  5    160 ms    190 ms    191 ms  sl-bb51-sea-0-2.link.net [154.232.5.36]
  6    161 ms    180 ms    160 ms  sl-bb3-sea-4-0-0.ink.net [154.232.5.21]
  7    170 ms    200 ms    200 ms  Hssi5-2-
0.BR1.FOO1.ALTER.NET [147.39.243.50]
  8    210 ms    201 ms    190 ms  105.ATM3-
0.XR2.FOO1.ALTER.NET [156.188.199.72]
  9    161 ms    190 ms    200 ms  294.ATM4-
0.TR2.FOO1.ALTER.NET [156.188.199.123]
 10    230 ms    251 ms    260 ms  110.ATM5-
0.TR2.FOZ1.ALTER.NET [156.188.136.75]
 11    270 ms    290 ms    311 ms  198.ATM6-
0.XR2.FOZ1.ALTER.NET [156.188.242.111]
 12    271 ms    300 ms    290 ms  194.ATM8-0-
0.GW1.FOZ1.ALTER.NET [156.188.242.145]
 13    861 ms    871 ms    892 ms  bnet-gw.customer.ALTER.NET [167.130.64.82]
 14   1012 ms    941 ms    931 ms  mang.bnet.zm [186.7.240.110]
```

Note that the Web server (186.7.240.110) is running a variant of BSD. We know this because NMAP, a tool developed by Fyodor, reports NetBSD 1.1–1.2.1; Telneting to the Web server reports FreeBSD/i386. In addition, according to NMAP, the router (167.130.64.82) is a Cisco router running IOS 10.3–11.1.

A superb visual trace route tool called VisualRoute is available from *www.visualroute.datametrics.com*. Figure 12-4 shows an example of using the tool to get a route from Herndon, Virginia, to Wellington, New Zealand.

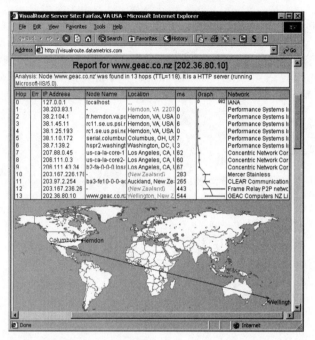

Figure 12-4. *Using VisualRoute.*

Distributed DoS Attacks

Recently, a new type of attack has made the headlines—the distributed denial of service (DDoS) attack. It works like this:

1. An attacker compromises a large number of computers using well-known vulnerabilities in unpatched computers.

2. The attacker installs special DDoS software on each compromised computer. The software listens for commands from the attacker.

3. The attacker uses special client software to send commands to all the compromised computers to direct them to flood a victim's network with data.

You should note that DDoS tools use three layers of computers. The lowest layer takes instructions from the middle layer and performs the attacks. The lowest layer requires the IP address of the middle layer in order to get instructions. Attackers don't want to embed their own IP addresses in the instructions, so they need the middle layer. Commands go from the attacker to the middle layer and then to the lowest layer. Each layer has a different name, depending on the type of DDoS tool.

Three major DDoS tools have been used:

- Tribe Flood Network (TFN), which performs the following distributed attacks:

  - ICMP flood

  - SYN flood

  - UDP flood

  - Smurf

    For more information, go to *staff.washington.edu/dittrich/misc/ tfn.analysis*.

- Trinoo, which performs distributed UDP flooding attacks. For more information, go to *staff.washington.edu/dittrich/misc/trinoo.analysis*.

- Stacheldraht (German for barbed wire), which combines features of TFN and Trinoo and adds communication encryption between the attacker's client software and the Stacheldraht software. It performs the same attacks as TFN does. For more information, go to *staff.washington.edu/dittrich/ misc/stacheldraht.analysis*.

The main computers performing the attacks (unbeknownst to their administrators) were vulnerable Sun Solaris computers with buffer overruns in unpatched versions of statd (network status monitor), cmsd (calendar manager service), and ttdbserverd (ToolTalk database).

If you think that your Web site might become the victim of a DDoS attack, you should set the Registry values listed in Table 12-3 to increase the TCP/IP stack's resistance on your servers. You can set these options using the hisecweb.inf Security Configuration Tool template included with this book and described in Appendix F in the companion CD's e-book. They're also described in detail at *www.microsoft.com/ technet/security/dosrv.asp*.

Registry Key	Recommended Value
Tcpip\Parameters\SynAttackProtect	2
Tcpip\Parameters\TcpMaxHalfOpen	100 (500 on Advanced Server)
Tcpip\Parameters\TcpMaxHalfOpenRetried	80 (400 on Advanced Server)
Tcpip\Parameters\EnablePMTUDiscovery	0
NetBt\Parameters\NoNameReleaseOnDemand	1
Tcpip\Parameters\EnabledDeadGWDetect	0
Tcpip\Parameters\KeepAliveTime	300,000
Tcpip\Parameters\Interfaces\PerformRouterDiscovery	0
Tcpip\Parameters\EnableICMPRedirects	0

Table 12-3. *Recommended TCP/IP Registry settings to help withstand DDoS attacks.*

For additional information about countering DDoS attacks, go to *www.cert.org/ incident_notes/IN-99-07.html* and *www.cert.org/reports/dsit_workshop.pdf*.

Attack Summary

You might notice that many of the common attacks relate to the TPC/IP protocol suite. They exploit flaws in the implementation of the protocols or in the design of TCP/IP itself, or they create malicious congestion. The biggest concern with TCP/IP is it was never designed to be secure. Packets can be forged, altered, and sent in an unauthenticated manner. Internet Protocol Security (IPSec), an IETF technology included in Windows 2000, addresses these issues by providing packet authentication, packet integrity, and packet privacy. You can also configure a server to never accept connections from non-IPSec clients.

You'll find an excellent summary of the more common IP-level attacks at *www.zdnet.com/devhead/stories/articles/0,4413,2172746,00.html*.

HOW TO DETECT WHETHER YOU'RE UNDER ATTACK

The simplest way to detect whether you're under attack is to use audit logs and an intrusion detection tool.

Enabling Audit Logs

It's paramount that you enable logging in Windows 2000, IIS, and Microsoft SQL Server, as described in the following sections.

Auditing in Windows 2000

In Windows 2000, you can set auditing policy on a local machine if it's not running in a domain. If the machine is running in a domain, you can make the policy global. Take the following steps:

1. In the Security Policy tool, navigate to Local Policies, Audit Policy.

2. Set the policy you want by using the settings listed in Table 12-4.

Policy	Setting
Audit account logon events	Success, Failure
Audit account management	Success, Failure
Audit directory service access	Failure
Audit logon events	Success, Failure
Audit object access	Failure
Audit policy change	Success, Failure
Audit privilege use	Failure
Audit process tracking	No auditing
Audit system events	No auditing

Table 12-4. *Windows 2000 audit settings.*

Auditing in IIS

You can configure audit logging in IIS by following these steps:

1. In the IIS Microsoft Management Console (MMC) snap-in, right-click the Web site in question (such as the Default Web Site node) and choose Properties from the context menu.

2. Be sure that Enable Logging is selected and that the active log format is W3C Extended Log File Format.

3. Click the Properties button next to the Active Log Format drop-down list box.

4. Select a new log time period. Select the Use Local Time For Naming And Rollover option if you don't want to use the default UTC (or GMT) timing.

5. Click the Extended Properties tab.

6. Be sure that the following are enabled:

    ❑ Client IP Address

    ❑ User Name

    ❑ Method

    ❑ URI Stem

    ❑ URI Query

    ❑ Protocol Status

    ❑ Win32 Status

    ❑ Bytes Sent (optional)

    ❑ Bytes Received

    ❑ Time Taken (optional)

    ❑ User Agent

7. Click OK twice.

Auditing in SQL Server

You can configure security logging in SQL Server 7 as follows:

1. In the SQL Server Enterprise Manager, choose Microsoft SQL Servers, SQL Server Group.

2. Open the server in question.

3. Right-click the server, and choose Properties from the context menu.

4. Click on the Security tab.

5. Be sure that Audit Level: All is selected, and then click OK.

Analyzing IIS logs

The first logs you should look at if an attack is Web-based are the IIS logs. People often try to perform attacks using scripts for old vulnerabilities that have been fixed. Examples of such attacks are listed in Table 12-5.

Attack	Comments
"::$DATA" bug	Allows the attacker to view the source code of ASP files.
"." bug	Same as above, but the file being accessed has a "." at the end.
".htr" buffer overflow	A specially crafted request to an .htr file executes arbitrary code in the security context of the Web server.
RDS exploit	A specially crafted Remote Data Services request executes arbitrary code at the server.
Samples	Some samples contain code for viewing source code. Never install samples on a production server.

Table 12-5. *Common attacks on IIS based on vulnerabilities that have been fixed.*

You might be under attack if you see any lines in your IIS logs that look like those listed in Table 12-6.

Attack	Log File Example(s)
"::$DATA" bug	15:59:09 218.216.157.240 – W3SVC1 207.46.171.196 80 GET /default.asp::$DATA
"." bug	15:59:09 218.216.157.240 – W3SVC1 207.46.171.196 80 GET /default.asp. (Note the "." at the end of default.asp.)
".htr" buffer overflow	15:59:09 218.216.157.240 – W3SVC1 207.46.171.196 80 GET / iisadmpwd/aexp.htr (You should consider access to any file ending in .htr suspicious.)
RDS exploit	16:55:54 228.153. 98.189 – W3SVC1 207.46.171.196 80 POST /msadc/msadcs.dll hr=800a1004,CSoapStub::HttpExtensionProc, 200 271 679
	18:48:21 216.118.25.150 – W3SVC1 207.46.171.196 80 GET / msadc/msadcs.dll - 404 3395 387
	15:33:57 219.213.116.121 – W3SVC1 207.46.171.196 80 GET /msadc/msadcs.dll/ VbBusObj.VbBusObjCls.GetRecordset+HTTP/1.1 – 401 3417 460
	15:35:45 219.123.163.22 – W3SVC1 207.46.171.196 80 GET / msadc/msadcs.dll/AdvancedDataFactory.Query+HTTP/1.1 – 401 3417 452 (All of the above are valid RDS entries and should all be treated as suspicious.)
Samples	15:59:09 218.216.157.240 – W3SVC1 207.46.171.196 80 GET / IISSamples

Table 12-6. *Examples of suspicious activity recorded in the IIS logs.*

You can use the following Perl code to look for these attempted attacks on your server. Save this file as Attacks.pl; usage is *Attacks.pl logfile(s)*. You can use wildcards in the names of log files.

```perl
$SUMMARY_ONLY = 0; # Set to 0 to display all offending lines.

%hits=(RDS            => 0,
       DOLLAR_DATA    => 0,
       DOT            => 0,
       SAMPLES        => 0,
       SHOWCODE       => 0,
       HTR            => 0,
       DOT_DOT        => 0,
       SAM_ACCESS     => 0,
       INDEX          => 0,
       BOOT_INI       => 0);

foreach (<$ARGV[0]>) {
    print "Opening log $_\n";
    warn unless open FILEHANDLE, "<" . $_;

    # Read each line.
    while (<FILEHANDLE>) {
        print "$lines lines processed.\r" if ++$lines % 500 == 0;

        if (/msadcs/i) {
            print "[RDS EXPLOIT] $_\n" unless $SUMMARY_ONLY;
            $hits{RDS}++;
        } elsif (/::\$DATA/i) {
            print "[::\$DATA EXPLOIT] $_\n" unless $SUMMARY_ONLY;
            $hits{DOLLAR_DATA}++;
        } elsif (/.*GET \/.*\.asp\./i) {
            print "['.' EXPLOIT] $_\n" unless $SUMMARY_ONLY;
            $hits{DOT}++;
        } elsif (/sam\._/i) {
            print "[ACCESSING SAM] $_\n" unless $SUMMARY_ONLY;
            $hits{SAM_ACCESS}++;
        } elsif (/\.ida|\.idq|\.htw/i) {
            print "[INDEX SERVER] $_\n" unless $SUMMARY_ONLY;
            $hits{INDEX}++;
        } elsif (/boot\.ini/i) {
            print "[ACCESSING BOOT FILE] $_\n" unless $SUMMARY_ONLY;
            $hits{BOOT_INI}++;
        } elsif (/iissamples/i) {
            print "[SAMPLES] $_\n" unless $SUMMARY_ONLY;
```

```
            $hits{SAMPLES}++;
        } elsif (/showcode\.asp/i) {
            print "[SHOWCODE] $_\n" unless $SUMMARY_ONLY;
            $hits{SHOWCODE}++;
        } elsif (/htr/i) {
            print "[HTR EXPLOIT] $_\n" unless $SUMMARY_ONLY;
            $hits{HTR}++;
        } elsif (/\.\./) {
            print "[\.\. EXPLOIT] $_\n" unless $SUMMARY_ONLY;
            $hits{DOT_DOT}++;
        }
    }

    close FILEHANDLE;
}

# Print the summary results.
print "\n\n--------------\nAttack Summary\n-------------\n";
print "$lines lines processed\n\n";
@keys = sort {int $hits{$b} <=> int $hits{$a} } keys %hits;
foreach $key (@keys) {
    $value = $hits{$key};
    $percent = ($value / $lines) * 100;
    printf "%12s = %7d (%0.4f%%) attempts\n",$key,$value,$percent;
}
```

You should run this script, available on the companion CD, regularly to determine whether you're being attacked or probed, but don't be too alarmed by occasional activity. To quote Chapman and Zwicky in their excellent book *Building Internet Firewalls,* "Once is an accident; twice is a coincidence; three times is enemy action."

BUFFER OVERFLOWS

You might have noticed that we referred to the ".htr" bug as a buffer overflow bug. A buffer overflow is simply a coding problem whereby a large amount of data is copied into a small space. Look at the following C/C++ code:

```
#include "stdio.h"
#include "string.h"

void CopyData(char *str) {
    char buff[64];
    strcpy(buff,str);
}
```

(continued)

continued

```
void main(int argc, char* argv[]) {
    char cLargeString[80];
    memset(cLargeString,'*',80);
    cLargeString[79] = 0;
    CopyData(cLargeString);
    puts("Data copied");
}
```

As you can see, when the *CopyData* function is called, it tries to copy at least 80 bytes into a 64-byte space. In the best case, an access violation occurs and the operating system shuts down the application. In fact, that's what this code does. In the worst case, the attacker might be able to execute arbitrary code. Here's how.

When one function calls another, it places (the correct term is *pushes*) the address of the next instruction onto the stack. When the function returns, it "*pops*" the address off the stack and continues execution at the new address. Look at the *buff* variable in *CopyData*. If you know C or C++, you know that this is a stack-based variable. In other words, *buff* is right next to the return address for this function on the stack. Also on the stack is the only argument to *CopyData*, a pointer to a series of characters: *char *str*. In memory, the stack looks like that shown in Figure 12-5.

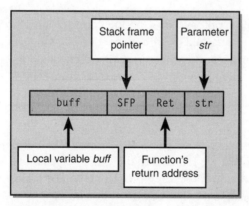

Figure 12-5. *A healthy stack.*

You'll notice another unit of data called the SFP, or stack frame pointer. We won't cover this, but you must take its size into consideration in a real attack.

The secret to an attack is the content of the 80-byte block, which is specially crafted so that it overwrites the return address to point to the contents of the 64-byte buffer. The attacker places executable assembly language instructions in the buffer. After a successful attack, the stack looks like that shown in Figure 12-6.

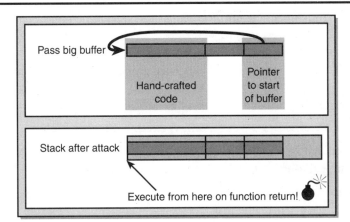

Figure 12-6. *A stack after an attack.*

This is often referred to as "smashing the stack." The preeminent paper on the subject is called "Smashing the Stack for Fun and Profit" by AlephOne in issue 49 of *Phrack* magazine (*www.phrack.com*). Another great article is "The Tao of Windows Buffer Overflow" by DilDog, available at *www.cultdeadcow.com/cDc_files/cDc-351.*

Analyzing Windows 2000 logs

You should also monitor the Windows 2000 logs; especially suspicious are the security events described in Table 12-7.

Security Event ID	Comments
612	The audit policy has changed, perhaps maliciously.
640	A change has been made to the SAM database. (Was it you?)
531	An attempt was made to log on using a disabled account. (Why would anyone want to do this?)
539	A logon attempt was made and rejected because the account was locked out. (Why would anyone want to do this?)
529	An attempt was made to log on using an unknown user account or using a valid user account but with an invalid password. (An unexpected increase in the number of these audits might indicate an attempt to guess passwords.)
517	The audit log has been cleared. (Is an attacker attempting to cover her tracks?)

Table 12-7. *Security event log entries that you should monitor.*   *(continued)*

Table 12-7. *continued*

Security Event ID	Comments
624	A user account has been created. (Was it created by a trusted person?)
628	A user account's password has been set. (Was this done by a trusted person?)

Note that you can filter the event log in Windows 2000. To monitor for 529 events, take these steps:

1. In the Event Viewer, right-click the Security log and choose New Log View from the context menu.

2. Select the new log view, press F2, and type *Security - 529*.

3. Right-click the new log view, and choose Properties from the context menu.

4. Click the Filter tab.

5. Set the following fields:

   ❑ Event Source: Security

   ❑ Category: Logon/Logoff

   ❑ Event ID: 529

6. Click OK.

You should set up a filter for any other events that are of interest to you.

If you deal with many computers, you might want to use the Dump Event Log (or Dumpel) tool that comes with the *Microsoft Windows 2000 Server Resource Kit*. This command line tool dumps an event log for a local or remote system into a tab-separated or comma-separated text file.

You can also use the tool to filter certain event types. For example, the following will dump security events 529 and 531 from the security event log on a server called \\major into a file called seclog.txt:

```
Dumpel -f seclog.txt -s \\major -l security
 -m security -e 529 531
```

You can then easily parse this file to look for suspicious activity.

Analyzing SQL Server logs

SQL Server has two log types, the Windows 2000 event log and its own text files, called errorlog.*nnn*, in the \MSSQL7\LOG directory. The event log entries are always the same regardless of whether the logon was validated; only the text varies. The entries are in the Application log. Source is MSSQLServer, Category is Logon, and Event ID is 17055. This makes them a little difficult to analyze. However, the text files are quite easy to analyze. They look something like this:

```
1999-12-17 12:48:16.16 logon     Login succeeded for user
 'DOM\Squirt'. Connection: Trusted.
1999-12-17 12:49:09.64 logon     Login failed for user
 'sa'.
1999-12-17 12:55:00.34 logon     Login succeeded for user
 'sa'. Connection: Non-Trusted.
```

The first entry shows a valid trusted connection from a user called Squirt on the DOM domain. Connection: Trusted means that the account was authenticated using Windows authentication. Connection: Non-Trusted means that the account used the built-in SQL Server authentication.

You can quickly parse these files by entering the following at the command line in the SQL Server log file directory:

```
findstr /i "login.failed" err*.*
```

Note the period between *login* and *failed*. Without it, *findstr* would look for the words *login* or *failed* in the files.

Using Performance Monitor to detect an attack

You should also consider monitoring resource load—most notably, CPU load—using Performance Monitor. If the system peaks at 100 percent CPU use, the computer might be under a DoS attack. Of course, the server might just be very busy!

Intrusion Detection Tools

Intrusion detection tools are programs that look for attack "fingerprints" and log the results in an audit file or notify an administrator. Thankfully, these tools are becoming commonplace in many organizations. A good analysis of these tools is available at *www.networkcomputing.com/1023/1023f1.html*.

There are many tools to choose from, including the following:

■ RealSecure from Internet Security Systems (*www.iss.net*)

■ BlackICE from Network Ice (*www.networkice.com*)

■ Intruder Alert and NetProwler from Axent Technologies (*www.axent.com*)

Figure 12-7 shows a computer monitored by BlackICE coming under serious attack.

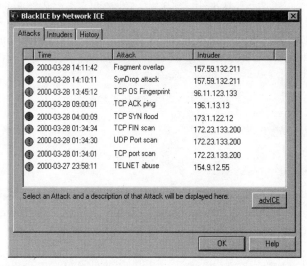

Figure 12-7. *The BlackICE intrusion detection tool showing a series of attacks.*

The seven oldest events are probes, not attacks, although the Telnet abuse might be one or the other. If the probes were just Telneting to port 80 to find out the Web server version, it's part of the information-gathering exercise; however, if they were typing in some illegal characters to, say, an RPC port to attempt to get the RPC service to crash, it might be an attack.

The TCP OS Fingerprint event is interesting. Operating systems can behave differently when they receive certain types of specially crafted IP packets. By sending these packets to a server and evaluating the response, a program can determine with some accuracy which operating system is running on the remote computer. The most common tool for performing this is called NMAP. For more details about OS fingerprinting and NMAP, go to *www.phrack.com/search.phtml?view&article=p54-9.*

The top two events, SynDrop and Fragment overlap, are attacks, both of which were mentioned in "Some Common Attacks."

Many tools also have excellent documentation explaining each attack in detail. Figure 12-8 shows an example of the BlackICE online documentation for a SYN flood attack.

It's quite easy to see whether you're under a SYN flood attack without an intrusion detection tool by using the netstat utility included with Windows 2000. This tool provides statistics about the TCP/IP protocol suite, but more importantly, it can display the status of all TCP/IP connections to and from your computer and the state of each connection.

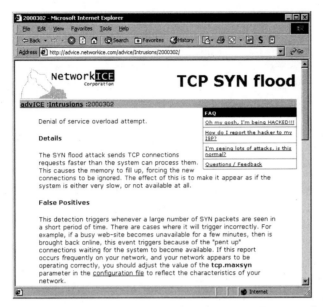

Figure 12-8. *BlackICE's online documentation for a SYN flood attack.*

For example, if you enter *netstat −n −p tcp* at the command line, you'll see output like this if you're under attack:

```
Proto  Local Address       Foreign Address     State
TCP    127.0.0.1:1030      127.0.0.1:1032      ESTABLISHED
TCP    127.0.0.1:1032      127.0.0.1:1030      ESTABLISHED
TCP    10.57.8.190:21      10.57.14.154:1256   SYN_RECEIVED
TCP    10.57.8.190:21      10.57.14.154:1257   SYN_RECEIVED
TCP    10.57.8.190:21      10.57.14.154:1258   SYN_RECEIVED
TCP    10.57.8.190:21      10.57.14.154:1259   SYN_RECEIVED
TCP    10.57.8.190:21      10.57.14.154:1260   SYN_RECEIVED
TCP    10.57.8.190:21      10.57.14.154:1261   SYN_RECEIVED
TCP    10.57.8.190:21      10.57.14.154:1262   SYN_RECEIVED
TCP    10.57.8.190:21      10.57.14.154:1263   SYN_RECEIVED
TCP    10.57.8.190:21      10.57.14.154:1264   SYN_RECEIVED
TCP    10.57.8.190:21      10.57.14.154:1265   SYN_RECEIVED
TCP    10.57.8.190:21      10.57.14.154:1266   SYN_RECEIVED
TCP    10.57.8.190:4801    10.57.14.221:139    TIME_WAIT
```

Note the number of connections in the SYN_RECEIVED state. Be aware that the foreign address is probably fake.

Another issue to be aware of is the coordinated or DDoS attack. Hosts around the world can coordinate to mount a massive attack on a single host. For more information, go to *www.cert.org/incident_notes/IN-99-07.html*.

Integrity tools

Another tool that you should seriously consider using is an integrity tool. Integrity tools check that resources such as files, access controls lists, and Registry settings haven't been tampered with. If they have, the tools can perform actions such as e-mailing administrative staff.

Two such tools we've used are

■ Tripwire from Tripwire Security Systems Inc. (*www.tripwiresecurity.com*). Tripwire is well known in the UNIX world and has been ported to Windows NT and Windows 2000. At the Tripwire Web site, be sure to get a copy of the excellent "Common Security Exploits and Vulnerability Matrix" poster, which is a superb reference.

■ Intact from Pedestal Software (*www.pedestalsoftware.com*). Intact was designed for Windows NT and Windows 2000. It not only monitors files, Registry entries, and ACLs, but it also monitors user and group account manipulation.

Here's some sample output from Intact 2.0 indicating that a file has been changed. (The file size has grown.) Was the change benign or malicious? Has a hacker left some new wording on your home page? You should check whether changes such as this were made by your Web development team!

```
INFO: MSG: CONFIG: Intact Intelligence Version 2.0
INFO: MSG: CONFIG: Current User EXAIR\WebAdmin
INFO: MSG: CONFIG: INTACT CHECK START 09/03/99 22:33:12

CHANGED: FILE: c:\Web\Default.html
Last write time changed:
   was: September 02, 1999 13:53:21
    is: September 02, 1999 23:12:54
Size has changed
   was: 1022
    is: 1431
DIGEST1 is different
   was: (MD5: 27 00 70 A8 DC C4 C6 D1 AE F0 08 92 C8 3B 39 C2)
    is: (MD5: 02 A9 25 77 87 E3 1E FD 0F 39 EA 6E 17 36 11 9D)
DIGEST2 is different
   was: (SHA1: 38 DE FA 26 78 7E 66 EB 88 D7 6B A7 21 46 A6 B1
A1 2F 0D 63)
    is: (SHA1: 71 FD 44 E8 FA 1A BC C8 81 E4 EE 01 8A 11 00 00
17 11 2B FE)
```

USER INPUT ATTACKS

Most Web applications take user input, manipulate the data, and create results based on the information. The most common way to gather user input in a Web application is with a Web form, which uses the *<FORM>* tag. However, few Web developers perform stringent validation of the posted data. The most common user input attacks take these forms:

- Posting HTML, script, or specially crafted input to the server
- Posting large amounts of data to the server

Let's look at both types of user input attack in turn.

Posting HTML, Script, or Specially Crafted Input to the Server

You must be cautious if your application uses any user input to create results that are displayed in a browser. You should inspect all user input before using it for output or before using it to access requested system resources. You might have the best firewalls and perimeter defenses, but HTTP and HTML traffic travels right through those defenses—they don't protect you from malicious user input.

> **AN IMPORTANT RULE OF THUMB** All user input is bad until proven otherwise!

A good example of an application that might be vulnerable to a user input attack is a guest book application. There are two main uses for a guest book application: to gather user input and to display the results for other users to see. An attacker can easily look at the source code (in Microsoft Internet Explorer, you right-click the page and then choose View Source from the context menu) of the data-gathering form to determine what sort of input the application expects and then attempt to post nonstandard data to the server. Any form that accepts text is a potential target for posting of HTML or script.

Let's look at a very common, real-life example. The attacker goes to the data entry page at *www.exair.com/comments.html* and looks at the source code. He sees that there are three fields: name, address, and comments. Each of these is a potential target. For fun, he enters his name as *<!--META HTTP-EQUIV="REFRESH"CONTENT="1" URL="www.advworks.com">* and clicks the Submit button, which posts the data to the Exploration Air Web server. After one second, any user viewing this person's "name" is whisked away from *www.exair.com* to *www.advworks.com*!

How did this work? It's actually very simple. When the comments were re-displayed, the tag he entered was executed by the client's browser and caused the browser to go to *www.advworks.com* after one second. This is a simple but irritating attack because no one can read the comments.

The easiest way to protect against this kind of attack is to parse all user input as it comes to the server, as described in the following sections. To restate the simple rule you should always follow: never use user input as output without checking it first.

REGULAR EXPRESSIONS IN VBSCRIPT AND MICROSOFT JSCRIPT

The following code samples use the RegExp object built into version 5 of the VBScript and JScript script engines. RegExp let's you use a search string—known as a *regular expression*—to search for or replace a pattern of text in a string. You should use RegExp—which debuted in late 1999—in your ASP files to parse and process user input before you use that input to query databases or to display data.

You'll recognize the syntax if you're familiar with Perl or grep regular expressions. The characters are described in Table 12-8.

RegExp Character	Comments
\	Marks the next character as a special character or a literal. For example, *"n"* matches the character *n*. *"\n"* matches a newline character. The sequence *"\\"* matches \, and *"\("* matches (.
^	Matches the beginning of the input.
$	Matches the end of the input.
*	Matches the preceding character zero or more times. For example, *"mi*"* matches *m* or *michael*.
+	Matches the preceding character one or more times. For example, *"mi+"* matches *michael* but not *m*.
?	Matches the preceding character zero or one times. For example, *"a??ve"* matches *alive*.
{n}	Matches a pattern exactly *n* times.

Table 12-8. *Abridged VBScript and JScript RegExp syntax.*

RegExp Character	Comments
{n,m}	Matches a pattern at least *n* times and no more than *m* times.
.	Matches any single character except a newline character.
(pattern)	Matches the pattern and remembers the match in the Matches collection.
x|y	Matches x or y. For example, *"g |food"* matches g or *food*. *"(g |f)ood"* matches *good* or *food*.
[xyz]	A character set. Matches any one of the enclosed characters. For example, *"[abc]"* matches the *a* in *plain*.
[^xyz]	A negative character set. Matches any character not enclosed. For example, *"[^abc]"* matches the *p* in *plain*.
[a-z]	A range of characters. Matches any character in the specified range. For example, *"[a-z]"* matches any lowercase alphabetic character in the range *a* through *z*.
[^m-z]	A negative range of characters. Matches any character not in the specified range. For example, *"[m-z]"* matches any character not in the range *m* through *z*.
\b	Matches a word boundary (the position between a word and a space). For example, *"er\b"* matches the *er* in *never* but not the *er* in *verb*.
\B	Matches a nonword boundary. For example, *"ea*r\B"* matches the *ear* in *never early*.
\d	Matches a digit character. Equivalent to [0-9].
\D	Matches a nondigit character. Equivalent to [^0-9].
\n	Matches a newline character.
\r	Matches a carriage return character.
\s	Matches any white space, including space, tab, and form-feed. Equivalent to *"[\f\n\r\t\v]"*.
\S	Matches any non–white space character. Equivalent to *"[^ \f\n\r\t\v]"*.
\w	Matches any word character, including the underscore. Equivalent to *"[A-Za-z0-9_]"*.
\W	Matches any nonword character. Equivalent to *"[^A-Za-z0-9_]"*.
\xn	Matches *n*, where *n* is a hexadecimal escape value. Hexadecimal escape values must be exactly two digits long. For example, *"\x41"* matches *A*. *"\x041"* is equivalent to *\x04* and *1*. Allows ASCII codes to be used in regular expressions.

Stripping a string of all characters other than 0–9, a–z, A–Z, and _

In some cases, you know you're dealing with a limited set of characters—for example, names or country names. In this case, you should remove all unnecessary characters from the string, as shown here:

```
Set reg = New RegExp
reg.Pattern = "\W+" ' Characters that are NOT 0-9,
                    '  a-z, A-Z, or _.
strUnTainted = reg.Replace(strTainted, "")
```

Stripping all text after pipe or redirect operators

Attackers often try to use pipe (|) or redirect (< and >) operators to invoke other programs after some data is processed, especially on UNIX platforms. For example, say that an ASP file takes a user's age as input and uses it to build an SQL query such as *select * from useraccounts where age = <%=age%>*. This code is flawed because if an attacker enters her name as *34 | someprogram.exe*, the following SQL is executed: *select * from useraccounts where age = 34 | someprogram.exe*, which executes someprogram.exe.

The following code strips out the < and > characters and has the side effect of rendering HTML tags useless.

```
Set reg = New RegExp
reg.Pattern = "^(.+)\<|\>|\|(.+)"
strUnTainted = reg.Replace(strTainted, "$1")
```

As a side note, if you want to specifically search for and remove HTML tags, don't search for them using the following expression:

```
' INCORRECT HTML parsing code.
Set reg = New RegExp
reg.Pattern = "\<.*\>" ' A < character followed by zero or
                       '  more characters then a > character.
StrUnTainted = reg.Replace(strTainted, "")
```

This expression works only if the post contains single lines of HTML—in other words, if the opening < and closing > are on the same line. However, it's legal HTML for these two characters to appear on different lines, so you must adjust the parsing code to search all the lines as a single unit, not separately:

```
' CORRECT HTML parsing code.
Set reg = New RegExp
reg.Global = True
reg.Pattern = "\<.*\>" ' A < character followed by zero or
                       '  more characters then a > character.
StrUnTainted = reg.Replace(strTainted, "")
```

Stripping invalid text from a filename

Windows 2000 has a function called *CreateFile* for creating and opening files. However, in Windows 2000 a file is more than a sequence of bytes on a disk drive; it can also be a printer or a serial port. If you use the *FileSystem* object (which uses *CreateFile*) from an ASP page, you should be sure that any data passed to you from a client that is used as part of the filename is valid and not the name of a printer or a serial port.

The following JScript code strips invalid filenames from a string called *strIn*:

```
var strOut = strIn.replace(/(AUX|PRN|NUL|COM\d|LPT\d)+\s*$/i,
    "");
```

This script removes all instances of strings matching AUX, PRN, NUL, COM*n*, and LPT*n* (where *n* is a number) and possibly followed by spaces.

A twist on malicious input: script injection and cross-site scripting

An attack on a Web server doesn't always affect the Web server itself, but might use the Web site as a catalyst for attacking other unsuspecting Web users. This type of attack relies on servers that create dynamic output based on user input. A Web site that is a victim of this attack creates malicious content for other unsuspecting Web surfers and makes them vulnerable to any number of attacks.

Let's say that Attacker A wants to attack User B. Here's how the attack works:

1. Attacker A finds a vulnerable Web site C, which takes script as input and includes the script in the output. For example, the Web site might take a request such as *www.exair.com/search.asp?searchfor=code*, where *code* is specially formatted code that will run in a client's browser. As you'll see, *code* will be sent to User B's browser because Web site C puts the input data into the output data without first checking its validity.

2. Attacker A sends User B an anonymous e-mail or a posting in a news forum that contains the specially formatted URL for User B to click. The URL contains malicious client code pointing to Web site C.

3. When User B clicks on the URL, his or her Web browser loads and attempts to connect to the URL.

4. Web site C receives the request and evaluates the text after the *?* in the URL.

5. Web site C creates a dynamic page that includes the results of the search and the initial data used in the search. It's common practice for search engines to include the search string in the output to the user.

6. User B's Web browser loads the dynamically generated HTML, but when it comes time to display the search string, the browser executes the code in the security context of User B. The code might do any of a number of things, such as update cookies on User B's machine (using JavaScript's *document.cookie* object) so that the attacks continue for a long time.

As you can see, it's utterly imperative that your Web sites parse all user input. Some user input might be an attempt to attack you, while other input might be an attempt to attack others and look like it came from you!

Reviewing ASP code for vulnerability

You can take the following steps to make sure that your ASP code isn't a catalyst in this type of attack:

- Look for all code that generates dynamic output—most notably, Response.Write and <%= %> tags.
- Determine whether the output includes input parameters from sources such as
  - ❑ Request.Form
  - ❑ Request.QueryString
  - ❑ Databases
  - ❑ Request.Cookies
  - ❑ Session

You must fix any code that creates output based on untested input, including

- Code that uses regular expressions (as described earlier)
- Code that uses Server.HTMLEncode to encode input parameters
- Code that uses Server.URLEncode to encode URLs received as input parameters

For more information about checking your ASP code, see Knowledge Base article Q253119 at *support.microsoft.com/support/kb/articles/q253/1/19.asp*. You can also find more information about this type of attack at *www.microsoft.com/technet/security/crssite.asp* and *www.microsoft.com/technet/security/CSOverv.asp*.

Some useful regular expressions

You can use the expressions listed in Table 12-9 in your code to check the validity of user input using the *RegExp.Test* method. For example, the following VBScript code checks a number:

```
Set reg = New RegExp
reg.Pattern = "\d+" ' One or more 0-9's.
bIsOK = reg.Test(strTainted)
```

Input Type	*Regular Expression*
U.S. telephone number Example: (abc) def-ghij	^\(\d{3}\) \d{3}-\d{4}$
U.S. zip code Example: 98006 or 98006-9111	^\d{5}(-\d{4}){0,1}$
Dollar amount Example: $34.12, 34.12, $34, or 34	^\${0,1}\d+(\.\d\d){0,1}$
IP address	/^([01]?\d?\d|2[0-4]\d|25[0-5])\. ([01]?\d?\d|2[0-4]\d|25[0-5])\. ([01]?\d?\d|2[0-4]\d|25[0-5])\. ([01]?\d?\d|2[0-4]\d|25[0-5])\$

Table 12-9. *Common regular expressions.*

IMPORTANT If you cannot use regular expressions to verify user input, you should consider using the <PRE> tag to display any output based on unparsed user input. Text displayed using this tag is not interpreted by the browser; it is displayed. <PRE> is often used to display HTML tags in Web pages for educational reasons.

Posting Large Amounts of Data to the Server

Look at this HTML form code:

```
<form method=POST action=Comments.asp
 enctype="application/x-www-form-urlencoded">

<table border=0 cellspacing=0 cellpadding=0>

<tr>
    <td width=131 valign=top>Name:</td>
    <td width=288 valign=top>
    <INPUT TYPE="TEXT" MAXLENGTH="64" SIZE="49" NAME="txtName">
    </td>
</tr>

<!-- Other fields, including address and comment -->
```

(continued)

```
<tr>
    <td><INPUT TYPE="SUBMIT" METHOD="POST"></td>
</tr>

</table>
</form>
```

Your browser prevents you from entering more than 64 characters of data into the name field. Unfortunately, many Web applications do no other data-size checking because they rely on the browser to do the work. An attacker can quite easily "handcraft" an HTML post to include a very large name—say, 64,000 characters long. If the data is unchecked by the server, all kinds of failures can occur, such as database errors if the data is written to a database or access violations if the data is used by a C++ COM component that has a fixed 64-byte array.

The following Perl code is an example of an attack of this kind:

```
use HTTP::Request::Common qw(POST);
use HTTP::Headers;
use LWP::UserAgent;

# Create a new, invalid request.
$ua = LWP::UserAgent->new();
$req = POST 'http://www.exair.com/comment.asp',
            [ Name => 'A' x 64000,
              Address => 'B' x 8192,
              Comment => 'C' x 8192
            ];
$res = $ua->request($req);

# Display the error from the server.
$err = $res->status_line;
print "$err ";

# If interested, display the body of the request.
print "Display body? (y/N)";
print $res->as_string if (getc == 'y');
```

The line that causes the damage is *$req = POST*. It builds up a post with long name (64,000 As), address (8192 Bs), and comment (8192 Cs) fields.

You should always check the size of posted data in your server-side code before you use it as input (to a database, for example). The following sample ASP code performs this task:

```
If Len(Request.Form("Address")) >= 128 Then
    Response.Write "Address is too long. Try again."
Else
    ' Normal processing.
End If
```

WHAT TO DO IF YOU'RE UNDER ATTACK

Imagine that your pager goes off at 3 A.M. and you find out that your home page has been defaced. Here are some simple steps you should consider. Note, however, that speed without haste is paramount. Don't panic.

- Find out what happened. What type of attack was it—DoS, disclosure, or integrity? Has the attacker broken into one of your systems? Is the attack still in progress? What changed? Take note of any dates and times and the impact of the attack.

- Consider pulling the power or the network connection. You might want to take the server(s) off line and replace them with a server displaying a "We will be back on line shortly" message. It's very important that you take the affected servers off line so you have clean evidence.

- Consider making a complete snapshot of the system. This is worth the effort if you think you might be pressing charges. You can work on the duplicate system without disrupting the original.

- Gather evidence. This includes data in all log files, including Windows 2000 logs, SQL Server logs, IIS logs, firewall logs, and intrusion detection tool logs. Take special note of any suspect IP addresses. Use tools such as Sam Spade (*www.samspade.org/t/*) to gather more information about the attacker. The Sam Spade site also has an excellent Internet Explorer 5 package that adds useful analysis tools to the browser. While you gather evidence, document who does what to what and when. It's important that you don't change file dates. Windows NT and Windows 2000 change the "last read" time and date if you read the files. NTObjectives (*www.ntobjectives.com*) has an excellent set of "forensics" tools that do not disrupt the file times. Have any new user accounts been added? An attacker might have added a special user account so he could come back later.

- Check with vendors. Talk to your vendors to see if they can provide information, especially if the vulnerability that led to the attack is already known to the vendor.

- Why did it happen? This is often a difficult question to answer. Unfortunately, many attacks occur because of administrative oversight. Perhaps the administrator did not install one or more of the intrusion detection tools mentioned earlier or was not paying attention to the security logs.

- Bring the system back on line. Use a trusted backup to restore the system to a healthy state. You might need to go to original media such as installation disks and CDs. Bringing the system to a healthy state might mean a new box with fresh software installation, including the operating system. A hacked computer cannot be trusted. It might have trojans or backdoors installed.

■ Change passwords. Make sure you change all passwords for all accounts that were accessible from the penetrated system, especially privileged accounts such as administrators and backup operators.

■ Try to make sure it doesn't happen again. This can be a somewhat difficult step to figure out. Some common remedies include

❑ Improving education

❑ Monitoring security newsgroups

❑ Taking security more seriously

❑ Monitoring logs actively

❑ Using intrusion detection tools

■ Document and learn. Write up what happened. Make sure the lessons learned are spread around the organization. Documenting the attack might also be important if you decide to take legal action.

STAYING UP-TO-DATE ON SECURITY ISSUES

Appendix F in the companion CD's electronic book describes some of the best practices for securing your Web server. However, you must thoroughly appreciate the single most important best practice: *staying up-to-date on security news*. Security is an ever-changing landscape. When new vulnerabilities are found in any software you use, regardless of vendor, you must take swift action. So keep current. If you're not up-to-date, you run the risk of being attacked as information about vulnerabilities and fixes spreads.

The following are some of the best places to go on the Web to stay current with security issues:

■ *www.microsoft.com/security*   The source for all Microsoft security-related information

■ *www.ntsecurity.net*   Another useful source of Microsoft-related security information

■ *www.sans.com*   A superb source for security best practices and education

■ *www.cert.org*   Carnegie Mellon University's CERT Coordination Center, a great clearinghouse of security information

- *www.hackernews.com*   Need we say more?

- *xforce.iss.net*   An updated list of vulnerabilities maintained by Internet Security Systems

You should also consider subscribing to a number of security-related newsletters:

- Microsoft security alerts: *www.microsoft.com/security/subscribe.htm*

- CERT alerts: *mailto:cert-advisory-request@cert.org*

- BugTraq from Aleph1 (probably the best source for day-to-day security issues): *www.securityfocus.com*

- BugTraq for Windows NT and Windows 2000, maintained by Russ Cooper: *www.ntbugtraq.com*

- The SANS digest: *www.sans.org/digest.htm*

- Security Alert for Enterprise Resources (SAFER): *safer.siamrelay.com*

Finally, a word of advice for the truly paranoid: if you have a Windows CE Pocket PC or handheld device, you should consider using Microsoft Mobile Channels or AvantGo (*www.avantgo.com*) to stay on top of security issues. You can easily keep current by keeping the latest Web pages on your PC companion. For example, one of us uses AvantGo to keep the latest Microsoft and CERT security pages on his Hewlett-Packard Pocket PC. He's been known to read them during meetings—it's more productive than playing games!

A Final Thought

Every client connecting to the Internet is a potential point of attack because with the TCP/IP protocol suite all clients are also servers and can therefore accept connections from remote hosts. A neighbor of one of the authors saw the following on his screen (please pardon the atrocious spelling) and asked the author what had happened:

> *Your computer is vonrable to hackers please add passowrd to your sharring acounts! If you dont do that people can conect to your computer and deleate everything on your hard drive or put a virus in your comput. mayby evan a trojan and after that he can furthur exploit your computer. so plz plz set up a password...*

> *No damage was dome by me!*

The attacker had connected to the server using NetBIOS, set the file containing this text in the Startup group, and remotely rebooted the computer! You can easily fix the problem by unbinding NetBIOS and/or adding passwords to any shares. Be especially careful of client computers that use DSL or cable modems, which are always connected to the Internet.

The lesson is a simple one: secure every computer connected to the Internet.

SUMMARY

The moment a server is placed on the Internet, it's vulnerable to attack. Don't for one moment think that you can "sneak" a Web server onto the Internet without anyone noticing!

For an attack to take place, the attacker must have the motivation (she just got fired from a company, for example), a justification (destroying the company's Web site is nothing compared to the anguish she's suffered), and the opportunity. Having the opportunity is easy on the Internet—an attack can be launched at any time from virtually anywhere.

Attacking a site involves finding the site and scanning for open ports using a tool downloaded from the Internet. The tool determines information about the system and can sometimes search for vulnerabilities.

A common type of attack is the IP-level attack. Most of these are DoS attacks. Many low-level IP attacks exploit weaknesses in the TCP/IP protocol suite because TCP/IP was never designed to be a secure protocol. IPSec is designed to remedy most of these issues.

Be ready for attacks coming through the HTTP port. As administrators reduce the number of open ports on their firewalls, more application vendors are tunneling data through port 80. Also, be sure to filter all content coming from users. You should consider all user input as bad until you've inspected it using regular expressions. You should be able to represent any data as a regular expression.

Constantly monitor your site for vulnerabilities. Try to break into it, and use some of the tests described in this chapter. Monitor the Windows 2000, IIS, and SQL Server logs and parse them to look for suspicious activity. Use a scanner tool to scan your site for vulnerabilities. (Go to *backoffice.microsoft.com/securitypartners* for an up-to-date list.)

To catch a thief, you must think like a thief! All computers, clients, and servers are potential attack victims, so be sure to adequately secure all Internet-connected computers. Finally, the most important precaution you can take is to stay current with security issues by subscribing to security newsletters and lists.

Part IV

Reference

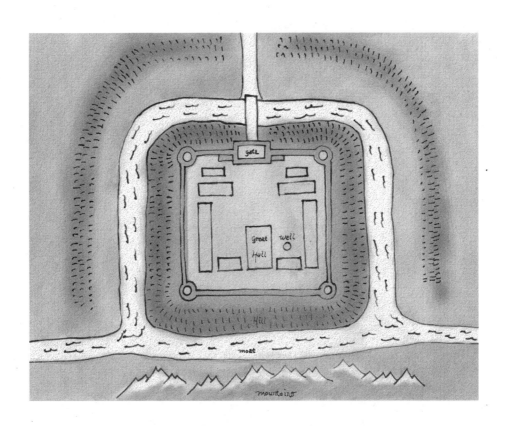

## Chapter 13

Security Administration with ADSI, WMI, and COM+

Configuring a group of servers with each server running multiple applications can be time-consuming. This chapter introduces the developer and administrator to some of the functionality available in Microsoft Windows 2000 to help build custom tools to manage complex Web-based applications. It's the authors' view that the best way to manage Windows 2000 networks programmatically—that is, from scripts—is to learn the following technologies:

- Windows Script Host (WSH): *http://msdn.microsoft.com/scripting*
- Microsoft Visual Basic Scripting Edition (VBScript) or Microsoft JScript: *http://msdn.microsoft.com/scripting*

■ Active Directory Services Interface (ADSI): *http://www.microsoft.com/windows2000/library/howitworks/activedirectory/adsilinks.asp*

■ Windows Management Instrumentation (WMI): *http://www.microsoft.com/windows2000/library/howitworks/management/wmioverview.asp*

■ Microsoft Component Object Model (COM and COM+): *http://www.microsoft.com/com*

When you use these technologies, there's little you cannot manage locally and remotely on a Windows network.

The main topics in this chapter are

■ What is WMI?

■ What is ADSI?

■ Example management and security configuration code, including Windows 2000 settings, Internet Information Services (IIS) 5 settings, Microsoft SQL Server 7 and SQL Server 2000 settings, miscellaneous COM+ scripts, and common IIS security-related ADSI settings

WHAT IS WMI?

Windows Management Instrumentation is the Windows implementation of the Web-Based Enterprise Management (WBEM) technology. Its aim is to make computer systems much more manageable and reduce the cost of managing distributed systems. WBEM is based on the Common Information Model (CIM) schema, an industry standard driven by the Desktop Management Task Force (DMTF). We strongly recommended that you download the WMI software development kit (SDK) from *http://msdn.microsoft.com/downloads/sdks/wmi* if you want to learn about WMI.

WHAT IS ADSI?

Active Directory Services Interface provides a simple, powerful interface to Active Directory, other directories (such as Novell NetWare Directory Services [NDS]), and the IIS metabase (a database used exclusively by IIS). ADSI makes it easy for programmers and administrators to create administrative programs by using high-level tools such as Visual Basic and JScript without having to worry about the underlying differences between the different technologies. ADSI enables you to build or buy programs that give you a single point of access to multiple directories in your network environment, whether those directories are based on the Lightweight Directory Access Protocol (LDAP) or another protocol.

ADSI's name might suggest that it works only with the Active Directory, but the following list of compatible technologies shows that this is not the case. ADSI is not an application development interface tied to any specific directory service.

- Microsoft Windows NT 4.0
- LDAP, which also works with Windows 2000 Active Directory
- Novell NDS
- Novell NetWare 3 Bindery
- Microsoft Exchange
- Microsoft Site Server
- Microsoft Internet Information Server

EXAMPLE MANAGEMENT AND SECURITY CONFIGURATION CODE

The following sections show how to administer different Microsoft technologies by using ADSI, WMI, and COM+. The technologies covered are Windows 2000, IIS, and SQL Server.

Windows 2000 Settings

The primary technologies for administering Windows 2000 are WMI and ADSI. All of the following samples are VBScript examples called from the WSH.

Retrieving computer information

The following code is useful for getting critical information from a possibly remote computer to determine its status. In this case, because the *DomainRole* value is *3*, the code is returning computers acting as member servers. Table 13-1 defines other values for *DomainRole.strServer = "."*

```
strQuery = & _
    "Select * from Win32_ComputerSystem Where DomainRole = 3"
Set compSet = & _
    GetObject("winmgmts:{impersonationLevel=impersonate}//" & _
    strServer & "/root/Cimv2").ExecQuery(strQuery)

For Each comp In compSet
    WScript.echo "Manufacturer: " & comp.Manufacturer
    WScript.echo "Model:        " & comp.Model
    WScript.echo "Name:         " & comp.Name
```

(continued)

```
WScript.echo "CPUs:        " & comp.NumberOfProcessors
WScript.echo "Owner:       " & comp.PrimaryOwnerName
WScript.echo "AdminPwdStat: " & comp.AdminPasswordStatus
WScript.echo "DomainRole:  " & comp.DomainRole

For Each role in comp.Roles
    WScript.echo "Role:       " & role
Next

Next
```

Value	Domain Role
0	Stand-alone workstation
1	Member workstation
2	Stand-alone server
3	Member server
4	Backup domain controller
5	Primary domain controller

Table 13-1. *Possible WMI DomainRole values.*

Enumerating groups

The following WMI code will display all the groups on a computer:

```
strServer = "."
strQuery = "Select * from Win32_Group"
Set grpSet = & _
    GetObject("winmgmts:{impersonationLevel=impersonate}//" & _
    strServer & "/root/Cimv2").ExecQuery(strQuery)

For Each grp In grpSet
    WScript.echo grp.Caption & " [SID=" & grp.SID & "]"
Next
```

Enumerating groups and users in the groups

The following code is a superset of the code in the previous section. It not only shows each group and the users in each group but also uses the *WinNT:* ADSI provider rather than WMI.

```
strComputer = "MyServer" ' Use '.' for the local computer.
Set oComp = GetObject("WinNT://" & strComputer & ",computer")
oComp.Filter = Array("group")

For Each group In oComp
    WScript.echo group.Name
```

```
    iCount = 0
    For Each member in group.members
        WScript.echo "  " & member.Name
        iCount = iCount + 1
    Next
    If iCount = 0 Then WScript.echo "  <none>"
Next
```

Viewing user account information

You can access user account information in many ways, including using the WMI provider, the LDAP provider, or the WinNT provider. The following code uses WMI to get a list of all locked-out accounts:

```
strServer = "myserver" ' Use '.' to access the local computer.
strQuery = "select * from Win32_UserAccount where Lockout = 0"
Set userSet =  & _
    GetObject("winmgmts:{impersonationLevel=impersonate}//" & _
    strServer & "/root/Cimv2").ExecQuery(strQuery)

For Each user In userSet
    WScript.echo user.Caption & " [" & user.SID & "]"
Next
```

This code uses the WinNT provider to list details about a specific account:

```
strComputer = "remotecomputer"  ' Use '.' for local computer.
strUser = "administrator"
Set oUser = GetObject("WinNT://" & strComputer & _
    "/" & strUser & ",user")
WScript.echo "Last Login: " & oUser.LastLogin
WScript.echo "Member of..."
For Each group in oUser.Groups
    WScript.echo " " & group.Name
Next
```

Accessing a user's certificate in Active Directory

The following ADSI example shows how to access a user's binary X.509 certificate. In this case, the user is *cheryl@explorationair.com*. Once you have the certificate, you can look at its contents by using the Certutil.exe tool described in Chapter 15, "An Introduction to Cryptography and Certificates in Windows 2000." Note that the *userCertificate* data is an array of bytes, so you might need to use another method other than the file system object (FSO), *scripting.filesystemobject*, to write out the data because FSO supports writing text only.

```
strDomain = "DC=ExplorationAir,DC=com"
strUser = "CN=Cheryl,CN=Users"
Set user = GetObject("LDAP://" & strUser & "," & strDomain)
cert = user.userCertificate
```

Configuring the Account Is Sensitive And Cannot Be Delegated option

The following code shows a number of options that can be set on a user object in Active Directory, including Account Is Sensitive And Cannot Be Delegated:

```
ACC_DISABLED = &H2
ACC_STORE_PWD_AS_CLEARTEXT = &H80
ACC_PWD_NEVER_EXPIRES = &H10000
ACC_SMARTCARD_REQUIREED = &H40000
ACC_TRUSTED_FOR_DELEGATION = &H80000
ACC_SENSITIVE = &H100000

StrDomain = "DC=explorationair,DC=com"
StrUser = "CN=MichaelH,CN=Users"
Set user = GetObject("LDAP://" & strUser & "," & strDomain)
user.userAccountControl=user.userAccountControl Or & _
    ACC_SENSITIVE
user.SetInfo
```

Changing a user's lockout property

It's not obvious how to read or set this property because the *IsAccountLocked* property is not accessible when using the LDAP provider—you must use the WinNT provider. The following code will read the lockout property by using the WinNT provider. If you want to set this property, you must call the *SetInfo* method on the *oUser* object after the property is set.

```
Set oUser = GetObject("WinNT://EXAIR/cheryl")
If oUser.IsAccountLocked Then
    Wscript.Echo "The account is locked out"
End If
```

Querying the Windows 2000 Security Event Log

The code following Table 13-2 uses WMI to query the Security Event Log on a remote computer to check whether any specific log entries have been written. In this case, we're searching for failed audit events that are not object access events (category 3). Note that *TimeGenerated* has an interesting format. It's not the number of seconds since a specific moment as in many other technologies—all dates and times in WMI use a fixed-length string. The string contains several fields:

yyyymmddHHMMSS.mmmmmmmsUUU

Table 13-2 describes each of these fields. Note that an asterisk can be used in an unused field.

Field	Comments
yyyy	Four-digit year (0000–9999)
mm	Two-digit month (01–12)
dd	Two-digit date (01–31)
HH	Two-digit hours based on the 24-hour clock (00–23)
MM	Two-digit minute (00–59)
SS	Two-digit seconds (00–59)
mmmmmm	Six-digit microseconds
s	"+" or "–", indicating positive or negative offset from Universal Time Coordinate (UTC) (that is, Greenwich Mean Time)
UUU	Three-digit offset from UTC in minutes

Table 13-2. *WMI date string formats.*

```
strServer = "myserver" ' Use '.' for local computer.
strQuery = "select * from Win32_NTLogEvent " & _
           "where Logfile = 'Security' " & _
           "and Type = 'audit failure' and Category <> 3"

Set oLog = & _
    GetObject("winmgmts:{impersonationLevel=impersonate}//" & _
    strServer & "/root/Cimv2").ExecQuery(strQuery)

For each oLogEntry in oLog
    WScript.Echo oLogEntry.Category
    WScript.Echo oLogEntry.TimeGenerated
    WScript.Echo oLogEntry.Message
Next
```

Internet Information Services 5 Settings

The main interface with IIS is ADSI, which is simply a wrapper on the lower-level COM+ metabase interface called *IMSAdminBase*. It's recommended that you use ADSI over the lower-level COM+ interface. Also, a tool exists called Adsutil.vbs in the InetPub\AdminScripts folder to set and enumerate all ADSI settings in IIS. For example, type the following at the command line to set the server comment on the default Web site to *"ExAir Marketing."*:

```
cscript adsutil SET W3SVC/1/ServerComment "ExAir Marketing."
```

You can view settings on the default Web site by typing

```
adsutil enum  W3SVC/1
```

You can find out more about the use of ADSI in IIS in the IIS online help at *http://localhost/iisHelp*.

Configuring a Web site to require a secure connection

The following code shows how to set the "secure" virtual directory to require Secure Sockets Layer/Transport Layer Security (SSL/TLS):

```
Set oIIS = GetObject("IIS://localhost/W3SVC/1/Secure")
oIIS.AccessSSL = True ' True enables SSL.
oIIS.AccessSSLFlags = AccessSSL128 ' Enable 128-bit crypto.
oIIS.SetInfo
Set oIIS = Nothing
```

Configuring a Web virtual directory to require Windows authentication

The following sample code shows how to set Windows authentication on a virtual directory named *Secure*.

```
Set oIIS = GetObject("IIS://localhost/W3SVC/1/Secure")

' Technically, this is wrong. Windows authentication
'   could be NTLM or Kerberos.
oIIS.AuthFlags = AuthNTLM
oIIS.SetInfo
Set oIIS = Nothing
```

Enabling/disabling CRL checking on a Web server

This simple example sets the certificate revocation list (CRL) checking status on a default Web server, Web server #1:

```
Set oIIS = GetObject("IIS://localhost/W3SVC/1")
oIIS.CertCheckMode = True ' Set to False if you want
                          '  to disable CRL checking.
oIIS.SetInfo
Set oIIS = Nothing
```

Setting a different anonymous user account on a virtual directory

This example code shows how you can set the anonymous user account to be a specific account on a virtual directory named Pricelist on the default Web server:

```
Set oIIS = GetObject("IIS://localhost/W3SVC/1/Pricelist")
oIIS.AnonymousUserName = "PriceListAnonUser"
oIIS.AnonymousUserPass = "WeakPassword1"
oIIS.SetInfo
Set oIIS = Nothing
```

Setting a logon type for Basic authentication users

The following sample shows how you can set the logon type for Basic authentication on a remote computer named \\merlin. This setting is the value IIS uses when it calls *LogonUser* internally. Note that the accounts logging on must have the privilege you chose or they will not be able to log on.

The default setting is *LOGON_LOCAL*. If you select *LOGON_NETWORK_CLEARTEXT*, the account will have the much more secure network logon privilege yet will still be able to access remote resources when using NTLM authentication rather than Kerberos. This will happen if the Web servers are not running in a Windows 2000 domain.

Note also that the constants defined in the code are not the same as the constants used in the call to *LogonUser*.

```
Dim oIIS
Const LOGON_LOCAL = 0x0
Const LOGON_BATCH = 0x1
Const LOGON_NETWORK = 0x2
Const LOGON_NETWORK_CLEARTEXT = 0x3
Set oIIS = GetObject("IIS://Merlin/W3SVC/1")
oIIS.LogonMethod = LOGON_BATCH
oIIS.SetInfo
Set oIIS=Nothing
```

Setting IP restrictions

The following code shows how to set IP restrictions on the Secure virtual directory on the default Web server such that only localhost (127.0.0.1) can access its resources:

```
' Get the IP Settings.
Set oVDir = GetObject("IIS://localhost/W3SVC/1/Secure")
Set oIP = oVDir.IPSecurity

' Set the IP grant list to 127.0.0.1.
Dim IPList(1)
IPList(1) = "127.0.0.1"
oIP.IPGrant = IPList

' Do not grant access by default.
oIP.GrantByDefault = 0

' Write the information back to
'   Internet Information Services and clean up.
oVDir.IPSecurity = oIP
oVDir.SetInfo
Set oIP = Nothing
Set oVDir = Nothing
```

SQL Server 7 and SQL Server 2000 Settings

SQL Distributed Management Object (SQL-DMO) is a collection of COM+ objects for administering SQL Server from programming and scripting languages. The most complete documentation can be found in the Microsoft SQL Server Books Online documentation.

Enumerating databases and tables

The following example shows how you can display all databases and tables on an instance of SQL Server, as well as the effective privileges and the row count of each table:

```
Set oSQL = CreateObject("SQLDMO.SQLServer")
oSQL.LoginSecure = true    ' Use Windows authentication.
oSQL.LoginTimeout = 30
oSQL.Connect "dbserver"    ' Use '.' to represent local
                           '  computer.

For i = 1 to oSQL.Databases.Count
    Set oDB = oSQL.Databases(i)
    WScript.echo oDb.Name

    For j = 1 to oDB.Tables.Count
        Set oT = oDB.Tables(j)

        If oT.Attributes <> 2 Then   ' 2 == System object.
            WScript.echo "  " & oT.Name & " (" & oT.Rows & ")"

            Set oPerm = oT.ListPermissions()
            For each p in oPerm
                WScript.echo "     " & p.PrivilegeTypeName
            Next
        End If
    Next
Next
```

Adding a new login to SQL Server

The following code shows how to use SQL-DMO to add a new login to SQL Server. The account added can be a SQL Server account or a Windows account. If you're adding a Windows account, you must provide the domain name and username.

```
Set oSQL = CreateObject("SQLDMO.SQLServer")
oSQL.LoginSecure = true   ' Use Windows authentication.
oSQL.LoginTimeout = 30
oSQL.Connect "."     ' Use '.' to represent local computer.
```

```
For i = 1 to oSQL.Logins.Count
    WScript.echo oSQL.Logins(i).Name
Next

Set oLogin = CreateObject("SQLDMO.Login")
oLogin.Name = "EXAIR\Cheryl"
oLogin.Type = 0 ' 0 = Windows account, 2 = SQL account.
oSQL.Logins.Add(oLogin)
```

Adding a login to a SQL Server role

The following example adds a user named Bob to the Security Administrators role:

```
Set oSQL = CreateObject("SQLDMO.SQLServer")
oSQL.LoginSecure = true     ' Use Windows authentication.
oSQL.LoginTimeout = 30
oSQL.Connect "dbserver"     ' Use '.' to represent local
                            '  computer.

Set oRole = oSQL.ServerRoles("SecurityAdmin")
WScript.echo oRole.FullName
' The Logon 'Bob' must already exist in SQL Server.
oRole.AddMember("Bob")
```

Miscellaneous COM+ Scripts

In this section, we'll describe two other ways you can use COM+ and script to administer your computers.

Querying security settings in the COM+ Catalog

COM+ exposes copious information in the COM+ Catalog—a combination of the Registry and the *RegDB* database that functions as a single logical entity—about COM+ applications. The following script displays relevant security information about all the applications on the current computer:

```
' Open the catalog and access the application data.
Set oCatalog = CreateObject("COMAdmin.COMAdminCatalog")
Set oApplications = oCatalog.GetCollection("Applications")
oApplications.Populate

Header
TAB = Chr(9)

For Each oApp In oApplications
    ' Get the settings.
    iAppChecks = oApp.Value("ApplicationAccessChecksEnabled")
    iAuth       = oApp.Value("Authentication")
```

(continued)

```
    iAuthCap   = oApp.Value("AuthenticationCapability")
    iImp       = oApp.Value("ImpersonationLevel")

    strInfo.= GetAuth(iAuth) & TAB & _
             GetAuthCap(iAuthCap) & TAB & _
             GetImp(iImp) & TAB & _
             iAppChecks & TAB & _
             oApp.Name

    WScript.Echo strInfo
Next

Function GetAuthCap(iAuthCap)
    strAuthCap = "Unknown  "
    Select Case iAuthCap
        Case &h00 : strAuthCap = "None"
        Case &h02 : strAuthCap = "Cloak"
        Case &h20 : strAuthCap = "DynCloak"
        Case &h40 : strAuthCap = "Reference"
    End Select
    GetAuthCap = strAuthCap
End Function

Function GetAuth(iAuth)
    strAuth = "Unknown"
    Select Case iAuth
        Case 0 : strAuth = "Default"
        Case 1 : strAuth = "None"
        Case 2 : strAuth = "Connect"
        Case 3 : strAuth = "Call"
        Case 4 : strAuth = "Packet"
        Case 5 : strAuth = "Intgrty"
        Case 6 : strAuth = "Privacy"
    End Select
    GetAuth = strAuth
End Function

Function GetImp(iImp)
    strImp = "Unknown"
    Select Case iImp
        Case 1 : strImp = "Anonymous  "
        Case 2 : strImp = "Identify   "
        Case 3 : strImp = "Impersonate"
        Case 4 : strImp = "Delegate   "
    End Select
```

```
    GetImp = strImp
End Function

Function Header
    WScript.Echo "-----------------------------------------" & _
        "----------------------------"
    WScript.Echo "Auth    Auth             Impersonate    App"
    WScript.Echo "Type    Cap's            Level          " & _
        " Checks  Name"
    WScript.Echo "-----------------------------------------" & _
        "----------------------------"
End Function
```

Determining whether a server has a "heartbeat"

The following script uses Windows Sockets (Winsock) to ping a server at regular intervals. If the server at the specified IP address is listening and replies within the predetermined timeframe, the server is considered to have a "heartbeat"—that is, to be "alive and functioning."

```
Dim iProtocol, iPort, dwSleep, strIP
strIP = Array("157.59.133.192", "157.59.133.193")
iProtocol = 0 ' TCP.
iPort = 80
dwSleep = 2000 ' 2 seconds.

Set o = CreateObject("MSWinsock.Winsock")
o.Protocol = iProtocol

Do
    For i = LBound(strIP) To UBound(strIP)
        o.Connect strIP(i), iPort
        WScript.Sleep dwSleep
        strDetail = strIP(i) & " is "

        If o.State = 9 Then strDetail = strDetail & "Dead"
        If o.State = 7 Then strDetail = strDetail & "Listening"

        strDetail = strDetail & " on " & iPort

        WScript.echo strDetail

        o.Close
    Next
Loop
```

Common IIS Security-Related ADSI Settings

Table 13-3 lists common security-related ADSI properties and objects used in IIS 5. Where applicable, the hexadecimal value of a setting is provided.

Setting/Object	Comments
AccessFlags	This setting determines the type of access to a Web resource. Valid settings are *AccessExecute (0x4)*, *AccessNoRemoteExecute (0x2000)*, *AccessNoRemoteRead (0x1000)*, *AccessNoRemoteScript (0x4000)*, *AccessNoRemoteWrite (0x400)*, *AccessRead (0x1)* (the default setting), *AccessScript (0x200)*, *AccessSource (0x10)*, and *AccessWrite (0x2)*.
	AccessScript allows Active Server Pages (ASP) pages to run. If set, the *AccessSource* flag grants source access to users, using the Web-based Distributed Authoring and Versioning (WebDAV) HTTP extensions.
	Remote access flags are valid only when the corresponding general access flag is set. For example, setting *AccessNoRemoteRead* has no effect unless *AccessRead* is set as well. If both are set, the local host can read the file, but the file cannot be read by the remote client.
	There is no way of setting the *AccessNoXxx* settings other than through ADSI; they are not available in the IIS administration tools.
AccessSSLFlags	This setting contains SSL/TLS requirements. Valid options are *AccessSSL (0x8)*, *AccessSSL128 (0x100)*, *AccessSSLMapCert (0x80)*, *AccessSSLNegotiateCert (0x20)*, and *AccessSSLRequireCert (0x40)*.
	If set, *AccessSSL* requires an SSL/TLS connection. *AccessSSL128* requires that the connection be 128-bit. *AccessSSLNegotiateCert* will request a client authentication certificate from the client but not require one. *AccessSSLRequireCert* requires the client to provide a certificate.
	Note that to require a client authentication certificate you must set *AccessSSLFlags* to *AccessSSLNegotiateCert + AccessSSLRequireCert*.

Table 13-3. *Security-related IIS ADSI values.*

Setting/Object	Comments
AccessSSLFlags (continued)	*AccessSSLMapCert* will map the provided client authentication certificate. To use this option, *AccessSSLFlags* must be set to *AccessSSLNegotiateCert + AccessSSLMapCert*. Refer to *SSLUseDsMapper* for more information about which certificate mapper is used: the IIS mapper or the Active Directory mapper.
AdminACL	This setting determines what access users have to the metabase. It is recommended that this not be changed.
AllowSpecialCharsInShell	This Registry value controls whether special characters (including | (, ; % < and >) are allowed when running batch files (.bat and .cmd files). These special characters can pose a serious security risk. If the value of this entry is set to 1, malicious users can execute commands on the server. The setting can be found at *HKEY_LOCAL_MACHINE\SYSTEM\ CurrentControlSet\Services\W3SVC\Parameters*.
AnonymousPasswordSync	This property indicates whether IIS should handle the user password for anonymous users attempting to access resources. See also *AnonymousUserName* and *AnonymousUserPass*.
AnonymousUserName	Sets the username for unauthenticated access to a Web resource. See also *AnonymousUserPass* and *AnonymousPasswordSync*.
AnonymousUserPass	Sets the password for the account used for unauthenticated access to a Web resource. See also *AnonymousUserName* and *AnonymousPasswordSync*.
AuthFlags	This property contains the authentication protocols supported when accessing a Web resource. Values include *AuthAnonymous (0x1)*, *AuthBasic (0x2)*, *AuthMD5 (0x10)*, and *AuthNTLM (0x4)*. *AuthMD5* is Digest authentication. *AuthNTLM* is the Negotiate protocol; it will use either NTLM or Kerberos. Note that *AuthMD5* is not in the IIS online documentation.

(continued)

Table 13-3. *continued*

Setting/Object	Comments
AuthPersistence	This property specifies authentication persistence across requests on a connection. Valid options are *AuthPersistSingleRequest (0x40)*, *AuthPersistSingleRequestIfProxy (0x80)* (the default value), and *AuthPersistSingleRequestAlwaysIfProxy (0x100)*. If *AuthPersistSingleRequest* is set, authentication persists for a single connection. *AuthPersistSingleRequestIfProxy* is the same as the above setting but only if the request is handled by a non-Microsoft proxy server. *AuthPersistSingleRequestAlwaysIfProxy* is the same as the above setting but for all proxy requests.
CertCheckMode	Determines whether to check the CRL associated with a Web browser. The default, 0, is to check for certificate revocation, while a non-zero value will not check for a CRL.
CheckCertRevocation	This Registry setting works with *CertCheckMode* and is used only when a Web server is upgraded from Internet Information Server 4. *CheckCertRevocation* overrides *CertCheckMode* if *CheckCertRevocation* is set to *True*. By default, it is *False*. The setting can be found at *HKEY_LOCAL_MACHINE\SYSTEM\ CurrentControlSet\Services\InetInfo\Parameters*.
CreateProcessAsUser	This property specifies whether a Common Gateway Interface (CGI) process will be created in the system context or in the context of the requesting user. The default value is *True* and should not be changed.
DefaultLogonDomain	This property specifies the default domain for logon when using Basic or Digest authentication. If this value is not specified (the default), the default domain will be the domain name in which the Web server resides. If the computer is not in a domain, the default domain will be the computer name.

Setting/Object	Comments
IIsCertMapper (object)	The *IIsCertMapper* object allows the ASP developer to write code to map X.509 client authentication certificates on to Windows 2000 user accounts.
IPSecurity (object)	The *IPSecurity* object allows the ASP developer to write code that imposes IP and DNS restrictions. Do not confuse this setting with Internet Protocol Security (IPSec), built into Windows 2000.
LogonMethod	This property specifies the logon method used for accounts logging on with Basic authentication. Valid settings are logon *locally (0), logon as a batch job (1), network logon (2)*, and *network logon with cleartext (3)*. Note that the last setting is not in the IIS online documentation.
NTAuthenticationProviders	This property contains a comma-delimited list of Windows authentication providers used by the Web service. This is also the list of authentication methods sent to a browser during an HTTP 401 error. Its default value is *Negotiate,NTLM*.
ProcessNTCRIfLoggedOn	This property enables processing of Integrated Windows (NTLM) authentication even if a user has already logged on using an alternate authentication scheme. The default value is *True*.
Realm	This property specifies the realm when the server requests that the client authenticate itself using Basic or Digest authentication. The default value is *""*, which sets the realm name to the name of the server.
SecureBindings	This property specifies a string that is used by IIS to determine which SSL/TLS IP addresses and ports to listen on. The format of the string is *IPAddress:Port:*. If *IPaddress* is missing, all IP addresses are assumed. The default value is *:443:* when SSL/TLS is enabled.
SSLCertHash	The hash of the certificate used when SSL/TLS is enabled. You can determine the hash of a certificate by looking at the certificate's thumbprint in the Certificate Properties box. Note that *SSLCertHash* is a binary value and cannot be set using ADSI from scripting languages—you must use a language like C++.

(continued)

Table 13-3. *continued*

Setting/Object	Comments
SSLStoreName	The name of the certificate store that holds the server's SSL/TLS certificate and private key. By default, this is My, and there's no reason to change it.
SSLUseDsMapper	This property specifies whether IIS uses the Active Directory Service certificate mapper or the IIS certificate mapper. The default value, *False*, means IIS certificate mapping will be used.
UNCAuthenticationPassthrough	This property enables user authentication pass-through for Universal Naming Convention (UNC) virtual root access when using delegable authentication protocols such as Kerberos.
UNCPassword	This property specifies the encrypted password used to gain access to UNC virtual roots when not using a delegable authentication protocol such as Kerberos.
UNCUserName	This property specifies the username used to gain access to UNC virtual roots when not using a delegable authentication protocol such as Kerberos.
UserTokenTTL	This Registry setting determines how long to cache a user's token once the user has logged on to IIS. Applies to non-Windows authentication protocols only. The default is 15 minutes, but for debugging purposes it's worthwhile to set it to 0. The value can be found at *HKEY_LOCAL_MACHINE\SYSTEM\ CurrentControlSet\Services\InetInfo\Parameters*.
WAMUserName	This property specifies the account name that IIS uses by default as the COM+ application identity for newly created Web applications requiring Medium or High protection. The default value is *IWAM_machinename*.
WAMUserPass	This property specifies the password that IIS uses by default as the COM+ application identity for newly created Web applications requiring Medium or High protection. The default value is generated when IIS is installed.

## Chapter 14

An Introduction to Kerberos Authentication in Windows 2000

In this chapter, we'll focus on the Kerberos authentication protocol used in Microsoft Windows 2000. However, our approach is a little different from most other books on the subject. Rather than covering the low-level details of the protocol, such as data packet contents, we'll cover higher-level aspects of the protocol as they apply to the sample application we built in Chapter 10, "Building a Secure Solution." Numerous sources of information exist regarding the intricate details of the protocol, and we don't want to duplicate that work, mainly because we believe that most people don't (and shouldn't) care about these intricacies.

We also promise not to mention the role of dogs in ancient Greek mythology!

In this chapter, we'll discuss the following topics:

- What is Kerberos authentication?
- How Kerberos authentication works
- Kerberos acronyms
- Helpful tools
- Kerberos ticket flow, in general and in the sample application

WHAT IS KERBEROS AUTHENTICATION?

Kerberos authentication is the default authentication protocol used by Windows 2000 for a Windows 2000 domain. Unlike many other implementations of the protocol, it's completely transparent to your users. As far as your users need to be concerned, they're just logging on to computers running Windows 2000 by using the usual logon techniques available in prior versions of the operating system.

Kerberos was originally developed at Massachusetts Institute of Technology (MIT), and the protocol is defined in RFC 1510, making use of security tokens defined in RFC 1964. Microsoft has implemented the PKINIT protocol to support smartcard-based logon. This is currently an Internet Engineering Task Force (IETF) draft: draft-ietf-cat-kerberos-pk-init.

Kerberos Supports Mutual Authentication

Unlike the previous default authentication scheme in Windows, NTLM, Kerberos authenticates the client and the server. This feature of Kerberos is referred to as mutual authentication. NTLM authenticates the user only. Because of this, when using NTLM a user accessing a server cannot guarantee that the server is the one it claims to be. Kerberos authenticates servers as well so that users can be confident that the server they are accessing is not an imposter.

NTLM is still supported by Windows 2000 for backward compatibility with prior versions of Windows, including Microsoft Windows NT, Windows 95, and Windows 98.

> **NOTE**   If you're completely new to Kerberos and want a lighthearted introduction to the protocol, see "Designing an Authentication System: a Dialogue in Four Scenes" at *http://web.mit.edu/kerberos/www/dialogue.html* and "The Moron's Guide to Kerberos" at *http://www.isi.edu/gost/brian/security/kerberos.html*.

Kerberos Supports Delegation

A feature of Kerberos used to great advantage in Windows 2000 is the concept of delegation, or the ability of a process to delegate a user's identity to another process possibly executing on another computer. The remote process can then act on behalf of the user, with the privileges associated with the user. This is somewhat similar in principle to the Windows NT notion of impersonation. The big difference is that a delegated identity can flow from machine to machine, assuming they are configured correctly. An impersonated account cannot leave a computer and access a remote resource as the impersonated user.

Figure 14-1 shows the difference between impersonation and delegation in Windows 2000.

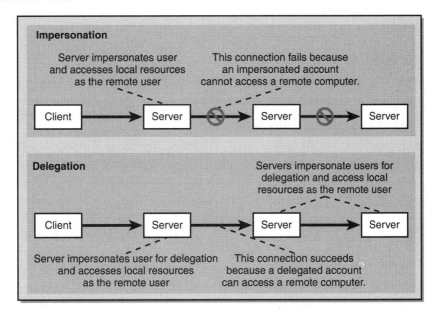

Figure 14-1. *The main difference between impersonation and delegation is how far the client's identity can "reach."*

Note that even in Windows 2000 delegation will not succeed if a Windows 2000 domain cannot be accessed, if the application acting on behalf of the user is not trusted to act as a delegate (that is, trusted for delegation), or if the user specifically requests that his identity never be delegated.

For example, COM+ applications default to impersonation rather than delegation when they take client requests. You can ask the operating system to provide a delegable identity when using remote procedure calls (RPCs) and calling the *RpcBindingSetAuthInfoEx* function. A named pipes client can also set the impersonation level in the call to *CreateFile* when it opens a remote pipe.

How Kerberos Authentication Works

Kerberos authentication uses a notion of tickets. A ticket is nothing more than a packet of information specific to Kerberos to aid in authentication. A ticket contains the client's identity, a session key, a timestamp, and other information. Sensitive parts of the ticket are encrypted with the server's key. However, before we dive into Kerberos ticket flow, let's take a moment to explain some of the acronyms used in Kerberos.

Some Kerberos Acronyms

You'll encounter many new abbreviations and acronyms when using Kerberos. This section of the chapter discusses each in detail.

Key Distribution Center (KDC)

The Key Distribution Center is at the heart of Kerberos. The KDC's job is to set up protected communication between client and server by assisting in the secure distribution of cryptographic keys that can then be used by the client and the server to protect their conversation.

In Windows 2000, the KDC resides in the Local Security Authority (LSA) process Lsass.exe on domain controllers. To an administrator, the KDC is implemented as a Windows service that is enabled on a Windows 2000 domain controller. It resides on a domain controller because Kerberos in Windows 2000 uses Active Directory as its account database.

The KDC is a mediator of sorts; all requests for all tickets come through the KDC. The KDC is a trusted third party; it knows about all the principals (users and computers) in the system and knows their passwords. (Yes, Windows 2000–based computers have passwords!)

The KDC is logically broken in two components, the authentication service and the ticket granting service, which are covered in the next two sections.

Authentication service (AS)

The authentication service's role is to authenticate principals and to grant tickets known as ticket granting tickets, described in a moment, which allow the principal to obtain further tickets from the ticket granting service, described next.

Ticket granting service (TGS)

The ticket granting service issues service tickets that are used by a principal to authenticate itself to another principal such as a server. Note that the TGS can issue ticket granting tickets also. Often these tickets are used when accessing other Kerberos realms (analogous to Windows 2000 domains); however, Windows 2000 also uses the TGS to get delegable ticket granting tickets. More on this a little later.

Ticket granting ticket (TGT)

A ticket granting ticket is a ticket issued by the AS to access the KDC itself. It is opaque to all principals other than the KDC. The reason TGTs exist is to reduce the number of times a user must present credentials to the operating system. So long as the TGT is valid and has not expired, it can be used to authenticate the user without having the user enter her username and password. The default lifetime for a TGT is 10 hours. TGTs form the basis of delegation; we'll discuss TGTs and delegation shortly.

Service ticket (ST)

Service tickets, also known as sessions tickets, are issued by the TGS. STs are used when a principal wants to authenticate itself to another principal. Figure 14-2 shows the layout of the KDC and the flow of STs and TGTs in Windows 2000.

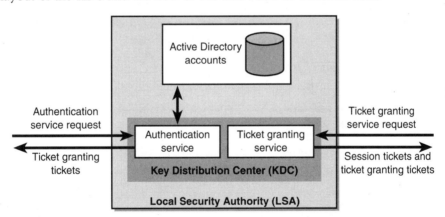

Figure 14-2. *The architecture of the KDC, and the flow of data in and out of the AS and TGD in Windows 2000.*

Service principal name (SPN)

A service principal name is the name by which services are identified. SPNs are used to support mutual authentication between a client application and a service. Remember that we mentioned that NTLM authenticates the client only? Using SPNs allows server services to be named, and hence they can also be identified and authenticated. The format of an SPN is

<service type>/<instance name>:<port number>/<service name>

Table 14-1 describes what each part of the SPN means.

Element	Comments
Service type	Type of service. For example, *HTTP* for Internet Information Services (IIS), *MSSQLSVC* for the Microsoft SQL Server service, *SMTPSVC* for the Simple Mail Transfer Protocol (SMTP) Server service, or *LDAP* for the Lightweight Directory Access Protocol (LDAP) service.
Instance name	The name of the server on which the service resides. Often the DNS name of the server.
Port number (optional)	Port number used by the service if it's different from the default for the service type. For example, if IIS is listening on another port other than port 80, this will need to be set.
Service name (optional)	Name of the service, if applicable. This option is used to locate replicated services.

Table 14-1. *Elements of an SPN.*

If the service name is the same as the instance name, which is common, and the port number is the default for the service, the SPN can be abbreviated to

<service type>/<instance name>

Table 14-2 describes some example SPNs.

Example SPN	Comments
HTTP/WEBSERVER HTTP/ webserver.explorationair.com	Two SPNs registered by the Web server services. One is an SPN for the NetBIOS name of the server, and the other is the DNS name of the server.
MSSQLSERVER/ dbserver.explorationair.com: 1433	An SPN for SQL Server. Note that we are interested in supporting mutual authentication only if the client accesses this server using DNS rather than NetBIOS. We have explicitly set the port number to which SQL Server is listening. This is important in the case of SQL Server 2000 because the technology allows multiple instances of SQL Server to run on a server, each listening on a different port.

Table 14-2. *Example SPNs.*

WHY REGISTER TWO SPNS?

If a client accesses a remote computer, he can access the computer by using either its NetBIOS name or its DNS name. Actually, he could use the IP address too, but IP addresses are not a secure way to authenticate a server. Because the two SPNs are registered, the client software can authenticate the service regardless of the name used to access the server.

Note that not all services need to be registered. Many service types will map to a default service type called HOST. Examples include HTTP, W3SVC, WWW, RPC, CIFS (file access), WINS, and UPS (uninterruptible power supply). For example, if your client software performs an HTTP connection to the Web server on the *middleware.explorationair.com* server by using an SPN of *HTTP/middleware.explorationair.com*, but this SPN is not registered on the server, the Windows 2000 domain controller will automatically map it to *HOST/middleware.explorationair.com*. This mapping applies only if the Web service is running as *LocalSystem*.

Before we discuss the ticket flow in Kerberos, let's look at three tools that help an administrator using Kerberos.

HELPFUL TOOLS

The *Microsoft Windows 2000 Server Resource Kit* includes tools to help you troubleshoot and configure Kerberos authentication. The most important ones are Kerberos Tray (KerbTray), Kerberos List (Klist), and SetSPN.

KerbTray and Klist

KerbTray is a graphical tool that displays ticket information for a computer running the Kerberos protocol. The KerbTray icon is located in the status area of your desktop and can be used to view tickets. Positioning your mouse cursor over the KerbTray icon will display the time left on your initial TGT before it expires.

Klist is a command line tool that enables you to view and delete Kerberos tickets granted to the current logon session. It is similar to KerbTray but more flexible. An updated version of Klist is included on this book's companion CD.

Both of these tools are handy for verifying the tickets you have.

SetSPN

SetSPN allows you to manage the SPN directory property for an Active Directory directory service account. SPNs are used to locate a target principal name for running a service. SetSPN allows you to view the current SPNs, reset the "host" SPNs, and add or delete supplemental SPNs.

It's usually not necessary to modify SPNs. SPNs are set up by a computer when it joins a domain and when services are installed on the computer. In some cases, however, this information becomes stale. For instance, if the computer name is changed, the SPNs for installed services would need to be changed to match the new computer name.

WHAT IS THE KRBTGT ACCOUNT?

If you look in the Active Directory Users And Computers tool, you might see an account named *krbtgt*, the name used by all KDCs. For example, the KDC for the *explorationair.com* account is named *krbtgt/explorationair.com*. In addition, a derivative of the password for this special account is used to encrypt TGTs issued by the KDC. The *krbtgt* account cannot be deleted or renamed.

Note that if a service runs as an account other than *LocalSystem*, you might need to register an SPN for the service. A good example is SQL Server 2000: It can run as *LocalSystem* or as a specific user account. If it runs as *LocalSystem*, you will not have to run SetSPN. But if the process runs as a specific user account, you'll have to run the following from the command line:

```
setspn -A MSSQLSvc/dbserver.explorationair.com:1433 DBUser
```

In this example, SQL Server is running on a server named DBServer and we're registering the DNS server name. The process runs as *EXAIR\DBUser*. This is configurable during SQL Server setup or in the SQL Server properties dialog box in the SQL Server Enterprise Manager.

KERBEROS TICKET FLOW

Let's look at the most basic Kerberos authentication overview. In the example illustrated by Figure 14-3, a client logs on to her workstation and then wants to access a remote server.

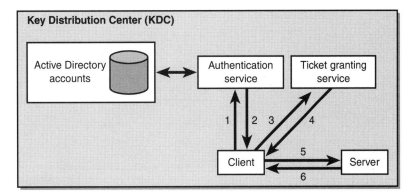

Figure 14-3. *Kerberos authentication flow.*

The following simplified steps take place when Kerberos authentication occurs:

1. Alice sends a request to the AS saying, "Hey, I'm Alice. Give me a TGT so that I can access other resources."

2. The AS sends a TGT and a special message encrypted with a key related to Alice's password. (This is not the case when using Kerberos preauthentication, but the spirit is right.) Both the TGT and the special message contain a (shared) session key that Alice and the KDC can use to converse securely.

3. Alice sends a request to the TGS saying, "Hey, it's me again. I want to access a remote server named WebServer."

4. The TGS sends an ST back to Alice along with a session key. The ST, encrypted with WebServer's password, also contains that session key—this is the secret that Alice and WebServer will use to protect their communications.

5. Alice sends the ST to the remote server.

6. The server verifies the ST and sends a data packet called an authenticator back to the client to verify its own identity to the client.

   NOTE Steps 1 and 2 happen only when Alice logs on to her computer or when the TGT expires. Steps 3 and 4 occur each time Alice accesses a server she has not accessed previously or if the ST for the server has expired.

Now that we have a basic understanding of how Kerberos authentication works and how TGTs and STs fit together, we'll look at an example.

Kerberos Ticket Flow in the Sample Application

Let's take a moment to reacquaint ourselves with the book's sample application. Figure 14-4 outlines its design.

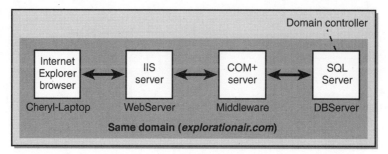

Figure 14-4. *The design of the sample application used in this book.*

Here are the major authentication parameters we'll focus on:

■ Alice logs on to a desktop computer called Cheryl-Laptop.

■ She is authenticated against a domain controller, running Active Directory on a server named DBServer.

■ Using Microsoft Internet Explorer 5, she wants to access an IIS 5 server running on WebServer. The Web server is configured to use Integrated Windows authentication.

■ The Web application accesses a remote COM+ component that resides on the Middleware server. The COM+ application startup account is *AppAccount*.

We'll show the Security Event Log entries you'll see if you're auditing for successful and failed account logon and successful and failed logon\logoff.

Alice logs on

Alice sits down at a laptop computer, presses Ctrl+Alt+Delete, and enters her username and password.

Domain controller authenticates Alice

Steps 1 and 2 occur as her computer contacts the AS at DBServer to request a TGT. If this phase of the process succeeds, you'll see the Security Event Log entries shown in Figures 14-5 and 14-6 at the domain controller.

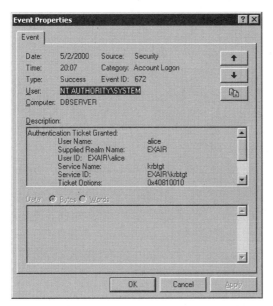

Figure 14-5. *The initial TGT being returned to Alice by the AS in the KDC.*

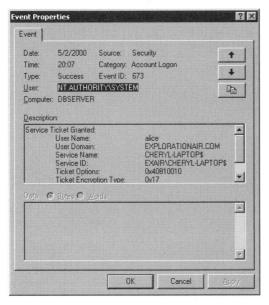

Figure 14-6. *Alice is given an ST to use on Cheryl-Laptop.*

Next, steps 3 and 4 occur as her computer requests an ST for Alice. You'll now see the Security Event Log entries shown in Figure 14-7.

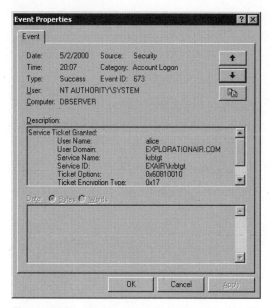

Figure 14-7. *Another ticket is returned to Alice by the TGS in the KDC to allow her to delegate her credentials.*

Finally, Alice is authenticated, as shown in Figure 14-8.

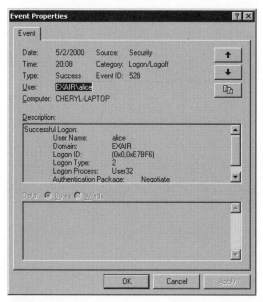

Figure 14-8. *The logon event at Cheryl-Laptop showing that Alice logged on.*

Using KerbTray, as shown in Figure 14-9, Alice can see what tickets are currently available to her.

Figure 14-9. *Alice viewing her tickets.*

Note there are two *krbtgt/EXPLORATIONAIR.COM* tickets. The highlighted ticket was issued by the AS; it is Alice's initial ticket. The second has different flags set—Forwarded is set, but Initial is not set. This ticket is used by Alice for delegation purposes when she accesses remote servers.

Alice accesses the Web server

Next, Alice starts Internet Explorer and accesses the Web server named WebServer. When this event occurs, she requests an ST to enable her to access the server. Figure 14-10 shows the Windows 2000 domain controller issuing an ST.

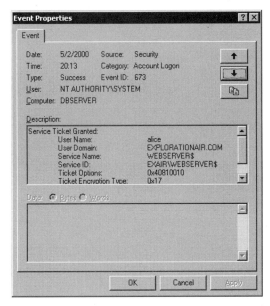

Figure 14-10. *The Windows 2000 domain controller issuing an ST to Alice so that she can access WebServer.*

Figure 14-11 shows Alice successfully logging on to the Web server.

Figure 14-11. *Alice viewing her tickets.*

As you can see in Figure 14-12, Alice now has another ticket available to her.

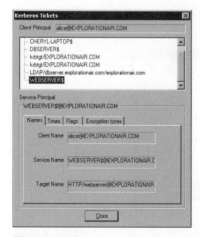

Figure 14-12. *Alice's tickets, including the new ticket to access WebServer.*

Web server invokes COM+ application

Finally, the ASP page on the Web server attempts to launch a remote COM+ component that resides on the Middleware server. The first step is for Alice to get an ST to access the Middleware server, as shown in Figure 14-13.

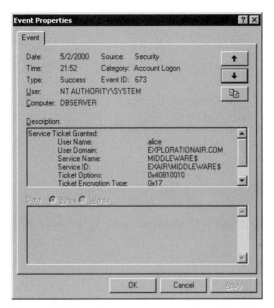

Figure 14-13. *Alice requesting an ST so that the Web server can access Middleware on her behalf.*

The next two steps are interesting. Figure 14-14 shows the *AppAccount* account, which is used as the identity for the COM+ application, requesting a TGT from the AS. Figure 14-15 shows the completion of the logon as *AppAccount* logs on to the Middleware computer.

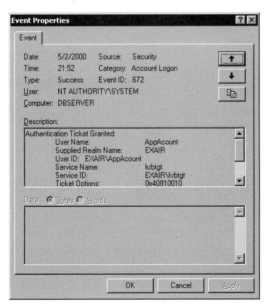

Figure 14-14. *The COM+* AppAccount *account requesting a TGT.*

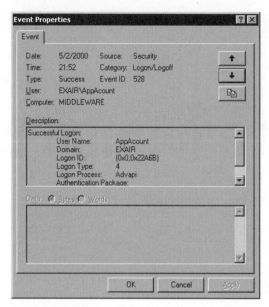

Figure 14-15. *The COM+* AppAccount *account logs on to the Middleware server.*

We haven't shown the request from Middleware to DBServer, but it's virtually the same as the request from WebServer to Middleware: Alice will get an ST, and the Middleware computer will use it to access the DBServer computer.

NOTE   To make identity delegation work, each ST request must include Alice's TGT. If it does not, Alice's identity cannot be delegated.

SUMMARY

Kerberos authentication is an industry-standard network authentication protocol initially designed at MIT. With Kerberos support, a fast, single logon process gives users the access they need to Windows 2000 Server–based resources, as well as to other environments that support this protocol. The Windows 2000 operating system implementation of the Kerberos protocol is designed for interoperability with other security services based on the MIT Kerberos version 5 reference implementation. Support for Kerberos includes additional benefits such as mutual authentication, in which the client and server must both provide authentication, and delegated authentication, in which the user's identity is passed from server to server. Internet Information Services 5, Internet Explorer 5, COM+, and SQL Server 2000 are Kerberos-aware and will use the protocol where possible to provide all of these benefits.

## Chapter 15

An Introduction to Cryptography and Certificates in Windows 2000

This chapter is an introduction to the fundamentals of cryptography. It explains how cryptography is used to create public key–based security solutions using certificates and how Microsoft Windows 2000 exposes public key functionality to both users and developers. The chapter isn't intended as a complete tutorial on the intricate details of cryptography. That's the subject of numerous excellent books, some of which are listed in the bibliography. Instead, the chapter will discuss the use of *pragmatic* cryptography in Windows 2000, from cryptographic basics to the use of certificates and the cryptographic and certificate technologies and products included in Windows 2000.

The topics covered include

- The fundamentals of cryptography
- The basics of certificates
- Cryptography and certificates in Windows 2000

If you already understand cryptography and how it's used to solve specific security problems, you might want to skip the next section and go straight to "The Basics of Certificates."

THE FUNDAMENTALS OF CRYPTOGRAPHY

Cryptography is a branch of computer science concerned with protecting information. Aspects of data protection include making data private, verifying the authenticity of data, and verifying that data hasn't been tampered with.

Data Privacy

Data privacy is usually provided by using *symmetric* encryption, in which two or more parties share a *secret,* usually referred to as a *key.* An *encryption algorithm,* also called a *cipher,* and the key are used to encrypt the data. The data is then sent to the recipient, who uses the same encryption algorithm and the same key to decrypt the data. As long as the key is kept secret, the data remains private. If the key is compromised, an attacker can decrypt the data with ease.

The term *symmetric* refers to the requirement that the same key be used for encryption and decryption. Symmetric key systems are often referred to as private key systems because the keys used must remain private. Figure 15-1 shows an example of symmetric key cryptography.

A CRYPTOGRAPHIC MAXIM

Keep private keys private.
As a colleague once said, the value of a secret key is inversely proportional to its accessibility. Put another way, a secret shared by many people is no longer a secret.

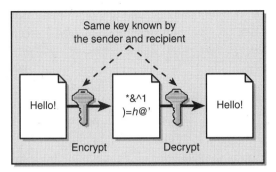

Figure 15-1. *Symmetric key cryptography.*

The ability of a symmetric system to withstand attack comes from the strength of the algorithm and the size of the key. Some encryption systems are strong, others aren't. By strong, we mean that the system is well designed, secure, and has withstood all previous attacks. Also, any vulnerability in the algorithm is known.

The size of the key is measured in bits; some cryptographic algorithms have 40-bit keys, some have 56-bit keys, some have 128-bit keys, and still others support variable-size keys. It takes longer to perform an exhaustive check of all possible keys if the key size is large. The number of keys in a symmetric cipher, also called the *keyspace,* is 2^x, where x is the key size. Using the same encryption algorithm, it takes longer to check all possible keys in a 56-bit key than it does in a 40-bit key—65,536 times longer, to be precise, because 56 bits (2^{56}) is 65,536 times larger than 40 bits (2^{40}).

Of course, an exhaustive key search might not be necessary if the cipher itself is weak.

WHAT IS AN EXHAUSTIVE KEY SEARCH?

An exhaustive key search is simply a test of every possible key available to an encryption algorithm. For example, let's say you receive a message and you know it was encrypted using a 56-bit cipher such as the Data Encryption Standard (DES). You don't know the key used to encrypt the message, so you muster all the computing power available to you and test all the keys—from 0 through $2^{56}-1$ or zero through 72,057,594,037,927,899 or, in hexadecimal, 0x0 through 0xFFFFFFFFFFFFFF. This is an example of an exhaustive key search.

To put key size into perspective, Table 15-1 shows various key sizes along with the corresponding number of keys in the keyspace and the time it takes to check all keys at 1.6 million keys per second and at 10 billion keys per second. We chose 1.6 million keys per second because this is the approximate speed at which a 600-MHz Pentium III can test RC5 keys. (RC5 is a popular symmetric cipher developed by Ron Rivest of RSA Data Security.)

Key Size (x)	Number of Keys (2^x)	Time to Check All Keys (at 1.6 Million Keys per Second)	Time to Check All Keys (at 10 Billion Keys per Second)
40	1,099,511,627,776	8 days	109 seconds
56	72,057,594,037,927,900	1,427 years	83 days
64	18,446,744,073,709,600,000	365,338 years	58.5 years
128	3.40282E+38	6.73931E+24 years	1.07829E+21 years

Table 15-1. *Key sizes and the time required to test all keys in the keyspace.*

As you can see, a 40-bit symmetric key is utterly insecure. Even a lowly PC can break a 40-bit encryption system in a matter of a few days. A 56-bit system can be broken in days by a moderate to large amount of CPU power.

Remember that each extra bit in the key size doubles the keyspace. A 41-bit key has twice as many keys as a 40-bit key.

Key-cracking competitions

Over the last few years, a number of cryptographic vendors have created contests in which they encrypt a message with a private key and challenge the Internet community to determine the message. Distributed.net is one group that has taken these challenges seriously and in a number of cases has successfully revealed the key using exhaustive key searches.

What makes the distributed.net work so interesting is that they've cracked the keys using thousands of small computers rather than "Big Iron" machines such as mainframe computers. This shows that if small-key cryptographic algorithms are susceptible to attack from small computers, imagine how vulnerable they are to large computers!

The process works like this: Each computer is assigned a small portion of the keyspace to check. If it doesn't find a probable key among its assigned chunk of keys, it informs a central key server that it hasn't found the key and downloads another set of keys to try. This process continues until the key is found.

For more information on key-cracking attempts, go to *http://www.distributed.net*.

How do you know when you've found the key?

This is an interesting question: if you're performing an exhaustive key search, how do you know you have the right key? In some cases, it's easy to tell because many common file formats begin with a well-known header. For example, let's say that Alice sends Bob an encrypted photograph in Graphic Interchange Format (GIF) format. The first three letters of a GIF graphics file are *G*, *I*, and *F*. If the program testing all keys finds these three letters at the start of the file, chances are good that you have found the key.

A CRYPTOGRAPHIC SANITY CHECK

Let's assume for a moment that the entire keyspace of an encryption algorithm can be tested in eight days at a cost of $2 million. The total cost depends on a number of factors, including the cost of the hardware and software. You must consider two issues:

- The value of the data

- Whether the data is relevant after the key search

For example, why would you spend $2 million testing all keys if the data is worth only $17? Worse, why would you spend eight days testing all keys if the data is stale after seven days? Let's say that you set out to determine the content of a competitor's message. After eight days, you find that the message was a secret press announcement. However, it was secret for only seven days, after which it made the headlines in all the national newspapers. All of your efforts and expenses were wasted.

Symmetric key cryptographic algorithms

Examples of symmetric key encryption systems include the following:

- DES, a common 56-bit algorithm

- Triple-DES (3DES), which is DES used three times with two keys to create an effective 112-bit keyspace or DES used with three keys to create a 168-bit keyspace

- RC2, RC4, and RC5, which are variable key-length ciphers developed by RSA Data Security

- IDEA, a 128-bit system used in Pretty Good Privacy (PGP)

- Skipjack, an 80-bit cipher used by the U.S. government for sensitive but nonclassified data

In the overall scheme of cryptography systems, symmetric key systems offer reasonably quick encryption and decryption. However, there's one big problem: how do Alice and Bob agree on a key to use when they're sending secure messages to one another? We'll answer that question a little later. For the moment, let's see how Alice can send a message to Bob and be sure that the message isn't tampered with.

ANOTHER CRYPTOGRAPHIC SANITY CHECK

A symmetric key can be any value that falls within the bounds of the keyspace. For example, DES has a 56-bit keyspace, so a DES key can be any value from 0 through 2^{56}. Passwords, on the other hand, tend to use a limited keyspace because they're normally restricted to printable characters, such as 0–9, a–z, A–Z, and punctuation so that they're easy for people to remember.

Many cryptographic solutions take a password and use it directly as the key to a cryptographic algorithm such as DES. This is much less secure than a 56-bit keyspace because the keyspace is no longer 0 to 2^{56} keys in size—it's a subset of the keyspace limited to 0–9, a–z, A–Z, and punctuation, which is substantially smaller than 2^{56}. If an attacker knows that the key is derived from a cleartext password, she knows that she doesn't have to test the entire keyspace.

Another way to look at this problem is to consider what happens when a homeowner decides to buy strong locks for the front door and then keeps the key under the doormat. An attacker won't attempt to pick the lock; he'll first look for the key—under a flower pot, under a window ledge, or, of course, under the welcome mat.

Verifying Data Integrity

Verifying that data hasn't changed or been tampered with is an extremely important aspect of data security. If Alice places an order for 100 widgets, she wants to be sure that the order isn't changed by an attacker to an order for 150 widgets.

Cryptographic systems use *hash functions,* also called *digest functions,* to provide such integrity checks. Simply put, a hash function takes a large chunk of data and produces a much smaller digest, usually 128 bits or 160 bits in length. Digests are somewhat similar to cyclical redundancy checks (CRCs) in data communication. Their main characteristics include the following:

■ A small change in the originating data creates a massive change in the resulting digest.

■ It isn't feasible to create data that exactly matches a specific digest.

■ It's impossible to determine the data based on just the digest.

A good analogy for a digest is your thumbprint. A thumbprint uniquely identifies you but tells nothing about you or about what you know. It's also unlikely that you'll find someone else with a thumbprint that matches yours.

It's common practice to hash all data before sending it to a recipient and then append the hash to the original data. On receipt, the recipient recalculates the hash of the data and checks it against the appended hash. If the two are the same, the data hasn't changed. Right? No, not really! There's nothing stopping an attacker from intercepting and changing the message, recalculating the hash, and appending the new hash to the changed message. However, we'll cover this issue in detail later when we discuss digital signatures.

Figures 15-2 shows Alice sending an order to Bob, and Figure 15-3 shows Bob verifying that the message was not tampered with.

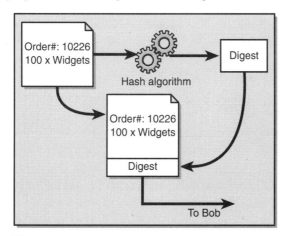

Figure 15-2. *Alice sends an order to Bob.*

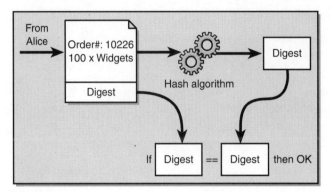

Figure 15-3. *Bob verifies that the order wasn't tampered with.*

Message Authentication Code, or MAC, also uses hash functions to provide evidence when data has been tampered with, and it also verifies the authenticity of the data.

For example, Alice and Bob agree on a secret key for their conversation. When Alice sends data to Bob, she hashes the data and then hashes the secret key with the resulting hash. The function looks like this:

```
MAC = HASH( HASH( data ), secret )
```

Upon receiving the data, Bob rehashes the document, applies the secret key to the result, and if the resulting MAC is the same as the MAC in the message, he knows that the data was not tampered with and that someone who knows the secret key sent the message.

Examples of common hash functions include

- MD4, created by RSA Data Security, which yields a 128-bit digest
- MD5, created by RSA Data Security, which yields a 128-bit digest
- SHA-1, created by National Institute of Standards and Technology (NIST), which produces a 160-bit hash

Hashing is a quick process, even with very large quantities of data.

Verifying Authenticity (Sort Of)

Another form of data encryption uses *asymmetric keys*; it's often called *public key* encryption. Rather than having two or more parties share one key, asymmetric systems use *key pairs*. Each party has two mathematically related keys, one called the *private key* and the other called the *public key*. Depending on the algorithm used, the two keys are usually two very large numbers. One feature of these systems is that knowing the public key doesn't mean you can easily determine the private key, and vice versa.

As the name implies, the public key can be made public, but the private key must remain private. In fact, the private key often doesn't leave the hardware on which it was generated.

HAVE KEYS, WILL TRAVEL

It's imperative that the private keys in an asymmetric or public key system remain private. The foundation of a public key infrastructure (PKI) is the protection of private keys. However, this leads to a significant problem: what happens if users need access to their private keys from multiple workstations? There are a number of solutions, some convenient, some secure:

- Store your private keys on each workstation. This leads to two problems: how to securely transfer the keys to each workstation and how to keep others from accessing the keys after the user logs off the workstation.

- Restrict users to using only one workstation. This is difficult to enforce, especially in a shared-workstation scenario.

- Store the keys on hardware devices such as PCMCIA cards or smartcards. This is a reasonable solution and is well supported by Windows 2000. In this scenario, the user need not store private key information on a computer. When a user wants to use another system, she must provide her hardware token in order to use her private keys. Fortezza PCMCIA cards are supported by Internet Information Services (IIS) 5 and Microsoft Internet Explorer 5; see the IIS documentation for further details about Fortezza. Smartcards are natively supported by Windows 2000, IIS 5, and Internet Explorer 5.

Public key cryptography also has the following important attributes:

- Data encrypted with the public key can be decrypted only with the private key.

- Data encrypted with the private key can be decrypted only with the public key.

If these two statements haven't sunk in, read them again!

If Alice receives a message from Bob and the message can be decrypted using Bob's public key, as shown in Figure 15-4, it must have been encrypted using Bob's private key and hence must have come from Bob because only Bob has access to Bob's private key. We've just proved the authenticity of a message, right? Actually, we haven't. How do we know that Bob's public key was used in the first place? We're on the right track, though. We'll explain how you can verify Bob's public key when we discuss certificates.

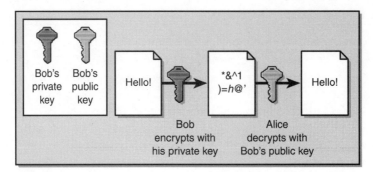

Figure 15-4. *Bob sends a message to Alice in such a way that Alice knows it could have come only from Bob.*

If Alice wants to send a private message to Bob (a message that only Bob can read), as shown in Figure 15-5, all she has to do is use Bob's public key (it's public, remember) to encrypt the message. Because only Bob has access to his private key and only the private key can decrypt the message, only Bob can decrypt the message. This is a way of sending a private message to Bob. (Actually, it isn't. How do we know it's Bob's public key? As just noted, however, we're on the right track. More about this later when we cover certificates.)

> **TWO SIMPLE RULES OF THUMB**   If you have a private key, you can send authenticated messages. If you have someone else's public key, you can send them encrypted messages.

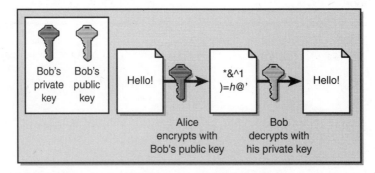

Figure 15-5. *Alice sends a message to Bob that only he can read.*

The most famous example of a public key encryption system is RSA, named after the three inventors of the algorithm, Rivest, Shamir, and Adleman. One downside of most public-key cryptography systems is they're extremely slow, so it's impractical to encrypt and decrypt large amounts of data.

Digital Signatures and Signing

Signing is a process that combines two cryptographic technologies—public key (asymmetric) encryption and hashing. Signing is a simple procedure. Alice's software hashes the document, such as an e-mail message, and then encrypts the resulting digest with her private key. The resulting *signature* is appended to the message. When the recipient, Bob, receives the e-mail, his software hashes the document and uses Alice's public key to decrypt the signature, as shown in Figure 15-6. If the two hashes match, we know two things:

- The document hasn't been tampered with. If it had, the hashes wouldn't match.

- The message must have come from Alice because only her public key can decrypt the signature; hence, she had access to the private key associated with the public key.

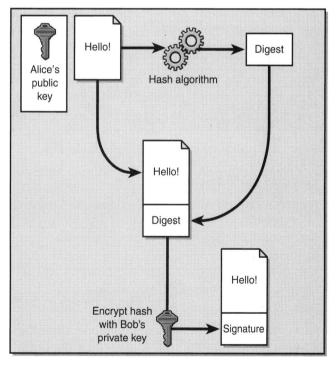

Figure 15-6. *Bob signs a document using his private key so that anyone with his public key can verify that the document came from him and was not tampered with.*

Again, we must ask how Bob knows that Alice is the sender. In other words, how does he really know that the public key belongs to Alice and no one else? We'll address this issue shortly.

Key Agreement

So how do Alice and Bob agree on a key? If asymmetric cryptography weren't slow, Alice could just encrypt a message using Bob's public key. However, encrypting even a small message is excruciatingly slow. Normally, Alice and Bob agree on a symmetric key used for bulk encryption and use that key to encrypt the message. Among the many mechanisms for doing this, we'll cover one: using public key encryption for key agreement.

Alice wants to send a large secret message to Bob. To do so, she thinks up a key to use to encrypt the message—or better yet, she lets her computer derive a random number to act as the key. This key is often referred to as a *session key* because it's used only for the duration of the communication. She encrypts the session key using Bob's public key and sends the encrypted blob to Bob. This is a reasonably quick process because a key is usually less than 128 bits in length. His software uses his private key to decrypt the blob and derives the secret key. Alice sends her messages to Bob using the session key that Bob now knows.

We've already mentioned the flaw here: how does Bob know that Alice sent the original message containing the key and how does Alice know that she's sending the key to Bob? In other words, how do Alice and Bob know that each other's public keys are valid? That is the purpose of certificates, our next subject.

THE BASICS OF CERTIFICATES

The three previous topics—symmetric cryptography, digest functions, and asymmetric cryptography—are important building blocks of all PKI-based solutions. Symmetric key cryptography can provide data privacy, digests can provide data integrity, and asymmetric cryptography can help provide message authenticity and provide for key exchanges. Sort of. In fact, asymmetric cryptography doesn't guarantee message authenticity because you don't know that Alice's public key is actually Alice's. Hence, you cannot assert that the person with Alice's private key is indeed Alice. You also don't know that a message is valid because a message digest can be tampered with. Certificates and the technologies surrounding them can help address many of these issues.

A Look Inside a Certificate

A certificate is a binary structure containing information about the holder of a public key. In technical terms, a certificate *binds* a name to a public key. The most common form of certificate is the X.509 certificate, of which there are three versions—1, 2, and 3. We'll focus mainly on version 3 certificates, which contain, at a minimum, the following information:

- **Version number**   The number 0, 1, or 2, which represents certificate version 1, 2, or 3, respectively.

- **Serial number**   A unique identifier for the certificate determined by the certificate issuer.

- **Signature algorithm**   The algorithm used to derive the digital signature, represented using an object identifier (OID). OIDs are discussed a little later.

- **Issuer name**   The name of the certificate issuer. Often, the name is expressed as an X.500 name; we'll discuss X.500 names in a moment.

- **Validity period**   The period during which the certificate is valid. Like a credit card, a certificate becomes valid on a given date and time and expires on a given date and time.

- **Subject name**   The name of the subject (the owner of the private key associated with the public key held in the certificate). Like the issuer name, the subject name is often expressed as an X.500 name.

- **Subject public key information**   The algorithm used to define the public/private key pair (expressed as an OID) and the actual public key data.

- **Signed hash of the certificate data**   The hashed contents of the certificate, which are encrypted using the issuer's private key, resulting in a *digital signature*.

Version 3 certificates can also contain other optional data, called *extensions*, which are extensions to a certificate not defined in the X.509 specification. Common extensions include alternate subject name, key usage, and certificate revocation list (CRL) distribution points, or CDPs.

An alternate subject name is another name by which the subject is known. For example, the common name in a certificate might be CN=Cheryl, but Cheryl might also be known by another name, such as her e-mail name, in which case altSubjectName might be E=Cheryl@exair.com.

Key usage determines what the private key associated with the certificate can be used for—for example, code signing, e-mail, server authentication, and logon. We'll explain key usage later in this chapter.

CDPs are lists of locations where software can check to see whether the certificate has been revoked by the issuer. Certificate revocation is also discussed later in this chapter.

NOTE The Internet industry standard certificate format is defined by the Internet Engineering Task Force (IETF) Public Key Infrastructure (PKIX) working group, details of which can be found at *http://www.ietf.org/html.charters/ pkix-charter.html*. The most important document is RFC 2459, "Internet X.509 Public Key Infrastructure Certificate and CRL Profile."

Figure 15-7 shows the composition of an X.509 certificate.

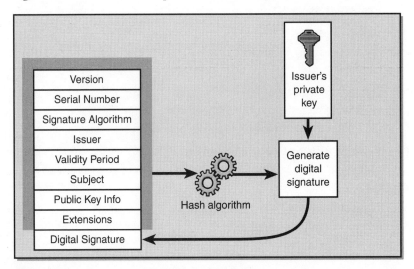

Figure 15-7. *The structure of an X.509 certificate.*

X.500 naming, X.509, DER, base64 encoding, OIDs, PKCS, and ASN.1 explained

We've already mentioned X.509, X.500 naming, and OIDs. When you use cryptographic and certificate-based solutions, you'll also hear about distinguished encoding rules (DER), base64 encoding, PKCS (Public Key Cryptography Standard) #5, PKCS

#7, PKCS #10, PKCS #12, and Abstract Syntax Notation One (ASN.1). Let's take a moment to look at each term in more detail.

X.500 naming is a standard way to unambiguously name an entity, such as a user. Its usage derives from the hierarchical X.500 directory services. A unique X.500 name is known as a *distinguished name* (DN). The most common format you'll see is of the type C=US, O=ExAir, OU=Development, CN=Cheryl, where C is country, O is organization, OU is organizational unit, and CN is the common name of the entity being named. As you can see, the naming structure is hierarchical and fits well into directory systems based on or derived from X.500.

Table 15-2 lists the typical DN components.

Component	Name	Example
C	Country	US
SP	State/Province	WA (Washington)
S	State	WA (Washington)
L	Locality	Redmond
O	Organization	ExAir
OU	Organizational Unit	Development
CN	Common Name	Cheryl
E	E-Mail	cheryl@exair.com

Table 15-2. *X.500 DN components.*

Note that version 3 certificates do not mandate X.500 naming for the subject or issuer names. Other possibilities include e-mail name, IP address, electronic data interchange (EDI) name, or URL.

X.509 is the industry-standard certificate type. Microsoft Windows 95, Windows 98, Windows NT, and Windows 2000 all natively support X.509 certificates. You can find more information about X.509 certificates in the RSA Security Crypto FAQ at *http://www.rsasecurity.com/rsalabs/faq* and the official X.509 certificate specification at *ftp://ftp.isi.edu/in-notes/rfc2459.txt*.

DER is a binary encoding format for certificates. For more information, go to *ftp://ftp.rsa.com/pub/pkcs/doc/layman.doc*. Windows 95, Windows 98, Windows NT, and Windows 2000 support DER-encoded certificates.

Base64 encoding is a text-based encoding system for binary data. It's the same coding scheme used by basic HTTP 1.0 authentication and is defined in RFC 1521 at *ftp://ftp.isi.edu/in-notes/rfc1521.txt*. Base64 encoding is often used to transfer certificates and certificate requests in e-mail because the data is textual rather than binary and many older e-mail clients and e-mail servers cannot process binary data correctly.

Windows 95, Windows 98, Windows NT, and Windows 2000 support base64-encoded certificates.

OIDs are a way to identify algorithms and attributes (such as parts of a distinguished name). OIDs are based on a hierarchical dot notation. For example, 1.2.840.113549.1.1.4 refers to the MD5/RSA digital signature algorithm. The parts of this OID are identified in Figure 15-8.

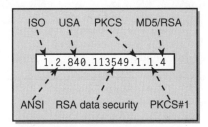

Figure 15-8. *An MD5/RSA OID in detail.*

You'll also come across OIDs if you use Active Directory. All identifiers in Active Directory, such as *userPrincipalName* (1.2.840.113556.1.6.655) and *cn* (common name; 2.5.4.3) are represented by OIDs.

To find out what an OID means, visit the invaluable Web site at *http://www.alvestrand.no/harald/objectid/top.html*. At the time of this writing, this site doesn't list security-related OIDs under 1.3.6.1.5, but it does list RSA-related OIDs under 1.2.840.113549.

PKCS #5, often referred to as *passphrase-based encryption*, is a standard and secure way of deriving a private key from a password and using the key to encrypt confidential data. For more information, go to *http://www.rsasecurity.com/rsalabs/pkcs/pkcs-5/index.html*. PKCS #7 is a binary format for defining encrypted and signed data such as certificates. For more information, go to *http://www.rsasecurity.com/rsalabs/pkcs/pkcs-7/index.html*. PKCS #10 is a binary format for creating certificate requests. For more information, take a look at *http://www.rsasecurity.com/rsalabs/pkcs/pkcs-10/index.html*. PKCS #12 is a binary format for storing certificates and their keys. The .pfx file format in Windows is a PKCS #12 blob. For more information, go to *http://www.rsasecurity.com/rsalabs/pkcs/pkcs-12/index.html*.

ASN.1 is a method and syntax for describing data precisely. For example, the data format of an X.509 certificate is defined using ASN.1 syntax. ASN.1 is somewhat similar in principle to BNF notation, which is familiar to those who know about the science of programming languages. The following is abbreviated ASN.1 syntax for an X.509 certificate taken from RFC 2459:

```
Certificate  ::=  SEQUENCE  {
    tbsCertificate       TBSCertificate,
    signatureAlgorithm   AlgorithmIdentifier,
    signatureValue       BIT STRING  }
```

```
TBSCertificate   ::=  SEQUENCE  {
     version          [0]  EXPLICIT Version DEFAULT v1,
     serialNumber          CertificateSerialNumber,
     signature             AlgorithmIdentifier,
     issuer                Name,
     validity              Validity,
     subject               Name,
     subjectPublicKeyInfo SubjectPublicKeyInfo,
     issuerUniqueID  [1]  IMPLICIT UniqueIdentifier OPTIONAL,
                           -- If present, version shall be v2 or v3.
     subjectUniqueID [2]  IMPLICIT UniqueIdentifier OPTIONAL,
                           -- If present, version shall be v2 or v3.
     extensions      [3]  EXPLICIT Extensions OPTIONAL
                           -- If present, version shall be v3.


     }
```

Finally, in the interest of building a sentence containing the most certificate-related acronyms possible: an X.509 certificate is defined using ASN.1 notation, the entities of which are identified using OIDs, and is usually stored as a PKCS #7 data structure in either base64 or DER encoding.

Certificates and the role of trust

Earlier we mentioned that a certificate binds a public key to a subject such as a computer or a user—in other words, a *principal*. But how do we know that the certificate is really the principal's certificate and not someone else's? It's all a matter of trust. Certificates are issued by issuers or authorities. An example of a well-known *certificate authority* (CA) is VeriSign. Thawte Consulting, based in South Africa, is another. At the time of this writing, Thawte was in the process of being purchased by VeriSign. Windows 2000 includes Microsoft Certificate Services, so in theory you can be a CA, too, but it's not quite as simple as that.

When a CA issues a certificate to a principal, it takes the following steps:

1. It performs background checks to verify that the principal (called a subject) is who it says it is. For example, for a user's certificate this might be a simple physical address check or perhaps a simple verification that the CA can receive the e-mail that the subject sent during the enrollment process. However, because certificates are often used for important and sensitive tasks, more stringent background checks are advisable.

2. It creates and signs a certificate using its private key.

3. It issues the certificate to the subject.

4. The CA (or the subject) makes the certificate known to all interested users.

HOW DO YOU ACCESS ANOTHER USER'S CERTIFICATE?

Certificates are public, so accessing another user's certificate is actually quite easy. You can ask the user to send it to you via e-mail or on a floppy disk. In fact, if the e-mail is a digitally signed Secure Multipurpose Internet Mail Extensions (S/MIME) message, the certificate is already available to you in the e-mail. The certificate might reside in an Lightweight Directory Access Protocol (LDAP)–enabled directory, such as Active Directory in Windows 2000.

Windows 2000 also enables you to find a VeriSign customer's certificate right from the shell. You simply take the following steps:

1. Choose Search from the Start menu.

2. Select For People.

3. In the Find People dialog box (Figure 15-9), select VeriSign Internet Directory Service in the Look In drop-down list box.

4. Enter the name or e-mail address of the user you want to find.

5. Click Find Now.

If the user exists, you'll see details about the user, including the user's certificate or certificates.

Figure 15-9. *The VeriSign Internet Directory Service in Windows 2000.*

So, how does Bob know that a message was sent by Alice? As you can probably guess, it's a trust issue. Let's look at an example:

1. Alice creates an e-mail message using Microsoft Outlook Express 5 and digitally signs it using the private key associated with the public key contained in a certificate she possesses. The certificate containing her public key is already publicly available.

2. Alice sends the e-mail message to Bob over an insecure medium such as the Internet.

3. Bob's e-mail software, Microsoft Outlook 2000, receives the message and verifies that the certificate is correct. It does this as follows:

   ❑ It verifies that the issuer of Alice's certificate is trusted. If the certificate is trusted, Outlook knows that the certificate of the issuer is stored on your computer.

   ❑ It verifies that the document hasn't been tampered with by hashing the original document and decrypting the signature on Alice's e-mail using Alice's public key from her certificate. If the two resulting hashes are valid, the message is valid.

   ❑ It verifies that the certificate hasn't expired.

   ❑ It verifies that the certificate hasn't been revoked.

   ❑ It verifies that the subject name in the certificate (Alice) matches the name of the e-mail sender (also Alice).

Here's what this process achieves: Bob's software determines that the message came from Alice and wasn't tampered with because Bob trusts the issuer of Alice's certificate and the digital signature is valid. Because Bob trusts the issuer, he trusts the issuer's public key and this public key is used to verify the signature on Alice's certificate.

Figure 15-10 shows the steps involved in checking that the certificate associated with the message is valid.

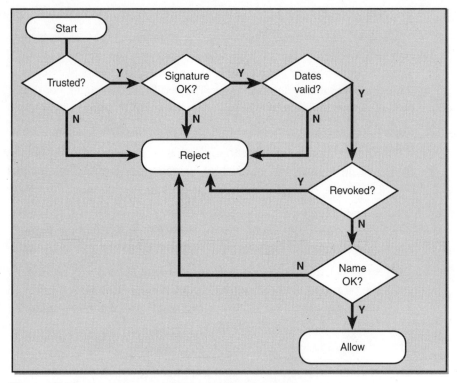

Figure 15-10. *Determining whether a certificate is valid.*

A HEALTHY DOSE OF PARANOIA

During a presentation that Michael gave on cryptography and certificates at Microsoft Web Tech·Ed in Palm Springs, California, in early 1998, an audience member raised his hand and asked, "How do I know that the VeriSign root certificates included with Windows really came from VeriSign?" Michael jokingly responded, "Trust me!"

Of course, the audience laughed and Michael quickly responded, "Seriously, though, that's a great question and it's these kinds of security assumptions you should constantly examine. However, if you don't believe or trust that the root certificates are really VeriSign's, then go to the VeriSign Web site and download them."

The same gentleman raised his hand again and said, "But how do I know it's the VeriSign Web site and not a rogue server acting as VeriSign and I'm being sent to the rogue site because someone has "poisoned" a DNS server?" Michael replied, "Phone up VeriSign and ask them to send you the root certificates on a floppy."

Obviously, the man wasn't happy with the answer and inquired, "How can I be sure that no one at the postal service changed the root certificates on the floppy to that of a rogue CA pretending to be VeriSign?"

Michael was impressed, but he had a quick answer. "Okay, when you install the root certificates from the floppy, you'll be given two thumbprints by Windows, an MD5 thumbprint and an SHA-1 thumbprint, both in hexadecimal. Telephone VeriSign and ask them to confirm the thumbprints." At this point, Michael showed the audience what the dialog box in question looked like (Figure 15-11).

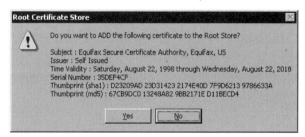

Figure 15-11. *Adding a new root certificate. (Note the two thumbprints, or hashes.)*

The man cleared his throat and said, "How can I be assured that no one at the telephone exchange is redirecting my call to a rogue CA? I'm still not convinced that the roots are from VeriSign."

At this point, Michael dryly commented, "Sir, are you sure you should be putting anything on the Web?" The audience erupted into laughter and Michael continued, with a big grin: "May I suggest you fly to VeriSign's offices and personally ask an engineer to load the root certificates onto a floppy and hand them to you. And by the way, if you ask me how do you know it's VeriSign's offices and not those of an imposter, I will personally escort you out of the hall!"

Of course, the man wasn't trying to be difficult, nor was he particularly concerned about the authenticity of the roots included with Windows. He was merely thinking through a series of trust decisions that have to be made and wondering at what point a person should be convinced that something is what it says it is and is trustworthy.

As you can see, trust in the root CA certificate is paramount. All parties must trust the root CA; otherwise, the system won't work. A common analogy is that of issuing a driver's license. Many businesses accept a driver's license as proof of identity and date of birth because they trust that the issuer performed appropriate checks on the person.

AN IMPORTANT NOTE ON ROOT CA CERTIFICATE TRUST

Windows 2000 ships with over 100 root CA certificates "baked in." In other words, if your software encounters a certificate issued by any of these companies, it will trust them. However, some of the companies you might not know, so you shouldn't trust them. Period. You should go through the list of trusted root certificates and remove the root certificates of all the companies you do not know or do not trust. Do not remove any Microsoft or VeriSign root certificates, however, because many components included with Windows 2000 are signed by Microsoft or VeriSign, and removing them might make the system unreliable.

In Windows 2000, you can enforce this certificate removal through policy. Also note that you must not remove the roots from the computer store because these are used by some applications, such as Microsoft SQL Server and Internet Information Services.

Certificate chains and hierarchies

Often, a series of certificates (often called *leaf* certificates) leads from the principal's certificate up to the root certificate; this is referred to as a *chain* or a *hierarchy*. The topmost certificate, the root, is also called a *self-signed* certificate because it's not issued by any other CA, it's issued by itself to itself.

It's quite normal to have more than one subordinate certificate issued by the root (or a high-level subordinate) because the subordinates might issue certificates based on differing organizational units, geographical location, or certificate usage. This has significant benefits, including

- **Flexible configuration** For example, the root CA might store its private key in expensive but very secure cryptographic hardware for maximum protection, while subordinate CAs store their private keys in software.

- **Reduced impact of CA key revocation** You can disable parts of the CA hierarchy without affecting the entire public key infrastructure. For example, if the private key of the Client certificate subordinate CA is compromised, only its key is revoked, not all CA keys in the hierarchy.

A common way to set up a subordinate CA is to base the configuration on key usage. For example, Figure 15-12 shows Exploration Air's CA hierarchy, which is based on certificate usage.

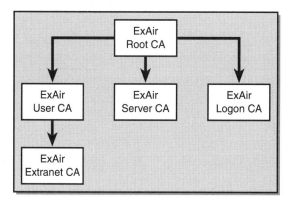

Figure 15-12. *Certificate hierarchy at Exploration Air.*

There is one root. The four subordinates are for

- Server authentication for use in Secure Sockets Layer/Transport Layer Security (SSL/TLS) (ExAir Server CA)

- Client authentication when using SSL/TLS and secure e-mail using S/MIME (ExAir User CA)

- Client authentication when using SSL/TLS and secure e-mail using S/MIME for extranet business partners (ExAir Extranet CA)

- Client logon using smartcards and Windows 2000 (ExAir Logon CA)

Arguably, the third is for more than key usage; it's for key usage for specific customers. Exploration Air issues certificates to its business partners using this CA.

Key usage

Certificates and their associated private keys are used for a number of things, but ultimately they're all about verifying identity. For example, a certificate might be used to verify the sender of an e-mail message or assert ownership of a piece of code. However, the most common scenario is verifying the authenticity of a Web site. It's important that the private key associated with the certificate be used only as intended.

As another example, take a look at Table 15-3, which lists Michael's certificates.

Subject	Issuer	Purposes
Michael Howard	Personal Freemail RSA 1999.9.16 (Thawte)	■ Client authentication ■ E-mail protection
Michael Howard	Windows 2000 Development Team	■ Encryption of data on the disk
Michael Howard	Windows 2000 Development User Enrollment	■ Client authentication ■ E-mail protection ■ Smartcard logon
http://mike-security	Michael's CA	■ Server authentication

Table 15-3. *Michael's certificates.*

Each certificate has an intended purpose for its associated private key. For example, the first three certificates are used to authenticate a user, and the fourth is used to authenticate a Web server called http://mike-security.

The first certificate can be used to authenticate the owner when the client is using SSL/TLS and the Web server requires that the user identify himself with a client authentication certificate. The certificate can also be used when the client sends secure electronic mail, such as S/MIME.

The second certificate, issued to members of the Windows 2000 development team, is used to encrypt and decrypt data on the disk using the Windows 2000 Encrypting File System.

The third, also issued to members of the Windows 2000 development team, can be used for SSL/TLS, e-mail (such as S/MIME), and logon to Windows 2000 using a smartcard rather than a password.

The fourth certificate was issued by the author's CA using Microsoft Certificate Services (included with Windows 2000) to his own intranet Web server. This is a purely experimental setup because no one has inherent trust in a personal CA.

As already discussed, it's common to have multiple certificate chains based on key usage. For example, the two Windows 2000 certificates in Table 15-3 have different issuers but they share the same root. (This isn't obvious from the table because the table includes only the issuers, not the full certificate chain.)

The full chains for each certificate are shown in Table 15-4.

Subject	Certificate Chain
Michael Howard	■ Thawte Personal Freemail CA (root)
	■ Personal Freemail RSA 1999.9.16 (Thawte)
Michael Howard	■ Windows 2000 Dev CA Root
	■ Windows 2000 End-User
	■ Windows 2000 Development Team
Michael Howard	■ Windows 2000 Dev CA Root
	■ Windows 2000 End-User
	■ Windows 2000 Development User Enrollment
http://mike-security	■ Michael's CA

Table 15-4. *Certificates and their certificate chains.*

Certificate trust

Notice the decreasing trust in the certificates listed in Table 15-4—the first certificate from Thawte carries more authority than the last certificate issued to Michael by Michael (which is a little like issuing a passport to yourself). Most people trust Thawte as a respected CA that issues certificates after performing some degree of due diligence. But few people will trust a certificate issued by an individual unless they know the individual personally. Think of it as a *sphere of trust* issue: how much trust is inherent in the issuer and to what degree is the issuer trusted? Thawte certificates have global trust, the internal Microsoft CA certificates are trusted within Microsoft, and Michael's CA is trusted only by Michael and those who know him.

Another implied aspect of trust is that CAs manage the certificates they issue—that is, they renew certificates when they expire and revoke certificates when required.

Certification revocation lists

A certification revocation list (CRL) is a data structure that maintains a list of certificates that have been revoked or invalidated before their expiration date. A CA might revoke a certificate for such reasons as these:

■ The associated private key has been compromised.

■ The user has left the organization or changed positions.

■ It's been discovered that the certificate was obtained through falsified means.

When a program requests a certificate from a principal, it can check the CRL to ensure that the certificate hasn't been revoked. It does this by checking the CDPs in the certificate, which might be a file stored on a file and print server, an FTP server, a Web server, or a server responding to LDAP requests such as Active Directory.

Data communication protocols that use certificates

Some of the common protocols that use certificates include

- SSL/TLS, a protocol for securing a connection between a client application and a server application (such as a Web browser and Web server). SSL/TLS requires a certificate at the server and optionally a certificate for each client if the server requires a client authentication certificate. Internet Explorer 5, IIS 5, Microsoft Exchange Server 5.5, SQL Server 2000, SMTP Server, and LDAP support on Windows 2000 all support SSL/TLS.

- S/MIME, a protocol for sending secure e-mail. If a user has a private key and an associated certificate, he can sign his e-mail to enable other users to verify the origin of the message. A user can send another user a private e-mail if he has access to the recipient's certificate. It's common to sign and encrypt e-mail. To do so, both parties must have a certificate and a private key. Outlook 2000 and Outlook Express 5 support S/MIME.

- IPSec (Internet Protocol Security), a computer-to-computer protocol that supports privacy, authentication, and data integrity. IPSec does not require certificates, but it's a very secure means of authenticating hosts. Windows 2000 supports IPSec.

Some myths about certificates

We've seen numerous articles explaining, erroneously, how simply using certificates can render a Web site impervious to attack. Certificates are useful for building certain security solutions, but they're no panacea.

Myth #1: certificates provide encryption.

This myth originates from the fact that the most common protocol that uses certificates is SSL/TLS, and SSL/TLS provides encryption—hence the misconception that certificates provide encryption. SSL/TLS works by authenticating the server first; this is where the certificate is used. Once the client authenticates the server, the client and server determine a symmetric key to use for the rest of the conversation. The key is used to encrypt the communication channel.

Myth #2: certificates are a perfect authentication scheme.

Certificates are an excellent form of authentication, especially when used in conjunction with smartcards. However, certificates have two weaknesses:

■ Your software trusts all certificates issued by the CA if you trust the CA. However, if the CA does an inadequate background check on the principal, the system breaks down.

■ Managing keys is a complex task, especially for users. In order for the system to be secure, the keys must never leave the user's computer, but many users have access to more than one computer. Unlike passwords, which are portable because you keep them in your head, private keys usually reside on a computer. Moving the keys to another computer is a relatively complicated undertaking for users, and it's also a security risk because the private keys might be exposed as they're being transferred.

Myth #3: the CA has your private key.

Most of the time, this isn't true, especially in the case of public CAs. When you want a new certificate and private key, the key pair is created at the client computer and the private key is securely stored locally. The certificate request is made and contains only the public key that will eventually be returned to the user as a certificate containing the public key.

Myth #4: certificates provide as much authentication as Web cookies.

We were surprised to hear this comment coming from an industry consulting organization. Cookies are a common way to authenticate users when they access your Web site, but they're a very weak form of authentication compared to public key certificates. Here are some of the differences:

■ A certificate is a public document. There is nothing in a certificate to protect or secure data. Cookies must be secured because they're private data.

■ A certificate is tamper resistant. No one can change a certificate without making it invalid. Cookies provide no such security.

■ Only the person who holds the private key can use the certificate for authentication. Others can use the certificate to verify your identity. A cookie, however, is much less secure and can easily be replayed. (A replay or *spoof* attack is a third party using packets captured from a successful connection to play back the remote client's response in order to gain an authenticated connection.)

- Certificates are issued only after some kind of verification of your iden-tity. Cookies come with no such assurances.

- Certificates and private keys can be stored on tamper-resistant devices such as smartcards; cookies are not stored on these devices.

- Cookies can easily be stolen by sniffing the connection between the cli-ent and the server. Private keys are much harder to steal because they rarely leave the computer on which they were generated.

- Private keys can be used to create digital signatures that assert that the possessor is the owner or producer of a piece of code or a document. Cookies cannot be used for such purposes.

CRYPTOGRAPHY AND CERTIFICATES IN WINDOWS 2000

Now let's turn our attention to how Windows 2000 implements cryptographic technolo-gies and how a user or administrator can use them. We'll look at the following topics: CryptoAPI, certificates in Windows 2000, and certificates in Microsoft Office 2000.

CryptoAPI

Windows 2000 has an extremely rich set of low-level cryptographic capabilities based on the Cryptographic API, or CryptoAPI for short. CryptoAPI provides services that allow developers to add certificate and cryptographic capabilities to their applications without having to understand the implementation details of cryptographic functions.

CryptoAPI implements cryptographic operations by calling CryptoAPI Service Providers (CSPs). When an application wants to perform a cryptographic operation, it asks CryptoAPI to use a specific CSP.

Windows 2000 ships with the following CSPs:

- Microsoft Base Cryptographic Provider, a general-purpose CSP that sup-ports data encryption and digital signatures. It supports RSA, RC2, and RC4 as well as MD5 and SHA1.

- Microsoft Strong Cryptographic Provider, an extension to the Microsoft Base Cryptographic Provider CSP. It supports all the algorithms in the

Microsoft Enhanced Cryptographic Provider, but the key lengths are the same as in the Microsoft Base Cryptographic Provider. It supports RSA, DES, 3DES, RC2, and RC4 as well as MD5 and SHA1.

■ Microsoft Enhanced Cryptographic Provider, which supports stronger security through longer keys and additional algorithms compared to the Base provider. It supports RSA, DES, 3DES, RC2, and RC4 as well as MD5 and SHA1.

■ Microsoft DSS Cryptographic Provider, which supports hashing, data signing, and signature verification using the SHA1 and Digital Signature Standard (DSS) algorithms.

■ Microsoft Base DSS and Diffie-Hellman Cryptographic Provider, a superset of the Microsoft DSS Cryptographic Provider that also supports Diffie-Hellman key exchange, hashing, data signing, and signature verification using the SHA1 and DSS algorithms.

■ Microsoft Base DSS and Diffie-Hellman/Schannel Cryptographic Provider, which is the same as the Microsoft Base DSS and Diffie-Hellman Cryptographic Provider but is used for SSL3 and TLS1 protocols when the application uses Diffie-Hellman key exchange.

■ Microsoft RSA/Schannel Cryptographic Provider, which is similar to the Microsoft Base DSS and Diffie-Hellman/Schannel Cryptographic Provider in that it works with SSL3 and TLS1, but uses the RSA suite of algorithms rather than Diffie-Hellman.

■ Schlumberger CSP and GEMPlus CSP (from the vendors Schlumberger and GEMPlus, respectively), which are used with smartcards.

CryptoAPI in Windows 2000 is actually two sets of functionality. CryptoAPI 1.0 provides the low-level cryptographic functionality, such as encrypting, decrypting, hashing data, and managing keys. CryptoAPI 2.0 isn't an upgrade to CryptoAPI 1.0— it provides additional functionality for managing certificates and manipulating PKCS #7 signed messages.

The general architecture of CryptoAPI is shown in Figure 15-13. (For more information about CryptoAPI, see the Microsoft Developer Network (MSDN) CDs or the MSDN Web site at *msdn.microsoft.com.*)

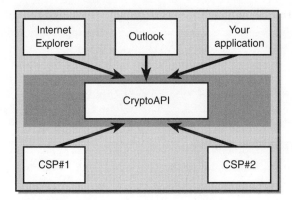

Figure 15-13. *The CryptoAPI architecture.*

NOTE Windows 2000 now supports 128-bit cryptography for all countries outside North America except countries embargoed by the U.S. government. You can get the High Encryption Pack for Windows 2000 from *http:// windowsupdate.microsoft.com* or by choosing Windows Update from the Start menu.

Certificates in Windows 2000

Windows 2000 provides excellent support for certificates at all levels of use through the following technologies: CryptoAPI 2.0, Microsoft Certificate Services, and certificate enrollment control.

Certificates and CryptoAPI 2.0

CryptoAPI 2.0 supplies services for storing certificates and their private keys as well as a user interface that makes manipulating certificates easy.

Certificate stores

Certificates and keys are stored in certificate stores. The location of a store is determined by the CSP used. In the case of the default Microsoft CSPs, they're held in a secure area of the Registry. The most commonly used stores are

■ The personal store (often called the MY store), which holds a user's or a computer's certificates and private keys

■ The root store, which holds self-signed root CA certificates

■ The trust store, which holds certificate trust lists (CTLs), which are signed lists of root CA certificates defined by an administrator as trustworthy within an organization.

■ The CA store, which holds intermediate CA certificates

Note that users, computers, and services can all have their own certificate stores.

Certificate user interfaces

The main user interface tools for manipulating certificate stores and certificates are the Certificate dialog box and the Certificates management tool. The former allows the user to view a certificate file (usually a file with a .crt or .cer extension) or a certificate in a certificate store.

If you double-click a certificate or view a certificate in a certificate store, you see the Certificate dialog box, as shown in Figure 15-14.

Figure 15-14. *Viewing the properties of a user's certificate.*

CRYPTOAPI'S CERTIFICATE FORMAT

The following C/C++ structure shows how CryptoAPI 2.0 defines a certificate:

```
typedef struct _CERT_INFO {
    DWORD                       dwVersion;
    CRYPT_INTEGER_BLOB          SerialNumber;
    CRYPT_ALGORITHM_IDENTIFIER  SignatureAlgorithm;
    CERT_NAME_BLOB              Issuer;
    FILETIME                    NotBefore;
    FILETIME                    NotAfter;
    CERT_NAME_BLOB              Subject;
    CERT_PUBLIC_KEY_INFO        SubjectPublicKeyInfo;
    CRYPT_BIT_BLOB              IssuerUniqueId;
    CRYPT_BIT_BLOB              SubjectUniqueId;
    DWORD                       cExtension;
    PCERT_EXTENSION             rgExtension;
} CERT_INFO, *PCERT_INFO;
```

You can also view all the certificates known to you by using the Certificates management tool. To use the tool, follow these steps:

1. Choose Run from the Start menu.

2. Type *mmc /a* and press Return.

3. Choose Add/Remove Snap-in from the Console menu.

4. Click Add.

5. Double-click the Certificates snap-in.

6. Select My User Account.

7. Click Finish, click Close, and then click OK.

You'll see all certificates known to you if you open the Personal node. In the Certificates node, you'll see all the certificates assigned to you. It's these certificates to which you also have the private key. To view a certificate, double-click the file from Windows Explorer or the shell.

Importing and exporting certificates and private keys

Windows 2000 allows the user to import a certificate or import a certificate and a private key into a key store. It also allows the user to export a certificate or export a certificate and private key to a file. If the file is a .cer or .crt file, it contains only a certificate, not a certificate and a private key. A certificate and private key are stored in a PKCS #12 file, which has the .pfx extension. Figure 15-15 shows the different icons.

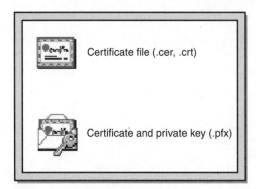

Figure 15-15. *Certificate and certificate/private key icons.*

You can import a .cer or .crt file by double-clicking it. In the Certificate Information dialog box, click Install Certificate to launch the Certificate Import wizard, which will help you install the certificate.

You can import a .pfx file by double-clicking on it. This launches the Certificate Import wizard. The Certificate Information dialog box doesn't appear because the file is encrypted and you must provide the password to successfully install the certificate and private key.

Internet Explorer 5 also has a certificate import option, which you can access as follows:

1. In Internet Explorer, choose Internet Options from the Tools menu.

2. On the Content tab of the Internet Options dialog box, click the Certificates button.

3. Invoke the Certificate Import wizard by clicking the Import button.

   Before you import a certificate, you have to make some important decisions:

■ Where to store the certificate and private key. Normally, you should let the wizard select the correct store.

■ Whether you want strong private key protection. This option isn't enabled by default, but it's highly recommended in secure environments. When you enable strong private key protection, you are prompted each time an application attempts to use the private key. Figure 15-16 shows the dialog box that appears when an application attempts to use a private key marked for strong private key protection.

■ Whether to allow the private key to be exported. By default, this option is disabled, so the private key can never leave the store in which it's saved. Any attempt to export the certificate and private key will fail.

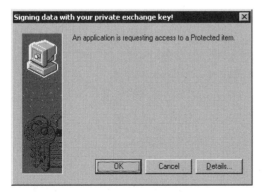

Figure 15-16. *An application is attempting to use a private key. You can click Details to see which application is performing the operation.*

You usually export a certificate to make a backup of the certificate and, optionally, the private key, or to copy the certificate to another computer. You export a certificate as follows:

1. In the Certificates Microsoft Management Console (MMC) tool, right-click on the certificate in question.

2. Select All Tasks.

3. Select Export. This launches the Certificate Export wizard, which guides you through the certificate and private key exporting process.

Exporting requires you to make some decisions:

■ Whether to export the private key. This option is available only if the certificate has a private key. For example, a root CA certificate can be exported from your store, but you won't have the private key—that's held securely by the CA.

■ The format in which to export the certificate and private key. If you're not exporting a private key, you have the following options:

❑ DER encoded binary X.509, a standard binary format for a single certificate saved with a .cer extension.

❑ Base64-encoded X.509, which is like the DER encoded format except that the binary data is encoded as a text base64 file with a .cer extension. This option is useful for transferring a certificate via e-mail.

❑ Cryptographic Message Syntax Standard - PKCS #7, which is also a binary standard but has the added advantage of being able to store the entire certificate chain. The file is saved with a .p7b extension.

■ If you're exporting a private key with the certificate, you export the data as a Personal Information Exchange - PKCS #12 file with a .pfx extension. You have the following options available to you:

❑ Including all the certificates in the path. This is similar to the PKCS #7 capability of saving the certificate chain.

❑ Enabling strong private key protection. This option uses PKCS #5 to make the password you enter harder to break should the encrypted exported data be stolen. Note that this is supported only by Windows NT 4 Service Pack 4 and later or Internet Explorer 5 and later. You should enable this option unless you plan to install the certificate and private key on Windows 95, Windows 98, or a Windows operating system prior to Windows NT 4 Service Pack 4 that doesn't have Internet Explorer 5 installed.

❑ Deleting the private key if the export succeeds. This option is disabled by default, but if you're exporting a certificate and private key for use solely on another computer, you should select this option.

You should be very careful about exporting and importing private keys between computers. You must be able to account for every copy of the private key and make sure that the keys are appropriately protected.

Let's now switch focus from the certificates themselves to the issuance and life cycle management of certificates using Microsoft Certificate Services in Windows 2000.

Microsoft Certificate Services

Certificate Services is an application for issuing and managing certificates that run on Windows 2000. It accepts PKCS #10 certificate requests and generates X.509 certificates in PKCS #7 format to be used for such diverse technologies as SSL/TLS, S/MIME, IPSec, and Code Signing, to name a few.

Certificate Services can be a root CA or a subordinate CA and can optionally integrate with Active Directory. When you use Active Directory, Certificate Services is referred to as an *enterprise CA* and it publishes certificates and CRLs to Active Directory, which makes managing the CA and certificates straightforward.

> **NOTE** Where does Certificate Services store its data? Certificate Services uses the same database technology as Active Directory and Microsoft Exchange Server to securely store certificate information.

You can access the Certificate Services administration tool as follows:

1. Choose Programs from the Start menu.

2. Select Administrative Tools.

3. Select Certification Authority. You'll see the opening screen of the Certificate Services tool, as shown in Figure 15-17.

DOES THIS MEAN I CAN CREATE A
CA LIKE VERISIGN OR THAWTE?

Yes and no. Yes, the Certificate Services technology is similar to that of VeriSign or Thawte, but these companies have built their reputations on trust. They are trusted third parties. Setting up a CA is more than technology. It's about trust, legal enforcement of policy, and in some cases backing the use of a certificate and private key with insurance—real money. It's not a trivial exercise.

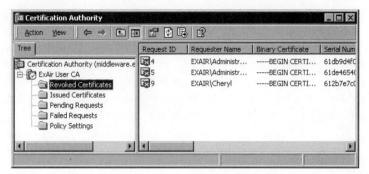

Figure 15-17. *The Certification Authority Administration Tool.*

From here, you can examine certificate properties by double-clicking on a certificate, back up and restore the CA database, manage the kinds of certificates you want to issue, and revoke certificates.

Certificate revocation lists

Like credit cards, all certificates have a useful lifetime. However, sometimes a certificate must be invalidated—for example, because the private key has been compromised or because the certificate owner leaves the company. Once again, the analogy to a credit card is useful—if you discover that someone has fraudulently used your credit card, you can revoke the card by contacting the issuer.

When a certificate is revoked, its serial number is added to a CRL maintained by the CA. A CRL contains the following information:

- Version number
- Issuer
- Effective date
- Next update
- Signature algorithm
- Signature
- Revocation list

The data is similar to that found in X.509 except for the effective date, next update, and revocation list. The effective date is the date and time that the list was last updated, next update is the date and time of the next update, and revocation list is the list of revoked certificate serial numbers and the date the certificate was revoked.

You can determine where to find the CRL for the CA that issued a certificate by looking at a CDP in the certificate.

Figure 15-18 shows a certificate issued by VeriSign. As you can see, VeriSign place its updated CRLs on the Web at *http://crl.verisign.com*. If you navigate to this URL with your browser, you'll see a number of files ending in .crl, one of which is named class1.crl. If the serial number of this certificate is in the CRL, this certificate has been revoked. (At the time of this writing, such action had not been taken on this particular certificate.)

Figure 15-18. *The CDPs in a VeriSign certificate.*

You can copy the CRL to your computer if you want to look inside it. Once you copy it, it appears on your computer with the icon shown in Figure 15-19.

Figure 15-19. *The CRL icon in Windows 2000.*

You can look at a CRL by double-clicking it from the Windows 2000 shell. Figure 15-20 shows the VeriSign CRL.

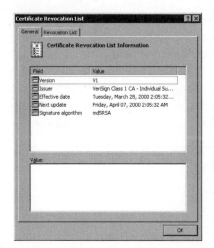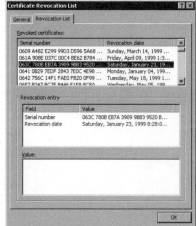

Figure 15-20. *A VeriSign CRL.*

Where does revocation checking occur?

Certificate revocation checking occurs at the host that requests the certificate. For example, if you have a Web browser that uses an SSL/TLS connection to a Web server, your browser will check that the Web server's certificate is valid. By default, Internet Explorer 5 doesn't perform CRL checking, but you can enable checking as follows:

1. In Internet Explorer 5, choose Internet Options from the Tools menu.

2. Click on the Advanced tab.

3. Scroll down to the Security node, and select the Check For Publisher's Certificate Revocation option and the Check For Server Certificate Revocation option. The former performs CRL checks on signed code, and the latter performs CRL checks on the certificates issued to Web sites.

If a Web server is configured to require client authentication certificates over an SSL/TLS connection, the Web server will check that the client's certificate is valid. In the case of IIS 5, a 403.13 error ("Client Certificate Revoked") is returned if the certificate has been revoked by the CA. By default, IIS 5 performs CRL checking.

When you use secure e-mail, the e-mail program will check whether the sender's certificate has been revoked. Outlook 2000 and Outlook Express 5 do not perform CRL checking by default, but you can enable this functionality.

In Outlook 2000, you take the following steps:

1. Using RegEdt32, open or create the following key: HKCU\Software\Microsoft\Cryptography\{7801ebd0-cf4b-11d0-851f-0060979387ea}.

2. Create a REG_DWORD PolicyFlags value and set it to 0x00010000.

3. Restart Outlook 2000.

In Outlook Express 5, you take these steps:

1. Choose Options from the Tools menu.

2. Click the Security tab.

3. Click the Advanced button.

4. In the Check For Revoked Digital IDs drop-down list, select Only When Online.

Revoking a certificate by using Certificate Services

Revoking a certificate is a simple process in Certificate Services:

1. In the Certification Authority tool, right-click the certificate in question.

2. Select All Tasks.

3. Select Revoke Certificate.

4. Specify the reason why the certificate is being revoked by selecting from the list of options.

It's important to realize that once you revoke a certificate, you cannot "unrevoke" it, so double-check that the certificate is the correct one.

A problem with CRLs

CRLs are updated at regular intervals called *publish periods*. By default, the publish period for Certificate Services is one week. What happens if a certificate is revoked within the one-week period? Clients might not pick up on the change until the next CRL update, as defined in the Next Update field in the CRL, because it's normal for client software to cache the CRL until the next update.

Because of this problem, you should set the CRL publish period to balance the cost of publishing a new CRL against the risk of a client missing a revoked certificate.

Note that you can reissue an updated CRL at any time using Certificate Services, but as we've already discussed, clients with cached CRLs might not use the updated CRL.

DOES THIS MEAN THAT CRLS WILL BECOME VERY LARGE OVER TIME?

Imagine if a CA had to add every revoked certificate to the CRL. Over time, wouldn't the CRL would grow very large? Luckily, the answer is no. Only certificates that haven't expired are added to a CRL. In fact, once a certificate expires, it can appear on the next CRL update, after which it's removed from the CRL.

To change the CRL publish period, take the following steps:

1. In the Certification Authority tool, right-click on Revoked Certificates and choose Properties from the context menu.

2. Enter the new publish period in the Publish Interval field.

> **NOTE**   Microsoft Certificate Services will extend the validity period of the CRL by 10 percent (up to a maximum of 12 hours) to accommodate directory replication latency.

Certificate enrollment control

The certificate enrollment control is a COM+ component that simplifies the building of solutions that request and process certificates. Because it's a COM+ component, you can use it from virtually any programming language, such as C++, Microsoft Visual Basic, or a scripting language such as Microsoft Visual Basic, Scripting Edition (VBScript) or JScript. Certificate Services in Windows 2000 includes a set of Active Server Pages (ASP) pages that call the certificate enrollment control to generate certificate requests for users.

The ASP enrollment pages are available at *http://yourserver/certsrv*.

HOW DO THE CERTIFICATE SERVICES ASP PAGES WORK WITH NETSCAPE CLIENTS?

Netscape browsers don't support COM+ components, but ASP pages work well with both Microsoft and Netscape browsers because they detect the browser type. If they detect Internet Explorer, they use the certificate enrollment control. If they detect a Netscape browser, they instead present Netscape-specific pages that contain a Netscape proprietary tag called *<keygen>*, which generates keys for the user. You can find out more about *<keygen>* at *http://developer.netscape.com/docs/manuals/htmlguid/tags10.htm#1615505*.

The control might also be called to create a PKCS #10 blob to be used with any CA, such as Thawte or VeriSign.

> **NOTE**   If you used Certificate Server 1 in the Windows NT 4 Option Pack, you might already be familiar with the certificate enrollment control. It had a different name in the Windows NT 4 Option Pack, however: XEnroll.

Using the certificate enrollment control, you can create your own custom certificate generation tools. The control takes user input, creates private and public key pairs, generates a PKCS #10 certificate request, and accepts PKCS #7 responses from the CA. It also manages the storage of the keys and certificates.

The following pseudocode creates a simple, custom application to request a client authentication certificate and store the result:

```
// Define objects.
oEnroll = CreateObject("CEnroll.CEnroll.1");
oRequest = New CCertRequest

// Build up cert request details.
// The OID represents a client authentication certificate.
strUsage = "1.3.6.1.5.5.7.3.2";
strDN = "CN=Cheryl, OU=Development, O=ExAir," & _
    " L=Redmond, S=WA, C=US";

// Build the cert request.
strReq = oEnroll.createPKCS10(strDN, strUsage);
fFlags = PKCS10 in BASE64 format;
strAttributes = "";
strConfig = "EXAIR\UserCA"
oRequest.Submit(fFlags, strReq, strAttributes, strConfig);

// Get the cert.
strCert = oRequest.GetCertificate(BASE64);
oEnroll.AcceptPKCS7(strCert);
```

Others ways to enroll for a certificate

The certificate enrollment control isn't the only way to enroll for a certificate. For example, IIS 5 includes a Web Server Certificate wizard that guides you through the process of building up a certificate request specifically for a Web server. The certificate can be sent directly to Certificate Services or can be saved as a PKCS #10 file to send to another CA.

You can also enroll for a client certificate using the Certificates tool:

- In the Certificates tool, right-click Personal and choose Request New Certificate from the All Tasks option.

- Follow the wizard.

This feature works only with online Certificate Services running as enterprise CAs.

The CertUtil tool

We'll close by looking at a useful tool for managing certificates called Certutil.exe. The tool can perform many tasks, including

- Displaying Certificate Services configuration information
- Displaying a file containing a request, a certificate, a PKCS #7 blob, or a CRL
- Decoding hexadecimal or base64 files
- Encoding files to base64
- Retrieving the CA signing certificate
- Revoking certificates
- Publishing or retrieving a CRL
- Verifying one or all levels of a certification path
- Verifying a public/private key set
- Determining whether a CA service is running
- Shutting down the server
- Converting a Certificate Services 1 database to a Certificate Services 2 database
- Backing up and restoring the CA keys and database
- Displaying certificates in a certificate store
- Displaying error message text for a specified error code

You should become familiar with this tool if you intend to work extensively with certificates and Certificate Services in Windows 2000.

Some of the most useful features of the tool include the ability to view the contents of a PKCS #10 certificate request file, a certificate, or a certificate chain in a PKCS #7 package or a CRL in PKCS #7 format. Figures 15-21 through 15-24 show some sample output.

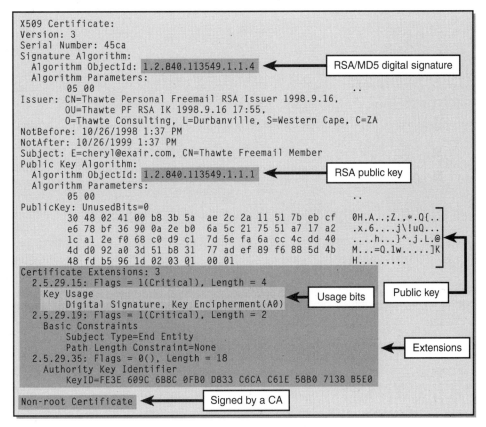

Figure 15-21. *A client certificate from Thawte in X.509 format.*

Other resources for Certificate Services

The Web pages listed in Table 15-5 have useful documentation on setting up and maintaining a PKI solution based on Certificate Services in Windows 2000. All the locations start with *http://www.microsoft.com/windows2000/library/planning/security/*.

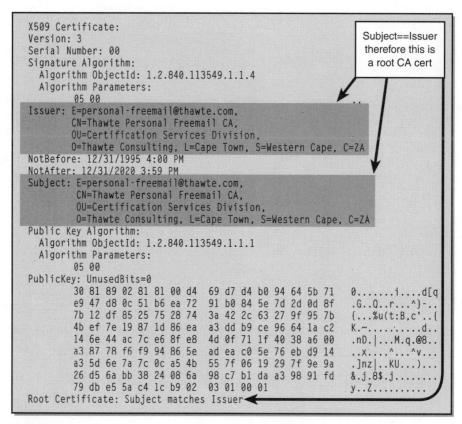

Figure 15-22. *A Thawte root CA certificate in X.509 format.*

Web Page Title	File
Step-by-Step Guide to Setting up a Certificate Authority	/casetupsteps.asp
Step-by-Step Guide to Certificate Services Web Pages	/cawebsteps.asp
Step-by-Step Guide to Administering Certificate Services	/adminca.asp
Step-by-Step Guide to Advanced Certificate Management	/advcertsteps.asp
Step-by-Step Guide to End User Certificate Management	/eucertsteps.asp
Step-by-Step Guide to Mapping Certificates to User Accounts	/mappingcerts.asp
Step-by-Step Guide to Public Key-Based Client Authentication in Internet Explorer	/pubkeyie.asp
Step-by-Step Guide to Public Key Features of Outlook 2000	/pubkeyol2000.asp
Step-by-Step Guide to Public Key Features in Outlook Express 5 and above	/pubkeyox.asp

Table 15-5. *Useful certificate-related documentation at http://www.microsoft.com.*

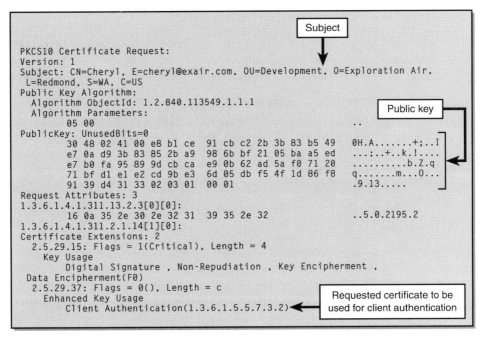

```
                                                    ┌─────────┐
                                                    │ Subject │
                                                    └─────────┘
                                                         │
                                                         ▼
PKCS10 Certificate Request:
Version: 1
Subject: CN=Cheryl, E=cheryl@exair.com, OU=Development, O=Exploration Air,
 L=Redmond, S=WA, C=US
Public Key Algorithm:
  Algorithm ObjectId: 1.2.840.113549.1.1.1
  Algorithm Parameters:                                        ┌────────────┐
    05 00                                          ..          │ Public key │
PublicKey: UnusedBits=0                                        └────────────┘
      30 48 02 41 00 e8 b1 ce  91 cb c2 2b 3b 83 b5 49   0H.A......+;..I
      e7 0a d9 3b 83 85 2b a9  98 6b bf 21 05 ba a5 ed   ...;..+..k.!....
      e7 b0 fa 95 89 9d cb ca  e9 0b 62 ad 5a f0 71 20   ..........b.Z.q
      71 bf d1 e1 e2 cd 9b e3  6d 05 db f5 4f 1d 86 f8   q.......m...O...
      91 39 d4 31 33 02 03 01  00 01                     .9.13.....
Request Attributes: 3
1.3.6.1.4.1.311.13.2.3[0][0]:
      16 0a 35 2e 30 2e 32 31  39 35 2e 32               ..5.0.2195.2
1.3.6.1.4.1.311.2.1.14[1][0]:
Certificate Extensions: 2
  2.5.29.15: Flags = 1(Critical), Length = 4
    Key Usage
         Digital Signature , Non-Repudiation , Key Encipherment ,
 Data Encipherment(F0)
  2.5.29.37: Flags = 0(), Length = c              ┌────────────────────────────┐
    Enhanced Key Usage                            │ Requested certificate to be│
         Client Authentication(1.3.6.1.5.5.7.3.2)◄┤used for client authentication│
                                                  └────────────────────────────┘
```

Figure 15-23. *A client authentication certificate request in PKCS #10 format.*

```
  X509 Certificate Revocation List:
  Version: 1
  Signature Algorithm:
    Algorithm ObjectId: 1.2.840.113549.1.1.4
    Algorithm Parameters:
      05 00                                              ..
  Issuer: OU=VeriSign Class 1 CA - Individual Subscriber,
   O="VeriSign, Inc.", L=Internet
  ThisUpdate: 2/16/2000 2:06 AM ◄──────────    ┌──────────────────┐
  NextUpdate: 2/26/2000 2:06 AM                │ Publishing period│
  CRL Entries: 931                             │   for the CRL    │
    Serial Number: 365d7d3209c977895866b3ec07f5c9└──────────────────┘
    RevocationDate: 1/8/1999 9:02 AM                         ┌──────────────┐
    Extensions: 0                                            │Two of the 931│
                                              ◄──────────────┤ CRL entries  │
    Serial Number: 3ec6e76c14972bb6e9728f4a046991            └──────────────┘
    RevocationDate: 4/28/1999 11:33 AM
    Extensions: 0

  <etc…>
```

Figure 15-24. *A CRL issued by VeriSign.*

Certificates in Microsoft Office 2000

Office 2000 does not require Windows 2000, but let's look at how Office 2000 uses certificates. Office 2000 uses certificates for securing e-mail in Outlook 2000 and for Visual Basic for Applications (VBA) code signing.

Securing e-mail in Outlook 2000

Outlook 2000 supports sending signed and encrypted e-mail using the secure e-mail standard S/MIME. You can access the S/MIME functionality as follows:

1. Choose Options from the Tools menu.

2. Click on the Security tab.

3. Click the Setup Secure E-Mail button. If the button is named Change Settings, you've already set up S/MIME.

You can now determine which certificate to use for signing and encrypting.

To send signed e-mail, you can choose to have all e-mail be signed (by selecting the Add Digital Signature To Outgoing Messages option on the Security tab) or you can choose to sign specific e-mail as you create the message (by clicking on the Options button on the message toolbar and then selecting the Add Digital Signature To Outgoing Message check box). The same applies to encrypted e-mail. However, to send encrypted e-mail, you must have the recipient's certificate added to your Contacts list.

For details about S/MIME support in Outlook 2000, see Knowledge Base article Q195477 at *http://support.microsoft.com/support/kb/articles/Q195/4/77.ASP*. For more information about S/MIME, go to *http://www.ietf.org/html.charters/smime-charter.html*.

VBA code signing

Office 2000 introduces digital signatures to help users distinguish legitimate script code from potentially harmful code. When you open an Office 2000 document and see a macro security warning with digital signature information, you can feel confident that the principal signing the macros also created them. You can choose to trust all macros signed by this person by selecting the Trust All Macros From This Source check box.

Office 2000 also includes a tool named SelfCert.exe that enables you to create a temporary certificate and key for signing VBA projects. The certificate is self-signed and has no inherent trust, and its key usage is for code signing only—you cannot use it for other purposes, such as secure e-mail or SSL/TLS.

> **NOTE**   The certificate and private key produced by SelfCert.exe isn't stored as a file; it's stored in the current user's MY store.

See Knowledge Base article Q206637 at *http://support.microsoft.com/support/kb/articles/Q206/6/37.ASP* for more information about signing macros and using digital certificates in Office 2000.

SUMMARY

Cryptography is an important technology for building secure Web applications, but you must use it properly. One of the best quotes from the movie *Sneakers* (Universal Studios, 1992) is the line, "You won't get in—it's encrypted." However, cryptography is only one part of the solution; you also need to consider how two or more parties exchange keys and where to store keys. Indeed, key management is one of the more complex aspects of cryptography.

Luckily, most cryptography is hidden from developers, users, and administrators alike in the form of built-in secure protocols such as SSL/TLS, IPSec, and S/MIME. You have little work to do other than enroll for a certificate.

X.509 certificates are a good, well-understood means of verifying authenticity, and Windows 2000 offers superlative certificate support for users, developers, and administrators.

Technologies included with Windows 2000 include CryptoAPI for building low-level cryptographic applications, usually from C or C++. CryptoAPI also provides an easy-to-use user interface for viewing and manipulating certificates. Windows 2000 also includes Microsoft Certificate Services, which allows you to deploy your own internal certificate infrastructure or perhaps an infrastructure between you and your business partners.

It's crucial that you review some of the online certificate service guidelines at *http://www.microsoft.com* before you build a public key infrastructure. You should be sure that you have a good understanding of why you're using cryptography and certificates before you deploy a solution.

"And they all lived securely ever after...."
—*Luke's Mom*

Bibliography

General Security

American Bar Association. *Digital Signature Guidelines: Legal Infrastructure for Certification Authorities and Electronic Commerce.* Chicago, IL: American Bar Association, 1996. This is a wonderful book outlining the legal aspects and pragmatics of using digital signatures in e-commerce. The real beauty of the book is that it isn't technical; it's a legal commentary. You can purchase it from the ABA Web site, or it's available for free at *www.abanet.org/scitech/ec/isc/dsgfree.html.* Well worth reading.

Biddle, C. Bradford, et al. "Web Security—A Matter of Trust," *World Wide Web Journal* 2, no. 3 (summer 1997). This journal is a collection of papers covering the Secure Sockets Layer (SSL) protocol, trust management, security in the Domain Name System (DNS) and BIND, and more. It's dry in places, but most of the authors are well known and well respected.

Burstein, Harvey. *Security: A Management Perspective.* Englewood Cliffs, NJ: Prentice Hall, 1996. Burstein's book covers an oft-overlooked aspect of security: how to budget for and prepare personnel for security. No technologies are covered in this book, but pick it up if you deal with management and need to convince them that money should be spent on securing the company.

Electronic Frontier Foundation. *Protecting Yourself Online.* New York: HarperCollins, 1998. This small book deals with what happens when you go on line as a user. It covers online hoaxes, privacy issues, free expression, anonymity, and intellectual property. It's a no-nonsense treatise and should be read by anybody going on line.

Garfinkel, Simson, and Gene Spafford. *Practical UNIX & Internet Security.* 2d ed. Sebastopol, CA: O'Reilly & Associates, 1996. This is a huge book and a classic. Although it focuses almost exclusively on security flaws and administrative issues in UNIX, its concepts can be applied to just about any operating system. It has a huge UNIX security checklist and gives a great rendering of the various Department of Defense security models as defined in the Rainbow Series of books.

———. *Web Security & Commerce.* Sebastopol, CA: O'Reilly & Associates, 1997. The best part of this book is its explanation of the SSL protocol. It covers certificates in detail, as well as cookie security, downloadable code implications, and common administration mistakes, but its coverage of SSL is superlative.

Kaeo, Merike. *Designing Network Security*. Indianapolis, IN: Cisco Press, 1999. This book is destined to be a classic. It's not a big book, but it covers virtually every aspect of building secure networks, including identity technologies, router configuration, VPNs, risk management, policy, firewall architectures, and much more. It comes highly recommended.

National Research Council. *Trust in Cyberspace*. Edited by Fred B. Schneider. Washington, DC: National Academy Press, 1999. This book is the result of a government security think-tank given the task to analyze the U.S. telecommunications and security infrastructure and make recommendations about making it more resilient to attack. It's a hard-to-read book but well worth reading.

Online Law. Edited by Thomas J. Smedinghoff. Reading, MA: Addison-Wesley Developers Press, 1996. This book gives an insightful rundown of the legal aspects of digital certificates, the state of current law relating to their use, privacy, patents, online cash, liability, and more. This is a recommended read for anyone doing business on line or anyone considering using certificates as part of an electronic contract.

Summers, Rita C. *Secure Computing: Threats and Safeguards*. New York: McGraw-Hill, 1997. A heavy read but very thorough, especially the sections about designing and building secure systems and analyzing security. Other aspects of the book include database security, encryption, and management.

Tung, Brian. *Kerberos: A Network Authentication System*. Reading, MA: Addison-Wesley, 1999. A small book that covers the Kerberos authentication well. It has a UNIX flavor but deals with some tools that are redundant in Microsoft Windows 2000, such as kinit. It covers the MIT APIs in detail and is therefore a good resource for developers.

Wood, Charles Cresson. *Information Security Policies Made Easy: Version 5*. Sausalito, CA: Baseline Software, 1996. Weighing in at over 500 pages, this is the best treatment of security policies the authors have seen. Every conceivable security policy is discussed in the book, including privacy, physical security, encryption, and personnel issues.

Public Key Infrastructure and Certificates

Adams, Carlisle, and Steve Lloyd. *Understanding the Public-Key Infrastructure*. Indianapolis, IN: Macmillan Technical Publishing, 1999. A new and complete book on X.509 certificates and the Public Key Infrastructure with X.509 (PKIX) standards. The authors consider this book the "IETF standards written in English." This is much more complete than Jalal Feghhi's book, but it is a more difficult read. That said, if your work with certificates will take you beyond the basics, consider purchasing this book.

Feghhi, Jalal, and Peter Williams. *Digital Certificates: Applied Internet Security*. Reading, MA: Addison-Wesley, 1999. The concepts behind digital certificates are somewhat shrouded in mystery, and this book does a great job of lifting the veil of secrecy. Quite simply, it's the best book there is on X.509 certificates and public key infrastructure (PKI).

Ford, Warwick, and Michael S. Baum. *Secure Electronic Commerce: Building the Infrastructure for Digital Signatures and Encryption*. Upper Saddle River, NJ: Prentice Hall PTR, 1997. Like *Digital Certificates: Applied Internet Security* by Jalal Feghhi and Peter Williams, this book explains X.509 certificates well. However, it goes further by delving into the effects PKI has on electronic commerce by covering some legal aspects also.

Secure Protocols

Ford, Warwick. *Computer Communications Security: Principles, Standard Protocols, and Techniques*. Englewood Cliffs, NJ: Prentice Hall PTR, 1994. Covers many aspects of communications security, including cryptography, authentication, authorization, integrity, and privacy, and has the best coverage of nonrepudiation outside of academic papers. It also discusses the Open Systems Interconnection (OSI) security architecture in detail.

Security Protocols. Edited by Bruce Christianson, et al. Berlin: Springer, 1998. This is a wonderful set of research papers on many aspects of secure communications. It's not for the weak-hearted—the material is complex and requires a good degree of cryptographic knowledge—but it's well worth reading.

Thomas, Stephen A. *SSL and TLS Essentials: Securing the Web*. New York: Wiley, 2000. A complete and readable explanation of the SSL and Transport Layer Security (TLS) protocols. Also covers the mysteries of ASN.1 syntax, as well as Microsoft Server Gated Crypto (SGC), the 128-bit exportable version of SSL. If you need to know the innards of SSL/TLS, consider this book. If all you need is a basic understanding of the principles of SSL/TLS, this book is overkill.

Security Theory

Amoroso, Edward G. *Fundamentals of Computer Security Technology*. Englewood Cliffs, NJ: Prentice Hall PTR, 1994. This is one of our favorite books. Amoroso has a knack for defining complex theory in a form that's useful and easy to understand. His coverage of threat trees is the best there is. He also explains some of the classic security models, such as the Bell-LaPadula disclosure, Biba integrity, and Clark-Wilson integrity models. The only drawback to this book is that it's somewhat dated.

Gollmann, Dieter. *Computer Security*. New York: Wiley, 1999. We consider this to be a more up-to-date and somewhat more pragmatic version of Amoroso's *Fundamentals of Computer Security Technology*. Gollmann covers security models left out by Amoroso, as well as Microsoft Windows NT, UNIX, and Web security in some detail.

Firewalls and Proxy Servers

Amoroso, Edward G., and Ronald Sharp. *PC Week Intranet and Internet Firewall Strategies*. Emeryville, CA: Ziff-Davis Press, 1996. This is a reasonable book if you're new to firewalls. The basics are explained in an easy-to-follow fashion. It also covers some of the commercial firewall offerings.

Chapman, D. Brent, and Elizabeth D. Zwicky. *Building Internet Firewalls*. Sebastopol, CA: O'Reilly & Associates, 1995. Probably the best and most comprehensive coverage of firewalls, presented in an easy-to-read format. The book also covers what to do in the case of an intrusion.

Cheswick, William R., and Steven M. Bellovin. *Firewalls and Internet Security: Repelling the Wily Hacker*. Reading, MA: Addison-Wesley, 1994. An old book but one of the best on firewalls.

Luotonen, Ari. *Web Proxy Servers*. Upper Saddle River, NJ: Prentice Hall PTR, 1998. Easy to read and complete, this is possibly the only book you'll need on proxy servers. Luotonen is a well-known proxy expert, having worked on the CERN and Netscape proxy products.

Hacking and Intrusion Detection

Amoroso, Edward G. *Intrusion Detection: An Introduction to Internet Surveillance, Correlation, Traps, Traceback, and Response*. Sparta, NJ: Intrusion.Net Books, 1999. This book takes off where Terry Escamilla's *Intrusion Detection* stops. It's a somewhat more academic book that offers some superb case studies to give a real-life flavor to intrusion detection (ID). Highly recommended.

Escamilla, Terry. *Intrusion Detection: Network Security Beyond the Firewall*. New York: Wiley, 1998. Wiley has produced some good security books, and this one is reasonable, too. It's an introductory text on the topic; you should read this to get a feel for the ID marketplace and the tools and technologies required. Once you've read this, read Edward Amoroso's *Intrusion Detection*.

Maximum Security: A Hacker's Guide to Protecting Your Internet Site and Network. 2d ed. Indianapolis, IN: Sams, 1998. Similar to *Hacking Exposed: Network Security Secrets and Solutions* but not quite as polished. However, it does list more tools and more vulnerabilities. You should consider having both books on your bookshelf.

McClure, Stuart, Joel Scambray, and George Kurtz. *Hacking Exposed: Network Security Secrets and Solutions*. Berkeley, CA: Osborne/McGraw-Hill, 1999. This book will make you realize how vulnerable you are to attack when you go on line, regardless of operation system! It covers security vulnerabilities in NetWare, UNIX, Windows 95, Windows 98, and Windows NT. Each vulnerability covered includes references to tools to use to perform such an attack. The book's clear purpose is to motivate administrators.

Shimomura, Tsutomu, and John Markoff. *Takedown: The Pursuit and Capture of Kevin Mitnick, America's Most Wanted Computer Outlaw—By the Man Who Did It*. New York: Hyperion, 1996. This is the story of the infamous hacker Kevin Mitnick and his attacks on various computer systems at The Well, Sun Microsystems, and others. It's a much slower read than Stoll's *The Cuckoo's Egg* but worth reading nonetheless.

Stoll, Clifford. *The Cuckoo's Egg*. London: Pan Macmillan, 1991. Not a reference or technical book, this book tells the story of how Cliff Stoll became a security expert by default while trying to chase down hackers attacking his systems from across the globe. A hearty recommendation for this easy and exciting read.

Cryptography

Electronic Frontier Foundation. *Cracking DES: Secrets of Encryption Research, Wiretap Politics & Chip Design*. Sebastopol, CA: O'Reilly & Associates, 1998. This book is presented in two big sections. The first deals with the Electronic Frontier Foundation's DES Cracking project, as well as with some political issues. The rest, indeed the bulk, of the book deals with the hardware and firmware required for a machine to perform as a brute-force DES cracking engine. It's an interesting read, but it's not really applicable to building applications.

Schneier, Bruce. *Applied Cryptography: Protocols, Algorithms, and Source Code in C*. 2d ed. New York: Wiley, 1996. Probably the best book there is on cryptography outside of academia. Easy to read, complete, and very big, it's the one to buy if you want only one book on cryptography.

Stallings, William. *Practical Cryptography for Data Internetworks*. Los Alamitos, CA: IEEE Computer Society Press, 1996. This is a gem of a book. If I were stranded on a desert island and had to choose one book on cryptography, this would be it. Comprising a series of easy-to-read papers, some from academia and some from the press, the book covers a myriad of topics, including DES, IDEA, SkipJack, RC5, key management, digital signatures, authentication principles, SNMP, Internet security standards, and much more.

———. *Cryptography and Network Security: Principles and Practice*. Englewood Cliffs, NJ: Prentice Hall, 1999. Stallings does a good job of covering both the theory and practice of cryptography, but this book's redeeming feature is the inclusion of security protocols such as S/MIME, SET, SSL/TLS, IPSec, PGP, and Kerberos. It might lack the cryptographic completeness of *Applied Cryptography: Protocols, Algorithms, and Source Code in C,* but because of its excellent protocol coverage, this book is much more pragmatic.

Windows NT and Windows 2000 Security

Blum, Daniel. *Understanding Active Directory Services*. Redmond, WA: Microsoft Press, 1999. If Active Directory is new to you, turn to this book. Not only is it an easy read, but it's very complete and surprisingly detailed for an "IT Professional" book. Highly recommended.

Edwards, Mark Joseph. *Internet Security with Windows NT*. Loveland, CO: Duke Press, 1998. The book is outdated now and covers an old version of Microsoft Internet Information Server. The good news: it is available on line at *www.ntsecurity.net,* and what it lacks in depth it makes up for in breadth.

Jumes, James G., et al. *Microsoft Windows NT 4.0 Security, Audit, and Control*. Redmond, WA: Microsoft Press, 1999. A reasonable checklist for configuring and administering a Windows NT 4 enterprise. It suffers from being outdated because so much has changed with Windows 2000 in the area of security and administration.

Microsoft Corporation. *Microsoft Windows 2000 Server Resource Kit.* Redmond, WA: Microsoft Press, 2000. An invaluable resource covering all aspects of Windows 2000, including security, Active Directory, host integration, deployment, TCP/IP networking, clustering, Internet Information Services, Microsoft Internet Explorer, and much more. At over 7000 pages, it's a massive and worthy reference.

Okuntseff, Nik. *Windows NT Security; Programming Easy-to-Use Security Options.* Gilroy, CA: R&D Books, 1997. This is the best reference available on using the Windows NT security APIs. It's written for Windows NT 4, but much of the information is pertinent to Windows 2000.

Rutstein, Charles B. *Windows NT Security: A Practical Guide to Securing Windows NT Servers and Workstations.* New York: McGraw-Hill, 1997. This book was cosponsored by the National Computer Security Association and is a reasonably complete look at security in Windows NT. It's somewhat out of date, but its principles are still valid. It's also very well written and easy to understand.

Windows NT Magazine Administrator's Survival Guide: System Management and Security. Edited by John Enck. Loveland, CO: Duke Press, 1998. A unique book made up of a collection of articles from back issues of *Windows NT Magazine,* all relating to systems management and security. Even if security is not your focus, you should consider purchasing this book because it covers many common administrative pitfalls and explains some of the esoteric aspects of Windows NT authentication.

TCP/IP Networking

Comer, Douglas E., and David L. Stevens. *Internetworking with TCP/IP: Vol. I.* 2d ed. Englewood Cliffs, NJ: Prentice Hall, 1994.

————. *Internetworking with TCP/IP: Vol. II.* 2d ed. Upper Saddle Hill, NJ: Prentice Hall, 1994.

————. *Internetworking with TCP/IP: Vol. III.* 2d ed. Upper Saddle Hill, NJ: Prentice Hall, 1994. These three books are all classics and well worth reading because many Denial of Service attacks utilize handcrafted IP packets and defending against such attacks requires an understanding of the TCP/IP protocol suite.

————. *Internetworking with TCP/IP: Vol. I-Windows Sockets Version.* 2d ed. Upper Saddle Hill, NJ: Prentice Hall, 1997. This is the same book as *Internetworking with TCP/IP: Vol. I.* 2d ed., but the samples use WinSock rather than Berkeley sockets.

Index

Italicized page numbers indicate figures or tables.

Special Characters

"." (dot) attacks, 365
".." (parent paths), 357
| (pipe operator), 378
< and > (redirect operators), 378
3DES (Triple Data Encryption Standard), 74, 428, 451
200 status code – no error, 103
401 error, 102–3, 116–17
401.2 unauthorized error, 331–32
401.3 unauthorized error, 332–33
401.4 authorization denied error, 333–34
403 errors, 116
403.13 client certificate revoked error, 334–35
403.15 forbidden: client access licenses exceeded error, 335

A

accepting threats, 21
access
  anonymous (*see* anonymous access)
  authenticated (*see* authentication)
  checks, 9
  control, 24, 217
  determination, 60–61
  identified, 100–101
access control entries. *See* ACEs (access control entries)
access control lists. *See* ACLs (access control lists)
AccessFlags setting, 402
AccessSSLFlags setting, 402–3
Access This Computer From The Network privilege, 105–7

access violations (AVs), 13
Account Is Sensitive And Cannot Be Delegated option, 69–70
Account Is Trusted For Delegation option, 70
Account Logon category, 318–20
accounts. *See also* groups; user accounts
  anonymous (*see* anonymous access)
  COM+ startup, 161
  IIS identity processes, 154
  IUSR_machinename, 104
  IWAM_machinename, 157–61
  krbtgt, 414, 419
  logon events log, 318–20
  managing, 51–53
  selection at logon, 173
  SIDs (Security Identifiers), 53–54
  startup, 161
  viewing with WMI and ADSI, 393
ACEs (access control entries), 57
  access determination, 60
  audit, 67–68
  Deny, 101–2
  Everyone, 250
  permission denied errors, 323–24
ACLs (access control lists), 9, 57–68
  access determination, 60–61
  ACEs (*see* ACEs (access control entries))
  for audit logs, 277
  Basic authentication, 106
  COM+ access, 201–3
  data-tampering threats, 250
  editing, 61
  groups with, 232
  IIS, 231–32

MICHAEL HOWARD

Michael Howard is a security program manager on the Windows 2000 team at Microsoft Corporation focusing on Internet security issues and secure design best practices. Prior to his current position, he was the Web infrastructure security program manager working on next-generation Web technology. He was also the security program manager for Internet Information Services 5. Before working on the Web server and Windows operating system teams, he was a senior consultant with Microsoft Consulting Services, working with large corporations, financial institutions, and government agencies on security-related technologies. He is a native of New Zealand and now lives in sunny Bellevue, down the road from the Microsoft campus, with his wife, Cheryl, and two Yorkies, Squirt and Major.

MARC LEVY

Marc Levy is a program manager in the BizTalk Server group. Before this, he was the program manager for Microsoft Transaction Server and COM+ 1.0 security. Prior to coming to Microsoft, Marc worked at OSF, where he developed his security background while working on the Distributed Computing Environment (DCE).

RICHARD WAYMIRE

Richard Waymire is the enterprise program manager for Microsoft SQL Server and owns overall security for SQL Server.

The manuscript for this book was prepared using Microsoft Word 2000. Pages were composed by Microsoft Press using Adobe PageMaker 6.52 for Windows, with text in Garamond and display type in Helvetica Black. Composed pages were delivered to the printer as electronic prepress files.

Cover Graphic Designer

Girvin | Strategic Branding & Design

Cover Illustrator

Glenn Mitsui

Interior Graphic Artist

Michael Kloepfer

Principal Compositor

Carl Diltz

Principal Proofreader/Copy Editor

Crystal Thomas

Indexer

Bill Meyers

MICROSOFT LICENSE AGREEMENT

Book Companion CD

IMPORTANT—READ CAREFULLY: This Microsoft End-User License Agreement ("EULA") is a legal agreement between you (either an individual or an entity) and Microsoft Corporation for the Microsoft product identified above, which includes computer software and may include associated media, printed materials, and "online" or electronic documentation ("SOFTWARE PRODUCT"). Any component included within the SOFTWARE PRODUCT that is accompanied by a separate End-User License Agreement shall be governed by such agreement and not the terms set forth below. By installing, copying, or otherwise using the SOFTWARE PRODUCT, you agree to be bound by the terms of this EULA. If you do not agree to the terms of this EULA, you are not authorized to install, copy, or otherwise use the SOFTWARE PRODUCT; you may, however, return the SOFTWARE PRODUCT, along with all printed materials and other items that form a part of the Microsoft product that includes the SOFTWARE PRODUCT, to the place you obtained them for a full refund.

SOFTWARE PRODUCT LICENSE

The SOFTWARE PRODUCT is protected by United States copyright laws and international copyright treaties, as well as other intellectual property laws and treaties. The SOFTWARE PRODUCT is licensed, not sold.

1. **GRANT OF LICENSE.** This EULA grants you the following rights:

   a. **Software Product.** You may install and use one copy of the SOFTWARE PRODUCT on a single computer. The primary user of the computer on which the SOFTWARE PRODUCT is installed may make a second copy for his or her exclusive use on a portable computer.

   b. **Storage/Network Use.** You may also store or install a copy of the SOFTWARE PRODUCT on a storage device, such as a network server, used only to install or run the SOFTWARE PRODUCT on your other computers over an internal network; however, you must acquire and dedicate a license for each separate computer on which the SOFTWARE PRODUCT is installed or run from the storage device. A license for the SOFTWARE PRODUCT may not be shared or used concurrently on different computers.

   c. **License Pak.** If you have acquired this EULA in a Microsoft License Pak, you may make the number of additional copies of the computer software portion of the SOFTWARE PRODUCT authorized on the printed copy of this EULA, and you may use each copy in the manner specified above. You are also entitled to make a corresponding number of secondary copies for portable computer use as specified above.

   d. **Sample Code.** Solely with respect to portions, if any, of the SOFTWARE PRODUCT that are identified within the SOFTWARE PRODUCT as sample code (the "SAMPLE CODE"):

      i. **Use and Modification.** Microsoft grants you the right to use and modify the source code version of the SAMPLE CODE, *provided* you comply with subsection (d)(iii) below. You may not distribute the SAMPLE CODE, or any modified version of the SAMPLE CODE, in source code form.

      ii. **Redistributable Files.** Provided you comply with subsection (d)(iii) below, Microsoft grants you a nonexclusive, royalty-free right to reproduce and distribute the object code version of the SAMPLE CODE and of any modified SAMPLE CODE, other than SAMPLE CODE, or any modified version thereof, designated as not redistributable in the Readme file that forms a part of the SOFTWARE PRODUCT (the "Non-Redistributable Sample Code"). All SAMPLE CODE other than the Non-Redistributable Sample Code is collectively referred to as the "REDISTRIBUTABLES."

      iii. **Redistribution Requirements.** If you redistribute the REDISTRIBUTABLES, you agree to: (i) distribute the REDISTRIBUTABLES in object code form only in conjunction with and as a part of your software application product; (ii) not use Microsoft's name, logo, or trademarks to market your software application product; (iii) include a valid copyright notice on your software application product; (iv) indemnify, hold harmless, and defend Microsoft from and against any claims or lawsuits, including attorney's fees, that arise or result from the use or distribution of your software application product; and (v) not permit further distribution of the REDISTRIBUTABLES by your end user. Contact Microsoft for the applicable royalties due and other licensing terms for all other uses and/or distribution of the REDISTRIBUTABLES.

2. **DESCRIPTION OF OTHER RIGHTS AND LIMITATIONS.**

   - **Limitations on Reverse Engineering, Decompilation, and Disassembly.** You may not reverse engineer, decompile, or disassemble the SOFTWARE PRODUCT, except and only to the extent that such activity is expressly permitted by applicable law notwithstanding this limitation.

   - **Separation of Components.** The SOFTWARE PRODUCT is licensed as a single product. Its component parts may not be separated for use on more than one computer.

   - **Rental.** You may not rent, lease, or lend the SOFTWARE PRODUCT.

   - **Support Services.** Microsoft may, but is not obligated to, provide you with support services related to the SOFTWARE PRODUCT ("Support Services"). Use of Support Services is governed by the Microsoft policies and programs described in the user manual, in "online" documentation, and/or in other Microsoft-provided materials. Any supplemental software code provided to you as part of the Support Services shall be considered part of the SOFTWARE PRODUCT and subject to the terms and conditions of this EULA. With respect to technical information you provide to Microsoft as part of the Support Services, Microsoft may use such information for its business purposes, including for product support and development. Microsoft will not utilize such technical information in a form that personally identifies you.

- **Software Transfer.** You may permanently transfer all of your rights under this EULA, provided you retain no copies, you transfer all of the SOFTWARE PRODUCT (including all component parts, the media and printed materials, any upgrades, this EULA, and, if applicable, the Certificate of Authenticity), **and** the recipient agrees to the terms of this EULA.

- **Termination.** Without prejudice to any other rights, Microsoft may terminate this EULA if you fail to comply with the terms and conditions of this EULA. In such event, you must destroy all copies of the SOFTWARE PRODUCT and all of its component parts.

3. **COPYRIGHT.** All title and copyrights in and to the SOFTWARE PRODUCT (including but not limited to any images, photographs, animations, video, audio, music, text, SAMPLE CODE, REDISTRIBUTABLES, and "applets" incorporated into the SOFTWARE PRODUCT) and any copies of the SOFTWARE PRODUCT are owned by Microsoft or its suppliers. The SOFTWARE PRODUCT is protected by copyright laws and international treaty provisions. Therefore, you must treat the SOFTWARE PRODUCT like any other copyrighted material **except** that you may install the SOFTWARE PRODUCT on a single computer provided you keep the original solely for backup or archival purposes. You may not copy the printed materials accompanying the SOFTWARE PRODUCT.

4. **U.S. GOVERNMENT RESTRICTED RIGHTS.** The SOFTWARE PRODUCT and documentation are provided with RESTRICTED RIGHTS. Use, duplication, or disclosure by the Government is subject to restrictions as set forth in subparagraph (c)(1)(ii) of the Rights in Technical Data and Computer Software clause at DFARS 252.227-7013 or subparagraphs (c)(1) and (2) of the Commercial Computer Software—Restricted Rights at 48 CFR 52.227-19, as applicable. Manufacturer is Microsoft Corporation/One Microsoft Way/Redmond, WA 98052-6399.

5. **EXPORT RESTRICTIONS.** You agree that you will not export or re-export the SOFTWARE PRODUCT, any part thereof, or any process or service that is the direct product of the SOFTWARE PRODUCT (the foregoing collectively referred to as the "Restricted Components"), to any country, person, entity, or end user subject to U.S. export restrictions. You specifically agree not to export or re-export any of the Restricted Components (i) to any country to which the U.S. has embargoed or restricted the export of goods or services, which currently include, but are not necessarily limited to, Cuba, Iran, Iraq, Libya, North Korea, Sudan, and Syria, or to any national of any such country, wherever located, who intends to transmit or transport the Restricted Components back to such country; (ii) to any end user who you know or have reason to know will utilize the Restricted Components in the design, development, or production of nuclear, chemical, or biological weapons; or (iii) to any end user who has been prohibited from participating in U.S. export transactions by any federal agency of the U.S. government. You warrant and represent that neither the BXA nor any other U.S. federal agency has suspended, revoked, or denied your export privileges.

For information about Microsoft Press®

products, visit our Web site at

mspress.microsoft.com